Information Technology and Computer Applications in Public Administration: Issues and Trends

G. David Garson
North Carolina State University

IDEA GROUP PUBLISHING
Hershey, USA • London, UK

Senior Editor: Mehdi Khosrowpour
Managing Editor: Jan Travers
Copy Editor: Terry Heffelfinger
Printed at: BookCrafters

Published in the United States of America by
    Idea Group Publishing
    1331 E. Chocolate Avenue
    Hershey PA 17033-1117
    Tel: 717-533-8845
    Fax: 717-533-8661
    E-mail: jtravers@idea-group.com
    Website: http://www.idea-group.com

and in the United Kingdom by
    Idea Group Publishing
    3 Henrietta Street
    Covent Garden
    London WC2E 8LU
    Tel: 171-240 0856
    Fax: 171-379 0609

Copyright © 1999 by Idea Group Publishing. All rights reserved. No part of this book may be reproduced in any form or by any means, electronic or mechanical, including photocopying, without written permission from the publisher.

Library of Congress Cataloging-in-Publication Data

Garson, G. David.
    Information technology and computer applications in public administration / G. David Garson.
        p.   cm.
    Includes bibliographical references and index.
    ISBN 1-878289-52-7
    1. Public administration--Data processing. 2. Information technology. 3. Information resources management. I. Title.
JF1525.A8G37 1998
351'.0285--dc21   98-43297
                                                        CIP

British Cataloguing in Publication Data
A Cataloguing in Publication record for this book is available from the British Library.

IDEA GROUP PUBLISHING
Hershey, PA, USA • London, UK

Series in Information Technology Management

The surge in information technology during the latter part of the 20th century has forced organizations to meet its challenges with an increased use and management of information resources. This series takes an in-depth look at trends, current practices, and problem resolution in information technology management and offers you a first-class source for expanding the reader's knowledge in this ever-growing field.

Books in this series:

- **Information Systems Innovation and Diffusion: Issues and Directions** (Tor J. Larsen and Eugene McGuire)
- **The Virtual Workplace** (Magid Igbaria and Margaret Tan)
- **Information Systems Success Measurement** (Edward Garrity and G. Lawrence Sanders)
- **Cases on Information Technology Management in Modern Organizations** (Jay Liebowitz and Mehdi Khosrowpour)
- **Collaborative Technologies and Organizational Learning** (R. Neilson)
- **Information Systems Outsourcing Decision Making: A Managerial Approach** (L.A. de Looff)
- **Information Technology and Organizations: Challenges of New Technologies** (Mehdi Khosrowpour)
- **Management Impacts of Information Technology** (Edward Szewczak)
- **Managing Information Technology Investments with Outsourcing** (Mehdi Khosrowpour)
- **Business Process Change: Reengineering Concepts, Methods and Technologies** (Varun Grover and William Kettinger)
- **Reengineering MIS: Aligning Information Technology and Business Operations** (Kevin Coleman, Jim Ettwein, Clelland Johnson, Dick Pigman and Deborah Pulak)

For more information, or to submit a proposal for a book
in this series, please contact:
Idea Group Publishing
1331 E. Chocolate Avenue
Hershey, PA 17033-1117
Tel: 1/800-345-4332 or 717/533-8845
Fax: 717/533-8661
E-mail: jtravers@idea-group.com
Website: http://www.idea-group.com

Author guidelines also available at http://www.idea-group.com

Other IDEA GROUP Publishing Books

- Measuring Information Technology Investment Payoff: Contemporary Approaches/ Mahmood/Szewczak 1-878289-42-X
- Information Technology Diffusion in the Asia Pacific: Perspectives on Policy, Electronic Commerce and Education/Tan 1-878289-48-9
- Managing Computer-Based Information Systems in Developing Countries: A Cultural Perspective/Abdul-Gader 1-878289-49-7
- Information Technology and Computer Applications in Public Administration: Issues and Trends/Garson 1-878289-52-7
- Telelearning via the Internet/Kouki/Wright 1-87828953-5
- Software Process Improvement: Concepts and Practices/McGuire 1-878289-54-3
- IT Investment in Developing Countries: An Assessment & Practical Guideline 1-878289-55-1
- Success and Pitfalls of IT Management/Khosrowpour 1-878289-56-X
- Effective Utilization and Management of Emerging Information Technologies/Khsrowpour 1-878289-50-0
- Information Systems Innovation and Diffusion: Issues and Directions/Larsen and McGuire **1-878289-43-8**
- The Virtual Workplace/Igbaria and Tan **1-878289-41-1**
- Information Systems Success Measurement /Garrity/ Sanders **1-878289-44-6**
- Cases on IT Management in Modern Organizations/Liebowitz/Khosrowpour **1-878289-37-3**
- Business Process Change: Reengineering Concepts, Methods and Technologies/Grover/ Kettinger 1-878289-29-2
- Cleanroom Software Engineering Practices/Becker/Whittaker 1-878289-34-9
- Collaborative Technologies and Organizational Learning/Neilson 1-878289-39-X
- Computer-Aided Software Engineering: Issues and Trends for the 1990s and Beyond/ Bergin 1-878289-15-2
- Computer Technology and Social Issues/Garson 1-878289-28-4
- Global Info. Infrastructure:The Birth, Vision and Architecture/Targowski 1-878289-32-2
- Global Issues of Information Technology Management/ Palvia/Palvia/Zigli 1-878289-10-1
- Global Information Systems and Technology: Focus on the Organization and Its Functional Areas/Deans/Karwan 1-878289-21-7
- Global Information Technology Education: Issues and Trends/Khosrowpour/Loch 1-878289-14-4
- The Human Side of Information Technology Management/ Szewczak/Khosrowpour 1-878289-33-0
- Information Systems Outsourcing Decision Making: A Managerial Approach/de Looff 1-878289-40-3
- IT and Organizations: Challenges of New Technologies/Khosrowpour 1-878289-18-7
- IT Management and Organizational Innovations 1-878289-35-7
- Managing Information & Communications in a Changing Global Environment 1-878289-31-4
- Managing Social and Economic Change With IT/Khosrowpour 1-878289-26-8
- Management Impacts of IT/ Szewczak/ Snodgrass/Khosrowpour 1-878289-08-X
- Managing Expert Systems /Turban/Liebowitz 1-878289-11-X
- Managing Information Technology in a Global Society/Khosrowpour 1-878289-13-6
- Multimedia Computing: Preparing for the 21st Century/Reisman 1-878289-22-5
- Partners Not Competitors: The Age of Teamwork and Technology/Oliva 1-878289-09-8
- Reengineering MIS: Aligning Information Technology and Business Operations/Coleman 1-878289-30-6
- Strategic Management: An Integrative Context-Specific Process/Mockler 1-878289-19-5

Receive the Idea Group Publishing catalog with descriptions of these books by calling, toll free 1/800-345-4332 or visit the IGP web site at: http://www.idea-group.com!

Excellent additions to your library!

Information Technology and Computer Applications in Public Administration: Issues and Trends

Table of Contents

PART I: MANAGING INFORMATION TECHNOLOGY IN THE PUBLIC SECTOR

Introduction 1
    G. David Garson
    North Carolina State University

Chapter 1
The Challenge of Teaching Information Technology 7
in Public Administration Graduate Programs
    Alana Northrop
    California State University-Fullerton

Chapter 2
The Political Dimensions of Information Systems in 23
Public Administration
    Bruce Rocheleau
    Northern Illinois University

Chapter 3
Information Technology and Organizational Change in the 41
Public Sector
    Sonal J. Seneviratne
    University of Southern California

Chapter 4
The Evolution of Information Technology Management 62
at the Federal Level: Implications for Public Administration
    Stephen H. Holden
    Internal Revenue Service

Chapter 5
**Strategic Planning for Public Sector Information Management 81
in State Government**
    Patricia D. Fletcher
    University of Maryland, Baltimore County

Chapter 6
**Managing Information Privacy and Information Access 99
in the Public Sector**
    George T. Duncan
    Carnegie Mellon University

Chapter 7
Electronic Governance on the Internet 118
    Michael Warren and Louis Weschler
    Arizona State University

PART II: COMPUTER APPLICATIONS
IN PUBLIC ADMINISTRATION

Chapter 8
**Leading Edge Information Technologies and Their 137
Adoption: Lessons from U. S. Cities**
    Donald F. Norris
    Maryland Institute of Policy Analysis and Research
    University of Maryland, Baltimore County

Chapter 9
Management Information Systems in the Public Sector 157
    Richard Heeks
    University of Manchester, England

Chapter 10
The Software Toolkit Approach for Public Administrators 174
    Carl Grafton and Anne Permaloff
    Auburn University at Montgomery

Chapter 11
**Computers, Survey Research, and Focus Groups in 196
Public Administration Research and Practice**
    Michael S. Vasu and Ellen Storey Vasu
    North Carolina State University

Chapter 12
Managing Geographic Information Systems in the Public Sector 220
    T. R. Carr
    Southern Illinois State University

Chapter 13
Legal Aspects of Electronic Mail in Public Organizations 231
    Charles Prysby
    University of North Carolina at Greensboro

    Nicole Prysby
    Attorney-at-Law, Charlottesville, VA

Chapter 14
World Wide Web Site Design and Use in Public Management 246
    Carmine Scavo and Yuhang Shi
    East Carolina University

Chapter 15
On-line Research for Public Managers 267
    G. David Garson
    North Carolina State University

About the Authors 293

Index 299

Introduction

by
G. David Garson
North Carolina State University

The readings which compose this volume are intended to constitute a survey of many of the most important dimensions of managing information technology in the public sector. Essays in Part I address general policy and administrative issues in this arena, while those in Part II are more applied and address information technology skills needed by public managers. Taken together, it is hoped that a contribution is made by these essays toward the knowledge and competencies needed by graduate students of public administration and by practitioners new to this field.

Part I: Managing Information Technology in the Public Sector

In "The Challenge of Teaching Information Technology in Public Administration Graduate Programs," Alana Northrop empirically reviews the level of computer and information management instruction in American public administration graduate programs and outlines prescriptive elements needed for curricular advance. Alana Northrop is a member of the faculty of California State University - Fullerton and is author of articles in Public Administration Review, Public Administration Quarterly, and other journals.

In "Political Dimensions of Information Systems in Public Administration," Bruce Rocheleau reviews the literature on political dimensions of public-sector information management;

covers both intra- and inter-organizational politics, illustrating major themes with examples and practical illustrations; outlines general strategies used by public managers to function effectively in political environments. Bruce Rocheleau teaches information management in the Division of Public Administration, Northern Illinois University, and has published numerous chapters and articles on information management in government in journals such as the *Public Administration Review*, *International Journal of Public Administration*, *Computers and Human Services*, and *Public Productivity & Management Review*.

In "Information Technology and Organizational Change in the Public Sector," Sonal J. Seneviratne reviews the literature about the relationship between organizational change and public sector information management, thereby drawing lessons for public sector managerial practice in a technological era. Sonal Seneviratne has had ten years experience in the information systems field both as an analyst and information systems manager, prior to becoming the Boaz Research Professor and Director of Organizational Development and Learning at the University of Southern California. His articles have appeared in *Public Administration Review* and the *Asian Journal of Business and Information Systems*.

In "The Evolution of Information Technology Management at the Federal Level: Implications for Public Administration," Stephen H. Holden notes that the federal government relies extensively on information technology (IT) to perform its basic missions. Arguably, the field of public administration should be driving the theory, policy, and practice for managing these increasingly important resources. This is especially true as public organizations move to electronic service delivery to improve mission performance and increase efficiency. This chapter reviews the literature from several academic disciplines and other sources covering IT management and comparing it to a normative model of management maturity. The review demonstrates that despite some maturation in the literature for managing IT, that public administration has contributed little to this effort. Other fields, such as information sciences and business administration, have done more work to inform IT management theory, policy, and practice at the federal level. This gap in public administration literature raises profound questions about the ability of public organizations to move into the information age. Stephen H. Holden is the National Director, Electronic Program Enhancements, for the Internal Revenue Service (IRS). He leads the development of new electronic filing, payment, and communications programs for the IRS. He joined the IRS in 1994 and has worked on their systems modernization efforts during his tenure. Prior to coming to the IRS, he worked for ten years at the Office of Management and Budget (OMB), doing a variety of policy, management, and budget analysis work. During that time, he served as the principal author of OMB's government-wide policy for information technology management. He earned his Ph.D. in Public Administration and Affairs from Virginia Tech in 1994.

In "Strategic Planning for Public Sector Information Management in State Government," Patricia D. Fletcher draws on data from national studies of state, county, and local level government information management to set forth the rationale, methodology, and management considerations involved in utilizing strategic planning to improve public sector effectiveness through information management. Patricia D. Fletcher teaches strategic planning and information resources management at the University of Maryland - Baltimore County. She has played major investigatory roles in three national studies of information resources management.

In "Managing Information Privacy and Information Access in the Public Sector," George T. Duncan discusses the manager's role as a data steward, with a focus on the federal legal and administrative context; shows how to develop a confidentiality plan for an agency; suggests means of resolving the tension between and privacy and data access; explores the implications of recent developments in information technology and telecommunications. George T. Duncan is Professor of Statistics in the Heinz School of Public Policy and Management, Carnegie Mellon University. He served as chair of the Panel on Confidentiality and Data Access of the National Academy of Sciences (1989-1993) and subsequently published the book *Private Lives and Public Policies: Confidentiality and Accessibility of Government Statistics*.

In "Electronic Governance on the Internet," Michael Warren and Louis Weschler discuss present and potential use of Internet-based technologies which impact access, governance, and democratic processes in public-sector environments. The chapter is based in ased in part on a doctoral dissertation by the lead author, who is also president of Electronic Archive Services, an information systems firm. Lou Weschler is professor of Public Affairs at Arizona State University, where he directs a study of the use of technology in community government.

Part II: Computer Applications In Public Administration

In "Leading Edge Information Technologies and Their Adoption: Lessons from U. S. Cities," Donald F. Norris bases his observations on a national study of the adoption of leading edge technologies. This essay surveys the range of information technology innovation in American cities and outlines the management and environmental characteristics associated with successful innovation diffusion and adoption. Donald F. Norris is director of the Maryland Institute for Policy Analysis and Research and is the author of numerous research studies on information technology. Dr. Norris is also Visiting Professor in the Department of Public Policy and Managerial Studies, DeMontfort University, Leicester, England.

In "Management Information Systems in the Public Sector," Richard Heeks explains the features of public sector monitoring and control systems using American and international examples; he provides a general information systems model, focusing on the management rationale for IS planning in the public sector. Richard Heeks is director of the Public Sector Management and Information Systems master's degree program at the University of Manchester (UK) and is author of three books and numerous articles on public-sector information systems.

In "The Software Toolkit Approach for Public Administrators," Carl Grafton and Anne Permaloff provide an overview of personal computer skills required of public managers, focusing on competencies associated with data analysis and data presentation. Carl Grafton and Anne Permaloff teach in the Public Administration Program of Auburn University - Montgomery. Carl Grafton also serves as Book Review Editor for the *Social Science Computer Review*.

In "Computers, Survey Research, and Focus Groups in Public Administration

Research and Practice," Michael S. Vasu and Ellen Storey Vasu provide an overview of the advantages and use of computer-based survey research tools for accomplishing basic public administrative tasks involving policy development, program evaluation, and impact assessment. Michael Vasu directs the Social Science Research and Computer Laboratory at North Carolina State University and consults widely on survey research. Ellen Vasu is an Associate Professor in the Department of Curriculum and Instruction at North Carolina State University and coordinates the graduate program in Instructional Technology.

In "Managing Geographic Information Systems in the Public Sector," T. R. Carr discusses the rapid evolution of public-sector GIS, reviewing primarily local level applications in education, public safety, and city planning; covers managerial issues and pitfalls. T. R. Carr is chair of the Department of Public Administration and Policy Analysis at Southern Illinois State University. His publications have appeared in *The International Journal of Public Administration* and *Labor Law Journal*, and he has coauthored a public policy text with St. Martin's Press.

In "Legal Aspects of Electronic Mail in Public Organizations," Charles Prysby and Nicole Prysby discuss public management opportunities and responsibilities in the age of electronic mail, outlining development of agency guidelines for use of electronic mail. Charles Prysby is chair of the Political Science Department at the University of North Carolina - Greensboro. Nicole Prysby is an attorney with interests in legal issues of electronic communication.

In "World Wide Web Site Design and Use in Public Management," Carmine Scavo and Yuhang Shi base their observations on data from a national study of American cities' use of the World Wide Web. This essay surveys the range of uses of the World Wide Web by American cities and outlines the practical management factors associated with successful implementation. Carmine Scavo is director of the Masters of Public Administration Program at East Carolina University.

Finally, in "Online Research for Public Managers," G. David Garson presents an overview of online research tools for public-sector practitioners and researchers. G. David Garson is professor of public administration at North Carolina State University, where he teaches courses on computer applications, GIS, and research methodology. Editor of the *Social Science Computer Review*, he is also author or co-author of 16 books and over 50 articles on public administration, computer applications, and political science.

Part I

Managing Information Technology in the Public Sector

Part 1

Advancing Information Technology in the Library Sector

1

The Challenge of Teaching Information Technology in Public Administration Graduate Programs

by
Alana Northrop
California State University
- Fullerton

This chapter first points out the need for a reader on information technology by reviewing the importance given computing education by M.P.A. programs and practitioners. Next, the chapter surveys current textbooks' and general public administration journals' treatment of the topic since 1985. Three highly respected public administration journals and six textbooks are reviewed. The journals are found to barely treat the topic of computing, whether as a main focus or as merely a mention in articles. The textbooks also barely mention computing. In addition, there was no consistent rubric or chapter topic under which computing is discussed. The need for a reader on information technology and computer applications in public administration is apparent. The chapter then turns to the consideration of what hands-on-skills in computer applications should be a mark of a graduate degree in public administration. It is suggested that there are six generic skills with a seventh one on the horizon. Finally, the chapter concludes by briefly discussing a range of issues that public administrators should be conversant with if they are to successfully utilize computer applications in the delivery of public sector services.

Introduction

In 1985, a special computing education committee recommended to the National Association of Schools of Public Affairs and Administration (NASPAA) that a sixth skill, comput-

Copyright© 1999, Idea Group Publishing.

ing, be added to the original five skills that must be taught in a MPA Program. This recommendation applied to the accreditation of schools starting in 1988. Now more than ten years have passed since the original recommendation. It seems an appropriate time to evaluate the progress that has been made and to reconsider what should be taught.

Computing Education in MPA Programs

There have been two published studies that surveyed MPA programs and assessed the level of computing education. Cleary (1990) mailed out questionnaires to 215 public affairs/public administration masters programs affiliated with the National Association of Schools of Public Affairs and Administration in 1989. Of the 80% returned, about one out of four reported that they had a course dealing with information systems/computer skills. The respondents were quick to note that the information systems/computer skills area needed more attention in the future. Yet, 1989 was a long time ago, especially when it comes to the massive changes in the computer field.

Brudney, Hy, and Waugh (1993) did a little more recent survey of MPA programs. Close to 90% of the programs said they use computers in their instruction. Over half of the institutions offer a course in computers, yet only 30% had made computing a requirement. The study also suggested that computing skills need to be taught beyond the typically taught statistical applications.

Without another survey of programs, one can only surmise, pretty safely, that computer use in MPA courses has greatly expanded. But what skills and management issues should be taught?

What PA Practitioners Advise in Computing Education

Four studies surveyed public managers. Lan and Cayer (1994) surveyed administrators in one state. The recommendations were that MPA programs need course work in computer literacy, specifically knowledge of applications and hands-on-skills. The respondents said they use information technology (unfortunately this includes phone and fax) on an average of 56% of their day. The respondents also said that they were involved with the management of the information system, so management issues as well as computer skills are important for PA students.

Crewson and Fisher (1997) surveyed 371 city administrators in the US. In terms of importance for public administrators in the future, 37% of the sample rated computer skills as most important with 57% giving such skills moderate importance. Similar ratings were given by the sample to knowing about computers.

An earlier study (Poister and Streib, 1989) of 451 municipal managers indicates the extensive diffusion of management information systems in the 1980s. Other indications of computer use can be obliquely inferred from usage of such management tools as revenue forecasting and performance monitoring.

A 1988 study of 46 technologically advanced cities was intended to predict the "common state" of computerization in US cities in the late 1990s (Kraemer and Northrop, 1989). That study indicated that no city department or staff role was spared from the diffusion of computers. In fact, 84% of managers responding and 85% of staff respondents indicated that their work involved major interaction with computers.

In essence, even taking into account that these studies are out of date, the word from public managers is know how to use computers and be ready to deal with management issues surrounding computerization.

Computing Education in Public Administration Journals and Textbooks

We know there is a need for computing education in MPA programs, as practitioners and both the 1985 recommendation and 1989 update pointed out (Kraemer and Northrop, 1989; NASPAA Ad Hoc Committee on Computers in Public Management Education, 1986). Yes, schools say they have integrated computing into their curriculum (Brudney, Hy, and Waugh, 1993). But how has the field of public administration pushed computing education in print?

One way to answer that question is to review research and textbooks in public administration. This third approach to looking at computing education is based on the theory of triangulation. Triangulation means using different data sources trained on the same problem, in this case computing education. Triangulation not only involves using data from different sources but also from different perspectives. In this section, the sources are general public administration journals and textbooks. The different perspective is the belief that one can learn about computing education not just from what university program directors say they teach, but also from looking at the published sources of information commonly available to public administration academics and professionals.

Professional Public Administration Articles

The journals were selected based on Forester and Watson's (1994) survey of all editors and editorial board members of 36 journals who mention public administration in general or public administration topics, such as personnel and finance, in their mission statements. The study used a 10-point scale, 10 representing the best journal in the field according to the respondents, a 0 indicating no respondent rates that journal in the top ten. The top five general public administration journals, whether you include or exclude the board members of those journals in the rankings were:

	All Respondents	Minus Board Members
Public Administration Review	8.34	8.19
Administration & Society	5.36	5.17
American Review of Public Administration	3.85	3.40
Journal of Public Administration Theory	3.20	2.78
Public Administration Quarterly	2.88	2.45

NOTE: There is a very clear drop-off in ratings for journals rated lower.

In deciding which journals to evaluate, the quality of the journal was considered as well as the requirement that the journal be recognized as one that dealt with the field of public administration in general. The latter requirement was based on the recommendation of the 1985 NASPAA committee that the computing topic be integrated into all courses versus segregated into one or a part of one course. Thus, the computing topic should be relevant to all academics and practitioners interested in public administration, not just those in a particular specialized area. The quality issue obviously speaks to the dissemination of information as well as the importance of computing as demonstrated by its acceptability as a topic in esteemed publishing outlets.

Clearly, *Public Administration Review (PAR)* and *Administration & Society (A&S)* stand out as the top general public administration journals and, in fact, as the top public administration journals, period (Forester and Watson, 1994). We also felt that *American Review of Public Administration (ARPA)* should be selected. Although it is closer in ratings to other lower-ranked journals than to the two leaders, it exceeds ratings' of the lower journals.

Table 1 shows how often computing appeared as a topic in the three selected journals over the thirteen year period since the NASPAA computing recommendations were made. There is no trend. Articles that mention computing or have computing as the main focus are rare, with no decided increase over time. It should also be noted that articles that mention computing may involve as little as a one sentence mention in the whole article.

PAR is obviously the main outlet for such articles of the three journals examined. Still assuming about eight articles per issue, less than 5 percent of the regular issue articles in *PAR* has dealt with computing. About 1 percent of articles published in *A&S* and *ARPA* since 1985 have dealt with computing to any degree. Of note is that in 1986, *PAR* published a special issue with 14 articles on computing issues.

In sum, while the academic field and the world of government practice increasingly recognize the importance of computing, the research world in terms of top quality journals does not.

The problem may be that only a few researchers or universities are interested in the topic. Of the 39 articles even somewhat dealing with computing noted in Table 1, authors represent a great variety of universities in a variety of states and the District of Columbia. In addition, a handful of authors were government employees. Moreover, all regions of the country except the Great Plains appear to be represented by the authors. Thus, it is not the case that computing as a research area is the publishing province of only a few universities in a handful of states. It may also not be the case that computing is the province of just a handful of people. While it is impossible to tell how many researchers are working on computing related questions and their proportion relevant to other areas of research, the 39 articles found were written by 51 authors.

Another issue of interest is the sex of the authors. Is computing a male-dominated field or reflective of other public administration topics in terms of sex of authors? Of the 39 articles cited in Table 1, 14 were written by women. From 1983 to 1994, 25% of the articles published in *PAR* had at least one female author (Young, 1995). By contrast, 36% of the computing articles had at least one female author; 43%

Table 1: Appearance of Computing Topic in Public Administration Journals

	1985	1986	1987	1988	1989	1990	1991	1992	1993	1994	1995	1996	1997
Administration & Society													
Number of articles that mention computing	0	0	0	0	1	0	0	0	0	0	0	0	0
Number of articles in which main focus is computing	0	0	0	0	0	0	0	0	1	0	0	0	1
American Review of Public Administration													
Number of articles that mention computing	0	0	0	0	0	0	1	0	0	1	0	0	1
Number of articles in which main focus is computing	0	0	0	0	0	0	0	0	0	1	1	0	0
Public Administration Review													
Number of articles that mention computing	3	0	0	0	1	2	1	1	0	0	0	2	4
Number of articles in which main focus is computing	1	2 (+14)[a]	1	0	1	3	1	1	1	2	2	2	0
Totals													
Number of articles that mention computing	3	0	0	0	2	2	2	1	0	1	0	2	5
Number of articles in which main focus is computing	1	2 (+14)[a]	1	0	1	3	1	1	2	3	3	2	1
Number of articles that mention computing or in which main focus is computing	4	2	1	0	3	5	3	2	2	4	3	4	6

[a] 1986 special issue with 14 articles on computing issues.

of the computing articles in *PAR* had at least one female author. So computing as a research topic is more likely to be written or co-authored by a female. Perhaps this uncharacteristic female interest in a public administration topic reflects that women are more recent entries into the academic and upper practitioner ranks and that computing is a more recent topic and skill.

The last factor considered was the empirical nature of the articles on computing published in the three journals. About half of the articles used data. While it may make sense that articles on computing are empirically based, such a high empirical basis is unusual in public administration research in the journals under consideration as well as in a wider sampling of public administration journals. In fact, Perry and Kraemer (1986), Houston and Delevan (1990), and Stallings and Ferris (1988) each decry the lack of empirical studies and evaluations of particular policies and programs. In contrast, it appears to be more in the nature of research on computing that the authors look to data to comment on the effectiveness of computing, relevant policies, and software packages.

Public Administration Textbooks

Professional public administration journal articles are a common outlet for academics and professionals to keep up on the latest research and trends in the field. Articles can be assigned in class or incorporated into lectures. Another common outlet on what is essential to the public administration field is textbooks. While one can "avoid" keeping up by not reading all journal articles, it is hard not to read the book assigned in class on both the professor's and student's sides. So if one were seeking to learn about the essential topics in the field of public administration, what would you learn by reading the textbooks?

In this instance, we looked at how often computers or information systems were mentioned in current public administration textbooks. Five of the texts were chosen since they were used in an earlier study (Bingham and Bowen, 1994). Stillman's (1996) textbook was added given its long history as a top textbook.

Table 2 indicates the remarkable lack of attention that these textbooks give to computing. Henry's (1995) textbook has the highest number of pages, eleven, representing a whopping three percent of the book treating computing as a topic or at least a mention. Similar to the three general public administration journals studied earlier, computing is just not a textbook topic of major or minor importance.

An additional concern, besides the amount of attention given to computing in these texts, is how it is treated. As Table 2 indicates, computing does not have its own chapter. Computing as a topic also appears not to have any consistent rubric under which it is treated. Computing is mentioned in a finance chapter, in two personnel chapters as well as in two decision-making chapters and appears in four eclectic chapters. Such inconsistent treatment suggests that computing has not been integrated into all areas of public administration and, in fact, has not even found a home in one area.

Need for a Book on Computing for Public Administrators

Without a doubt computing has permeated the practice of public administration at all levels of government in the United States. NASPAA has recognized this by requiring all accredited MPA programs to include in their programs information

Table 2: Appearance of Computing in Public Administration Textbooks

Textbook Name and Author	Number of pages Mentioning Computers or Information Systems and Percentage[a]	Name of Chapter in Which Pages Appear			
		Finance	Personnel	Decision-making	Other
Public Administration by Straussman (1990)	8 (2)		Chapter 5: "Public Management" (pp.88-89)	Chapter 10: "Information, Communication, & Decision-Making" (pp.230,231,236,241-242)	Chapter 15: "Evolving P.A." (p.368)
Contemporary Public Administration by Palumbo & Maynard-Moody (1991)	2 (.5)		Chapter 14: "Organizational Behavior" (pp.97-98)		
Public Administration Concepts and Cases by Stillman (1996)	0 (0)				
Public Administration Understanding Management Politics, and Law in the Public Sector by Rosenbloom (1998)	4 (.7)			Chapter 7: "Decision-making" (pp.355-356)	Chapter 13: "The Future" (pp. 567-8)
Public Administration: An Action Orientation by Denhardt (1995)	7 (2)	Chapter 5: "Budgeting & Financial Management" (pp.181-183)			Chapter 8: "Improving Public Productivity" (pp.279-282) [pp.282-283 deals with human fears & frustrations caused by new technologies, such as computers]
Public Administration and Public Affairs by Henry (1995)	11 (3)				Chapter 6: "The Systems Approach & Management Science" (pp.165-175)

[a] Percentages (in parentheses) are calculated using number of textbook pages as bases (i.e., excluding appendixes, references, and indexes.)

management, including computer literacy and applications. Yet in spite of the importance the work world and NASPAA has put on computing education, the two tables in this chapter show that textbooks and general public administration journals barely treat computing as a topic worthy of mention. Consequently, there is the strong sense that we all say computing is important, but it is more lip service than actual service. If it is truly accepted as important, computing should be a common research topic in our leading journals, a common topic in our textbooks, and thus a topic on which we are working hard to build a common body of knowledge. This is not true today, 13 years since we as a profession formally recognized computing's importance. How can there be a common theme or treatment to computing education if the textbooks and respected journals offer minuscule help or encouragement? A major way to begin correcting this dismal state is the present publication of an edited book on information technology and computer applications. This author also refers the reader to the articles that mention computers, listed at the end of this chapter.

Skills: Generic Applications

The Six Generic Applications

A person looking for a responsible job in city, county, state, or federal government will be expected to indicate computer skills on the resume. Experience with dedicated computer applications in one's area, such as human resources, will enhance one's employability. Of greater fundamental importance, there are computer skills that are commonly expected of all job applicants. These computer skills are generic because any job applicant would be wise to have them. The generic computer skills include word-processing, spreadsheet, graphics or data presentation, database management, e-mail, and internet. Geographic information systems(GIS) is a computer skill that is on the fast track to becoming a generic application too. There are also benefits to knowing a simple desktop publishing application; however, while desktop publishing is a nice and even a fun skill, it is not on the level of the other generic skills for PA professionals. One can develop a niche for oneself in an organization if one can produce a newsletter, but the niche is not an administrative one.

Wordprocessing

Word or WordPerfect are commonly both available in a governmental setting and have long histories. It would be wise to at least check out the wordprocessing system that one does not use. Talk with people who use each and see what they perceive as the advantages and disadvantages of Word versus WordPerfect. For example, some people like WordPerfect for its ability to easily insert spreadsheets within text. Also cited by users is the ease of footnoting. In contrast, Word users like its support from Microsoft and the frequent upgrades. Word's market dominance might also be an argument for becoming literate with the program. A wise rule would be to consider one's personal wordprocessing needs before learning WordPerfect if you are only comfortable with Word.

Spreadsheets

Spreadsheets are a data analysis application that has a myriad of uses and probably are taught or used in several public administration graduate courses. Obviously, the accounting function of any department or governmental unit is made easier through spreadsheets. But other functions also find the list nature and built in formula of spreadsheets useful. Human resource professionals can use spreadsheets to help in contract negotiations, and public works administrators can keep track of road repaving schedules.

Graphics

The ability to do graphics is a very important all-purpose tool. Pictures drive home a point better than words. Studies show that people remember what they have seen better that what they have heard. Graphics, therefore, can make a presentation clearer and more powerful. Graphics can also make a report clearer and more powerful. It is not uncommon for people to quickly skim a report right before a meeting or even look at it for the first time during the meeting. The net result is the subtleties of language are often overlooked or misunderstood. Graphical displays of main points are more likely to be looked at and become the foci of discussion or evaluation. Always keep in mind the audience for the report or presentation. What does the audience bring to the table and under what conditions? Will the audience have had time to carefully read the report? What do they want to learn from the report, are they familiar with the terms used, and what are the controversial or contentious aspects of the report? Plan graphical displays based on the answers to the above questions.

Database Management

Database management applications allow one to keep track of almost anything one can imagine. Inventory and mailing lists are excellent uses for such applications. One can link the data to spreadsheets and drop tables into a word-processing report. If one has too much related information to keep track of in one table, one can create relationships that tie two or more tables together. The query option is a powerful information search feature. For example, one can query for the names of the female senior citizens who called 911 in the last three months or the names of teenagers who have volunteered in a department in the last year.

E-mail

E-mail is helping offices cut down on paperwork and speed communication while saving money in terms of mail and phone costs and time savings. Of course, e-mail also has a down side. One's e-mailbox can also get filled with useless lists of jokes, reports that do not need to be widely shared, and personal mail. As no office can exist today without wordprocessing, the same can be said about e-mail. If one is to communicate, one needs to know how to send, respond to, copy others, customize address book, flag mail, etc. One point about the use of e-mail needs to be stressed. Communication that used to be done by phone or in person now is often done by e-mail. E-mail encourages people to talk more frankly, quickly (both in terms of number of words used and speed of reply), and equally. There are no cues from word inflections or facial expressions in e-mail. Keep this point in mind when one sends e-mail to people one does not communicate often with in person or by phone. Major misunderstandings can result from e-mail communication, and such misunderstandings take longer to catch or clear up.

Internet

The World Wide Web is exploding daily with sites that are used by or are maintained by government units, who started it in the first place. Cities and states in the U.S. use home pages to attract both businesses and visitors and to learn about their citizens through surveys. Home pages are used to provide services too. For example, cities and counties post job openings, building applications, bid requests, and low income housing applications. Information for the local citizenry from weather reports to lists of important dates and phone numbers to restaurant locations are just some of the information that can be found on home pages. Governmental units also use the World Wide Web to do research. For instance, when a city is considering a new ordinance, it can check out how other cities have dealt with the topic. Cities are also utilizing the Internet to spread the word about dangerous fugitives. A sound familiarity with the Internet is essential for anyone seeking to work in or learn about public administration. One should not only know how to surf the internet but also one should check out city, county, state, and federal sites. The magazine *Government Technology* gives yearly awards to the best government sites.

GIS

Geographic information systems initially were used in planning and public works departments. But the mapping uses have exploded as other departments have recognized the usefulness of GIS capabilities. Land can be mapped to show electrical and water lines, elevation, ownership, vegetation, parcel value, watercourses, erosion, soil type, wildlife habitat, pesticide and fertilizer application, rat population, type of crime, and such data can be connected and overlaid for multiple uses. In fact, cities have found that they can sell their GIS generated maps. The new hand held GIS systems with microphones open up even more possibilities. For example, the hand held voice activated systems allow inspectors driving down streets to automatically order work to be done or to cite code violators by just saying," stop sign down" or "pothole." Another benefit of GIS is the maps can really enhance public presentations.

Dedicated Applications

On the job or classroom experience in dedicated computer applications is also very helpful. However, unlike the generic applications, knowledge of specialized applications is not as versatile to all settings. There are many dedicated applications for hundreds of tasks such as case management, manpower, disaster recovery, and mapping. The point is that knowing one of these applications may not be potable to the same job but in a different organization. Applications are often tailored for an organization or custom-made. Moreover, applications have different impacts from one setting to another. Consider the varied uses for teleconferencing. Teleconferencing can be used for parole hearings or staff training or agency meetings. Each of these uses have different impacts and their effectiveness varies by the setting.

What is clearly useful is some familiarity with the types of applications used in the field in which one is planning to build one's career. Familiarity means awareness of basic features and strengths and weaknesses of applications for the line personnel, managers, and citizens. Database management issues should also be considered.

In a classroom setting, different students can present an overview of different specialized applications. This can be accomplished through overheads, handouts, or actual computer demonstrations. The overview could be based on the students' experiences, but definitely should include insights gained from interviewing several people who use the application on the job. The people chosen to be interviewed should have various years of experience with the application in the organization. Perspectives vary when one can include a before and after time frame as well as variability in job responsibilities. Presentations and related papers should touch on the strengths and weaknesses of the applications to do the work function and the ease of learning how to use the application.

Management Issues

A Master's in Public Administration signifies the recipient has the skills to manage people and tasks in an environment of both internal and external political demands and responsibilities. What are some key issues about which an MPA graduate should be conversant when it comes to managing in a computerized environment? First and foremost is the fact that computerization of a task does not necessarily lead to payoffs and more than likely will underachieve expectations. It is important to understand what factors affect payoffs and then address how to deal with them. The following section briefly points out factors that have been shown to influence the usefulness of computer applications.

Quality of Data

An absolute condition for achieving payoffs from computerization is that the data must be accurate. A system to control input errors and to change data must be instituted. In contrast, the length of time to get information from a computerized task does not need to be made as short as possible. Data that can be quickly retrieved is very nice, but data that many users think takes too long to be retrieved will still be used if it is considered useful.

Training

Training is also a key management issue. One obviously needs a training program to teach users how to use new applications. Another related consideration is having a way to train new hires in ongoing applications. In addition, an initial training program should not be considered the end of training. Follow-up training programs or help sessions need to be routinized; training should be considered an ongoing process.

Then there is the issue of who should do the training. There is no clear answer whether in-house trainers or external trainers are best, nor whether professional trainers or just experienced employees are best (Northrop et al., 1994). Professional trainers bring experience in conveying application knowledge, but sometimes an employee who uses the program is better at answering questions about how to use the program within the context of the work product.

Personnel

Employees bring skills to an organization and also gain skills on the job. The effectiveness and efficiency benefits of computerized applications are affected by the skills of the employees who use them. Some employees come with knowledge and experience with the computerized application; some do not. Some employees are more resistant than others to using and exploring a new or updated application. And, as is well known, employees vary in their work ethic, concentration, and diligence.

Hardware Compatibility

The computer field is known for its almost constant change. Upgrading or expanding a computer system is an expensive and disruptive proposition. There can be costs if one only upgrades the computers of some employees. Reports may no longer be able to be downloaded or sent to normal recipients if the upgrade results in computers that need to talk to each other are incompatible .

Resources

Computerized applications may be able to provide all sorts of new and valuable information to decision makers. But the information is only useful if the organization has the resources to take full advantage of the new information. To illustrate, a computerized manpower application system can outline where and how many police officers one needs to deploy at a certain time of day across the city. If the police department has that many officers available, all is well and good. If not, whether due to limits on force size or just scheduling variations, the computerized manpower information will not help much in the fight against crime.

What One Automates

When one is automating a task or upgrading a task system, the success of the present system to do the work needs to be considered. Often an organization just automates the way they presently do a task. If, for example, the present way of tracking the names of people who should be paying child support only finds and receives payment from 20 percent of the list, then the automated system will not likely do better. Therefore, an evaluation of the extent to which policy goals are currently being met should be required before a task is automated or upgraded.

Who to Involve in Adoption Decisions

Oddly enough, some organizations never consult the very employees who will use the new computer application to see what they need and to get their input on the weaknesses of the old application. Employees from all levels who will use the application should be asked for their input, from line personnel to managers.

Purchasing a Customized System

Experience at the federal, state, and local level point out that purchasing an information system is rife with risks. Millions have been spent on systems that were delivered years after being promised or that never worked. Choosing a company and writing a contract should be done with much care. Consider that purchasing a customized system as similar to choosing and working with a contractor to remodel one's house. Payments should not be made till each stage is approved. A final payment should be held back till the developer fixes the little problems in the system. Expect to pay more if the organization changes its specifications of the system, but build into the contract a cost. A bonus can be offered if the system is finished before the agreed upon date, and penalties can be assessed if the system is delivered after the expected date. Above all, ask for references and check them. Send a representative to other organizations that have contracted with the system development company. Do not just call. Remember line staff may have a different perspective than a manager; all input is relevant.

Management Support

Management must be supportive of the computer application. Staff personnel have been known to just not use the application because management has given the indirect signal that they do not see the usefulness of the application. One way that management can effectively show support is to actively use the application or the generated reports. If staff have a question about the application, management should be able to answer the question, even if this only means referring the staff to someone else who can help. Management must show they care about staff knowing and effectively using the application. It is up to management to sell the usefulness of the application to employees.

Security

Security has been considered a major management concern since the early computerization of data. If data are accessible and changeable by inappropriate personnel, the usefulness of the computerized database is compromised by major legal issues involving rights. Depending on the department or agency, security issues vary. For example, police field reports once entered should not be able to be changed at will by any patrol officer. Incident reports must be protected from being expunged or altered to protect the integrity of the court case from bribes or favoritism. Personnel files need to be more widely accessible to change to update job title, benefits, and addresses. But extent of access to personnel information must also be limited. The security needed for some national computer databases, such as Social Security, is monumental.

Conclusion

A public administration graduate needs hands-on-skills in computer applications, both mastery of generic applications and familiarity with dedicated applications. Said graduate also needs to be conversant with the issues involved in successfully managing information technology and computer applications.

Professional journals do offer useful articles on information technology, even if few in number. But general PA textbooks are not a source for building one's knowledge in this important area. Thus, edited books like the present one, are critical for universities to provide a common grounding in computer education for their PA graduates.

References

Bingham, R. D., and Bowen W. M. (1994). Mainstream? Public administration over time: A topical content analysis of *Public Administration Review*. *Public Administration Review*, 54, 204-208.

Brudney, J., Hy, R. J., and Waugh W. L. (1993). Building microcomputing skills in public administration graduate education: An assessment of MPA programs. *Administration and Society*, 25, 183-203.

Cleary, R. (1990). What do MPA programs look like? Do they do what is needed? *Public Administration Review*, 50, 663-673.

Forester, J. P., and Watson, S. S. (1994). An assessment of public administration journals: The perspective of editors on editorial board members. *Public Administration Review*, 54, 474-482.

Houston, D. J., and Delevan, S. M. (1990). Public administration research: An assessment of journal publications. *Public Administration Review*, 50, 674-681.

Kraemer, K. L., and Northrop, A. (1989). Curriculum recommendations for public management education in computing: an update. *Public Administration Review*, 49, 447-453.

Lan, Z. and Cayer, J. (1994). The challenges of teaching information technology use and management in a time of information revolution. *The American Review of Public Administration*, 24, 207-222.

NASPAA Ad Hoc Committee on Computers in Public Management Education. (1986). Curriculum recommendations for public management education in computing. *Public Administration Review*, 46, 595-602.

Northrop, A., Kraemer, K. L., Dunkle, D. E., King, J. L. (1994). Management policy for Greater Computer Benefits: Friendly Software, Computer Literacy, or Formal Training. *Social Science Computer Review*, 12, 383-404.

Perry, J. L., and Kraemer, K. L., (1986). Research methodology in the *Public Administration Review*, 1975-1984. Public Administration Review, 46, 215-226.

Poister, T., and Streib, G. (1989). Management tools in municipal government: trends over the past decade. 49, 240-248.

Stallings, R. A., and Ferris, J. A. (1988). Public administration research: Work in *Public Administration Review*, 1940-1984. *Public Administration Review*, 48, 580-587.

Young, C. D. (1995). An assessment of articles published by women in 15 top political science journals. *PS: Political Science and Politics*, 23, 525-533.

Journal Articles That Mention Computers

Allcorn, S. (1997). Parallel Virtual Organizations. *Administration and Society*, 29 (4), 412-439.

Botner, S. B. (1985). The use of budgeting, management tool by state government. *Public Administration Review*, 45, 616-619.

Bretschneider, S. (1990). Management information systems in public and private organizations: An empirical test. *Public Administration Review*, 50, 536-545.

Brudney, J., and Selden, S. C. (1995). The adoption of innovation by smaller local governments: The case of computer technology. *The American Review of Public Administration*, 25, 71-86.

Brudhey, J. L., Hy. R. J., and Waugh, W. L., Jr. (1993). Building microcomputing skills in public administration graduate education: An assessment of MPA programs. *Administration And Society*, 25, 183-203.

Buyers, K. M., and Palmer, D. R. (1989). The microelectronics and computer technology corporation: An assessment from market and public policy perspectives. *Administration And Society*, 21, 101-127.

Carroll, J. D., and Lynn, D. B. (1996). The Future of Federal Reinvention: Congressional Perspectives. *Public Administration Review*, 56, 299-304.

Cats-Baril, W., and Thompson, R. (1995). Managing information technology projects in the public sector. *Public Administration Review*, 55, 559-566.

Caudle, S. L. (1990). Managing information resources in state government. *Public Administration Review*, 50, 515-524.

Cleary, R. (1990). What do MPA programs look like? Do they do what is needed? *Public Administration Review*, 50, 663-673.

Cleveland, H. (1985). The twilight of hierarchy: Speculations on the global information society. *Public Administration Review*, 45, 185-195.

Crewson, P.E. and Fisher, B.S. (1997). Growing Older and Wiser: The Changing Skill Requirements of City Administrators, *Public Administration Review*, 57, 380-386

Danziger, J. and Kraemer, K. L. (1985). Computerized data-based systems and productivity among professional workers: The case of detectives. *Public Administration Review*, 45, 196-209.

Danziger, J., Kraemer, K. L., Dunkle, D., and King, J. L. (1993). Enhancing the quality of computing service: Technology, structure, and people. *Public Administration Review*, 53, 161-169.

Fraumann, E. (1997). Economic Espionage: Security Missions Redefined. *Public Administration Review*, 57, 303-308.

Gianakis, G. A. and McCue, C. P. (1997). Administrative Innovation Among Ohio Local Government Finance Officers. *American Review of Public Administration*, 27 (3), 270-286.

Globerman, S. and Vining, A. R. (1996). A Framework for Evaluating the Government Contracting Out Decision with an Application to Information Technology. *Public Administration Review*, 56, 577-586.

Grizzle, G. A. (1985). Essential skills for financial management: Are MPA students acquiring the necessary competencies? *Public Administration Review*, 45, 840-844.

Hendrick, R. (1994). An information infrastructure for innovative management of government. *Public Administration Review*, 54, 543-550.

Kraemer, K. L., Guraxani, V., and King, J. L. (1992). Economic development, government policy, and the diffusion of computing in Asia-Pacific countries. *Public Administration Review*, 52, 146-154.

Kraemer, K. L. and King, J. L. (1987). Computers and the constitution: A helpful, harmful or harmless relationship? *Public Administration Review*, 47, 93-105.

Kraemer, K. L. and Northrop, A. (1989). Curriculum recommendations for public management education in computing: An update. *Public Administration Review*, 49, 447-453.

Lan, Z., and Cayer, J., 1994. The challenges of teaching information technology use and management in a time of information revolution. *The American Review of Public Administration*, 24, 207-222.

Lee, R. D., Jr. (1997). A Quarter Century of State Budgeting Practices. *Public Administration Review*, 57, 133-140.

Levin, M. A. (1991). The information-seeking behavior of local government officials. *The American Review of Public Administration*, 21, 271-286.

Lewis, D. L. (1991). Turning rust into gold: Planned facility management. *Public Administration Review*, 51, 494-502.

Nedovic-Budic, Z. and Godschalk, D. R. (1996). Human Factors in Adoption of Geographic Information Systems (GIS): A Local Government Case Study. *Public Administration Review*, 57, 554-567.

Newcomer, K. E., and Caudle, S. (1991). Evaluating public sector information systems: More than meets the eye. *Public Administration Review*, 51, 377-384.

Norris, D. G., and Kraemer, K. L. (1996). Mainframe and PC Computing in American Cities: Myths and Realities. *Public Administration Review*, 56, 568-576.

Northrop, A., Kraemer, K. L., Dunkle, D., and King, J. L. (1990). Payoffs from computerization: Lessons over time. *Public Administration Review*, 50, 505-514.

Poister, T. H. and Streib, G. (1989). Management tools in municipal governments: Trends over the past decade. *Public Administration Review*, 49, 240-248.

Regan, P. M. (1986). Privacy, government information, and technology. *Public Administration Review*, 46, 629-634.

Relyea, H. C. (1986). Access to government information in the information age. *Public Administration Review*, 46, 635-639.

Roberts, N. (1997). Public Deliberation: An Alternative Approach to Crafting Policy and Setting Direction. *Public Administration Review*, 57, 124-132.

Rocheleau, B. (1992). Information management in the public sector; taming the computer for public managers. *Public Administration Review*, 52, 398-400.

Rocheleau, B. (1994). The software selection process in local governments. *The American Review of Public Administration*, 24, 317-330.

Slack, J. (1990). Information, training, and assistance needs of municipal governments. *Public Administration Review*, 50, 450-457.

Ventura, S. J. (1995). The use of geographic information systems in local government. *Public Administration Review*, 55, 61-467.

Williams III, F. P., McShane, M., and Seehnst, D. (1994). Barriers to effective performance review: The seduction of raw data. *Public Administration Review*, 54, 537-542.

2

The Political Dimensions of Information Systems in Public Administration

by
Bruce Rocheleau
Northern Illinois University

Many information management and generalist managers ignore the political aspects of managing information systems. But this chapter shows that political factors are often the most crucial in determining how successful information technology is. The purpose of the chapter is to provide awareness of the political context of information systems decisions. The political aspects of computing are discussed with respect to two major categories: (1) Internal, organizational politics concerning issues involving organizational members; (2) External politics concerning how the governmental organization relates to its councils or boards, external groups, and general citizenry. Several examples of internal politics are given including the structuring of the information function, the purchasing of information systems, interdepartmental sharing of information, and communication flows. External examples of politics are given concerning relationships with legislatures and citizenry such as disputes over funding, computer disasters, privatization, the Internet and telecommunications planning.

Introduction

Generalist administrators perceive computing as a technical area separate from the hurly burly of politics. We argue in this paper that the critical success factors for information management practitioners are nontechnical issues involving organizational and external politics. In order to be

Copyright© 1999, Idea Group Publishing.

effective, information managers and the generalist administrators to whom they report need to give more attention to these political issues than they have in the past. Otherwise, these managers are unlikely to achieve important goals with their systems.

In part, this traditional, technician's view of computing derived from the fact that, in the past, computing was constrained to the production of routine reports and billings. A major empirical study in the 1980's (Lucas, 1984) found that information service departments had little prestige and visibility in most organizations. Decisions about information systems did not constitute a critical success factor for most private or public organizations. Consequently, decisions about information technology (IT) could be safely delegated to technicians and generalist managers did not need to be involved much.

Over the past decade, computing has become much more important in governmental as well as private organizations. This is not to say that computing was ever nonpolitical. Detailed studies of cities in the 1970's (Laudon, 1974) & 1980's (Danziger et al., 1982) found cases involving computing and politics. But computing was less central to public organizations then. Most employees had minimal contact with computing. Computing is now used as a major means of communication (e.g., use of e-mail and the Internet) and for support of major decisions (e.g., what if analyses for budgeting and labor negotiations, forecasting of revenues). As the importance of and expenditures devoted to computing have grown, IT has involved more organizational and external politics.

The purpose of this paper is to help both generalist and information managers understand the political context of computing. Politics concerns issues of power rather than technical issues. We break the politics of computing into two major different categories: (1) Internal, organizational politics concerning issues involving organizational members; (2) External politics concerning how the governmental organization relates to its councils or boards, external groups, and general citizenry. We have avoided giving many prescriptions to managers on how to behave politically not only because research about politics is sketchy but also due to the fact that politics is highly contextual . The course of action that should be pursued depends on the complex interplay of political resources of the actors involved, ethical concerns, legal issues, as well as economic and technical factors.

A Note on Sources and Methods

Our study makes use of our own experiences as well as drawing on literature concerning public information management. We found very little formal research in recent years that explicitly focuses on the politics of information management. Indeed, most of the major and rigorous academic studies that have focused on the politics of computing date back to the mainframe era (e.g., Danziger, 1977; Dutton & Kraemer, 1985). In some more recent studies of computing, political aspects are touched on and we draw on examples drawn from the literature to illustrate our points. Due to its lack of coverage in traditional academic journals, we make use of periodicals such as computer magazines and newspaper articles concerning computing. Also, many of our examples are based on our own 18 years of experience and study of public organizations at the municipal, state, and Federal levels to illustrate our points. Our study is an initial attempt at identifying relevant issues and to illustrate them.

Information Systems and Internal, Organizational Politics

Although almost any decision about computing can become embroiled in politics, our experience is that the most prominent and important political issues involve questions of control and power over the following kinds of decisions:
- Information Management Structures: How should information management be structured? Where should control over information be placed in the organizational structure?
- Hardware and Software Acquisitions: What should be the nature of the process? How centralized should it be? Who should be involved?
- Information Management, Sharing Information, and Interdepartmental Relations: What process should be used to determine information sharing and exchange? How will computing influence and be influenced by other aspects of interdepartmental relations?
- Communication Flows: How does computing influence information flows in organizations? What, if any, rules and procedures should be established?

Although each of these decision areas has technical aspects, nontechnical issues such as concerns about autonomy and power often dominate decisions about these issues. Below, we outline how each of these decision areas involves important political aspects. Many information managers have technical backgrounds and prefer to avoid these political aspects. Likewise, generalist managers such as city managers have often ignored direct involvement in these decisions due to their lack of expertise concerning computers. As a consequence, it has been our experience that these decisions are often dominated by persons other than information system or generalist managers. Consequently, these issues are often decided without adequate attention from those with the most expertise or broadest perspective.

Information Management Structures

In the days of the mainframe, there was often little interest on the part of most employees as to how computing was structured. Due to the fact that computing was used to perform routine tasks such as water bills and routine accounting reports, in many municipal governments, the computing function was placed originally under the control of the Budget/Finance department. Computing was often done on a mainframe machine and the development of applications was controlled by data processing departments. End users tended to have little involvement in computing decisions. As the importance of computing has grown and spread along with decentralization due to microcomputers and distributed computing, the original structures have become outmoded. When the information systems department starts to make decisions as to what software and hardware they can use, then other departments begin to care more about how computing is organized.

But there is no consensus as to the best method of organizing computing. How centralized or decentralized should computing be? There are advantages and disadvantages to centralization of computing so that one major review of centralization-decentralization debate (King, 1983) concluded that "political factors" are paramount in decisions on how to structure computing. Business organizations have encountered the same dilemma. Markus (1983) has described how business departments have resisted efforts at integration of information systems. Davenport et al. (1992) found several reasons behind information politics including: (1) Units that share information fully may lose their reason for existence; (2) Weak divisions may be reluctant to share information when they are sensitive about their performance.

Where should computing be placed in the organizational structure of a public organization such as a city? Should it be a separate, line department, a subunit of another department (e.g., budgeting/finance), or a staff unit to the manager/mayor? Should mayors/managers require that the head of computing report directly to themselves or should they place a staff member in charge? There are no universal answers to these questions. The centrality of computing to all departments would suggest that information management should not be structurally placed under a single department such as budget/finance. But managers, both computing and generalist, need to think carefully about the implications of these different arrangements. In the past, many local government executives have complained about the feeling that the information they need to run a city exists somewhere, but that they can't seem to access it effectively (Danziger, 1977). Ackoff (1967) long ago pointed out that managers who took a hands off approach to computing would suffer from "management misinformation systems." Decisions concerning the structure will be based on a number of factors, including the degree of interest of the generalist managers in computing as well as what goals managers have for IT.

In the private sector, there has been a secular trend to organization of information technology under a person labeled a Chief Information Officer (CIO). A major rationale for the existence of a CIO (as opposed to a traditional data processing manager) is that (s)he will not be restricted to technical issues but act as a change agent, politician, proactivist, and integrator as well (Pitkin, 1993). Recently, the Federal government (Koskinen, 1996; Pastore, 1995) has moved towards the use of CIO in order to improve information management. Will it have a positive impact? Should the CIO model be followed in municipalities and other public organizations?

Merely assigning the CIO title does not ensure that these functions will be performed. For example, a study (Pitkin, 1993) of CIOs in universities found that, despite their title, they did not view themselves as executives and often do not perform these non-technical roles. Without a push from a CIO, public organizations may fail to make good use of information technology. For example, one study found that police regularly used their database systems for reports to external agencies, but rarely for internal management purposes (Rocheleau, 1993). There is evidence that CIO performance in the private sector has not been viewed favorably by their fellow managers (Freedman, 1994) and that CIOs in both public and private sector are blamed for failures (Newcombe, 1995; Cone, 1996).

In our experience, there is a wide variety in the amount of attention devoted by managers to structural issues concerning computing. In one city, a city manager was very much focused on information management and devoted great attention to decisions made concerning computing by the city, in effect acting as the municipality's CIO. When this manager left for another city, he was succeeded by another manager who paid very little attention to computing. Devoting great attention to computing can be counterproductive. The first manager devoted to computing issues became embroiled in severe struggles with his new board and organization over computing that contributed to his resignation from his new job.

Although there is no single right way of organizing computing, each manager needs to ensure that the structure will provide relevant, timely and reliable information. Kraemer and King (1976: 25) argue that public executives spend too much of their time on decisions concerning the purchase of equipment and too little on other important information management issues that have less visibility but are equally important. They (Kraemer & King, 1976) emphasized the need for generalist managers to take personal responsibility for computing and to be engaged in the following decisions: how to structure computing, the purposes to be served by computing, and implementation issues such as the goals of computing and the structures used to achieve them.

Some experts (e.g., Severin, 1993) argue that the Chief Executive Officer (CEO) of an organization should be the CIO. Mayor Stephen Goldsmith of Indianapolis is an example of a CEO who does appear to have taken charge of the information technology function and instituted a number of important policy changes such as privatizing many IT functions as well as encouraging e-mail from any employees directly to himself (Poulos, 1998). John Kost (1996) was appointed to be CIO of the State of Michigan by Governor Engler and instituted several policy goals of Engler's such as consolidation of state data centers, establishment of statewide standards, and reengineering of IT including its procurement process. It is notable that Kost did not have any IT background at all (Kost, 1996). Kost maintains that it is more important that the CIO understand the business of government than have a strong technology background (Kost, 1996:30). Kost proceeded to do a major reengineering of IT in Michigan and claims that they successfully achieved many of the goals set by Engler.

Paul Strassmann served as director of defense information at the Defense Department from 1991 to 1993 where he was in charge of a $10 billion annual budget for IT and instituted major changes in the procurement process. Strassmann subsequently published a book entitled *The Politics of Information Management* (Strassmann, 1995: xxv) in which he argues that managing IT is "primarily a matter of politics and only secondarily a matter of technology." Strassmann goes on to hold that only the technical aspects of information can be safely delegated to computer specialists. Strassmann (1995: xxix) supports a federalist approach to information management, "delegating maximum authority to those who actually need to use the information." Strassmann (1994: 10) believes that it is the duty of the CEO to establish general principles: "Without a general consensus about the principles and policies of who does what, when, and how, you cannot create a foundation on which to construct information superiority." Strassman says that the CEO should never delegate the responsibility for information management to a CIO because it is the CEO who must decide how to apply information systems.

Control over Hardware and Software Acquisitions

When direct use of computing was restricted to computer programmers, there was little interest in other departments concerning decisions about hardware and software. But as end-user computing has grown, end users have enjoyed the freedom to innovate and strong centrifugal forces have resulted. Centrifugal forces are strong. Employees often have strong personal preferences and feelings concerning software and hardware purchases. Part of the ethos of end user computing is the ability to make your own decisions about software and hardware. Allowing each end user (or end user department) to make decisions about software is likely to lead to multiple hardware and software platforms. In some cases, the case for a separate standard is based on strong technical reasons. For example, Unix workstations have been used by engineering departments in cities while the rest of the city is likely to use IBM PCs. Until recently, only these Unix workstations had the power and software to perform the graphics required for the engineering jobs. Consequently, engineers often used Unix-based machines while the rest of the municipality usually employed IBM PC microcomputers and this multiplicity of platforms was justified by technical considerations.

However, in many cases, generalist and information managers allowed user departments to make decisions about which PC software they would use and consequently we know of small cities that had several different spreadsheets and word processor programs. We have come across cities where there were strong divisions between Macintosh and IBM-compatible PC-users. For example, in one municipality, the city manager's office uses Macintosh computers while the rest of the city runs IBM PCs. The situation has led to the necessity for the Macintoshes to have a special board (costing a thousand dollars each) installed to enable easy-sharing of data base files. There are other tradeoffs between allowing each department to use its preferred software and hardware versus centralization. Multiple platforms complicate training, backup, and maintenance too. The existence of "platform zealots" is not unusual and can lead to conflict (Hayes, 1996). In our experience, these problems with multiple platforms have led certain managers toward establishing a single platform and also centralized control over hardware and software acquisitions. In some cases, this author has seen an interdepartmental committee established to make purchasing decisions which exceed some threshold of expenditure. In other cases, the review process is done alone by the person heading the information management function. In some cases, local control of IT purchases may be difficult or impossible if the funding source for hardware and software is from another level of government (e.g., state or Federal funding). Regardless of what approach is taken, information management and generalist administrators need to provide the centripetal force needed to integrate information management in public organizations. If they don't do it, no one else will. But this integrating role is not popular and it requires that the manager use powers of persuasion, negotiation, bargaining, and sometimes authority and threats.

Many generalist managers may want to establish a general policies that influence purchasing choices of departments such as the following: (1) Some governments take a position that data processing functions should be privatized as much as possible; (2) Many governments are instituting on-line purchasing and forms of purchasing pools which departments may be required to adhere to; (3) Some governments are establishing special arrangements with a small number (e.g., one or two) computer vendors with the idea of achieving advantageous pricing arrangements. Both the Federal and many state governments have been revamping the purchasing process with more emphasis on speeding the process and emphasizing value rather than lowest cost. Kost (1996: 8) believes that the CIO and CEO need to take charge of the purchasing process if they are to achieve goals such as privatization and value-purchasing:

> For example, a policy advocating privatization is doomed unless the purchasing process allows privatization to occur .... An intransigent purchasing director can often do more to thwart the direction of the administration than a policy-maker from the opposite political party.

At the Federal level, Strassmann implemented a corporate information management (CIM) initiative that was aimed at streamlining the military's information system purchases and, for example, using the same systems across the different services. Strassmann enunciated the following principle which the technicians were expected to follow: enhance existing information systems rather than "opt for new systems development as the preferred choice" (Strassmann, 1995: 94). In one case, this CIM approach killed an $800 million Air Force system and replaced it with a similar one that was used by the Army (Caldwell, 1992). The Air Force had already spent 28 million dollars on their system and resisted the move. Observers of the process noted that it was a "turf issue" and a GAO report concluded that CIM required centralization and a "cultural change" that were difficult for the Defense Department (Caldwell, 1992: 12-13).

The acquisition and implementation of new systems often engender resistance. One of the basic principles of planning for new computer systems is to involve the people who will be using the system in its design, testing, and implementation phases. Indeed, there are entire books written concerning the principles of participatory design (Kello, 1996). An apparent example of user resistance occurred recently in Chicago when a new computer system was introduced to speed the building permits process. Since the system has been implemented, lengthy delays have drawn widespread criticism (Washburn, 1998) and the delays have caused a bottleneck during a time of booming construction. The new system tracks permit applications, allows scanning in of plumbing, electrical, and other plans so that the plans can be viewed simultaneously on several screens. There have been some technical problems acknowledged by city officials. For example, some staff had trouble seeing plan details on their screens and on-the-spot corrections were not possible due since applicants were not present when reviews were done. But officials argue that many of the complaints are due to the fact that the system has changed the process of handling permits. Permits are now done on a first-in-first-out basis while before expediters used to "butt into line" and now fear their loss of influence under the new system (Washburn, 1998). They contend that the expediters are deliberately spreading false rumors about extensive delays in an attempt to "torpedo the new system." In such cases, it is clear that generalist and information system managers will have to be sensitive to organizational politics and employ their personal and political resources to achieve change.

Computing, Sharing Information, and the Politics of Interdepartmental Relations

In addition to purchasing issues, there are many other interdepartmental issues that need to be dealt with by CIOs and generalist managers in order to establish an effective information system. For example, computing creates the possibility of free and easy exchange of information among governmental organizations. But information is power and organizations tend to be sensitive about giving out information to outsiders, especially if it reflects on the quality of the organization's operations. Many agencies prefer to maintain autonomy over their data. For example, we worked with the job training agency of a state agency in a project that was to employ data bases drawn from several state agencies to evaluate the state's job training programs. However, despite obtaining verbal agreements from the top managers of the agency, the lower level programming staff delayed the sharing of data for months. It became clear that they saw our requests as an additional burden on them that would make their job more difficult if such requests were to become routinized.

Some new technologies such as geographic information systems (GIS) are forcing changes in computing structures and procedures among departments. Although many geographic information systems are initiated by a single department, the systems are expensive and the software is relevant to many different departments. When Kansas City decided to build a GIS (Murphy, 1995), they found it necessary to form a GIS committee (made up of representatives of four participating departments: Public Works, Water, City Development, and Finance) to conduct an interdepartmental needs assessment and resolve problems such as how to resolve conflicts in data bases and how to minimize data base development costs. Although such developments do force structural changes, there is still wide latitude in regard to the nature of the structure. Sharing data can lead to conflict. In a study of exchange of information between municipal department such as fire and police, Rocheleau (1995) found that a large percentage fail to exchange information despite overlaps in their job responsibilities concerning problems like arson and emergencies. The author studied one city where the fire department, clerk's office, and building department all shared responsibility for entering information about buildings, but each department tended to point its finger at others when mistakes in the data were discovered. A major task of generalist and information managers is to deal with departmental concern with autonomy over the databases. If they defer to the status quo, information management will be less effective. Bringing about changes required to achieve integration may aggravate such conflicts. Overcoming these obstacles requires negotiating, political and organizational skills.

Top managers may force the exchange of information via command. However, employees often find ways to resist change. For example, they may provide poor quality information which renders the exchange useless. Markus and Keil (1994) provide a case study of a new and improved decision support system designed to help sales persons that failed because it worked counter to underlying organizational incentives.

Knights and Murray (1994) have conducted one of the few careful studies of the politics of information technology. In their detailed study of IT in an insurance company, they concluded that the success and failure of the systems was closely tied to the careers of managers. Consequently, these managers often attempted to control the perception of the success of these systems because perception is reality (Knights & Murray, 1994: 172):

> The secret of success lies in the fact that if enough people believe something is a success then it really is a success...it was vital for the company and for managerial careers that the pensions project was a success.

Another detailed case study (Brown, 1998) of the implementation of a new computer system in a hospital found that different groups (the hematology ward, hematology laboratory, and information technology team) had very different perspectives on the reason for the failure of a new computer system. Moreover, each of the three groups used the common goal of patient care to legitimate their view of the system. Brown (1998) concludes that the study shows that participants were influenced by attributional egotism in which each person and group involved attributes favorable results to their own efforts and unfavorable results to external factors. Similar to Knights and Murray (1994), Brown concludes that many of the actions are taken to protect individual autonomy and discretion.

The lesson of the above cases is that, prior to implementing new systems, information managers need to assess the organizational context and determine how proposed systems will be affected by incentives, informal norms, resistance to change and sharing, as well as other forms of organizational politics. Many of these factors may be addressed by including end users in the planning process. Managers will often have to be involved in exerting political influence and engage systems outside their direct control in order to assure a successful outcome. For example, Kost (1996) describes how the Michigan Department of Transportation decided to change from a mainframe to a client/server environment which endangered the jobs of a dozen mainframe technicians. The logical step was to retrain the mainframe technicians to do the new tasks but the civil service rules and regulations required that the mainframe workers be laid off and new employees be recruited to fill the client/server positions (Kost, 1996). Thus, in order to have an effective information system, generalist and information managers will often have to seek to change rules, procedures and structures. These changes may bring information managers into conflict with other departments.

Computing and Communication Patterns:

Information technology such as e-mail can affect organizational communication patterns. Changes in communication flows can be extremely political. For example, if a subordinate communicates sensitive information to others without clearing it with her/his immediate supervisor, strife is likely to result. The current Mayor of Indianapolis, Stephen Goldsmith, encourages every police officer and other public employees to contact him directly via email (Miller, 1995a). He claims to read 400 e-mail messages a day. Should mayors/managers encourage such use of direct contacts from employees? Although such communication can and does occur via phone and face-to-face communication, e-mail communications are different from face-to-face communications—there is less rich information and many people act differently in e-mail than they do in person.

Many managers are scornful of those who use email for certain purposes (e.g., reprimands) and there has been evidence that managers retain face-to-face communication for crucial tasks such as those involving negotiations (McKinnon & Bruns, 1992). On the other hand, some recent research (Markus, 1994) found that more effective managers made greater use of e-mail. The point is that computing is changing the communication patterns of organizations. These changes have the capacity to improve communication flows. There are also important legal issues concerning e-mail records as e-mail in public organizations may be regarded as public records (Miller, 1995b; Quindlen, 1993). New technologies bring new problems. E-mail exchanges concerning policy and political issues may be obtained as part of Freedom of Information Act requests in many states.

The establishment of e-mail and other communication policies involves sensitive organizational issues. For example, if one employee sends a printed memo to an employee in another department concerning a matter of interest to his/her bosses, it is often expected that the sending employee will send a copy of the memo to the bosses. Should the same policy hold for e-mail exchanges? Is e-mail more like a formal memo where such a procedure is expected or more like an informal phone call where copying is not done? Such policies will likely lead to debate and perhaps conflict. Legal assistance such as corporate lawyers needs to be sought in order to make these decisions. However, many of these policies are so new that no clear legal guidelines exist and a generalist will have to make the decision based on what is best in terms of ethical, organizational, and political considerations. Generalist and information managers need to be actively involved in making these decisions.

External Politics And Computing

There are several ways in which computing can become involved with external politics. Here are some examples:

- Legislatures, Councils and Boards of public agencies may contest the purchasing decisions of public organizations. In one case, disagreements between the city council and board were one of the major reasons behind the resignation of a city manager of a large city in Illinois. Likewise, the award of computer contracts may involve political rewards.
- Public computer records may be used for partisan politics. For example, in one Illinois city, the water bills of a village trustee were released based on the accusation by another official that the trustee had been allowed (unlike other village residents) to have unpaid bills for more than a year. Data residing in municipal and other databases may be sought to be used for political campaigns.
- The rise of the World Wide Web and related developments create the potential for many political implications. For example, some cities have employed email (Cooke, 1997) and developed discussion forums so that public officials and citizenry may interact online. However, in some cases, these forums have resulted in "high-tech lynchings" and public officials have withdrawn from them, feeling that they were under constant attack (Conte, 1995).
- Major computer disasters or failures can bring negative attention to public organizations. For example, the failure of the Federal Aviation Administration

(FAA) to successfully implement a new air traffic system and the resulting loss of power, threatening air travelers, has resulted in severe criticism of the agency (United States General Accounting Office, 1991).

- In some cases, use of computing may help to reduce the amount of ad hominem politics and give more attention to the underlying facts of cases. This was discovered by Dutton and Kraemer (1985) who studied the use of fiscal impact models on development decisions. They found that the computing models did not eliminate politics. Developers and anti-developers employed competing models with different assumptions. But the focus on the computer models helped to direct attention to facts of the case and away from personalities and unverifiable assumptions, thus facilitating compromise and agreement.

Many city managers attempt to defuse controversies over the purchasing process by involving council/board members in developing the proposals. Thus decisions will not be brought up for decision until strong council/board support exists. Achieving such a consensus may be more difficult these days because board members are more likely to be involved with computing in their own organizations (e.g., Pevtzow, 1989). When computing was restricted to mainframes and data processing departments, council/board members were less likely to feel knowledgeable and able to challenge purchases. Rocheleau (1994) found that there could be conflicts over purchasing, even if there is a consensus on what type of technology to use. For example, there may be tensions about whether to purchase from local vendors versus outside vendors.

The move to privatize information systems can create external conflicts with legislative bodies as well as unions. For example, the State of Connecticut's administration has decided to sell the state's entire system from mainframes to the desktop and hire an external vendor to handle every aspect of the information function (Daniels, 1997). Several other states have considered privatization including Indiana, Iowa, and Tennessee. In order to implement such plans, the managers will have to negotiate with legislatures and unions in order to negotiate agreements. For example, the Connecticut administration (Daniels, 1997) moved to assure jobs of the state IT workers for a period of two years at the same salary and benefits in order to have the privatization move approved.

Although privatization may be used to achieve positive goals, it can also be used for political rewards and result in problems. One such example occurred recently when a computer vendor, Management Services of Illinois Inc. (MSI), was found guilty of fraud and bribery connected with the State of Illinois awarding a very favorable contract to them (Pearson & Parsons, 1997). MSI had legally donated more than $270,000 in computer services and cash to Illinois Governor Edgar's campaign. The jury found that the revised contract had cheated taxpayers of more than $7 million. Campaign donations as well as the flow of governmental and political staff between government and private vendors can influence the awarding of contracts.

At the same time that many states and municipalities are exploring privatization of their information management function, there are several municipalities which are moving to become telecommunication owners which leads to political controversy. For example, Tacoma's (Washington) municipal power company is aiming to build and provide cable services to homes and thus put it in competition with the local phone and cable companies (Healey, 1997). Many other cities including several small communities such as Fort Wright (Kentucky) are also planning to build telecommunication networks (Newcombe, 1997) in the U.S. and are also providing telecommunication services for businesses and private homes in their communities. The rationale behind these moves is that the private cable and local phone companies have a poor record of providing up-to-date service (Healey, 1997). These moves have often been labeled as "socialism" and opposed by the local cable and/or phone companies. But, in the Tacoma case, most local business leaders are backing the municipality because of the desire to have better technology (Healey, 1997). Some states (e.g., Texas, Arkansas, and Missouri) have prohibited municipal organizations from becoming telecommunication providers (Healey, 1997). The state of California is in the process of privatizing its state telecom system (Harris, 1998). But, in Iowa, many municipalities have been laying fiber to deliver cable in competition with cities. The first suit brought by a phone company was found in favor of the municipality (Harris, 1998). Although many information managers prefer to avoid controversy, telecommunications issues such as cable and access to the internet have become so central to legislatures, councils, and the public that it will be difficult to avoid involvement concerning privatization or public ownership strategy.

It is likely that the majority of computer problems and disasters remain unknown to the public and even legislative bodies. However, certain disasters have so much impact on key operations that they do become public and create crises for generalist and information managers. For example, the delay in the opening of the new Denver Airport was due to software problems controlling the baggage system for the new airport. Likewise, the State of Illinois Medicaid program encountered many computer system failures; the system assigned patients to inappropriate health care providers (Krol, 1994).

Many disasters are beyond the control of managers and there is little they can do other than plan for emergencies. However, in many cases, disasters appear to result from overly high expectations for new computer systems and a lack of understanding on how difficult it is to implement a new system. This author has reviewed a large number of computer problems and failures (Rocheleau, 1997). Both the Federal Aviation Administration (FAA) and Internal Revenue Service (IRS) have experienced major failures that have led to threats from Congress to defund systems (Cone, 1998). Another example is the State of Florida's new human services system which encountered much higher-than-projected costs and slower-than-expected implementation (Kidd, 1995). The perceived disaster led to the loss of job of the state official in charge of the new system along with threatened legal action. But over the long run, it appears that the system actually worked and has helped to reduce costs. Information management officials need to ensure that executives and the public have a realistic expectations of system costs and performance. Computer problems and disasters are likely to occur more often as computing becomes central to governmental performance and communication with its constituents. In these situations, managers cannot avoid dealing with computing even if they have removed themselves from any decisions concerning it.

In contrast to the disaster cases, some politicians and managers make use of notable achievements in computing to boost their reputation for innovation and effectiveness. However, it can be dangerous for politicians or managers to claim success for large-scale new systems until the systems have been fully implemented and tested. For example, State of Illinois Comptroller Loleta Didrickson introduced a powerful new computer system that was aimed at speeding the issuance of checks as well as improving access to on-line information during June of 1997 (Manier, 1997). But soon afterwards, there were complaints that checks were arriving behind schedule and that matters had not improved (Ziegler, 1997). The agency stated that it was just taking time for workers to get used to the new system. The lesson for managers is clear: new computer systems that are large-scale and introduce major changes usually experience significant startup problems and claims of success should be muted until success can be proven.

Most information managers prefer to avoid the release of information with political implications. But often they cannot avoid releasing such information and need to have a defensible policy in this regard. Freedom of Information Act (FOIA) requests cover computer records in most states. Issues of privacy and public interest often collide and managers are often forced to make unpleasant choices. Although these problems existed prior to computers, the existence of computing has made it possible for outsiders to conduct very detailed critiques of the practices of public agencies with emphasis on pointing out their failures and questionable decisions on the part of public agencies. For example, the *Chicago Tribune* did a reanalysis of computerized information from the Illinois Department of Public Aid to do an expose of fraud and waste in its Medicaid system (Brodt, Possley & Jones, 1993). The extent, magnitude, and speed of their analysis would have been impossible without access to computerized records.

Generalist and information managers picture technology as a way to better services but they should be aware that same technologies and databases are likely to be employed for political purposes. For example, many municipal and state governments are now constructing powerful geographic information systems (GIS) that are aimed at improving services to citizens through the mapping of integrated databases. However, GIS systems and their data are now being used for "cyber ward heeling" in the 1990s and facilitate such traditional functions like the mapping of volunteers, canvassing of voters, and location of rally sites (Novotny & Jacobs, 1997). Politicians are likely to seek data from these public information systems to conduct their political campaigns. For example, databases allow the targeting of campaigns so that candidates can use several different messages and conduct "stealth campaigns" without alerting their opponents. Thus, the richer and more powerful local GIS systems become, the more attractive they will be as databases for political activities; this could lead to controversy.

The impact of the World Wide Web has especially important implications for politics. Researchers such as Robert Putnam (1995) point out to a substantial decrease in some forms of civic participation on the part of the public. Many people are frightened to speak at public hearings. The Web offers a way of increasing public participation in community decisions (Alexander & Grubbs, 1998). Many people see us entering a new age of cyberdemocracy (Stahlman, 1995). Shy people and stutterers would be able to provide testimony electronically and their arguments would be judged based on content rather than their appearance or public-speaking skills (Conte, 1995). Municipalities may help to develop useful networks such as senior citizen discussions. Parents can use the system to update themselves on student homework assignments.

But, as noted above, there are several drawbacks to teledemocracy and development of interactive Internet applications:

- There is less inhibition in telecommunications than in person communications against intemperate statements. Consequently, electronic forums often degenerate into "flaming" wars. The originator of the Santa Monica (California) on-line discussion system argued that, if he were to do it over again, he would like to have a moderator for the system and charge user fees (Schuler, 1995; Conte, 1995).
- Many people lack the computing technology and/or skills to participate in these electronic discussions (Wilhelm, 1997).
- It is feared by some that easing access to public testimony and input to public officials may result in such a massive and discordant amount of input that democracy would be stymied and that gridlock would increase.
- The Internet raises fears about privacy. Efforts to improve access can often lead to resistance. For example, the Social Security Administration (SSA) made interactive benefits estimates available over the Internet but was forced to withdraw the service due to privacy issues (United States General Accounting Office, 1997; James, 1997). Social security numbers are not very private and all someone needed was the number plus the recipient's state of birth and mother's maiden name to gain access to earnings and benefits information.
- Public online systems may become campaign vehicles for certain politicians as occurred in one case with Santa Monica's PEN system (Schmitz, 1997).

A detailed account (Schmitz, 1997) of a discussion group concerning homelessness on Santa Monica's PEN system made the following points about the successes and failures of on-line groups: (1) The discussion group was successful in bringing together for discussion purposes people on an equal basis people who would never have exchanged in face-to-face meetings; (2) But electronic media demand keyboarding and writing skills. Thus there are many obstacles to the successful participation of the poor. One recent study by Gregson (1997) found that even politically active citizens were not able to transfer their activism to a community network without substantial training and experience. It is instructive to look at the City of Santa Monica's on-line (http://pen.ci.santa-monica.us/pen/cityhall/telcomm/execsumm.htm) telecommunications plan and how it seeks public involvement:

(1) They employed a community survey, focus groups and interviews with providers of communication services to solicit input. They found the computer penetration at 60 percent.
(2) They did an internal needs assessment which, among other things, studied the coordination of right of way management so that costs and annoyance can be minimized from repairs, construction, and the placement of antenna structures.
(3) They explicitly considered construction of a full-service network to act as direct competition to the local phone and cable company which they rejected due to costs and vagaries of the environment. They decided to construct a municipal fiber network to connect major city and school facilities.

It is important that governments construct formal plans concerning their intended uses for information technology and solicit wide participation and comment. Such plans are not just for technicians.

Both generalists and information management staff need to give careful consideration to the possibilities and drawbacks of teledemocracy. If they decide to support electronic discussion groups, should they employ a moderator and, if so, who should act as a moderator? Would a moderator's censoring of input be a violation of the right to free speech? Fernback (1997) argues that most people accept moderation not as "prior restraint but as a concession" for the good of the collectivity. How can the argument that teledemocracy is elitist be handled? Is the provision of public places (e.g., in libraries) for electronic input sufficient to deal with this objection? Will input via the Web overwhelm public employees and officials? How will public employees allocate their workload — should they give equal priority to electronic as to in person or phone requests or treat them as of equal importance?

Conclusion

Failure to become engaged and knowledgeable about internal politics can undermine the efficacy of information managers. We know of cases where managers with good technical skills lost their jobs due to their failure to master organizational politics. When engaged in non-technical issues, information managers will have to rely on political skills. They may need to negotiate, bargain, dicker and haggle with other departments. They may need to formal coalitions and engage in logrolling in order to achieve their goals. A good information manager needs good political skills to be effective. We have drawn from a number of resources to illustrate the politics of information management but there exists little systematic research concerning the topic as Strassmann (1995) has pointed out. We need more research concerning the crucial issue, both in-depth qualitative case studies and as well as surveys concerning how managers employ politics in their dealings with information technology.

Generalist managers can no longer afford to ignore IT. Internal political issues such as those we have discussed above (structures, purchasing, sharing information, and electronic communication) have become so central that managers will find questions about these issues demanding attention and decision. External political issues will also grow as the Web and cyberpolitics become more prominent. Information is power and information management is political.

References

Ackoff, R. (1967). Management misinformation systems. *Management Science*, 14(4), 319-331.

Alexander, J. H. & Grubbs, J.W. (1998). Wired government: Information technology, external public organizations, and cyberdemocracy. *Public Administration and Management: An Interactive Journal* (online), 3(1), http://www.hbg.psu.edu/Faculty/jxr11/alex.html

Brodt, B.; Possley, M.; & Jones, T. (1993). One step ahead of the computer. *Chicago Tribune*, November 4, pp. 6-7.

Brown, A. (1998). Narrative politics and legitimacy in an IT implementation. Journal of *Management Studies*, 35(1), 1-22.

Caldwell, B. (1992). Battleground: An attempt to streamline the Pentagon's operations has triggered a fight for control. *Informationweek*, November 30, 12-13.

Cone, E. (1996). Do you really want this job? *Informationweek*, August 12, 63-70.

Cone, E. (1998). Crash-Landing ahead? *Informationweek*, January 12, 38-52.

Conte, C. R. (1995). Teledemocracy: For better or worse. *Governing*, June, 33-41.

Cooke, K. (1997). *Government use of e-mail to solicit public comment*. Paper presented at the 58th national conference of the American Society for Public Administration, Philadelphia, Pennsylvania, July.

Daniels, A. (1997). The billion-dollar privatization gambit. *Governing*, November, 28-31.

Danziger, J. N. (1977). Computers and the frustrated chief executive. *MIS Quarterly*, 1 (June), 43-53.

Danziger, J. N.; Dutton, W.H.; Kling, R. & Kraemer, K.L. (1982). *Computers and politics: High technology in American local governments*. New York: Columbia University Press.

Davenport, T.; Eccles, R.G. & Prusak, L. (1992). Information politics. *Sloan Management Review, Fall*, 53-65.

Dutton, W. H. & Kraemer, K.L. (1985). *Modeling as negotiating: The political dynamics of computer models in the policy process*. Norwood, New Jersey: Ablex Publishing Company.

Fernback, J. (1997). The individual within the collective: Virtual ideology and the realization of collective principles (pp. 36-54). In S.G. Jones (Ed.), *Virtual Culture: Identity and Communication in Cybersociety*. London: Sage Publications.

Freedman, D. H. (1994). A difference of opinion. *CIO*, March 1, 53-58.

Gregson, K. (1997). Community networks and political participation: Developing goals for system developers. *Proceedings of the ASIS Annual Meeting*, 34, 263-270.

Harris, B. (1998). Telcom wars. *Government Technology*, 11(March), pp. 1, 38-40.

Hayes, M. (1996). Platform Zealots. *Informationweek*, August 19, 44-52.

Healey, J. (1997). The people's wires. *Governing*, August: 34-38.

James, F. (1997) Social Security ends web access to records. *Chicago Tribune*, April 10, pp. 1 and 12.

Kello, C. T. (1996). Participatory design: A not so democratic treatment. *American Journal of Psychology*, 109(4), 630-635.

Kidd, R. (1995). How vendors influence the quality of human services systems. *Government Technology*, March, 42-43.

King, J. L. (1983). Centralized versus decentralized computing: Organizational considerations and management options. *Computing Survey*, 15(4), 319-349.

Knights, D. & Murray, F. (1994). *Managers divided: Organisation politics and information technology management*. Chichester: John Wiley & Sons, 1994.

Koskinen, J. A. (1996). Koskinen: What CIO act means to you. *Government

Computer News, July 15, 22.

Kost, J. M. (1996). *New approaches to public management: The case of michigan.* Washington, D.C.: The Brookings Institution, CPM Report 96-1.

Kraemer, K. L. & King, J. L. (1976). *Computers, power, and urban management: What every local executive should know.* Beverly Hills, CA: Sage Publications.

Krol, E. (1994). State's health plan for poor comes up short. *Chicago Tribune,* June 24, pp. 1, 15.

Laudon, K.C. (1974). *Computers and bureaucratic reform: The political functions of urban information systems.* New York: Wiley.

Lucas, H. C. (1984). Organizational power and the information services department. *Communications of the ACM,* 127 (January), 58-65.

McKinnon, S. M. & Bruns, Jr., W. J. (1992). *The information mosaic.* Boston: Harvard Business School Press.

Manier, J. (1997). State endorses powerful machine. *Chicago Tribune,* June 27, pp. 1, 5.

Markus, M. L. (1983). Power, politics, and MIS implementation. *Communications of the ACM,* 26 (June), 430-444.

Markus, M.L. (1994). Electronic mail as the medium of managerial choice. *Organizational Science,* 5(4), 502-527.

Markus, M. L. and M. Keil. (1994). If we build it, they will come: Designing information systems that people want to use. *Sloan Management Review,* 35(Summer), 11-25.

Miller, B. (1995a). Interview with Indianapolis mayor, Stephen Goldsmith. *Government Technology,* April, 24-25.

Miller, B. (1995b). Should agencies archive E-Mail? *Government Technology,* February 1995, 22.

Murphy, S. (1995). Kansas city builds GIS to defray costs of clean water act. *Geo Info Systems,* June, 39-42.

Newcombe, T. (1995). The CIO-Lightning rod for IT troubles? *Government Technology,* October, 58.

Newcombe, T. (1997). Cities become telecomm owners. *Government Technology,* March, online version at http://www.govtech.net/.

Novotny, P. & Jacobs, R.H. (1997). Geographical information systems and the new landscape of political technologies. *Social Science Computer Review,* 15(3), 264-285.

Pastore, R. (1995). CIO search and rescue. *CIO,* December 1, 54-64.

Pearson, R. & Parsons, C. (1997). MSI verdicts jolt Springfield. *Chicago Tribune,* August 17, pp. 1, 12.

Pevtzow, L. (1989). Bitterly divided Naperville leaders decide computer strategy. *Chicago Tribune,* July 8, p. 5.

Pitkin, G. M. (1993). Leadership and the changing role of the chief information officer in higher education. *Proceedings of the 1993 CAUSE Annual Conference.* Boulder, Colorado: CAUSE, 55-66.

Poulos, C. (1998). Mayor Stephen Goldsmith: Reinventing indianapolis' local government. *Government Technology,* special edition (May), 31-33.

Putnam, R. D. (1995). Bowling alone revisited. *Responsive Community,* Spring,

5(2), 18-37.

Quindlen, T. H. (1993). When is e-mail an official record? Answers continue to elude feds. *Government Computer News*, June 7, pp. 1, 8.

Rocheleau, B. (1993). Evaluating public sector information systems: Satisfaction versus impact. *Evaluation and Program Planning*, 16: 119-129.

Rocheleau, B. (1994). The software selection process in local governments. *American Review of Public Administration*, 24(3), 317-330.

Rocheleau, B. (1995). Computers and horizontal information sharing in the public sector. In H. J. Onsrud & G. Rushton (Eds.), *Sharing Geographic Information* (pp. 207-229). New Brunswick, New Jersey: Rutgers University Press.

Rocheleau, B. (1997). Governmental information system problems and failures: A preliminary review. *Public Administration and Management: An Interactive Journal* (online). 2(3), http://www.hbg.psu.edu/Faculty/jxr1l/roche.html

Schmitz, J. (1997). Structural relations, electronic media, and social change: The public electronic network and the homeless. In S. G. Jones (Ed.), *Virtual culture: Identity and communication in cybersociety* (pp. 80-101). London: Sage Publications.

Schuler, D. (1995). Public space in cyberspace. *Internet World*, December, 89-95.

Severin, C.S. (1993). The CEO should be the CIO. *Informationweek*, October 11, 76.

Stahlman, M. (1995). Internet democracy hoax. *Informationweek*, December 25, 1995, 90.

Strassmann, P.A. (1995). *The politics of information management*. New Canaan: The Information Economics Press.

United States General Accounting Office. (1991). *FAA information resources: Agency needs to correct widespread deficiencies*. Washington, D.C.: U.S. General Accounting Office, GAO/IMTEC-91-43.

United States General Accounting Office. (1997). *Social Security Administration: Internet access to personal earnings benefits information* (GAO/T-AIMD/HEHS-97-123).

Washburn, G. (1998). Building-permit delays spur city shakeup. *Chicago Tribune*, May 18, pp. 1, 10.

Wilhelm, A.G. (1997). A resource model of computer-mediated political life. *Policy Studies Journal*, 25(4), 519-534.

Zeigler, N. (1997). Agencies say kinks worked out of new state computer system. *Daily Chronicle* (Dekalb, Illinois), p. 1.

3

Information Technology and Organizational Change in the Public Sector

by
Sonal J. Seneviratne
University of Southern California

The adoption of Information and Communication Technology (ICT) to organize, integrate, coordinate and manage various activities has become the catalyst for organizational change. The impact of these changes in the public sector have been to change the type of work being performed, demand new levels of productivity and efficiency from those performing the work, and call for a fundamental restructuring of the public sector to reflect the value systems of an information age. The literature on the organizational impacts of Information and Communication Technology have pointed to mixed findings about the success of information technology enabled organizational change, suggesting that the success of such change efforts depends on the combination of technical and social influences. Despite any potential for organizational change in the private sector, information technologies have not been associated with organizational transformation in the public sector. It is suggested that for the public sector to begin reaping the benefits of Information and Communication Technology, public sector managers are going to need to become change agents and manage the change process by managing the technology.

As with most industrial nations, the United States is witnessing a shift from an industrial-based economy to an information-based economy in which information is intrinsic to organizational functioning. Driven by the need to acquire, manipulate and distribute information, the last two decades have seen an exponential growth in Information and Communication Technology investments by both public and private institutions. Often described as a characteristic of the 'information revolution', this increasing rate of investment in technology has also been fueled by both the decreasing costs and increasing capabilities of technological hardware and software. Given all of these events, there is little doubt that our society has become increasingly dependent on Information and Communication Technology.

The adoption of Information and Communication Technology to organize, integrate, coordinate and manage various activities has also been a catalyst for organizational change. For example, new business processes such as telecommuting and teleconferencing have emerged as a result of advances in Information and Communication Technology. Changes such as these have subsequently impacted individual and organizational behaviors, the outcomes of which are now being scrutinized. The private sector has been trying to manage information technology related changes since the early days of the information revolution. This is evident by the abundance of literature focusing on the subject of information technology and organizational change in private corporations. Unfortunately, not as much attention has been given to managing change in public sector organizations, even though they too have been experiencing organizational stresses due to the adoption of Information and Communication Technology.

In recent years, advances in information technologies such as the Internet and the World Wide Web have led to a growing interest within the public sector toward developing a new and innovative model of service delivery based on information technology. Much of the focus, however, has resided in just the technical merits of using information technologies in creating new mechanisms for service delivery. If cyberspace is going to provide the infrastructure for a public service delivery model of the future, it would behoove those interested in public management to not only treat Information and Communication Technology as the catalyst that is driving change, but to also treat it as the solution base from which to address the public sector managerial challenges of operating in an increasingly electronic environment. This chapter is intended to help public sector managers, and others interested in public management to broaden their understanding of the relationships between information technology and organizational change. In doing so, it is hoped that they will be better prepared to learn how to use the tools associated with Information and Communication Technology not only to initiate organizational change, but to manage the change process and the technology itself.

The Information Revolution

A century ago, the United States was beginning to shift from an economy based on agriculture, forestry, and fishing, to an economy based on the transformation of raw materials into manufacturing goods. Today, we are undergoing another major transformation — one that is taking us from the industrially-based economy of the 20th century to a service based economy built around the creation, manipulation and distribution of information. Integral to this 'information revolution' has been the development of Information and Communication Technology (ICT). Sometimes used instead of Information Technology (IT), the expression ICT explicitly includes communications technologies, thereby making it clear that the information revolution includes computer hardware, software and communications equipment. Whether we use the term IT or ICT, it is clear that this group of technologies has rapidly diffused throughout the world, where they have created a presence responsible for initiating various industrial and economic changes that have led to globalization.

The Development of Electronic Computing Technology

Generally speaking, computing technologies have been around for hundreds of years. For example, during the 17th century, Blaise Pascal invented an adding machine that operated like a digital calculator, but was only made up of mechanical gears, levers and counting wheels. Devices such as this paved the way for the mechanical business machines of the late 18th and 19th centuries. The first successful electronic computers began appearing in the 1940s when the development of computer technology became a more focused effort. By the early 1950s, the first commercial computer in the United States, the UNIVAC, was being used by a handful of corporations. During the early part of the 1960s, America began experimenting with digital signal processing — the process by which numbers, letters, sounds and images could be rapidly and accurately transformed into strings of electronic pulses. Much of this research laid the foundation for the digitalization of communications and the transformation of computers from large devices made up of vacuum tubes to large devices made up of integrated circuits. It was during the 1970s however, that society witnessed two of the most defining moments in the history of the development of Information and Communication Technology. First, and perhaps the most important, was the development of the micro chip which would later become the core component of the personal computer. The second development came about from the merging of telecommunications and computer technology to forge the concept of computer networking. Most of the ICT developments during the 1980s centered on making personal micro computers smaller, faster and more powerful. In addition, there was increased emphasis on developing powerful software packages to work with the personal microcomputers; as well as research and development into improving network technology. By the late 1980's and early 1990's, the world witnessed the commercialization of the Internet followed by the birth of the World Wide Web. Both of these revolutionary technologies have changed and are continuing to change the way we do business today. As the rate of technological developments continue to increase beyond expectation, there appears to be no end in sight to what Information and Communication Technology will have to offer society.

The evolution of information and communication technologies have also been described in terms other than that of a technological development framework. For example, Earl (1989) has described information technology as moving through a number of distinct stages such as the 'data processing' stage and presently the 'information processing' stage. Using an organizational point of view, Zuboff (1988) has described the stages of information technology development as having been the 'automate' stage where computers were primarily used for automating manual processes; and now the 'informate' stage where computers are presently being used for information processing purposes. A third stage called the 'transformate' stage has been suggested to describe the transformational impacts of modern information and communication technologies on organizations. The stages described by both Earl and Zuboff are essentially technology driven and assume that ICT develops independently of the organizations that use it. Friedman and Cornford (1989) have suggested an alternative perspective to describe the development of ICT. Their approach does not depict technological determinism, and is based on the notion that the use of information technologies is directly influenced by the needs of the organization, and is controlled through both technological and organizational constraints. According to this model of technological evolution, hardware constraints dominated the first phase in the mid-1960s, and problems with software constrained the next development phase that lasted until the late 1970's. Issues regarding end user relations were predominantly the constraining factor until the late 1980's, while the current phase is now being constrained by issues of the organization's environment.

The Information Revolution and its Influence on the Public Sector

Government by nature is an information intensive organization. Large amounts of information are required to deliver public benefits such as pensions, unemployment benefits, and other social services. The information collected by these welfare programs must be stored, protected and made available when access is requested. Before the use of computer technology, the information processing functions in the public sector were primarily manual and decentralized. For the most part, departments within public agencies did their own data processing, maintained most of their own records and manually prepared most of their own reports. The introduction of computer technology into the public sector in the 1960s began to change the previously decentralized nature of data processing. With computers becoming more efficient, it meant that large amounts of data could be processed in a shorter time. As a result, electronic systems gradually began to replace manual systems. However, because early computers were large and expensive, every agency could not afford its own computer, so it became necessary to centralize the data processing operations.

Until the late 1970s, basic record keeping and financial functions were the primary activities that were automated. This is not surprising given the data processing characteristics of mainframe computers (e.g.,. storage, speed, and accuracy) and, the operational needs of public agencies (e.g,. billing, record keeping, financial accounting). In keeping with the trends of the information revolution and those occurring in the private sector, government agencies began investing in personal computers by the early 1980's. Innovative use of personal computers soon began to include the processing of information for planning analysis and decision making. Meanwhile, as private corporations began to invest more heavily in ICT, they also began to examine their business processes in terms of ICT with the hopes of finding more innovative uses of ICT. The public sector, however, took a more conservative approach. They kept up with the basic technological developments, but their use still remained primarily in the arena of centralized records management and financial applications.

By the late 1980s, public agencies were feeling the pressures of citizen demands for new and improved services. Citizens and businesses increasingly demanded that government programs made sense and worked efficiently. They began to expect better levels of service instead of the fragmented, duplicative and lengthy processes that had come to characterize government operations. Success in the private sector's use of ICT to improve customer service also led to demands for better service in the public sector. People wanted to know why the banking industry could give them their account balance and process transactions at any time, but government still could not figure out how to streamline the simple process of getting a driver's license renewed. It was felt that government's use of modern information technology had not kept pace with the private sector (Otten, 1989), not just in terms of service delivery, but also with regards to its use of technology for improving internal administrative functions.

The public sector's conservative approach to its use of ICT began to change in the 1990s. With new software applications and more powerful hardware, the old inflexible technologies of the prior decades were being replaced by more flexible systems that relied on networks and new methods of electronic communication. Technologies such as electronic mail, document imaging, and data exchange had made their way into public agencies and were making possible the processing and sharing of information in ways that were unimaginable prior to the 1990's. Technology was now being viewed as a key component in improving the way the public sector conducted its business and provided service to citizens.

One of the more promising technological developments that holds a lot of potential for the public sector has been the evolution of the World Wide Web. This technology offers virtually unlimited access to information, and seems perfectly suited for the government which is all about service and information delivery. In fact, the World Wide Web is slowly becoming a warehouse for federal, state and local government information. By transcending time and distance, the Web has removed barriers that have often hampered effective service delivery in the past. The World Wide Web and the concept of electronic commerce are now being regarded as the wave of the future for government. Although private corporations have viewed electronic commerce as simply a way to shop for goods on-line, public sector managers are viewing it in broader terms. Many agencies are thinking about going on line, or have done so already. For example, the IRS offers static information such as tax forms and publications over the Web. The next step in the interactive process requires government to provide access to information such as whether tax refunds have been mailed. This is more of a policy issue than a technological issue, and once such policy issues are addressed, perhaps government will finally be able to actually conduct two-way business transactions and will eventually do most of its business on-line. The World Wide Web not only holds promise for improving public service functions, but also for improving the internal administrative functions of government agencies. Experiences from the private sector have shown productivity improvements through the use of Intranets. Likewise, Intranets can be used by public sector agencies to link remote offices to central agency databases, and provide organizational information to staff, thereby enhancing organizational development.

It is apparent that the information revolution will continue to change the work environment in all organizations. The impact of these changes in the public sector have been to change the type of work being performed, and to demand new levels of productivity and efficiency from those performing the work. Thus the fundamental restructuring of the public sector to reflect the value systems of an information age will become a necessity. The government's success in being able to use new technologies such as the Internet and World Wide Web will depend on its ability to grapple with policy, management and other organizational challenges, as well as its ability to adapt to the new technologies themselves. Public managers will have to optimize the use of information technologies so as to improve productivity in the administrative functions that occur within their departments. In doing so, they will have to contend with the challenge of restructuring their organizations. It seems that the information revolution in the public sector has reached a new stage - one where managers must now confront the organizational changes that have accompanied the introduction of new powerful information and communication technologies.

Information Technology and Organizational Change

Until the late 1980's, Information and Communication Technology had generally been applied to strictly defined areas or functions such as accounting, administration or production. Since then, ICT has become increasingly connected with comprehensive organizational change efforts (Coombs and Hull, 1995). It has become commonly assumed that information technologies have the potential to transform organizations and render traditional organizational structures obsolete. In many industries, there is a growing belief that the flexibility and versatility of new information technologies provides new opportunities for organizations to survive the turbulent business environments of today. With the emergence of processes associated with IT-enabled organizational change, many organizations feel that they can achieve flatter organizations, enhance productivity and develop new markets through the innovative use of new information and communication technologies.

Organizational Change Methodologies Based on Information Technology

In the past, three common organizational change approaches have been used to introduce Information and Communication Technology into organizations (Thach and Woodman, 1994). These have been identified as: 1) Technical Installation; 2) Systems Approach and 3) Gap Analysis. The Technical Installation model has perhaps been the most widely used model and is simply a management initiated technical installation. Top management usually makes the decision to install ICT equipment for the purposes of improving productivity, and delegates the implementation to the Information Systems Department. With technically-oriented staff leading the installation, the change process usually becomes tailored in nature, with little emphasis being given to relationships between people, processes and training. The second approach, referred to as the Systems Approach, recommends that managers leading the change process examine five domains of the organization before implementation. These domains are: 1) behavioral (e.g. attitudes, values, behaviors); 2) technical; 3) process (e.g. decision making and communication processes); 4) systems (e.g. protocols) and 5) structure. Each of the domains has a list of ten factors that managers need to consider in their planning process. Thus, managers are encouraged to concentrate on the relationship between people, processes, structure and technical issues. An alternative form of the systems approach identifies six key elements for organizational transformation. These are: 1) vision; 2) organizational design; 3) core competencies; 4) work redesign; 5) rewards and 6) change management. Again, managers leading the technological change effort are encouraged to examine variables from each of these elements as they plan for the implementation of Information and Communication Technology. Finally, the third change approach referred to as Gap Analysis calls for top management to view ICT as a strategic implementation that requires a vision of the future organization. Management is required to evaluate the current state of the organization, propose a vision for the future and conduct an analysis of the steps necessary to achieve the vision. An implementation plan is then developed that involves all aspects of the organization.

A more recent manifestation of information technology enabled organizational change has been an approach referred to as Business Process Re-engineering (BPR). With the growing belief that IT was a crucial organizational resource, and the notion that business strategy was increasingly tied to the potential of IT to secure competitive advantages, researchers began to investigate ways of aligning business and IT strategies (Lederer and Mendelow, 1988; Finnegan and Fahy, 1993). BPR assumes that information systems could be utilized to increase empowerment; that networks could enable cross functional communication thereby improving coordination, collaboration and integration between departments; and, that new systems such as shared databases could facilitate the storage and analysis of information to promote the sharing of experience. Based upon a technical framework that resonated with concepts of taylorism and scientific management, a partnership framework that presented information technology as a partner to individuals rather than the organization and, a benevolent framework that focused on the organizational impacts of information technology, BPR became synonymous with radical organizational transformation. While the rhetoric of BPR relied heavily on the partnership and benevolent frameworks of computing, its techniques and tools were still firmly rooted in the technical framework. As a result, BPR has not been as successful as hoped, and has encountered significant problems not only due to a lack of commitment, but also due to implementation problems, and due to problems associated with the integration of change management with the introduction of redesigned processes. Basically, BPR has been seen as being too technical, too hard and too reliant on what is essentially an engineering perspective of human processes and actions.

Regardless of the change methodology used, it is apparent that if ICT implementation occurs in the most productive fashion, and all aspects of the organization's environment are taken into account, there is no doubt that organizations will be significantly affected by ICT. How these changes will manifest themselves, and whether they have positive or negative connotations, will vary from organization to organization. Also, the question of what additional organizational change techniques will be necessary to facilitate IT-enabled organizational change will vary with other variables in the environment and the organization.

Organizational Impacts of Information Technology

The impact of IT is often felt across the entire organization from top to bottom. Technological change is transforming the role of management (Gutek et al, 1984;

Ang & Pavri, 1994), the characteristics of organizational structures (Fitzgerald, 1993) and the work environment of employees (Zuboff, 1985; Gattiker, 1990). As a result, we sometimes find ourselves with institutions that made sense when they originated, but which may now be incompatible and inconsistent with the technological organizations of the present era. Much of the empirical research in the area of information technology and its impacts on organizations has occurred in the private sector. Unfortunately, there has not been as much empirical research in the public sector, and the limited research that does exist often focuses on specific areas such as dealing with finance or planning. Overall, research relating to the impacts of IT on organizations can be grouped into several areas of interest:

1) Impacts on organizational structure and processes: Environmental pressures and the development of powerful and flexible information technologies are converging to create an impetus for major change in structure, function and processes of business organizations (Grover & Goslar, 1993; Forrest, 1994). Recent research investigating the link between IT and organizations has shown that effective and efficient utilization of IT requires the alignment of IT strategies with business strategies. For example, an organization with a conservative business strategy may possess a more centralized information system than an organization with a more aggressive strategy (Tavakolian, 1989; Luftman, Lewis, & Oldach, 1993). Thus, if organizations are to benefit from using IT effectively, they should have an organizational structure and a set of business strategies that reflect the interdependence of organizational strategy and IT capabilities (Luftman et al,. 1993). Many organizations have turned to re-engineering to realign their IT and business strategies. Instead of using technology to automate the way tasks were done in the past, re-engineering first redefines the process, and then automates the new process (Hosseini, 1993). Research has also shown that information technology promotes traditional organizational structures to give way to cross functional structures that are often flat and flexible (Mahnke, 1990; Halal, 1994). In some organizations, however, the absence of traditional hierarchical structures have resulted in confusion about how to unite their parts. This unexpected consequence has been amplified due to organizational boundaries becoming less distinct as a result of the far-reaching nature of information technology (Coulson-Thomas, 1990; Henke 1991).

2) Impacts on individual attitudes and behavior: Research in the areas of individual attitudes and perceptions such as anxiety and fear (Torkzadeh & Angulo, 1992; Henderson et al., 1995) have indicated that in addition to reducing anxiety, the quality of information technology, especially that of software, has strongly effected individual attitudes toward technology. It has also been found that managerial support of technology affected workers' attitudes in a positive way. Culpan (1995) suggested that an individual's acceptance of information technology is influenced by their perception of the impact of automation on their discretion in performing their jobs. The argument that social and behavioral changes usually follow the introduction of new information technologies has also been supported by Sainfort (1990) and, Yang and Carayon (1995) who have examined the effects on behavior due to job demand and stress of using technology.

3) Impacts of workflow and work: The introduction of computer mediated communication technologies such as electronic mail and computer conferencing groupware has proven to alter the flow of information exchange within an organization and between organizations, thereby creating different methods of communication. (Barnes & Greller, 1994; Reynolds 1994). Workflow is also hypothesized to be influenced by technologies that are easy to use (Trevino & Webster, 1992). There has also been a general consensus that as information technology continues to evolve, it will also continue to have a marked and increasing impact on the nature of work (Olson, 1989; Olson, Card, Landauer et al., 1993). These technological impacts will in turn affect the character of jobs (Senker, 1992; Gleckman, 1993), and as a result, an adaptive change effort will be required of workers and organizations if they are to master and use the new information technology.

Information Technology Enabled Organizational Change

The literature on the organizational impacts of IT have pointed to mixed findings about the success of IT enabled organizational change (Robey, 1977; Nelson, 1990; Davenport & Stoddard, 1994). This lack of consensus is partly attributed to the fact that while researchers share some perspectives on the impacts of ICT on organizations, they also tend to focus on different aspects of the relationship, thereby arriving at different conclusions. According to some researchers, it appears that organizational change is not accomplished through the installation of new IT alone. Instead, the success of technology enabled organizational change depends upon a combination of technical and social influences (Robey & Sahay, 1996; Thach & Woodman, 1994). Not only must new information technologies meet necessary technical requirements, but the existing social environment must be receptive to change if the organizational transformation is to occur. Sometimes the intended transformations may occur, while in other instances, older forms of the organization may persist or some combination of new and old organizational forms may arise. Alternatively, Lui et al. (1990) have indicated that new information technologies have immediate impacts on the nature of work, but do not modify existing organizational forms. In time, the original organizational design becomes increasingly sub-optimal with respect to the opportunities that the new technologies have created, thereby forcing changes to the organization. Regardless of whether the relationships between IT and organizations is direct or mediated by other factors such as those found in the social environment, the fact remains that IT is key to transforming organizations.

Despite their potential for organizational change in the private sector, information technologies have not been associated with the radical transformation of public organizations (Robey & Sahay, 1996). To the contrary, the evidence suggests the persistence of existing formal structures and political alignments when IT is introduced into public agencies (Danziger, Dutten, Kling & Kraemer, 1982; Kraemer, 1991; Pinsonneault & Kraemer, 1993). In summarizing the findings of an extensive research program on the effects of computers in government, Kraemer (1991) concluded that computing reinforced existing power structures and played little role in changing organizational structures. Theoretical support for this is also found in the meta-analytic research on the impacts of planned organizational change in private versus public sectors (Robertson & Seneviratne, 1995). Their examination of planned organizational change observed that, regardless of the change agent, organizing arrangements (e.g., formalized bureaucratic elements of the organization such as formal structures, administrative procedures, goals and reward systems) change more readily in the private sector than in the public sector.

Although many experts feel that IT will make traditional organizational structures obsolete (Thach & Woodman, 1994), it appears that this may not necessarily be the case in the public sector. However, if the traditional pyramid and matrix hierarchical structures tend to obstruct the true value of IT, and if all organizations need to be transformed in the future so that computer based electronic technologies can be effective (Morton, 1991), then the public sector needs to begin to carefully examine its impediments to organizational change.

In the early stage of the adoption of computers by large bureaucratic agencies, the possibility of conflict with traditional organizational forms had not been seriously considered. On the whole, computer technology was primarily in the form of centralized mainframes, and was seen as an instrument which would reinforce centralized decision making and exercise closer control by management. With the arrival of personal computers, the growth of end user computing produced a strong tendency towards autonomy and decentralized computing in the midst of a centralized organizational structure. The balance between centralization and decentralization is not a new issue. It has been an old organizational dilemma that is now appearing under a new context of information technology and its impacts on organizations. With the public sector highly enthusiastic about using Web-based technologies to deliver services, and given the notion that efficient utilization of technology requires the alignment of organizational structure with IT strategy, and business strategy, it becomes imperative that managers take a look at information technology and its impacts on organizational change.

Centralization Versus Decentralization: An Old Debate In A New Context

At the beginning of the century, Max Weber regarded the bureaucratic organization as the most advanced expression of rationality in human affairs. The logic of control that it embodied based upon the expertise of specialists, hierarchical progression and centralized authority had been the guiding principle for public organizations. The basic technology of Weber's administrative system was primitive however. The means of communication within and between organizational levels was slow. The rate and quality of information transmissions were governed by human capacity, with little help from mechanical devices. Today, the development of ICT is viewed as having the capability of transforming this image. The consequences of such transformation will include the increased speed and volume of information flow, reduced labor costs and changes in skill requirements. Many of these changes however, are philosophically opposed to the traditional bureaucratic structures that are characterized by slow information flow and static skill requirements. This means that all existing assumptions about structures of control, location of specialization within the hierarchy, and the hierarchical structure itself are called into question by the potentials of ICT.

An organization's structure can be defined as the way an organization divides its labor or differentiates its parts. For example, organizations may be differentiated horizontally into departments and groups, and vertically into management hierarchies. With the ability of ICT to extend lines of communication and break down barriers of time and distance, it has been observed that traditional organizational structures are bound to be transformed by ICT. Unlike the private sector, the transformation of organizational structure has been more difficult to achieve in the public sector due to Weberian bureaucracy and hierarchical relationships becoming highly institutionalized. Compounded by a political system that is resistant to change, a government structure that allows change only when there is agreement among a number of individuals or institutions, and the sheer complexity of a governmental system characterized by separation of powers and various jurisdictions (local, state and federal), IT-enabled change has proven to be quite a challenge, but a critical one to overcome if the enthusiasm for an IT-based electronic service delivery mechanism is to become a successful reality.

Traditionally, the nature of the technology dictated the degree of centralization both in terms of the technology and the organizational structure in which it was used. Control over IT was centralized because the nature of large mainframes placed information processing control in the hands of data processing professionals. In this environment, users were dependent on a centralized data processing department for all their computing needs. There was a hierarchical chain of command to follow if new applications or modifications to existing applications were required. This was very much in line with the bureaucratic nature of public organizations as a whole. With IT strategies being aligned similarly to organizational strategies, public agencies were able to use their information technologies to achieve their business goals. When the public sector began investing in personal microcomputers, this relationship between technology and organization began to change. Many agencies could now afford powerful, personal microcomputers for use in word processing, financial modeling, database management and other information oriented tasks. The increasing variety of software applications and the growth in personal computer abilities has put tremendous computing power in the hands of the end users, thereby leading to technological decentralization. The resulting organizational environment can be described as a traditionally centralized bureaucratic organization, attempting to use highly decentralized information technologies to fulfill a combination of centralized and decentralized goals. This change in alignment between ICT strategy and business strategy has created an organizational stress that needs to be addressed before the public sector can think of fully benefiting from decentralized ICT. It is expected that technological developments will continue to give end users increasing control over their own computing environment and thereby, exacerbate the centralization versus decentralization issue.

Interestingly, some researchers have argued that new technology does not have a decentralizing effect but quite the opposite. According to Sitarski (1991), improved automation within the public sector has improved the flow of information in all directions. As the time and distance barriers to operational data flow shrink, the appeal of having centralized policy making authority increases. It becomes easier for those higher in the chain of command to identify transgressions of directives, standards and budgets by using the new technologies. Although public agencies and personnel may have autonomy in the use of information technology, this same technology can be used to hold these departments responsible thereby centralizing power at the top of the government pyramid structure. Whether or not ICT is really centralizing control has yet to be determined. Most of the literature continues to promote the decentralizing effects of ICT.

The trend towards decentralized computing has the potential to intensify the fragmentation within public organizations, especially at a time where the importance of integration is increasing. The issue at hand can be framed in terms of public managers having to search for organizational forms which have a balance between maintaining centralized control and providing decentralized tools/facilities. While governments are encouraging managers to take advantage of the benefits of automation, the implementation of information technology not only increases process efficiency, but also changes the locus of knowledge, placing it with the line staff. In the eyes of the managers, this equates to changing the locus of power, and is often considered threatening to managers. If IT-enabled organizational change is to succeed, managers need to overcome their fear of change, and become change agents. Clearly managers have a role to play in determining how IT impacts organizations, and it would behoove managers to look towards the management of technology as a way of assisting IT-enabled change.

Managing Technological Change

The adoption of Information and Communication Technology into an organization is the initial step in the growth of computing within that organization. Often, it is also the first step in an organizational transformation process whereby the organization may begin to take on a new form and function. Concurrently with the adoption process begins the incorporation of ICT as a part of the ongoing activity in routine organizational life. With the expansion of computing applications to include more tasks, the information infrastructure becomes more complex, and larger numbers of employees become dependent on its use. Accompanying this burgeoning growth are a host of problems faced by managers who have to make sure that the technology is assimilated successfully, is accepted by the staff, and is being effectively used. While some of these problems can be rendered trivial and painless, others are more serious and intractably related to the effective use of the technology. The private sector has been dealing with such problems for quite sometime. Public sector managers, however, must still try to master the changes wrought by information technology on the people and the organizations within government.

Problems Facing Public Sector Managers

The public sector manager need only look around the office to see the effects of information and communication technologies. For example, while clerical staff can often be found busy using wordprocessors, analysts are busy using sophisticated spreadsheet applications to develop forecasts and financial models of future expenditures and revenues. As the use of information technology increases, there has become a growing awareness that, along with the potential benefits of technology, comes problems that confound its application.

According to King and Kraemer (1985), the growth of information technology in public sector organizations has produced at least three generic areas of concern for those who must manage technology in routine organizational life. The first involves the control of the technology. Control usually refers to the question of who gets to set policy regarding information technology use; who gets to implement the policies and who determines the way in which the policies can be changed to meet new organizational conditions. These problems of control were not as complex when technology was centralized. With the responsibilities for ICT falling on the director of the data-processing department, public managers did not have to worry about technology control. With the decentralization of ICT, many of the decisions regarding the management of ICT now affect the managers. Related to the issue of control, managers have begun to face a recent problem associated with productivity. Managers may be prepared to deal with productivity problems related to a lack of training and complex technology. But what about productivity problems related to having too much access to technology? One of the growing problems managers have to contend with these days is that the World Wide Web is becoming the tool by which staff are apt to waste time. Surfing the Web for personal reasons during work is becoming an issue that managers are finding difficult to handle, especially when it is hard to differentiate between personal surfing and work-related surfing. A second concern is related to the effective and efficient use of the technology. Information processing is technology dependent, but the technology is not always stable. As with all technologies, ICT is in a state of continued flux, especially as new developments are made. Upgrading to newer technologies may create problems of incompatibility with existing technologies, and create new learning curves for employees. Hence, knowing when and how to utilize new technology, especially given the costs of a change over, is not an easy task. Managers often have to decide on whether having the latest and best technology is more important than technological stability. On the other hand, using outdated technology can impede daily operations. Reliability is a critical issue to managers and users who depend on the consistent and timely performance of technology in their daily work. A third generic concern for managers is the problem of matching the requirements and capabilities of information and communications technologies to the requirements and capabilities of the staff and the functions they perform. For example, assuming that staff are adequately trained in performing their tasks, it is critical that they have the appropriate levels of technology to complete their tasks. On the other hand, it's also important that staff not be stressed by technology that is overly complex for the requirements of their job. As ICT becomes designed for increasingly complex tasks, organizational success will depend on how effectively users can operate the technology. Optimal use of ICT necessitates a good match between people and machines. In the decentralized computing environment, it often becomes the manager's job to make these types of determinations.

In addition to these generic problems, other problems facing managers include dealing with questions about what kind of computer-related training to provide staff, and how to manage technical support issues so as to expedite the effective assimilation of ICT by the users. Another problem that continually challenges managers involves the lack of knowledge by both managers and their staff about the technology and what it can do. In the case of the manager, this problem usually refers to a lack of understanding about the potentials and limitations of computing. With the case of end users, it usually applies to uncertainty about how to adapt to the tasks impacted by information technology. Employees often have a difficult time making genuine adaptation to new technologies. They experience emotional problems at having to learn so many new tasks, and this quickly leads to technostress. Understanding the resistance to technological change is more challenging and important than ever before.

In short, the task of managing the evolution and use of computing in organizations is complex and difficult. Managers are ultimately responsible for coordinating people and computers in the office so as to meet business objectives. The use of new technology has created a new learning curve, which invariably increases the potential for complicated and unpredictable results. The growing recognition that management of computing is a difficult undertaking has been accompanied by a growth in the literature containing recommendations about how to manage computing effectively. Although most of the literature has been geared to private sector managers, some of it is also applicable to public managers.

Managing on the Edge of Cyberspace

Much of the literature on the management of information technology and its impacts on organizations is grounded in the belief that computing is manageable in a rational manner. The fact that computing can be managed in organizations is demonstrated by the fact that many organizations, at least to some extent, do get the results they desire from information technology. But at the same time, it is apparent that managers find it difficult to cope with the problems of control, technology and human factors that plague the use of information technology. The highly rationalistic assumptions that underlie many of the recommendations for management of information technology are appealing. They seem to make sense and are consistent with the goals of improving efficiency and effectiveness of organizations, but have to compete with the sometimes irrational behavior of the human side of technology assimilation.

There is an abundance of literature about the technical side of how to use information technology. Vendors and consultants often provide technical advice on how to plan and implement automation in the workplace. Unfortunately, the literature related to managing information technology and its impacts on organizational change has not been as forthcoming. What little literature that does exists on management of information technology has focused on sectoral shifts in employment attributed to technological change, and identifying sources of innovation and potential use. It is only recently that there has been a concerted effort to focus on management of the organizational impacts of ICT. With information technology impacting organizational structures, managers now have to change their management styles so they can maintain organizational harmony and fulfill their managerial tasks while operating in an increasingly electronic environment. If managers try to manage the old way in the new environment, a lot of organizational stress can be created. Instead, managers need to learn to use the technology that has created the organizational changes in order to actually manage the change process.

In the past, management of technology was limited to data processing. The manager would simply provide guidance to the data processing director to ensure that user needs were being addressed. Now, however, users themselves are determining methods and strategies for managing information and the technologies unique to their function. Technology management becomes as much a bottom-up process as a top-down process. As end users become more knowledgeable, managers need to be able to strike a balance between stifling enthusiasm and maintaining effective control.

The next century will demand government managers who are as knowledgeable and well trained in information management and computer technology as they are in personnel and financial management. Managers will need to think in terms of dealing with managing technology on two fronts. Firstly, all managers need to deal with managing the technology internal to their department i.e., the technology that they and their staff use to perform their administrative work. Secondly, managers need to deal with the technology that is used to provide service to the public. For example, the information superhighway will provide the government with the opportunity to reach many communities, but its complexity will also increase managerial stress. Regardless of whether public managers are dealing with technology from the internal or external aspect, the following recommendations are provided as guidelines for managers to manage the technology that is changing their environment.

To approach today's working environment with the technology of tomorrow, one must make a commonplace approach to redefine the working environment, the workers and their functions which are under great pressures of change. As the new functions of the government office are redefined, great care has to be taken not to define the functions as they currently exist, then automate them using higher levels of technology. Rather, managers must examine and possibly redefine the functions so as to take maximum advantage of the new technologies.

Guidelines For Managing Information Technology

1) Public sector managers must become more information efficient. They must define their information needs. This is the simplest yet the most overlooked requirement. They should not expect someone else to tell them about what they need. If they do, more often than not, they will not be told what they need, but sold a bill of goods that they did not need. Managers must see to it that the resources at their disposal are applied efficiently and effectively to enable the completion of their responsibilities.

2) Managers need to clarify the current organizational baseline. They should try to document costs and productivity using existing systems. Based upon this information, managers can then make decisions on how to change operating procedures, create new organizational forms and realign technology strategies with business strategies. Managers should attempt to improve the current system using common-sense management techniques. For example, simplify forms and requirements and make sure that information flow is efficient. Managers should try and establish procedures to audit their department for effectiveness and be prepared to upgrade as organizational needs, technology or both change in time.

3) Managers should train and prepare their staff for a new electronic environment. When managers procure new computing technology without properly preparing their staff for it, usually the new installation fails. Managers should be prepared to redefine job categories and requirements and insist that the vendors of the new systems provide users with adequate training and a strong technical overview of their equipment. When technology was centralized, support for dealing with technical problems was often entirely centralized. With the trend toward decentralized computing, managers should have their staff trained to some degree in various aspects of technology so that they can become some-

what self sufficient. A recommended approach is that of running a triage model. Having staff prepared to handle the daily front-line problems of computing alleviates the time lost in waiting for the systems department to respond. This model provides the greatest opportunity for coordination and long term stability, but may require some substantial reorganizations.

4) Managers need to undertake a well-defined procurement process with special attention being given to maintenance, support and training. It should be kept in mind that technology will keep on changing and that the organization's technology should be able to follow suit. It is important that managers allow their staff to candidly discuss how they believe the changes will affect technical goals, the social system, rewards and policies

5) A great deal of management is accomplished through implied rules, especially in the form of myths and organizational culture. With information technology creating a level playing field in regards to management information, public managers will have to define new unspoken rules that will allow them to manage the democratizing values accompanying ICT.

6) Integration of technologies is an absolute necessity for the future. Managers must stop thinking of computers in stand-alone terms, and start thinking in terms of networks, modular design, emphasizing the strengths of each type of technology and maximizing the synergy that can be achieved. This mode of thinking then needs to be transferred to management styles. Managers must be prepared to reorganize their management thinking around the flow of information, and take advantage of ICT to improve the speed of communication between managers and subordinates thereby increasing effectiveness of the organization.

7) Managers need to motivate employees to become self starters and efficient users of these information handling tools that are most appropriate for increasing individual productivity in the context of organizational mission, goals and objectives. To motivate subordinates to use information technology, managers should set an example and become proficient in the use of these tools themselves.

New information technologies have the tremendous promise to reduce the administrative distance between the information produced, handled and disseminated in the organization and the user of that information, thereby strengthening the function of government. According to King and Kraemer (1985), information technology has offered considerable potential for assisting public sector managers in running the public affairs of government. These basic advantages of computerization lie in the ability to gather information about the many sources and analyze them to provide alternatives for making planning and policy decisions on issues of concern. If the public sector is going to be able to harness the potential of ICT to provide better service, managers must begin to take advantage of the abilities of ICT not only to provide better service, but to manage their organizational environment.

Summary and Conclusions

During the last three decades, numerous predictions have been made about the information revolution and its impacts on organizations and society (Toffler, 1980;

Naisbitt, 1984). Although some of the potential benefits of the information revolution may have been over exaggerated, there is no doubt that there have been considerable improvements to society, and that organizations have experienced significant change. On the basis of past research in organizational change methods used, and the resulting changes to organizational structure and communications patterns, several concepts have emerged as being critical for future IT management. For example, it is important to have a flexible and customized change model that can be adapted to different organizational settings. IT-enabled organizational change needs to be considered from a socio-technical systems view and be customized to fit the social network of the specific organization.

The new millennium implies all kinds of images including a new government workplace. Government organizations have withstood and will continue to withstand the numerous changes that it faces. As the public becomes more and more dependent on government to provide leadership, service and support, those in government are charged with finding new ways and means to do so. The expansion of management information systems is one of the most significant developments in the field of public administration. IT is now being credited with enhancing program delivery and improving accessibility to information using cyberspace. The thing we have to start recognizing is that cyberspace is more content-driven than technology-driven. Employing the World Wide Web as a universal interface to government services offers a number of advantages over the traditional methods of service delivery. These include more immediate and convenient public access to information and services and opportunities for increased collaboration amongst government agencies.

Enthusiasm for the opportunities offered by technologies such as the World Wide Web must be tempered with an understanding of the challenges and limitations imposed by rapidly changing technology. The issue is not so much as to whether or not the technology is available to accomplish such a vision—it is here and advancing. The more difficult and fundamental question lies elsewhere. Do we have or can we develop the organizational structures, management tools, business processes, information products and policies to take advantage of the set technologies and direct their use to achieve important public goals? Will public departments be willing to share pertinent and timely information? Will agencies be willing to relinquish solitary control over programs? Can traditional hiring and training programs allow the public workforce to acquire and maintain new skills? From what we have seen, it appears that this can be done. The extensive use of information technology will bring greater complexity to the public sector, and complexity is often dynamic and difficult to manage. The primary obstacle will be the willingness of public managers and staff to go through the change process and create a new organizational culture, one that does not have to contrast with the traditional bureaucratic structure, but one that has been molded and adapted to the new electronic environment.

Whether it is creating new shared databases for welfare tracking, or crafting new methods of managing information technology, today's government managers are at the helm in the effort to transform government for the new millennium. And with them, stands technology. Managers are in a position to use information technology and need to be thinking in terms of collaboration and service to the public. They need to be thinking about removing barriers and enhancing the speed and agility of government services where technology is the vehicle for the inertia, but human vision and commitment are the drivers. While the public servant must become qualified to be a productive information worker, for managers this translates into the need for additional competencies in the ability to take advantage of computers and to be able to decide on the use of information tools from a new perspective. As Ducatel and Millard (1996) have stated, managers must mobilize the new potential of these technologies rather than implementing rationalization and retrenchment

The challenge to public sector managers is to strike a balance between giving their staff the opportunity to explore and benefit from decentralized computing power, while still realizing the efficiencies of organization-wide coordination and standardization. Managers need to take on the responsibility of change agents. They need to assess the current levels of ICT readiness, develop visions of how the new ICT will affect the organization and link these to the new IT, thus enabling change.

To exploit the potential of new technologies and to master its risks, it is not enough to make adjustments to traditional organizational forms. A new way to think about organization, and a new paradigm needs to be developed as a substitute for the models of Weber and Taylor . These are still the dominant models of organizing. It is still too early to say if the emerging paradigm will follow through to completeness because many adjustments to change still need to be made. In the spirit of the new paradigm, the shift required in the minds of many is a very large one that has not yet come to culmination but is occurring and shows promise.

Bibliography

Ang, J. & Pavri, F. (1994). A survey and critique of the impacts of information technology. *International Journal of Information Management,* 14(2), 122-133.

Barnes, S. & Greller, L.M. (1994). Computer mediated communication in the organization. Communication Education, 43(2), 129-143.

Coombs, R. & Hull, R. (1995). BPR as 'IT-enabled organizational change': an assessment. *New Technology, Work and Employment,* 10(2), 121-131

Coulson-Thomas, C. (1990). The responsive organization. *Journal of General Management,* 15(4), 21-32.

Culpan, O. (1995). Attitudes of end users towards information technology in manufacturing and service industries. *Information and Management,* 28(3), 167-176.

Danziger, J.N., Dutton, W.H., Kling, R. & Kraemer, K.L. (1982). *Computers and Politics.* New York: Columbia University Press.

Davenport, T.H. & Stoddard, D.B. (1994). Reengineering: Business Change of Mythic Proportions? *MIS Quarterly,* 18, 121-127.

Ducatel, K. & Millard, J. (1996). Employment and innovation in advanced communication technologies: Strategies for growth and the growth of employment. *Futures,* 28(2), 121-138

Earl, M.J. (1989). *Management Strategies for Information Technology*, Englewood Cliffs: Prentice Hall.

Finnegan, P. & Fahy, M.J. (1993). Planning for information systems resources? *Journal of Information Technology*, 8, 127-138

Fitzgerald, N. (1993). Crucial to the design (information technology as a driver for organizational change and corporate strategy). *CA Magazine (Scotland)*, 97(1045), 6-9

Forrest, D. (1994). Winds of change? More like a hurricane in IT. *Computing Canada*, 20(9), 22-23

Friedman, A.L. & Cornford, D.S. (1989). *Computer Systems Development: History, Organization and Implementation*, John Wiley.

Gattiker, U. & Howg, L. (1990). Information technology and quality of work life: Comparing users with non-users. *Journal of Business and Psychology*, 5(2), 237-260.

Gleckman, H. (1993). The technology payoff: a sweeping reorganization of work itself is boosting productivity. *Business Week*, 3323 57-63.

Grover, V. & Goslar, M. (1993). Technical correspondence; information technology for the 1990's: the executives' view. *Communications of the ACM*, 36(3), 17-22.

Gutek, B.; Bikson, T. & Mankin, D. (1984). Individual and organizational consequences of computer based office technology. *Applied Social Psychology Annual*, 5, 321-254.

Halal, W. (1994). The transition from hierarchy to ... what? (organizational structures in the information age). *Technological Forecasting and Social Change*, 45(2), 207-211.

Henderson, R.D., Deane, F.P. & Ward, M.J. (1995). Occupational difference in computer related anxiety: implications for the implementation of a computerized patient management information system. *Behavior & Information Technology*, 14(1), 23-54.

Henke, J.W. (1991). An emerging organizational structure: A study of levels and information needs. *Systems Research*, 8(4), 67-75.

Hosseini, J. (1993). Revisiting and expanding Taylorism, business process redesign and information technology. *Computers and Industrial Engineering*, 24(1), 533-536.

King, J.L. & Kraemer, K.L. (1985). *The Dynamics of Computing*. New York: Columbia University Press.

Kraemer, K.L. (1991). Strategic Computing and Administrative Reform: In C. Dunlop and R. King (Eds.), *Computerization and Controversy*. (pp. 167-180), New York: Academic Press

Lederer, A. L. & Mendelow, A. L. (1988). Information Systems Planning: Top Management Takes Control. *Business Horizons,* 31(3), 73-78

Luftman, J.; Lewis, P. & Oldach, S. (1993). Transforming the enterprise: the alignment of business and information strategies. *IBM Systems Journal,* 32(1), 198-222.

Mahnke, J. (1990). Companies move to implement cross-functional structure: integrated organization married with MIS strategy garners profound results. *MIS Week,* 11(19), 29-31.

Morton, M.S. (1991). *The Corporation of the 1990's.* New York: Oxford University Press.

Naisbitt, J. (1984). *Megatrends: ten new directions for transforming our lives.* New York: Warner Books.

Nelson, D.L. (1990). Individual Adjustment to Information-driven Technologies: A Critical Review. *MIS Quarterly,* 14, 79-98.

Olson, M. (1989). Work at home for computer professionals: current attitudes and future prospects. *ACM Transactions of Information Systems,* 7(4), 317-339.

Olson, J.S.; Card, S.K.; Landauer, T.K.; Olson, G.M.; Malone, T. & Leggett, J. (1993). Computer supported cooperative work: Research issues for the 90's. *Behavior & Information Technology,* 12 (2), 115-129.

Otten, K.W. (1989). A changing information environment challenges public administrations. *Information Management Review,* 4(4), 9-16.

Pinsonneault, A. & Kraemer, K.L. (1993). The Impact of Information Technology on Middle Managers. *MIS Quarterly,* 17, 271-292.

Reynolds, M. (1994). Decision making using computer conferencing: A case study. *Behavior & Information Technology,* 13(3), 239-252.

Robertson, P.J. & Seneviratne, S.J. (1995). Outcomes of Planned Organizational Change in the Public Sector: A Meta Analytic Comparison to the Public Sector. *Public Administration Review,* 55(6), 547-558.

Robey, D. (1977). Computer and Management Structure: Some Empirical Findings Re-examined. *Human Relations,* 11, 963-976.

Robey, D. & Sahay, S. (1996). Transforming Work Through Information Technology: A Comparative Case Study of Geographic Information Systems in County Government. *Information Systems Research,* 7(1), 93-110.

Sainfort, P. (1990). Job design predictors of stress in automated offices. *Behavior & Information Technology,* 9(1), 3-16.

Senker, P. (1992). Technological change and the future of work - an approach to analysis. *Futures,* 24(4), 351-363.

Sitarski, C. (1991). Conceptual issues in the study of centralization and information technology. *Canadian Public Administration,* 34(4), 641-663.

Tavakolian, H. (1989). Linking the information technology structure with organizational competitive strategy: a survey. *MIS Quarterly,* 13(3), 308-318.

Thach, L. & Woodman, R.W. (1994). Organizational Change and Information Technology: Managing on the Edge of Cyberspace. *Organizational Dynamic,* 23(1), 30 - 46.

Toffler, A. (1980). *The Third Wave.* New York: Morrow.

Torkzadeh, G. & Angulo, I.E. (1992). The concept and correlates of computer anxiety. *Behavior and Information Technology,* 11(2), 99-108.

Trevino, L.K. & Webster, J. (1992). Flow in computer mediated communication: electronic mail and voice mail evaluation and impacts. *Communication Research,* 19(5), 539-573.

Yang, C.L. & Carayon, P. (1995). Effect of Job demands and social support on worker stress: a study of VDT users. *Behavior & Information Technology,* 14(1), 32 - 40.

Zuboff, S. (1985). Automate / Informate: The two faces of intelligent technology. *Organizational Dynamics,* 14(2), 5-18.

Zuboff, S. (1988). *In The Age of the Smart Machine: The Future of Work and Power,* New York: Basic Books.

4

The Evolution of Information Technology Management at the Federal Level: Implications for Public Administration

by
Stephen H. Holden
National Director, Electronic Program Enhancements, for the Internal Revenue Service*

*For identification purposes only. This article is independent of any association with the U. S. Internal Revenue Service.

Federal agencies rely extensively on information technology (IT) to perform basic missions. Arguably, public administration should be driving the theory, policy, and practice for managing these increasingly important resources. This is especially true as public organizations move to electronic service delivery to improve mission performance.

However, despite some maturation in the literature for managing IT in federal agencies, public administration has contributed little to this effort. Other academic fields, such as information sciences, business administration, and practitioners, have done more to improve IT management at the federal level.

This chapter analyzes federal IT management literature from several academic disciplines and government documents. The analysis compares federal IT management with a normative model of management maturity focusing on the strategic objectives for IT and related management approaches. Public administration's lack of contribution to federal IT management raises profound questions whether federal agencies will be prepared for the information age.

Given the growing importance of effective information technology (IT) management to the basic functioning of most public programs, the sophistication of the policy, theory, and practice in this area should be evolving quickly. Unfortunately, that is not so (Holden, 1996; Holden & Hernon, 1996). As a result, it is quite possible

Copyright© 1999, Idea Group Publishing.

that the current generation of public administration scholars and practitioners may be ill-equipped to face the challenges of the information age in which we find ourselves trying to govern.

A mere gap in IT management theory might not be fatal, but in reality, the implications for the practice of public administration, and therefore governance, are quite grim. Press accounts of the possibility of the year 2000 computer problem causing chaos in air traffic control present one example of how integral IT has become to the safety and economic well-being of the country. While the billions of dollars currently spent by the federal government on IT make up an insignificant portion of the budget, IT underpins almost the whole budget directly or indirectly. Just ponder the implications to the government's cash flow if the Internal Revenue Service could not collect taxes or the Social Security Administration could not post employee earnings.

This chapter compares the federal IT management literature with a normative model of management maturity, examining the strategic objectives for IT and the related management approaches. The academic disciplines that contribute to an understanding of the management of IT in the federal government include business administration, state and local government management, information sciences, and public administration. Although the analysis of the literature does include government publications, it does not discuss the pertinent public law or government-wide policy (See instead Beachboard & McClure, 1996; Holden, 1994 ; Plocher, 1996).

Like public administration more generally, IT management draws on several different sources. Unlike other management topics in public administration, though, the literature covering IT management lacks breadth and maturity. The following quotation from Weber (1988, p. 68) summarizes the state of the literature as of 1990.

> Much of the literature still presents heresy, speculation, opinions, or evidence gathered by parties with vested political interests. Unfortunately, carefully conducted theoretical and empirical research studies are still scarce, and even those works are frequently plagued by incomplete, conflicting and counter intuitive results. (Northop, 1990, p. 505)

While the chapter documents some progress in the field in the last decade, it also points to continuing shortcomings. It is particularly troubling that disciplines besides public administration are responsible for the few recent developments in IT management literature. Compared against the management maturity model presented below, there is clearly much work left to do.

A Model for Information Technology Management Maturity

This analysis of federal IT management literature proceeds in an order that reflects the maturation of the strategic objectives for IT and the attendant management philosophy over the last 40 years. As a normative standard, this analysis adapts a model of maturation of theory and practice that Donald Marchand (1985) first used for the field of information management (Holden, 1994). He identified four stages of evolution for information management, encompassing the 20th century.

This chapter adapts his model as an organizing principle in several ways. First, since this analysis deals with the management of IT, it does not include his Stage 1, which addresses the physical control of information before automation in the 1950s. Second, Marchand discusses the evolution of information management for five distinguishing characteristics: (a) precipitating forces, (b) strategic objective, (c) basic technologies, (d) management approaches, and (e) organizational status. This chapter stresses how strategic objectives for and management approaches to IT have evolved, placing little emphasis on the other three characteristics. Third, since Marchand covers information management, which is broader than IT management, the names for the stages differ. Finally, the stages used to organize this chapter reflect the stage of development of the literature, despite the date of its publication. In contrast, Marchand's demarcated stages by time periods, assuming that all activities within a specified period of time conform to the same stage of development in management.

Stage 1 - Management Information Systems

This stage, which Marchand labeled "Management of Automated Technology," spans the 1960s through the mid-1970s. Then, business and public sector professionals often used the term management information systems (MIS) to describe IT. The management of technology dominated this era at the expense of management of information. Because the management of the technology was limited to the data center, there was little concern for relating those resources to other facets of management in organizations.

The management approaches for IT of this era reflected the isolation of the IT professional from broader functional and executive oversight. Organizations used IT to automate backroom operations, with the primary strategic objective being to improve the efficiency of clerical activities (Zuboff, 1988). Personnel in the data processing function took primary responsibility for the management of these resources and focused on the development of applications and systems. Typically, these systems consisted of applications run by data processing professionals in centralized processing facilities that consisted of mainframe computers. Users had few direct contacts with these systems other than to fill out punch cards, do manual key entry, and receive printouts from the data processing department. As a result, line functions in the organization rarely controlled their own computing resources (Ackoff, 1967).

The early MIS literature dealt almost exclusively with private-sector applications. It was not until much later that public administration adapted MIS literature to public-sector theory and practice. In 1986, Bozeman and Bretschneider articulated a case for a separate body of literature to address the unique information needs of public organizations. They proposed that this body of theory and practice fall under the heading of public management information systems (PMIS).

To support this argument, they asserted that MIS literature ignores variables external to the organization, such as the political environment and the annual appropriation process. The political control of public organizations, which entail uncertain and variable goals, means that public- and private-sector methods for establishing IT performance indicators differ dramatically. Though private and public organizations can acquire the same hardware and software, they contend different organizational environments require unique system design techniques. While this notion of PMIS brought attention to the use of IT in the public sector, it had limited applicability as a management approach. Instead of viewing IT as a strategic resource for public-sector organizations, this perspective examined the development of one application at a time.

Some public administration research has examined the availability of IT at the state and local government levels. For instance, the International City Management Association (ICMA) (1986) surveyed local and county governments' use of computers several times. Kenneth Kraemer (1989) and his associates at the University of California have published several works resulting from the Urban Information Systems (URBIS) research project. These initial efforts addressed the use of IT in local governments, placing much less emphasis on the management of those resources or their strategic importance.

Some theoretical work in evaluating information systems has surfaced nonetheless, which applies generally to public-sector organizations. Newcomer and Caudle (1991) provide some insights into how and why the evaluation of information systems in the public sector should go beyond mere return-on-investment criteria. In particular, they offer a framework for evaluation that includes qualitative and quantitative measures and recognizes the multiple uses of most public information systems. Although this framework does not help agency decision makers choose between competing projects, it nonetheless broadens the theoretical base for evaluating individual systems projects.

Stevens and McGowan's work (1985) presents an overview of information systems management for public administrators from the local to the federal level. Their book adapts contingency-based organization theory to explain how public organizations must process information effectively to respond to their environment. For the most part, the book focuses on managing single applications and makes illustrative points through the discussion of three case studies. Although it does cover a variety of topics, including management, policy, and technology, it does not provide an organization-wide or strategic view of managing IT.

Through the early 1980s to the middle of the 1990s, the Office of Management and Budget (OMB) used its annual five-year plan to publish analyses and views of federal agencies' efforts to manage IT. These analyses reflect an oversight perspective on what agencies should be doing to comply with government-wide policy (OMB, 1984). Therefore, OMB does not ground these publications in academic literature or theory.

Several years after the passage of the Paperwork Reduction Act (PRA), Congress's Office of Technology Assessment (OTA) (1986) published a report that included a chapter attempting to assess the status of IT management in the federal government. Through a network of contractors, OTA collected data on the use of IT in 13 cabinet departments and 20 independent agencies. Using these data, OTA's report made recommendations for future Congressional oversight of executive branch activities, including applications for IT, information dissemination, and computer security.

The General Accounting Office (GAO) prepared a summary report that highlighted IT as a major management issue facing the incoming Bush administration. Their review of agency plans and budgets led GAO to conclude that agency planning was either nonexistent or ineffectual. GAO asserted that the agencies' inadequate use of strategic planning for IT was leading to ill-focused investments, plans that were not linked to the budget processes, and projects that lacked sufficient return to justify the investment (GAO, 1986).

The Information Resources Management Service (IRMS) of the General Services Administration (GSA), exercising its Brooks Act (1962) authorities then, oversaw federal agency management of IT. Based on this oversight experience, GSA (much like GAO) published reports that attempt to generalize from its agency-specific IT acquisition reviews. GSA's publications, by design, were not anchored by a strong theory base. Instead, these documents pointed out pitfalls for agencies to avoid and, to a lesser extent, identified "good practices" (Information Resources Management Service, 1990).

GSA also published an analysis of what it called "grand design" implementations for systems modernization. It found that all-encompassing projects that combined hardware replacement and massive software development often experienced schedule delays and cost overruns. GSA contracted with a consulting firm to produce a document outlining alternatives to such all-encompassing projects. While this product was not grounded in an identifiable theory base, it did provide case study analysis of how public- and private-sector organizations have broken IT projects into more manageable pieces to isolate and minimize risks (American Management Systems, 1991).

Despite some maturation of the literature during the MIS stage, theory was apparently not meeting the needs of practice. There were two notable contributions to the literature during this period. First, an emerging view recognized that IT required broader management attention. Second, management approaches matured to recognize that private-sector IT management might not suffice for public sector managers. Even in the private sector, the MIS philosophy fell prey to vocal criticism as the developers rarely interpreted user needs accurately, and even if they did, it took so long to write the programs to run the systems, that the original user requirements changed. After corporate managers spent millions of dollars to buy and subsequently upgrade MIS that did not provide the expected results, this criticism became more widespread.

Frustration found a voice in John Dearden (1972), who wrote that MIS would never meet managers' expectations or needs. He asserted that:

> The notion that a company can and ought to have an expert (or a group of experts) create for it a single, completely integrated supersystem—an MIS—to help govern every aspect of its activity is absurd (p. 92).

After fixating on the technology and the life cycle, evidently organizations still did not build the information systems they needed. A new, broader perspective for managing IT emerged as an alternative to MIS in the early 1980s.

Stage 2 - Information Resources Management

Ironically, the private sector did not lead the next phase of IT management theory. Stage 2, signaled the replacement of MIS with a theory of information resources management (IRM). The federal government ushered in this new state of IT management with the passage of the original Paperwork Reduction Act (PRA) (1980). The PRA articulated a need for the federal government to manage information and IT as a resource, much like financial and human resources (Caudle, 1987). Though the PRA created requirements for managing both information and IT in the federal government, Marchand uses the term IRM to refer to a philosophy for managing IT more generally, as does this chapter.

IRM, as the Stage 2 perspective for managing IT, reflected change in both the technical and the external environments of organizations from the mid-1970s to the mid 1980s. Information technology began to move out of the data center with the arrival of minicomputers and the introduction of microcomputers. With this decentralization of computing power, management approaches had to shift from the data center to include user organizations. Strategic objectives for IT also changed as line organizations began to realize that they could use IT for more than just backroom functions. As a result, program offices often acquired their own IT when data processing organizations could not keep pace with their needs. These changes, combined with the increasing level of spending on IT in organizations, brought these resources to the attention of a broader range of managers (Marchand, 1985).

In response to the disillusionment with a management perspective focused on single applications mentioned earlier (i.e., MIS), private-sector organizations and business schools began to think more about how to tie together disparate systems to form an organization-wide perspective. Often, data processing organizations call such perspectives "architectures." This view represented a departure from the earlier philosophy of managing IT because it assumed that systems existed outside the physical and management control of a central data center.

McFarlan and McKenny (1983) also took an organization-wide view of managing IT, which they called "the Information Systems (IS) function." Their work distinguished itself in recognizing that organizations, especially large ones, often manage many information systems projects at once. As a result, it dealt with issues arising from coordinating several systems projects, going beyond exerting life cycle management control over individual projects.

McFarlan and McKenny (1983) acknowledged that cultural (what they call environmental) factors often determine the effectiveness of control mechanisms for managing information systems. These factors include: (a) the penetration of information systems in the working environment, (b) the level of maturity of information systems development efforts, and (c) the planning style of the organization. More specifically, McFarlan and McKenny asserted that the effectiveness of information systems planning depends on the perceived importance and status of the systems manager, the physical proximity of the systems group and the general management team, the corporate management style, and organizational size and complexity.

International Business Machines (IBM) (1984) developed a systems planning methodology called Business Systems Planning (BSP) that offered a framework for managing a collection of information systems across organizations. Specifically, BSP provided organizations, public or private, with a method for creating an information systems plan.

Experience has shown that BSP can be applied to all institutions in the public sector and all industries in the private sector, because the requirements for developing information systems are similar no matter the business served or the products and services provided. (IBM, 1984, p. I)

Even thought BSP does not address the planning or use of individual systems, it does create a framework for linking systems planning to the broader purposes of the organization.

IBM's stated intent in creating BSP was to develop a methodology for creating a plan that would overcome the historic weaknesses of information systems implementation, generally attributed to a lack of planning. In part, IBM built on its own attempts to deal with the plethora of systems that each of its own functions had developed over time. The keys to this new method, as IBM espoused them, were using top-down planning and analysis of organizational processes, relying on bottom-up implementation, translating organizational objectives into information systems requirements, and using a structured methodology (IBM, 1984).

Over time, the BSP process matured in two ways. First, IBM developed an automated version of BSP that it called Information Quality Analysis (IQA). Similar to BSP, the IQA technique concentrated on ensuring that information systems plans relate to the business plan of the firm. The technique involved interviewing key top executives, distinguishing between essential and nonessential data, establishing points of auditability for data accuracy and timeliness, and designing system outputs that pay attention to the needs of the ultimate data consumer (Vacca, 1984).

Second, a more recent version of BSP included an "enterprise analysis" phase. Earlier versions of BSP referred to "business" as the generic term for the organization entity under study, whereas it appears that the term "enterprise" has taken on that meaning. This is the genesis for the term "enterprise" that has crept into the systems planning lexicon as a way to describe planning that spans all parts of an organization. Other than changing the label for the organization-wide perspective from business to enterprise, the BSP has not changed much (Schouw, Jeltma, & Hanson, 1987).

Consistent with IBM's view that BSP methods applied to both public- and private-sector organizations, collections of articles on IRM issues appeared during this stage of the literature. For instance, Rabin and Jackowski (1988) edited a volume that touches on a variety of IRM issues, including information systems management, data administration, and applications such as decision support systems and data bases. While sections of the volume dealt with public-sector IRM (Marchand & Kresslein, 1988), the balance of the work was so general that applying it to any particular kind of organization is difficult. Specifically, it devoted little attention to federal government.

GSA's Federal Systems Integration and Management Center (FEDSIM) has also published several guides on IT management. These documents are similar to the IRMS documents described earlier in that they are grounded primarily in practice instead of theory. However, the nature of their practice makes these documents quite different. Instead of conducting oversight like GSA's IRMS, FEDSIM gave federal agencies technical support to plan and analyze IT projects. As a result, its publications reflect its experiences preparing projects and documentation that comply with GSA and OMB policy requirements.

These publications, best described as handbooks, provide operational advice on how agencies can organize the IRM function and prepare basic documents required by OMB and GSA policy. For instance, FEDSIM (1987) published two versions of a handbook that laid out a process for preparing the five-year information systems plan required by the PRA. These guides are so "hands on" that they include appendices with layouts for particular parts of the document and a notional table of contents. In the second version of the handbook, FEDSIM tried to show how an agency might link the development of its five-year plan with budgeting, analysis, and life cycle management activities.

Simultaneously, FEDSIM (1986, 1988) published a two-part guide on information systems planning. This guide differed from the handbooks in that it did not focus on the preparation of a five-year plan that would comply with the requirements of the PRA. The information systems planning handbook laid out a process for an agency to create both information and information systems architectures. This guide adapted the BSP methodology, with minor changes, to reflect some requirements of federal law.

In response to a request from the House Committee on Government Operations, GAO's Information Management and Technology (IMTEC) Division (1992d) compiled a report that highlighted some problems it consistently found in federal agency management of information resources. It identified eleven themes across 132 agency-specific reports that spanned the period between October 1, 1988, and May 31, 1991. Of those 11 themes, eight dealt with IT management and two addressed agency-wide management and control of information resources, including IT and data management. GAO did not set out to find root causes to these broadly-defined problems, but did identify several plausible explanations in the report. For management mechanisms such as life cycle management, project evaluation, and coordination of information resources, GAO found that agencies lacked sufficient policy controls or did not effectively use the controls that existed.

Based on its experiences reviewing agency-specific IT projects, IMTEC developed what it described as a generic framework for developing systems architectures. In the preface to the report describing this framework, IMTEC expressed hope that the framework would help to address a prevalent problem of agencies trying to manage IT projects, which is the lack of planning and analysis of alternatives. While this report provided a very high level view of the steps an agency should consider in developing a particular systems project, it did not address how to provide cohesiveness to information systems efforts across the agency (GAO, 1992c).

To date, only two academic studies have addressed the implementation of the PRA by federal agencies. Caudle (1987) conducted the first study, documented in a report for the National Academy of Public Administration (NAPA). This report included the results of interviews with federal IRM officials in cabinet-level agencies, selected subagency organizational units, and the central oversight agencies. She used these interviews to learn how agencies had organized to meet the mandates of the PRA and to assess whether the principles contained in the Act had begun to pervade agency attitudes and behavior. In addition, her study presented agency views on OMB and GSA's policy-making mechanisms for overseeing achievement the PRA and the Brooks Act.

Caudle's work provided a groundwork for subsequent public administration advances in IT management. In particular, she found that agency staff identified the strategic planning and budget processes as the "dominant IRM management control mechanisms." This attitude manifested itself in the respondents viewing IT management as guiding a project through the acquisition approval process at GSA and the budget approval process at OMB. In the conclusion to the report, Caudle recommended future research into control mechanisms for information resources. Such mechanisms, she noted, might differ from those used for financial and human resources. Additionally, her work serves as the foundation for GAO's Strategic Information Management study discussed later.

The second study, conducted by Levitan and Dineen (1986), also relied on interviews with selected federal IRM officials. This research differed from the Caudle's (1987) report for NAPA in that Levitan and Dineen first established a model of what they called "integrative IRM" and used that as a basis for assessing the state of the art of integration of federal IRM in 1985. In the authors' view, managing IT is complex because such management issues transcend normal organizational boundaries. Specifically, Levitan and Dineen cited strategic planning, implementation of technology, and interaction with the organizational constituencies as examples of integrative issues for federal IRM.

Having constructed this model of the integrative nature of federal IRM, the authors conducted interviews with representatives from several federal agencies and one bureau of a federal agency. They posed questions about whether managing information resources in the organization extended beyond information systems to include information management (e.g., functions such as dissemination and records management) and whether notions of IRM extended to the program offices.

The findings confirmed several of those cited by Caudle (1987) in her study published by NAPA. For the most part, agencies had not fulfilled the mandate of the PRA by integrating the management of information systems and information content. The federal IRM offices represented in the interviews cited the management of information systems as their major concerns overwhelmingly. This reflected the information systems background of those staff who had risen to management positions in IRM. Agencies relied on task forces to achieve integration of IRM issues across normal organizational boundaries. Levitan and Dineen found no consistent patterns of whether agencies had succeeded in integrating IRM as a management discipline in program operations.

Bishop, Doty, and McClure (1989) prepared a compendium of views on federal IRM from the two aforementioned studies, and academic literature, and GAO, OMB, and GSA publications that went beyond just the carrying out of the PRA. Their paper presented a matrix of various observers' critiques on the status of IRM in the federal government. Comparing these critiques, they identified strong agreement on several points such as: (a) insufficient integration of IRM at the agency level, (b) insufficient integration of IRM with agency mission and program management, and (c) a need for better planning. Only one index dealt with the management of IT, and the respondents split evenly on the issue of whether IRM suffered from an overemphasis on technology.

Several other contributions from information sciences bring more insight into state of IRM policy development and, to some extent, implementation. Beachboard and McClure (1996) point out some inherent inconsistencies among the various federal oversight bodies and policy instruments. To help deal with weaknesses in IRM policy, Beachboard and McClure advocate changes in IRM policy, federal agency commitment to IRM as a management discipline, and further empirical research into the lack of effectiveness of IRM policy and practice.

A similar publication on federal IRM finds that neither policy nor practice seems able to bring federal agencies into the information age, thereby enabling wide-scale electronic service delivery (Bertot, McClure, Ryan, & Beachboard, 1996). Without much empirical grounding, the authors offer a mix of policy, organizational and investment choices that they assert will enhance the effectiveness of federal IRM policy and practice. These contributions add a certain richness to an understanding of federal IRM policy, but despite some hints of loftier strategic objectives for IT (i.e., electronic service delivery), offer little in the way of concrete management process to make that vision a reality.

Consistent with the maturing view of IRM, the research on local governments' use of IT began to explore the benefits from investments in automation. An analysis of survey data collected from 46 U.S. cities found that payoffs accrued in fiscal control, cost avoidance, and improved service delivery mechanisms. This study also found that it took longer than anticipated to realize some benefits and that expected payoffs in better information for management and planning had yet to appear (Northop, 1990).

Other research has included IT management as part of an examination of IRM in state governments. The Syracuse University School of Information Studies (1989) produced a nationwide study on the maturity of IRM in state governments. This study used data collected from a survey of 2,200 program managers and information systems directors to characterize their views on the state of the art across several IRM activities, including IT usage and acquisition. It did not, however, discuss management techniques for IT or the strategic role of IT for stage governments.

A consistent theme emerges from the literature of Stage 2, covering IRM. The application of theory and practice from this era has been very uneven. The federal government, in particular, still relies extensively on centralized, mainframe information processing and a similarly centralized management approach, which does not support the sharing and integration envisioned by IRM proponents. A lack of agreement on the meaning and relevance of IRM, as manifest in the publications advocating continued changes to basic federal law and government-wide policy for IRM continues to thwart the adoption of the core management principles. This may be in part because researchers outside public administration, most notably information sciences, have done most of the research on IRM policy. What little research there is on IRM implementation points to mixed results at best and is mostly still exploratory.

The strategic focus for IT remains largely the same—efficiency. Although efficiency of government service delivery to the public, compared to the efficiency of backroom functions, represents some progress, the ultimate goal remains lower costs. These notions of IRM as a management philosophy and strategic focus for IT remain mostly inwardly focused to the organization, except for preliminary discussions of electronic service delivery. Despite, or perhaps because of, the limited success of IRM, a new era for managing IT has begun to emerge.

Stage 3 - Managing Information Technology in an Information Age

While many organizations strive to make the transition from Stage 1 (MIS) to Stage 2 (IRM), further developments in managing IT are forming the outline of a new stage. Marchand calls this stage "knowledge management" to highlight the shift in emphasis from the physical management of technology and information to the management of information content. He contends this stage of development began in the mid-1980s and will continue through the 1990s. While the management of information content is emerging as a new skill, the successful application of IT makes it possible to maximize the benefits of information content (Marchand, 1985).

At the outset, though, a more precise definition of the term "information age" is in order. "Information age" has crept into the day-to-day language used in most organizations and the popular press. It is generally used to describe a future state where information will be quickly and universally accessible in electronic form. In reality, however, there is a lack of agreement on what the information age means or what future conditions it purports to describe. The following provides a brief explanation of how the term is used in this chapter and is used for this third state of IT management.

The first reference to the term "information age" appears to date back to a book edited by Hammer (1976), which included contributions from library science academics and practitioners. In the introduction, Hammer defines the term somewhat, acknowledging that humans have used information throughout the civilized era. For the purposes of the book, he demarcated the information age "as being most reflective of the interests and passions of the 1965-1975 librarians and information scientists." (p. vii)

Dizard (1985) described his view of an information age, but implied that our society has not yet arrived there. Even in 1989, he states a revised edition of the book was "an interim report" because the U.S. was only then entering the most mature phase of an information age. The mature phase, which he believed would arrive in the 1990s, would entail the mass availability of IT and technology-based information services to consumers in their homes.

This third stage would be made possible by the existence and use of a broad network of networks for sharing information between individuals—not only large organizations and businesses. Many of these new services would be made available, not through the personal computer, but with existing appliances in many homes — the television and the telephone. To a great extent, this third stage of the information age is becoming a reality quicker than even Dizard might have envisioned. For that reason, this part of the chapter uses that description of the term "information age" to help frame the most mature management philosophy for IT.

As an indication of how powerful the notion has become, the Clinton administration described an information age initiative promoting new uses for IT in federal agencies (Office of Science and Technology Policy, 1993). This report brought a new strategic focus to the uses of IT for federal agencies as a service delivery vehicle, requiring new management approaches and supporting policies. The Clinton administration envisioned the federal government will use IT to make agencies more responsive and service-oriented. Instead of using automation to make government operations more efficient for internal processing, agencies would use IT to reach out the public to provide more timely and higher quality service.

Comparing differences between an information age philosophy and IRM point to the maturation of management approaches for federal IT management. One difference is a more robust understanding the importance of the technological infrastructure in the information age. Emerging and maturing technologies such as graphical user interfaces, client/server computing, and workstations create a foundation for more substantial user involvement in management. Additionally, this reality requires a recognition that technology cannot be managed effectively from the mainframe data center to the exclusion of management of the desktop and everything between.

Corporate information management (CIM) is among the most prominent additions to the literature on how to manage information systems from an organization-wide perspective. Although the Department of Defense (DOD) made the CIM acronym well known in the federal IRM community, many CIM ideas come from Paul Strassman's experiences in the private sector. Strassman served on the Executive Level Group (ELG) for Defense Corporate Information Management, which created the charter for CIM (Executive Level Group for Corporate Information Management, 1990). This document mirrors many facets of a 137-item policy checklist found in Strassman (1990), which is based on the private sector work he did before coming to the Department of Defense.

Several themes emerge from Strassman (1990) which extend the IRM view of managing information systems from an organization-wide perspective. He stresses that the policies for managing information systems should place responsibility in the hands of the users—not the IRM specialists. These policies include: (a) using economic analysis that promotes trading off between information resources and other resources and (b) providing mechanisms that charge users for information and information systems. He also introduces the notion that organizations should examine and redesign work processes before automation to ensure that automation does not speed up archaic and unneeded functions. The unifying theme presented by his list of policies is to ensure that investments in information systems add measurable value to the core missions of the organization.

Without identifying it as such, Strassman's approach of aligning information resources to organizational missions falls under the rubric of strategic management. Strategic management represents an effort by private and public-sector managers to make strategic planning more useful in meeting the short-run needs of organizations. Much like Strassman, business authors writing about strategic management talk about aligning corporate resources and missions to take advantage of opportunities in the market. Strategic management emphasized looking at resource allocation processes and support systems to see how they added value to a business (Hax & Majluf, 1984).

One example of a strategic management approach used by a consulting firm specializing in organization effectiveness is McKinsey's 7S Model, which identifies the following factors as contributing to organizational effectiveness: (a) structure, (b) strategy, (c) systems, (d) style, (d) staff, (e) skills, (f) strategy, and (g) shared values (Gluck, 1986). For use in the public sector, public administration authors have adapted these models for differences in civil service traditions in political environments (Nutt & Backoff, 1992). Much like the McKinsey model, some public-sector models of strategic management explicitly include and highlight the role of IT in strategic management processes (Adler, McDonald, & MacDonald, 1992; DeLisi, 1990).

Other public-sector strategic management models, though, do not include information technology as a strategic resource. For instance, one particular public-sector strategic management model focuses on human resources to the exclusion of IT (Eadie, 1989). This is somewhat ironic given that the impetus for viewing human resources as a strategic resource comes from "modern production systems" that require new knowledge skills (McGregor, 1988). In other publications, a public administration author might acknowledge IT as a strategic resource requiring special management attention, but then would do little to help the reader put the observation into action (Kraemer, 1989). Even more troubling, a well-known text on strategic planning in the public sector does not even mention a role for managing information systems as a strategic resource (Bryson, 1989). Despite this lack of emphasis in public administration literature, strategic management of information systems is receiving some attention in the practitioner community for the federal government.

GAO's IMTEC sent Congress a transition report for the incoming Clinton administration that touched on information resources as a strategic management responsibility. This transition report on federal IRM issues added several new items to the Bush administration report discussed earlier for Congress and OMB to consider in their policy making. GAO stressed a principle from DOD's CIM, namely that agencies should streamline work processes before applying automation. Additionally, the report pointed out the lack of incentives for agency project managers to report management problems truthfully to oversight organizations such as GAO, congressional committees, and OMB. GAO described this problem as inherent to complex systems modernization projects. GAO also questions whether changes to acquisition management and budgeting policies might have encouraged problem identification and resolution instead of the current practice of encouraging project managers to gloss over problems until they become so large that a project fails (GAO, 1992a).

To probe further into the causes of agencies' well-documented problems in managing IT, IMTEC convened a panel of experts to discuss perceived barriers to effective management of information resources. This panel, made up of private-sector and federal agency IRM managers, identified institutional barriers as a significant impediment to effective management of information resources. These institutional barriers include shortcomings in agency content and use of internal policy in areas such as life cycle management, performance measurement, and strategic planning. The panel report also stressed that some of these institutional barriers resulted from inconsistently applying IRM policies across all bureaus of an agency (GAO, 1992b).

More recently, GAO has gone a step further and taken a more preventive approach to dealing with federal agency problems managing IT (GAO, 1994). In doing so, GAO not only presents a new management approach for IT grounded in systematic research, it also brings the new strategic objective of mission performance into discussions of why the successful management of IT is so important. Within the federal IRM community, GAO's work in this area often goes by the label of its "best practices" study (Caudle, 1996).

Part of what separates this GAO effort from "typical" GAO reports is the rigor of the analysis supporting GAO's recommendations for change. GAO went to some lengths to find case study examples of effective IT management practices in both the private and public sectors and included federal agencies beyond state governments. Throughout the process of deriving the key best practices from the case study research, the GAO team consulted with federal IRM executives and oversight organizations such as Congress, OMB, and GSA to help ensure that the practices were applicable in the federal environment. As part of the case study analysis, the research also went to great lengths to point to empirical proof of improved mission performance resulting from, or at least relating to, the application of the best practices.

While not explicitly linking the research or the findings to a particular body of literature, it becomes apparent from viewing the list of practices that GAO has created a strategic management framework specifically for managing IT. The practices GAO advocated are:

(a) directing IRM changes; (b) integrating IRM decision making in a strategic management process; (c) linking mission goals and IRM outcomes through performance management; (d) guiding IRM project strategy and follow-up through an investment philosophy; (e) using business process innovation to drive IRM strategies; and (f) building IRM/line partnership through leadership and technical skills. (Caudle, 1996)

Although some of the language and the term IRM pervade best practices report, GAO's work has clearly brought both federal IT theory and practice to another level of management maturity.

Compared with the model of management maturity posited earlier, GAO's research, the resulting report, and the associated toolkits contribute new viewpoints to the strategic objectives and management approaches for IT. The strategic objective for the GAO's best practices work is unambiguously clear with the discussion of both strategic planning and mission performance, grounded in related program effectiveness measures. In effect, this implies a life cycle management approach to linking IT plans, investments, and results. The mission focus also becomes apparent as the management approach seeks high alignment of IT investments with strategic plans and greater partnership between IRM and program staff. An investment management philosophy, grounded in the budget process, gives the whole management approach "teeth" and helps to guard against the tendency for more traditional IT plans to lie unused.

It becomes apparent that GAO not only offered a new management approach and strategic focus, but it also changed the content of IT management policy at the federal level. Looking at the recent changes in federal law (i.e., the Information Technology and Management Reform Act (1996) and the amended Paperwork Reduction Act (1995)) and supporting government-wide policy (i.e., the revised OMB Circular No. A-130) (OMB, 1994) reveals the influence of the GAO work. In affecting all these policy-making efforts, GAO has helped to address some policy inconsistencies pointed out by researchers in information science that contributed to the IRM literature discussed earlier. The question remains, though, whether GAO's work will become accepted theory, policy, and practice for public administration scholars and practitioners alike. It is still too early to tell despite finding ourselves now in the middle of an information age.

Is Public Administration Ready for the Information Age?

Debating what constitutes the information age is not productive at this point. The administration of public programs reflects the reality of an information age. Various disciplines discuss federal IT management, but public administration's contributions continue to lack both depth and rigor. In particular, little public administration research has addressed the management of IT as a strategic resource for serving the public and improving program effectiveness.

It is quite apparent how integral IT has become to administering federal programs specifically and all public programs more generally. Relegating this management domain to "computer people" is no longer sufficient. Since governance is an information-rich endeavor, public administrators need to understand how to manage the infrastructure that collects, processes, stores, and disseminates information about and for public program delivery.

Advancements in federal IT management theory, policy, and practice have come from outside public administration. In particular, business administration leads public administration in identifying the strategic role of IT in supporting organizational missions. Information sciences have done the most in-depth research into federal IRM policy. GAO has contributed greatly to the development of new federal IT management policy and practice.

As documented by the lack of contributions to the maturing literature for federal IT management, public administration does not recognize of the critical importance of IT to deliver public programs. The depth and rigor of public administration research in budgeting, personnel, and organization theory compared to IT management points to a need to reexamine the core management competencies for public administration. The management of IT should be viewed as a competency as important as the management of human and financial resources within public administration.

Public administration should provide a vision for federal agencies as they move from a technology base and management philosophy grounded in concepts of management information systems and information resources management to a more mature notion of an information age. This more mature notion should recognize that as IT becomes even more widely available and used by the public, citizens will demand changes in the way they interact with their governments. Increasingly, the public will ask, if not demand, to "do business" with the federal government electronically. As a result, it is imperative that IT management theory, policy, and practice mature more quickly to enable the electronic service delivery the public will demand and the information age enables. It remains to be seen whether public administration will contribute to this maturation any more than it has in the past.

References

Ackoff, R. (1967). Management Misinformation Systems. *Management Science, 14*, B147-156.

Adler, P. S., McDonald, W., & MacDonald, F. (1992). Strategic Management of Technical Functions. *Sloan Management Review, 33*(Winter 1992), 19-37.

American Management Systems. (1991). *Alternatives to Grand Designs for Systems Modernization.* Washington, DC: General Services Administration.

Beachboard, J. C., & McClure, C. R. (1996). Managing Federal Information Technology: Conflicting Policies and Competing Philosophies. *Government Information Quarterly, 13*(1), 15-34.

Bertot, J. C., McClure, C. R., Ryan, J., & Beachboard, J. C. (1996). Federal Information Resources Management: Integrating Information Management and Technology. In P. Hernon, C. R. McClure, & H. C. Relyea (Eds.), *Federal Information Policies in the 1990s: Views and Perspectives* (pp.105-136). Norwood, NJ: Ablex.

Bishop, A., Doty, P., & McClure, C. R. (1989). *Federal Information Resources Management (IRM): A Policy Review and Assessment.* Paper presented at the 52nd Annual Meeting of the American Society for Information Science.

Bozeman, B., & Bretschneider, S. (1986). Public Management Information Systems: Theory and Prescription. *Public Administration Review, 46*(Special Issue), 475-487.

Bryson, J. M. (1989). *Strategic Planning for Public and Non-Profit Organizations.* San Francisco: Jossey-Bass.

Caudle, S. L. (1987). *Federal Information Resources Management: Bridging Vision and Action.* Washington, DC: National Academy of Public Administration.

Caudle, S. L. (1989). *Managing Information Resources: New Directions in State Government.* Syracuse: Syracuse University School of Information Studies.

Caudle, S. L. (1996). Strategic Information Resources Management: Fundamental Practices. *Government Information Quarterly, 13*(1), 83-97.

Dearden, J. (1972). MIS is a Mirage. *Harvard Business Review, 50*(January/February), 90-99.

DeLisi, P. S. (1990). Lessons From the Steel Axe: Culture, Technology, and Organizational Change. *Sloan Management Review, 32*(Fall 1990), 83-93.

Dizard, W. P., Jr. (1985). *The Coming Information Age: An Overview of Technology, Economics, and Politics.* (1st ed.). White Plains, NY: Longman.

Dizard, W. P., Jr. (1989). *The Coming Information Age: An Overview of Technology, Economics, and Politics.* (3rd ed.). White Plains, NY: Longman.

Eadie, D. C. (1989). Building the Capacity for Strategic Management. In J. L. Perry (Ed.), *Handbook of Public Administration* (pp. 162-175). San Francisco: Jossey-Bass.

Eugene B. & McGregor, J. (1988). The Public Sector Human Resource Puzzle: Strategic Management of a Strategic Resource. *Public Administration Review, 48*(November/December), 941-950.

Executive Level Group for Corporate Information Management. (1990). *A Plan for Corporate Information Management for the Department of Defense*. Washington, DC: Department of Defense.

Federal Property and Administrative Services Act (Brooks Act), 40 U.S.C. secs. 759 and 487 (1962).

General Accounting Office. (1986). *Information Technology Issues* (GAO/OCG-89-6TR). Washington, DC: General Accounting Office.

General Accounting Office. (1992a). *Information Management and Technology Issues* (GAO/OCG-93-5TR). Washington, DC: General Accounting Office.

General Accounting Office. (1992b). *Percieved Barriers to Effective Information Resources Management: Results of GAO Panel Discussions* (GAO/IMTEC-92-67). Washington, DC: General Accounting Office.

General Accounting Office. (1992c). *Strategic Information Planning: Framework for Designing and Developing Systems Architectures* (GAO/IMTEC-92-51). Washington, DC: General Accounting Office.

General Accounting Office. (1992d). *Summary of Federal Agencies' Information Resources Mangement Problems* (GAO/IMTEC-92-13FS). Washington, DC: General Accounting Office.

General Accounting Office. (1994). *Improving Mission Performance Through Strategic Information Management and Technology* (GAO/AIMD-94-115). Washington, DC: General Accounting Office.

Gluck, F. W. (1986). Strategic Management: An Overview. In J. R. Gardner, R. Rachlin, & H. W. Sweeny (Eds.), *Handbook of Strategic Planning* (pp. 1-36). New York: John Wiley.

Hammer, D. P. (1976). *The Information Age: Its Development, Its Impact.* Methuchen, NJ: Scarecrow Press.

Hax, A. C., & Majluf, N. S. (1984). *Strategic Management: An Integrative Perspective.* Englewood Cliffs, NJ: Prentice-Hall.

Holden, S. H. (1994). *Managing Information Technology in the Federal Government: New Policies for an Information Age.* Unpublished Doctoral dissertation, Virginia Polytechnic and State University, Blacksburg.

Holden, S. H. (1996). Managing Information Technology in the Federal Government: Assessing the Development and Application of Agency-Wide Policies. *Government Information Quarterly, 13*(1), 65-82.

Holden, S. H., & Hernon, P. (1996). An Executive Branch Perspective on Managing Information Resources. In P. Hernon, C. R. McClure, & H. C. Relyea (Eds.), *Federal Information Policies in the 1990s: Views and Perspectives* (pp. 96-100). Norwood, NJ: Ablex Publishing Corporation.

Information Resources Management Service. (1990). *A Guide for Requirements Analysis and Analysis of Alternatives.* Washington, DC: General Services

Administration.

Information Technology and Management Reform Act of 1996 (Clinger-Cohen Act), 40 U.S.C. Chapter 25 (1996).

International Business Machines. (1984). *Business Systems Planning Guide* (GE20-0527-4). Atlanta: International Business Machines, Inc.

International City Management Association (Ed.). (1986). *Local Government Yearbook: 1986*. Washington, DC: International City Management Association.

Kraemer, K. L. (1989). Managing Information Systems. In J. L. Perry (Ed.), *Handbook of Public Administration* (pp. 527-544). San Francisco: Jossey-Bass.

Kraemer, K. L., King, J. L., Dunkle, D. E., & Lane, J. P. (1989). *Managing Information Systems: Change and Control in Organizational Computing*. San Francisco: Jossey-Bass.

Levitan, K. B., & Dineen, J. (1986). Integrative Aspects of Information Resources Management (IRM). *Information Management Review, 1*(4), 61-67.

Marchand, D. A. (1985). Information Management: Strategies and Tools in Transition. *Information Management Review, 1*(Summer), 27-34.

Marchand, D. A., & Kresslein, J. C. (1988). Information Resources Management and the Public Administrator. In J. Rabin & E. M. Jackowski (Eds.), *Handbook of Information Resources Management* (pp. 395-456). New York: Marcel Dekker.

McFarlan, F. W., & McKenny, J. L. (1983). *Corporate Information Systems Management: The Issues Facing Senior Executives*. Homewood, Ill: Richard D. Irwin, Inc.

Newcomer, K. E., & Caudle, S. L. (1991). Evaluating Public Sector Information Systems: More than Meets the Eye. *Public Administration Review, 51*(September/October), 377-384.

Northop, A. (1990). Payoffs from Computerization: Lessons Over Time. *Public Administration Review, 50*(September/October), 505-514.

Nutt, P. C., & Backoff, R. W. (1992). *Strategic Management of Public and Third Sector Organizations: A Handbook for Leaders*. San Francisco: Jossey-Bass.

Office of Management and Budget. (1984). *A Five-Year Plan for Meeting the Automatic Data Processing and Telecommunications Needs of the Federal Government*. Washington, DC: Office of Management and Budget.

Office of Management and Budget. (1994). Management of Federal Information Resources, Transmittal 2, *OMB Circular No. A-130* (Vol. 59, pp. 37906-37928). Federal Register: Government Printing Office.

Office of Science and Technology Policy. (1993). *Technology for America's Economic Growth: A New Direction to Build Economic Strength*. Washington, DC: Office of Science and Technology Policy.

Office of Software Development and Information Technology. (1986). *Information Systems Planning Handbook* (OSDIT/FPSC-87/00). Washington, DC: General Services Administration.

Office of Software Development and Information Technology. (1987). *Strategic Information Resources Management Planning Handbook* (OIT/FPSP-85/001). Washington, DC: General Services Administration.

Office of Software Development and Information Technology. (1988). *Information Systems Planning Handbook: Phase II*. Washington, DC: General Services

Administration.

Office of Technology Assessment. (1986). *Federal Government Information Technology: Management, Security and Congressional Oversight* (OTA-CIT-297). Washington, DC: Office of Technology Assessment.

Paperwork Reduction Act of 1980, 44 U.S.C. 3501 et seq (1980).

Paperwork Reduction Act of 1995, 44 U.S.C. 3501 et. seq (1995).

Plocher, D. (1996). The Paperwork Reduction Act of 1995: A Second Chance for Information Resources Management. *Government Information Quarterly, 13*(1), 35-50.

Rabin, J., & Jackowski, E. M. (Eds.). (1988). *Handbook of Information Resource Management.* (Vol. 31). New York: Marcel Dekker.

Schouw, D., Jeltma, B., & Hanson, L. (1987). *Business Systems Planning for Strategic Alignment (BSP/SA): Concepts and Overview.* Los Angeles: IBM Advanced Business Institute.

Stevens, J. M., & McGowan, R. P. (1985). *Information Systems and Public Management.* New York: Praeger Publishing.

Strassman, P. A. (1990). *The Business Value of Computers: An Executive's Guide.* New Caanan, CT: Information Economics Press.

Vacca, J. (1984, December 10, 1984). IBM's Information Quality Analysis. *Computerworld, 18,* 45-47.

Weber, R. (1988). Computer Technology and Jobs: An Impact Assessment and Model. *Communications of the ACM, 31*(January), 68.

Zuboff, S. (1988). *In the Age of the Smart Machine: The Future of Work and Power.* New York: Basic Books.

5

Strategic Planning for Information Technology Management in State Governments

by
Patricia Diamond Fletcher
University of Maryland
Baltimore County

The importance of having a formal strategic plan for managing the information architecture is analyzed in the context of state government. Necessary elements of a successful strategic plan are delineated. The dimensions of strategy and an articulation of a strategic stance are defined and analyzed. The value of information technology and the strategic management of the technology as a valuable organizational asset is assessed in a state government environment. Internal and external variables pertinent to state government are explored and developed with a focus on their import to strategic information technology planning. The strategic plans of three state governments are described and analyzed to provide exemplars of proactive and innovative management of information resources.

Information resources management (IRM) has been a part of the government landscape since the Paperwork Reduction Act (PRA) of 1980 (44 U.S.C. Chapter 35). This law assigns the Director of the Office of Management and Budget (OMB) the responsibility to maintain a comprehensive set of information resources management policies and to promote the implementation of information technology to improve the use and dissemination of information in the conduct of Federal programs. The PRA was reauthorized in 1986 with some changes, then revised again in 1995. The goals of productivity, efficiency, and effectiveness of Federal programs, facilitated by the strategic management of

Copyright© 1999, Idea Group Publishing.

information resources, are at the heart of the PRA

To fulfill these responsibilities, OMB originally issued Circular No. A-130, Management of Federal Information Resources (52730-52751, 1985; revised 50 FR 52730, December, 1995). Circular A-130 provides the operational policy framework for Federal information resources management. The Circular is a strong message as to the value of information to the Federal government. It also places an emphasis on the need for Federal agencies to manage their information resources as economic assets and within a life-cycle framework. The intent and development of an IRM environment in these two policy pieces will be used to establish the context for strategic information technology planning in state government. States can and have borrowed heavily from the Federal initiatives in creating and nurturing their own versions of information resources management. Thus, an understanding of the basic concepts of these two Federal policies provides a beginning to this chapter.

The need to establish policy particular to information resources and the management thereof is clearly defined in Circular A-130.

> Government information is a valuable national resource. It provides the public with knowledge of the government, society, and economy—past, present, and future. It is a means to ensure the accountability of government, to manage the government's operations, to maintain the healthy performance of the economy, and is itself a commodity in the marketplace. The free flow of information between the government and the public is essential to a democratic society.

The definitions and guidelines assigned by the Circular to key constructs of IRM will be used here to create a context and frame the analysis of state and local strategic planning for IRM. Circular A-130 defines the term *information* as "any communication or representation of knowledge such as facts, data, or opinions in any medium or form, including textual, numerical, graphic, cartographic, narrative, or audiovisual forms." The concept of *information resources* includes the information technologies—computer and telecommunications hardware and software—and the actual government information. *Information management* is defined as the application of a life cycle approach the planning, budgeting, analyzing, dissemination, and controlling of an organization's information resources. The concept of *information resources management* is defined in the Circular as "the process of managing information resources to accomplish agency missions. The term encompasses both information itself and the related resources, such as personnel, equipment, funds, and information technology." Finally, *strategic IRM planning* is designated as a management tool to aid organizations in the improvement of the operation of their programs.

OMB Circular A-130 clearly envisions information resources as a set of tools to be applied in support of an organization's mission. Thus, the development and use of information resources should be integrated fully into an organization's strategic plan. According to Circular A-130, strategic planning for information technology promotes the responsible use of information throughout its life cycle "to maximize the usefulness of information, minimize the burden on the public, and preserve the appropriate integrity, availability, and confidentiality of information." Information resources are thus, accorded to management level status in an organization with all attendant management processes to be applied to them.

These two policy instruments are mandates for Federal agencies, but the applicability and value of the IRM framework that they establish is equally relevant at the state and local levels of government. Recent trends in management have contributed significantly to raising the importance of the information technology architecture in all levels of government. Business process reengineering, best practices, performance measurement, benchmarking, and Federal, state and local mandates to reinvent government are all part of a management environment which depends heavily on information technology to achieve mission goals. There is an intense focus today on managing government for results. Accountability and service are seen as important goals. Elected officials see IT as a top-priority tool to create a more effective government. Information technology is a vehicle that enables any government to leverage scarce resources while at the same time removes barriers to citizen access. These are desired capabilities for today's political agendas.

Strategic Planning

The value of having a strategic direction and plan for an organization has come into prominence since the mid-1960s. It was at this time that the body of knowledge about strategy began to build rapidly (Thompson, Fulmer, & Strickland, 1992). The importance and use of strategy, however, has a much longer history, going back more than 2000 years with the teachings of Sun Tzu. In reference to the value of having a strategic plan, Sun Tzu asserted that:

> Strategy is important to the nation — it is the ground of death and life, the path of survival and destruction, so it is imperative to examine it. There is a way of survival, which helps and strengthens you; there is a way of destruction, which pushes you into oblivion.

This sentiment is especially relevant today in the government arena where "doing more with less" is a business practice and the competition for scarce resources is an annual challenge. To work without an effective formal strategy is to sail without a rudder. A strategic plan can not only be an aid to survival, but can further, be a means to success for an organization.

Dimensions of Strategy

Formal strategies and their attendant plans imply a deliberate procedure, one that is *a priori* in nature. According to Mintzberg and Quinn (1991) there are three necessary elements to an effective strategy: a delineation of the strategic goals to be realized, an articulation of the policies which facilitate or limit ability to be strategic, and a determination of the critical programs necessary to carry out the organization's strategy. In addition to these necessary elements, other dimensions are relevant to the design of good strategies. Strategies should be focused on those few important directions which an organization deems as essential. Strategies must also incorporate the notion of an uncertain and basically unknowable future; a future that will have an unpredictable impact on the organization. Thus, the organization must craft a strategy that builds a strong posture or stance from which to respond to the external uncertainties which will affect it in unforeseeable ways. Finally, strategies should be developed in a hierarchical manner with higher level strategies informing the lower level ones, and the lower level strategies supporting the enactment of the higher level ones.

Organizations can build their strategic plans around certain positions or foci. These positions serve to carve out a niche for the organization and to define their focus in a broad or narrow manner. Porter (1996) delineates three distinct sources from which the strategic postures of an organization will emerge. These postures are not independent and often can be seen to occur in conjunction with each other. First, there is the variety-based position, one which is guided by the service or product which the organization chooses to distinguish itself. This could be a strategy represented by the goal of manufacturing the best quality, high end workstation, or providing low cost, accessible higher education to customers solely through the Internet. Second is the needs-based position where the organization directs its resources and attention to meeting a range of needs for a select customer segment. This is the most likely position for a government. It has a definable population of service which has a range of needs for data and services which the government agencies are mandated to provide. Third is the access-based position whereby the customer base is segmented into categories which reflect differing subsets of needs. An example of this would be a strategic targeting of rural versus urban customers, which must include an attention to the differences in what drives or motivates these two groups.

Organizations need strategies to set direction, or minimally keep them from harm in uncertain environments. A strategy gives meaning to an organization, it creates not only a plan, but a perspective for the organization. The strategic plan enables the organization to direct and coordinate the activities of its members, giving rise to a collective action which is based on a sense of mission. The strategy becomes the raison d'être, with organizational enactment of the plan its effect.

Strategy in the Public Sector

An important distinction to consider for government, in any formulation of strategy, is the significance of being public. Bozeman (1984) and later, Bozeman and Straussman (1990) have created a model of publicness which accounts for critical differences in approaches to strategic management in organizations. Central to the notion of publicness is the concept of political authority and the influence of political authority on all organizational behaviors. The influence is seen in the constraints placed on public organizations and public management. Included here are external variables such as policy creation and enactment, the posturing and agenda-setting activities of elected and appointed officials, and the constitutional basis of government which engenders a range of citizen responses to public activities. Byproducts of the presence of political authority include a short time frame for strategy development and implementation, innate ambiguities in definition and measurement of performance of strategic programs, and the particular effect of the annual budget process as a rein on any long-term programmatic orientation. A blending of the attention to the external forces which shape a public organization with a focused perspective on the organization's major functions can create a comprehensive vision which can then be translated into effective strategy (Barkdoll, 1992).

Gabris (1992) notes that the process of public sector strategic planning is "akin to pulling teeth" (p. 79), often as a result of the constraints of political authority. He argues, however, that important benefits can occur by engaging in the strategic planning process. Public sector organizations involved in the development of a strategic plan gain a perspective on their goals and on the specific activities to carry out the goals that they would otherwise lack. He further asserts that engaging in the strategic planning process itself is beneficial to public organizations, complementing and facilitating the importance of cooperative decision making in a public management context. At the macro-level of an organization, a strategic planning process that is participative in nature offers a context for and content to the mercurial and political aspect of public management (Golembiewski and Gabris, 1995).

The effects of this process go beyond the creation of a cooperative environment for policy makers and policy implementers. The strategic planning process, as a formative activity, can be seen to create a sense of enthusiasm and mission when the management staff are active participants in the strategy setting process. This can be an incentive to action for the policy implementers who, by virtue of being in a public organization, lack the monetary incentives, autonomy and flexibility, and clear and rewarded performance expectations that are typical in private organizations (Nutt and Backoff, 1993). It can be seen that there are secondary gains to be accrued from strategic planning in public organizations, along with the more important consideration that without attention to the constraints of political authority, any strategic planning process is doomed to fail.

Strategy and Information Technology

The development of a formal and considered approach to an organization's information technology (IT) architecture goes hand-in-hand with the strategic planning process. The strategic plan is the vision of where an organization is headed; the information technology is a value-added resource in achieving the vision. The impact of IT on business and government in the past 30 years has been dramatic. Information technology has changed the rules of business and the boundaries of competition (Porter and Millar, 1985; Laware, 1991). The strategic role of IT in an organization merits a place for it in the strategic planning process. In the earlier mentioned hierarchy of strategies inherent to any strategic plan, the IT plan is seen as a critical layer which supports the overarching strategic goals of an organization. It is also understood that to successfully manage and use IT, it must be an integral part of any organization's strategic plan. Success is directly tied to use and outcomes, hence the need to include in any strategic plan, a structure for the IT to facilitate the organization's goals and objectives (Ein-Dor and Segev, 1978).

Bozeman and Bretschneider (1986) envision the role of IT in public organizations as essential in anticipating external contingencies. They assert that planning for IT needs to be both comprehensive and forward looking in an effort to anticipate the influence and direction of public authority. Attention to political cycles and agendas, as well as to the legal and statutory constraints in the public organization's environment, can be facilitated by strategic use of IT.

Two more arguments for the value of information and IT in public organizations are set forth by Marchand and Kresslein (1988). First, they assert that "government is a large multiproduct firm that processes information either as a direct product or as a necessary aspect of delivering its services to citizens" (p. 396). Their second contention is that government depends on its IT to carry out its business. Information technology is a necessary and basic tool in government today. The decision to invest in,. maintain, and upgrade IT is no longer an option; it is a fundamental and continuos process in organizations. Given this critical role, it makes sense that developing and implementing a strategic IT plan is part of any successful management process. Anderson and Dawes (1991) reinforce this second argument with the fact that investing in IT is no trivial matter for an organization. Considerable human and capital resources are invested over extended periods of time in the development of information systems. Information technology represents a complex, large, and expensive investment; one which is high risk and rapidly evolving. These factors alone make a compelling case for strategic planning.

A recent report from the United States General Accounting Office (GAO/T-AIMD, 1997) reflects the current environmental drivers for strategically managing and using IT in public organizations. This report clearly targets the key reasons that a strategic approach towards information technology is important. First, the climate of urgency which permeates government today creates a need for government leaders to facilitate successful mission attainment. As IT is pervasive and critical in government today, it becomes a smart tool for enabling success if it is linked to an organization's goals. The second key factor has to do with the public perception of government services. Citizens today are used to a high level of service quality from the private sector, much of this enabled by the strategic use of information technology. They expect and demand the same level of performance from their government agencies. Information management is thus elevated from its more mundane operational role in government. A third factor is the current focus on performance and accountability for results. This makes visible the management and uses of the IT architecture in public organizations. The IT enables superior performance and tracks accountability, if it is used in a strategic manner that supports the organization's goals.

IT Strategy in State Government

Many state governments can today serve as benchmarks for the use and management of information technology. Florida, Minnesota, Texas, and California served as examples of leading IT organizations in a U.S. Government Accounting Office report (GAO/AIMD, 1994) on how to improve agency performance by strategically managing information technology. Florida, Kentucky, Minnesota, New Jersey, South Carolina, and Virginia served as case study examples of strategic information resources management in state governments in a seminal national study (Caudle, Marchand, Bretschneider, Fletcher, and Thurmaier, 1989). California, Kentucky, Ohio, Texas and Oregon are often mentioned award winners cited by government technology trade magazines for their IT innovations and management practices.

The drivers for statewide IT planning have changed over the past decade (Fletcher and Foy, 1994). Initial impetus for planning was often instigated by the state legislatures. Florida is a good example of this (Davies and Hale, 1986). In 1983, the

Florida legislature passed the Florida Information Technology and Planning Act (S. 282.301). This Act represented a major revision in how information technology would be administered statewide. The Act in itself was strategic in nature, implementing a structure that would guide policy development over a ten-year period. The legislation established the Florida Information Resource Commission (IRC), a policy and planning body composed of elected and appointed members including the Governor and members of the Cabinet. This clearly established the strategic intent of the Act. The legislation mandated the development of a formal statewide IT planning process within a biennial framework. Planning was to include consideration of computer hardware and software, IT personnel, facilities management, IT training, and the maintenance of the information resources. For its time, this was a broad and extensive management approach for a function more commonly referred to as data processing, with only computer hardware and software in its purview.

The Act required the development of a plan that aligned the State's information resources with its strategic goals, with an eye to both acquisition and use of the information resources in a planned and value-added manner. A direct link was established between the goals of the State agencies and the use of the information resources. In other words, the goals for the use of IT had to directly relate to the attainment of the State agencies' goals. The IRC was charged with the with the review and approval of all IT acquisitions, a move to insure the Act's integrity and its strategic focus. In 1985, the IRC issued two major reports providing guidance for planning and policy development related to the IT resources. An umbrella statement of statewide IT direction was included in this report, establishing a baseline for uniform IT policy development and creating an operating policy for the use of IT resources. The reports also served as a control for the State agencies to insure compatibility in the statewide IT plans.

In a national study of state information resources management practices, Caudle et al. (1989) noted that the trend towards executive or legislative mandates for strategic IT management was a major one. At that time, 33 states had some form of statewide IT plan. Of these states, 14 were legally required to prepare IT plans. These plans all pertained to the data processing component, computer hardware and software. Only 20 states required a communications or telephone plan be developed on a statewide basis, with three of these charges reflecting legislative intent. Twenty-three states had a high level decision making/advisory group at the time of the study, with a range of oversight authority and responsibility. The earliest instance of a high level decision making group was in Massachusetts with the establishment of the Governor's Advisory Committee on Information Technology established in 1976. This group was charged with the development of a strategic IT and telecommunications plan.

Caudle reported a number of planning trends that were evident at the time of the national study. These major trends indicated:

1. Most of the plans that did exist were concentrated on the data processing component of IT; they were not all-encompassing of information resources.
2. The mandate to develop and maintain strategic IT plans was on the state executive agencies. The judicial and educational departments were generally exempt.

3. Only a few states (Kentucky, Florida, and South Carolina) had an individual designated to manage the planning process for their state.
4. A small number of the states included local governments in their IT plans in recognition of the growing intergovernmental nature of services.
5. The statewide IT plans tended to emphasize more short-term goals centered on the annual budget cycle and procurement concerns.
6. Some of the states (Florida, California, Kentucky, and South Carolina) were revising their planning guidelines to develop a more strategic approach to information management. Many other states were in the process of deliberations on the intent of their IT planning process, with indications that there was a move afoot to make the IT plans more comprehensive and accountability for them placed at the executive level of the state.

These initial forays into IT planning were characterized by their dynamic flexible approaches. The early planning attempts were seen as educational and as the states gained more expertise in IT planning, the subsequent documents reflected what they had learned.

Finally, Caudle analyzed the major initiatives that were covered in the statewide master plans for information technology. These initiatives reflect the goals the various states held for the performance of their information resources. The eight major categories of IT strategies focused on (a) administrative system improvement or development, (b) end-user policies and support, (c) developing standards to share the basic information technology applications and data across agencies, (d) exploring emerging IT for statewide value and efficiency, (e) integrating library and records management functions into the IT architecture, (f) exploring statewide telecommunications systems, (g) developing the human resource talent, and (h) taking an enterprise approach to procurement, inventory, planning and evaluation.

At least half of the states that had IT master plans also had a vision for technology. One of the more important themes of the visions was the notion that information and information technology were strategic assets to state organizations and needed to be managed as such. This theme would emerge as a universal belief in the 1990s.

Current Strategic Planning for Information Technology

It can be seen from this review that state governments, when they did have an awareness of the value of IT, directed the management and use of IT from the executive or legislative level of government. This top level involvement set the stage for the states to begin to develop strategic IT plans which would incorporate all information resources in supporting the agency missions. This trend would be rapidly diffused across state governments in the following years, aided and abetted by the strong influence of a professional organization, the National Association of State Information Resources Executives (NASIRE).

NASIRE got its start in 1969 as the National Association of State Information Systems, an organization for data processing directors in state agencies. In 1989, there was a major change in direction for the organization most visibly reflected in the name change. The move to "information resources executives" indicated a much more strategic orientation to IT, elevating it to a top management concern. The organization recognized the need to proactively move into the 1990s. Membership includes any senior official from one of the three branches of state government who has executive level authority and control for the state's information resources. Today they have a wide range of initiatives including electronic commerce, intergovernmental relations, statewide leadership, and procurement reform. One of their new roles is research. NASIRE publishes a biennial report on information management across the 50 states, six U.S. territories, and the District of Columbia. This report has tracked the evolution of strategic planning since 1992.

In the latest biennial report (1996) a number of changes can be seen from the time of the Caudle study in the strategic management of information resources. Thirty-one states have an IRM commission with partial or full authority over some or all of the three branches of state government. The domain of this authority is primarily over the approval of all statewide IT plans, policies, and standards. Thirty-six states now have a Chief Information Officer (CIO), another indicator of the elevation of IT's role. The CIOs in 31 of these states have approval over all IT plans, policies, and standards. Twenty states have a statewide information resources management office charged with the IT planning function, with authority to set policy and standards for statewide management and use of information technology.

These management changes reflect the growing awareness of the value of IT to the attainment of statewide goals (Fletcher and Foy, 1994). These changes also are indicative of the more current drivers for today's IT planning ventures. As mentioned earlier in this chapter, IT has become a high priority item visible on the agenda of elected officials. State officials have embraced IT as a valuable tool to enable a more effective and efficient government (NASIRE, 1995). The importance of having a planned statewide information architecture which supports public access and leverages state resources is a goal of state governors and legislators, an important part of the political authority constraint system.

This attention to IT is also a part of the reengineering government trend which has diffused down from the Federal government to the states. State policymakers are relying on IT to create a solution to the paradox of downsizing and budget declines, demand for results and accountability, increased mandates on state level service responsibilities, and the public's demand for quality customer service. These factors can be seen to drive state governments towards a needs-based posture for strategy development. The attention to a wide range of customers with a wide range of needs is creating a specific focus for the use of information technology. Technology today is seen as the tool that can deliver more and enhanced services to the public. This is a new direction for IT planning and one that is rapidly becoming a standard at all levels of government. Information technology has become faster, less expensive, more sophisticated and flexible. End users have become accustomed to the benefits of technology use. The public is demanding quality in all levels of goods and service. Hence the convergence of strategy, information resources, and statewide plans.

Current IT Strategic Plans

In order to illustrate this new direction for IT planning, three state strategic IT plans will be described. Their strategic context will also be included to provide an understanding of their management framework. The choice of these three states is somewhat arbitrary, although all three have been consistently in the forefront of strategic IT management and use. We will revisit the State of Florida, mentioned earlier in this chapter as an exemplar of top management attention to the strategic use of information resources. All three states, Florida, Kentucky and Minnesota, were chosen as case studies in Caudle's national study of state information resources management based on their innovative and strategic management of information technology.

Florida

The State of Florida allocates 1.34 percent of its total state budget to expenditures for information resources. This is on the lower end of percent-of-budget allocated across state governments (NASIRE, 1996). There is a Chief Information Officer for information management; the Executive Director of the Information Resources Council. The CIO is charged with approval of all State IRM plans and policies, and the approval of departmental IT budgets. As noted earlier in this chapter, Florida has a statewide planning and policy group, the Information Resource Commission (IRC). This group has decision authority over the State IRM plans and policies as well as the IT budgets for State departments. In Florida, there is no State agency dedicated to provision of IT services.

The Florida IT plan, Preparing for the millennium: *Florida's State strategic plan for information resources management, 1996/1997—1999/2000* (http://mail.irm.state.fl.us/pubs/ssp96.html) is prepared by the Information Resourced Commission. The plan contains a long-term vision for how Florida will meet its major information management challenges and opportunities. The plan is directly linked to the State Comprehensive Plan, thus connected to the statewide initiatives and goals. The plan contains a vision, strategic goals for the State, policy guidelines, a section devoted to the telecommunications forecast, and an articulation of projects critical to mission achievement. Florida's vision for IT recognizes the need for "wise management of the substantial and growing investment in information technology critical to meeting the business needs of the State" (p. 3). The IT infrastructure is expected to provide better decision making and an ability to meet the increased service demands, to help manage the growing environmental complexity, to assist the departments in attaining their missions, and enable direct access to citizens and by citizens to critical government data.

Florida ties its strategic IT goals to four areas: the State's business needs, the strategic value of information, the ability to facilitate service delivery, and the need to effectively leverage the IT investment for the good of the State. A further articulation of these goals provides a better understanding of what IT means to the State. For the first goal, support of statewide business needs by efficient and effective use of the IT, the plan requires all State agencies to implement and maintain a formal IT planning process. Planning methodologies have been developed to ensure consistency in use and to enable the State agencies to better utilize their IT. This reflects an attention to the importance of a standard approach to the management of information technology to benefit the State as a whole, and not just the stovepipes of individual agencies. The second goal points to using information as a valuable strategic asset. This ties directly to public access to State data. Florida has a history of strong policy entitling public access to information and the plan seeks to continue this policy in an electronic age. It is recognized not only that the public has a right to data, and that the data must be accurate and current to maximize its value.

The third strategic goal envisions IT as a catalyst for the provision of new and effective service provision. Here the values of electronic commerce, utilization of emerging technology, and the rapid and continuous implementation of mission critical systems are elaborated. In the discussion on electronic commerce, the State notes that this is a vehicle not only for better service to all suppliers, manufacturers, and retailers, but also will enhance inter-agency data sharing as the State agencies adapt an electronic commerce approach to doing business with each other. The fourth goal envisions the use of the IT architecture as a comprehensive asset to not only State agencies, but also corporations, citizens, universities, communities, and other governmental bodies. This is to the achievement of economic development, educational advancement, freedom of information, business growth, and public-private partnerships. These four goals are broad yet integrated into the State's vision to enhance all aspects of quality of life in Florida.

Florida's plan includes an assessment of the current operating environment and those conditions which will present future challenges to the State. It acknowledges both internal and external characteristics which create the opportunities and constraints which define action. Prominent among the current external drivers of strategy is the growth of networked technologies and the subsequent demands they have created for better public service, more public service, and fast and accessible service to the public. The consequences of the Internet are detailed as they affect the State's ability to provide universal access to data and transform itself to an electronic commerce model of business.

An important component of the Florida IT plan is the enumeration of policy guidelines. There are ten specific enterprise-wide information areas designated here. Included as worthy of policy level attention are:

1. Geographic information systems.
2. E-mail systems.
3. Electronic document management.
4. IRM budget development.
5. User requirements analysis for major systems.
6. Risk assessment.
7. Paperwork reduction.
8. Capacity upgrade assessment measures.
9. Client/server, distributed and networked computing standards.
10. Access to public records.

The attention to defining critical IT management issues reflects a continuation of Florida's long history with IRM. The current strategic plan, in its attention to an informed and standard approach to the development and use of its IT architecture, carries on the legislative intent established in 1983 with the Florida Information and Planning Technology Act. The level of sophistication in the current statewide IT plan is a result of years of legislative and executive management recognition of the value of their information infrastructure. This plan goes beyond the scope of the more usual five-year forecast for acquisition of new information technologies, a recipe for a fast-food approach to technology strategy. The Florida plan looks beyond the predictable to ensure a strong statewide stance to information technology rather than a shopping list based on today's goods.

Kentucky

The Commonwealth of Kentucky allocates 4.03 percent of its annual State budget to information resource expenditures, the third largest allocation amount when viewed across all 50 states (NASIRE, 1996). The CIO is the Commissioner of the Department of Information Systems. The CIO has approval over all statewide policies, standards, statewide IT acquisitions, and State agency IT acquisitions. The statewide information resources policy group is the Kentucky Information Resources Management (KIRM) Commission. KIRM is an independent State agency responsible for establishing the policy, strategic planning, and coordination of IT for the executive branch and public universities in the Commonwealth. KIRM's charter is specifically to develop the statewide strategic IT plan which includes the design of the State's IT architecture and standards to support the architecture. KIRM has approval of all statewide IT plans and policies. There is also a statewide IRM organization in Kentucky with authority over information management and day-to-day IT operations.

The current Strategic Information Technology Plan (SITP) was approved by KIRM in 1997. An important feature of the SITP is its connection to a gubernatorial initiative for a one-time appropriation of $103 million for the "EMPOWER Kentucky" Technology Fund. (http://www.state.ky.us/agencies/gov/empower/powrmenu.htm) This initiative is focused on the redesign of State business processes, utilizing IT to generate revenue, save cost, and improve services to the public. The SITP establishes five guiding principles for the management of information resources. The principles are to:

1. Support the business objectives of the Commonwealth government.
2. Conduct Commonwealth business electronically.
3. Treat information as a strategic resource.
4. View technology investments from an enterprise perspective.
5. Ensure electronic access to information and services while maintaining privacy. (http://www.state.ky.us/kirm/strpln.htm)

When reading the plan, it is clear that the intent is to create and maintain an information infrastructure which supports all State agencies and the goals of the Commonwealth. The plan states that the role of information technology is "to support the business objectives of the Commonwealth and to facilitate agency efforts to provide efficient and effective services to the citizens of the Commonwealth" (p. 4). While this role may appear to be rather mundane in today's business environment, it takes on significance when paired with the current organizational restructuring going on statewide from a stovepipe functional organization to one that is aligned with business processes. This requires an IT architecture that is based on statewide standards, interoperable, and consistent with supporting the emerging process structure. Within the SITP framework, the IT vision is migrating to one which facilitates an enterprise-wide strategic use of IT to focus on the customer. This vision is in line with the current trends in the private sector; enterprise strategies and customer service.

The SITP defines the critical success factors for its success. These include top level support and leadership, involvement of State agencies in setting the IT direction, adherence statewide to the IT standards, cultural change, and training and education. An interesting feature to the Kentucky plan is the inclusion of a SWOT analysis, a review of the State's IT strengths, weaknesses, opportunities, and threats. While SWOT analyses are common in business, it is not the norm to see them applied to government management practices. Using the SWOT as an analytic tool enables the developers of the SITP to better target potential areas for success and those current practices needing special attention. Thus, they can build on the already existing strengths of their current IT environment while looking outside the organization to take advantage of relevant emerging IT trends. The focus on defining critical success factors and the use of the SWOT are evolutions in state strategic IT plans. They reflect an attention to the management practices in the business sector and their relevance to public organizations. While some of the noted critical success factors are directly attributable to political authority constraints, others are more generic, enabling the State to utilize best practices from the private sector. The SWOT reflects the emerging attention to the rapidly changing external environment of the State and the rapidly changing IT environment as well. It enables the State to be flexible in its strategic responses so as to understand its environment and appropriately and effectively apply the current IT as well as assess emerging information technologies.

Minnesota

The State of Minnesota allocates 2.6 percent of its annual budget expenditures to information resources. This is a modal value when viewed across all fifty states (NASIRE, 1996). Minnesota is one of the 20 states that does not have an IRM commission or decision-making body. It does have a chief information officer in its Assistant Commissioner for the Office of Information Policy. The CIO approves the plans, policies, and standards for statewide IT use. The CIO also has decision authority over statewide and departmental IT acquisitions. Minnesota has a Cabinet level agency, the Office of Technology, in the executive branch of government. This is a statewide IRM organization. The mission of this Office is to provide direction and leadership for a statewide information and communication technology architecture.

The Minnesota plan, *Beacon to our future: Developing a master plan for information technology in Minnesota*, represents the first phase in the State's response to creating a new IT vision for the 21st century (http://www.ot.state.mn.us/feature/feature.html). Minnesota's plan has a clear eye towards a global future where citizens, communities, schools, and businesses will take part in an emerging competitive landscape, create a technologically literate public, and rise to meet the challenges and opportunities of public-private partnerships. This direction is a far cry from the more prosaic goals of the past. It emerges from an attention to their external environment and to the opportunities created by modern information technology applications. The State sees information technology as a tool to meet key social needs. The IT master plan thus addresses the role of IT in enabling a well-educated public, a responsive public sector organization, and a healthy economy.

The IT master plan reflects, in a novel way, the political constraints which affect strategies. It calls for regulatory attention to facilitate the State's transition to a competitive marketplace. The challenge here is stated as a need to "ensure that consumers are informed and effective decision makers in a genuinely competitive market" (p. 2). The State recognizes this new marketplace as one which has been enabled by network technologies and changes in business practices. Rather than react to this dynamic environment, the State plans to capitalize on it. This is an instance of crafting a strategy which enables them to control the uncontrollable, to reduce uncertainty.

Another unusual aspect of the Minnesota IT master plan is the strategic recognition of public-private partnerships as devices to expand the use of information technology. This is stated as a fundamental principle of the plan. It reflects an attention to external constituencies and the value to be gained by collaborative business practices. This is a current awareness issue which the State has managed to incorporate into an overall strategy.

Minnesota's IT vision, as stated in the master plan, reflects a needs-based driver of strategy. The vision is directed at citizens, communities, business, and other governments, a constituency of varying needs. The vision offers these constituencies the opportunity to incorporate information and communication technology into all aspects of their lives, to enhance and empower them equally. It recognizes the evolution to a knowledge society connected seamlessly by a network of technology and information, removing barriers of time and distance to learning and self-actualization. To attain this vision, the Office of Technology must provide an electronic infrastructure open to all constituents.

The IT master plan sets forth five strategic goals. A series of strategies are articulated for each of the goals. First is the goal of enabling a technologically literate and competent public. Strategies are based on a lifelong learning paradigm which will enhance the lives of the State's constituents. Second is the creation and maintenance of an efficient and effective State government. Here tactics include a movement toward quality measurement and continuous process improvement. The third goal is for easy and affordable access to government information and services. Information technology needs to adhere to standards, be portable, scalable, and interoperable. The use of IT to stimulate economic development is the fourth goal. Electronic commerce figures prominently in the strategies for this goal. The final goal is to improve the quality of life for all who live and work in Minnesota. Information technology is envisioned as an enabler of better cultural, educational, and health experiences.

With the IT master plan, Minnesota is clearly poised to take advantage of whatever opportunities will be afforded to those who are prepared for a global digital economy. This is a very forward-looking plan based on a strong public ethic and an anticipation of emerging technologies. There is a very strong people component to the IT master plan, unique in its focus on its public as both a resource, or input to the government process, and as an asset, or value-added recipient of government services. There is an implicit understanding here that IT is only successful if it is used well, a strategic variable indeed.

New Directions in State IT Plans

State governments are not exempt from the market pressures and management concerns brought to bear in a highly competitive and global environment. They too have a customer base, one that is becoming more sophisticated and more demanding. State governments are also affected by the recent and rapid advances in information technologies which are changing the rules of business and creating new services.

They are also heavily influenced by the special constraints inherent in being a public organization. The state legislatures control the purse strings. They also influence the choices available for any course of action through their legislative intent. The public and the press create issues and demands which require state government responses. The elected officials set forth short-term agendas which define the short-term frameworks in which the state agencies must act. Federal and state regulations, special interest groups, social values, and trends all shape and constrain the sphere for governmental action.

The development and deployment of IT has had a critical and constant influence on how state governments act. Information technology has evolved from a closely-held chattel of finance departments to being a pervasive and all-encompassing tool for government administration and service delivery. It has changed the rules of engagement with the public. The evolution of strategic IT plans reflects this development of IT, from being a static and limited resource, to being a dynamic driver of how governments do business.

While this chapter was confined to the analysis of only three strategic IT plans, they are illustrative of state governments which are sensitive to the nuances of publicness and the strategic value of IT. They are all proactive in their visions and strategies for their futures, not content with redefining the status quo as a sufficient basis for management of information resources. This, in essence, defines their strategic posture, one that will enable them to effectively meet the unknown challenges of IT development and public sentiment. They plan to respond to the uncertainties in their future in a flexible, outward-looking, yet interoperable manner. The specific technologies that will be used are not as important as what the technologies are envisioned achieving for these states and their constituents.

The strategic plans examined in this chapter incorporate the three necessary elements to an effective strategy (Mintzberg and Quinn, 1991). Each plan delineates a critical set of strategic goals. Kentucky has five guiding principles. Florida has four strategic objectives. Minnesota has five strategic goals. The second necessary element for effective strategy is the attention to policies and external variables which constrain and direct action. Florida's IT plan clearly articulates its current operating environment and external characteristics that might create future challenges. Kentucky formally assess its strengths and weaknesses, and the opportunities and threats to survival. Minnesota takes a proactive stance on their role in a global competitive market. The state defines the regulatory barriers and strategies needed to effectively respond to constituent needs. Finally, an effective strategy requires the instantiation a clear programmatic direction to meet the strategic goals. Again, all three state IT plans contain this element. Florida designates ten program areas for policy attention and designates five major IT projects for special monitoring. Kentucky outlines its key implementation tactics and their attendant timelines. Minnesota clearly defines its statewide information and communication technology projects and puts these in the context of how they support state goals and strategies. Each state IT plan, in its own unique manner, sets out the strategic vision for IT; a vision which is then delineated in a hierarchy of strategies which enable the state to achieve its overarching mission.

The strategic IT plans create the environment and actions which will facilitate mission success. With these plans in hand, each of the three states can assertively and cogently create their futures. The names that these three states have accorded their IT plans are indicative of a vital and forward stance vis their IT. "Empower Kentucky," "Preparing for the Millennium," and "Beacon to our Future" paint a picture of states that are out there, actively facing and creating their futures, rather than passively waiting for the future to happen to them. This is indeed, strategic.

Glossary

Electronic Commerce: Conducting business electronically through computer hardware and software, modems, networks, the Internet, extranets, and emerging networked technologies. Information is exchanged and processed in a seamless and real-time manner to facilitate the exchange of materials, goods, and services.

Information: Data that has been made useful for decision making.

Information Architecture: The technical blueprint for an organization's enterprise wide development of its hardware, software, telecommunications or network components, and corporate data structures. The architecture defines the standards and policies for use of the information components.

Information Resources: The information itself and related resources such as IT personnel, facilities, computer and network hardware and software, and budget.

Information Resources Management: The process of managing the information resources to accomplish agency goals and objectives. Processes include planning, budgeting, evaluating, implementing, and operating,

Information Technology: Any information and communications hardware and software which creates, stores, and transmits data and information.

Strategy: The art of devising or employing tactics to meet a goal. A pattern of action which integrates mission goals, policies, and activities into a comprehensive gestalt.

Strategic Plan: The formal set of goals, objectives, and activities to be followed to achieve one's mission.

References

Anderson, D.F., and Dawes, S.S. (1991). *Government information management: A primer and caseboook.* Englewood Cliffs, NJ: Prentice-Hall, Inc.

Anderson, D.F., Belardo, S., and Dawes, S.S. (1994). Strategic information management: Conceptual frameworks for the public sector. *Public Productivity & Management Review*, XVII (4), 335-354.

Barkdoll, G.L. (1992). Scoping versus coping: Developing a comprehensive agency vision. *Public Administration Review*, 52 (4), 330-338.

Bozeman, B. (1984). Dimensions of publicness: An approach to public organization theory. In B. Bozeman and J. Straussman, eds. *New directions in public administration*. Belmont, CA: Crooks/Cole, 46-62.

Bozeman, B., and Bretschneider, S. (1986). Public management information systems: Theory and prescription. *Public Administration Review*, 46, 475-487.

Bozeman, B., and Straussman, J.D. (1990). *Public management strategies: Guidelines for managerial effectiveness.* San Francisco: Jossey-Bass.

Caudle, S.L. (1996). Strategic information resources management: Fundamental practices. *Government Information Quarterly*, 13 (1), 83-97.

Caudle S.L., Marchand, S.I., Marchand, D.A., Fletcher, P.T., and Thurmaier, K. (1989). *Managing information resources: New directions in state government.* Syracuse, NY: Syracuse University.

Commonwealth of Kentucky. (1996). EMPOWER Kentucky Homepage. Retrieved June 13, 1998 from the World Wide Web: *http://www.state.ky.us/agencies/gov/empower/powrmenu.htm*

Davies, T.R., and Hale, W.M. (1986). Implementing a policy and planning process for managing state use of information technology resources. *Public Administration Review*, 46, 516-521.

Ein-Dor, P., and Segev, E. (1978). Strategic planning for management information systems. *Management Science*, 24 (15), 1631-1641.

Fletcher, P.D. (1997). Local governments and IRM: Policy emerging from practice. *Government Information Quarterly*, 14 (3), 313-324.

Fletcher, P.T., and Foy, D.O. (1994). Government and information: State and local perspectives on information management. In M. Williams (Ed.), *Annual review of information science and technology*, Vol. 29. Medford, NJ: Learned Information Company. 243-275.

Gabris, G.T. (1992). Strategic planning in municipal government: A tool for expanding cooperative decision making between elected and appointed officials. *Public Productivity & Management Review*, XVI (1), 77-93.

Golembiewski, R.T., and Gabris, G. (1995). Tomorrow's city management: Guides for avoiding success-becoming-failure. *Public Administration Review*, 55 (3), 240-246.

Information Resources Commission. (1996). *Preparing for the millennium: Florida's State strategic plan for information resources management.* State of Florida. Retrieved June 10, 1998 from the World Wide Web: http://mail.irm.state.fl.us/pubs/ssp96.html

Kentucky Information Resources Management Commission. (July 7, 1977). *Empower Kentucky: Strategic information technology plan.* Commonwealth of Kentucky. Retrieved June 13, 1998 from the World Wide Web: http://www.state.ky.us/kirm/strpln.htm

Laware, G.W. (1991). Strategic business planning: Aligning business goals with technology. *Information Systems Management*, 8, 44-49.

Marchand, D.A., and Kresslein, J.C. (1988). Information resources management and the public administrator. In J. Rabin and E.M. Jackowski, eds. *Handbook of Infromation Resource Management.* NY: Marcel Dekker, Inc. 395-456.

Minnesota Office of Technology. (1996). *Beacon to our future: Developing a master plan for information technology in Minnesota.* State of Minnesota. Retrieved June 13, 1998 from the World Wide Web: http://www.ot.state.mn.us/feature/feature.html

Mintzberg, H., and Quinn, J.B. (1991). *The strategy process* (3rd ed.). Englewood Cliffs, NJ: Prentice-Hall, Inc.

National Association of State Information Resource Executives. (1995). *The state chief information officer: NASIRE issue focus report.* Released in conjunction with the 1995 NASIRE Midyear Meeting, May 11-12, 1995. Rapid City, SD.

National Association of State Information Resource Executives. (1996). *State information resource management organizational structures: 1996 Biennial Report.* Lexington, KY: author.

National Association of State Information Resource Executives. (1998). Who we are. Retrieved June 8, 1998 from the World Wide Web: *http://www.nasire.org/who/index.html*

Nutt, P.C., Backoff, R.W. (1993). Organizational publicness and its implications for strategic management. *Journal of Public Administration Research and Theory,* 3 (2), 209-231.

OMB Circular A-130. 1993. The management of Federal information resources. *Federal Register,* 50, 52730.

Porter, M.E. (1996). What is strategy? *Harvard Business Review,* 74 (6), 61-78.

Porter, M.E., and Millar, V.E. (1985). How information gives you competitive advantage. *Harvard Business Review,* 63 (4), 149-160.

Poister, T.H., and Streib, G. (1989). Management tools in municipal government: Trends over the past decade. *Public Administration Review,* 49 (3), 240-248.

Streib, G. (1992). Applying strategic decision making in local government. *Public Productivity and Management Review,* XV (3), 341-354.

Thompson, A.A., Jr., Fulmer, W.E., and Strickland, A.J., III. (1992). *Readings in strategic management,* 4th ed. Boston: Richard D. Irwin, Inc.

U.S. Government Accounting Office. (1994). *Improving mission performance through strategic information management and technology.* (GAO/AIMD Publication No. 94-115). Washington, D.C.

U.S. Government Accounting Office. (1997). *Managing technology: Best practices can improve performance and produce results.* (GAO/T-AIMD Publication No. 97-38). Washington, D.C.

6

Managing Information Privacy and Information Access in the Public Sector

by
George T. Duncan
H. John Heinz III School of Public Policy and Management
Carnegie Mellon University

Government agencies collect and disseminate data that bear on the most important issues of public interest. Advances in information technology, particularly the Internet, have multiplied the tension between demands for evermore comprehensive databases and demands for the shelter of privacy. In mediating between these two conflicting demands, agencies must address a host of difficult problems. These include providing access to information while protecting confidentiality, coping with health information databases, and ensuring consistency with international standards. The policies of agencies are determined by what is right for them to do, what works for them, and what they are required to do by law. They must interpret and respect the ethical imperatives of democratic accountability, constitutional empowerment, and individual autonomy. They must keep pace with technological developments by developing effective measures for making information available to a broad range of users. They must both abide by the mandates of legislation and participate in the process of developing new legislation that is responsive to changes that affect their domain. In managing confidentiality and data access functions, agencies have two basic tools: techniques for disclosure limitation through restricted data and administrative procedures through restricted access. The technical procedures for disclosure limitation involve a range of mathematical and statistical tools. The administrative procedures can be implemented through a variety of institu-

Copyright© 1999, Idea Group Publishing.

tional mechanisms, ranging from privacy advocates, through internal privacy review boards, to a data and access protection commission

The Tension Between Private Lives and Public Policies

An Environmental Scan

In its normal activities, the public sector captures enormous amounts of data, stores it in very large databases, analyzes some of it, and disseminates information products to individuals, governments, businesses, and other organizations. Much of these data are obtained directly from respondents in surveys and censuses or through building systems of administrative records based on a variety of citizen interactions with government. Surveys include:

- Face-to-face interviews, as with the National Longitudinal Surveys of Young Women conducted by the Bureau of Labor Statistics
- Telephone surveys, as with the Behavioral Risk Factor Surveillance System conducted by the Center for Disease Control, which estimates current cigarette smoking and use of smokeless tobacco
- Mail-back responses (including electronic mail), as with the reactions to their web site obtained by Inland Revenue of the Government of New Zealand (see http://www.ird.govt.nz/survey.htm).

Administrative records include:

- Employer-furnished data, as with Social Security Administration earnings records
- Licensing data, as with state Departments of Motor Vehicles and local building permits
- Individual and firm submitted data, as with Internal Revenue Service tax returns.

The Internet has accelerated the demand for access to government information services, primarily by broadening the range of potential data users. Access demand is in commensurate tension to concerns about privacy and confidentiality. The National Science Foundation in its Digital Government program announcement (NSF 1998), affirms, "Given the inexorable progress toward faster computer microprocessors, greater network bandwidth, and expanded storage and computing power at the desktop, citizens will expect a government that responds quickly and accurately while ensuring privacy." This article focuses on ways the public sector can resolve the growing tension between the demand for government data and concerns for privacy protection.

Government databases are rich in information and have evident practical utility for planning, marketing, and research. Still, many would-be users complain they cannot obtain the data they need, often thwarted by confidentiality concerns (Smith 1991). On the other hand, privacy advocates warn of the dangers of unfettered data capture and dissemination. Their arguments are ethically based. "Individuals in the Western world are increasingly subject to surveillance through the use of data bases in the public and private sectors, and these developments have negative implications for the quality of life in our societies and for the protection of human rights." (Flaherty

1989: 1) From a more utilitarian standpoint, public policy would be affected by declining survey participation rates. In 1992, for example, 31 percent of Americans refused to answer at least one survey, compared with 15 percent in 1982 (Leftwich 1993; also see Dalenius 1993). Acrimonious public debates rage about proper use of mailing lists, credit records, medical histories, and Social Security Numbers (Flaherty 1989). The media highlights privacy concerns in the use of ever-larger computer databases—those of terabyte size, labeled "data warehouses".

Broad access to data supports democratic decision-making. Access to government statistical information supports public policy formulation in areas ranging through demographics, crime, business regulation and development, education, national defense, energy, environment, health, natural resources, safety, and transportation. Thrust against the evident value of data access is the counter value that private lives are requisite for a free society. This article deals with an important aspect of the tension between information privacy and data access—the proper handling of personal information that is collected by government. Other privacy issues such as video surveillance, telephone interception or 'bugging,' Internet censorship, protecting children, encryption policy, and physical intrusion into private spaces are outside my purview.

A variety of governmental agencies have important roles in collecting, storing, analyzing, and disseminating information. Certainly this is the case with the federal statistical agencies, such as the U. S. Census Bureau, National Center for Health Statistics, and the Bureau of Labor Statistics. But it is also true of state public health organizations and functional agencies such as departments of motor vehicles. Each agency is tasked with the dual responsibilities of protecting privacy and confidentiality while disseminating information to client users, often including the general public. (Duncan, Jabine, and de Wolf 1993; Duncan and Pearson 1991).

What are some contentious issues in the clash between demands for information privacy and data access? To address this question, we examine a classification of some of the bills submitted in the 105th Congress. Besides general privacy and data access concerns, bills were introduced addressing medical record privacy, the sale of consumer records, mandating databases, and copyright protection of databases.

- *General Privacy And Data Access Concerns*
  HR 1330. American Family Privacy Act of 1997. Prohibits Federal officers and employees from providing access to Social Security account statement information, personal earnings and benefits estimate statement information, or tax return information of an individual through the Internet or without the written consent of the individual, and to establish a commission to investigate the protection and privacy afforded to certain Government records.
  HR 1367. Federal Internet Privacy Protection Act of 1997. Prohibits Federal agencies from making available through the Internet certain confidential records with respect to individuals, and to provide for remedies in cases in which such records are made available through the Internet.
  S. 144. Commission to Study the Federal Statistical System Act of 1997. Creates a commission to look at statistical agencies. The commission will look at privacy implications of collection and use of statistical information.
  S. 522. Taxpayer Browsing Protection Act. Criminalizes "browsing" of tax

records by IRS employees.

S. 1865. Safeguard of New Employee Information Act of 1998. Creates penalties for abuse of information in New Hires Database. Requires data be deleted after 24 months.

- **Medical Records Privacy** (see also, Duncan 1997)

  HR 3299. Family Genetic Privacy and Protection Act. Sets limits on disclosure and use of genetic information in connection with group health plans and health insurance coverage, prohibits employment discrimination on the basis of genetic information and genetic testing.

  S. 24. Health Care Assurance Act of 1997. Creates "centrally located" national database of health insurance information for processing all claims and outcomes. Gives grants to states to create and operate health care cost containment and quality information systems that contain clinical and treatment data on patients.

  S. 422. Genetic Confidentiality and Nondiscrimination Act of 1997. Defines the circumstances under which DNA samples may be collected, stored, and analyzed, and genetic information may be collected, stored, analyzed, and disclosed, to define the rights of individuals and persons with respect to genetic information, to define the responsibilities of persons with respect to genetic information, to protect individuals and families from genetic discrimination, to establish uniform rules that protect individual genetic privacy, and to establish effective mechanisms to enforce the rights.

  S. 1499. Health Insurance Consumer's Bill of Rights Act of 1997. Requires managed care group health plans to establish written policies and procedures for the handling of medical records; ensure the confidentiality of specified enrollee information; and prevent release of any individual patient record information, unless such a release is authorized in writing by the enrollee or otherwise required by law.

- *Sale of Consumer Records*

  HR 49. Postal Privacy Act of 1997 to prevent the United States Postal Service from disclosing the names or addresses of any postal patrons.

- **Mandating Databases**

  HR 102. A bill to require the national instant criminal background check system to be established and used in connection with firearms transfers.

  S. 103. United States Worker Protection and Illegal Immigrant Deterrence Act of 1997. Requires President to recommend creation of national workplace verification system within 90 days.

- *Copyright Protection of Databases.*

  H.R.3048. Digital Era Copyright Enhancement Act. Implements WIPO (World Intellectual Property Organization) Treaty. Ensures "fair use" of copyrighted materials.

It is evident from this listing that a variety of issues are currently on the forefront

of public debate. (Such legislative activity is monitored for example by the Electronic Privacy Information Center (EPIC); see http://epic.org/privacy/privacy_resources_faq.html). The key issues include:
- restricting access to database information to those with a need to know
- struggles with how to provide access to information through the Internet while protecting confidentiality
- dealing with so-called universal identifiers, especially the Social Security number
- abuse of databases by government employees
- establishing health information databases
- special problems about genetic information
- ensuring consistency with international standards.

While federal government agencies and certain other private sector organizations operate under federal legislative constraints related to privacy, that is not the case for other major record systems. No federal law ensures the confidentiality of medical records, and state laws vary. Similarly unprotected are insurance files, credit card transactions, most state government records, criminal records, employment records, and phone bills. The legislative environment for privacy and information issues is currently in flux, and likely will change. Organizations that monitor legislation in this area suggest that some one thousand bills were introduced in this area at the federal and state level in 1993 alone. In the next section, we examine legislation that is already on the books that both attempts to protect government data and constrain its use by agencies.

- *Relevant Legislation*

Some agencies are guided by specific legislation. The U.S. Census Bureau, for example, is governed by Title 13 of the U.S. Code, which provides for tight controls on individually identifiable data. In particular, Section 9 provides that

(a) Neither the Secretary, nor any other officer or employee of the Department of Commerce or bureau or agency thereof, or local government census liaison, may, except as provided in section *8* or *16* or chapter 10 of this title - (1) use the information furnished under the provisions of this title for any purpose other than the statistical purposes for which it is supplied; or (2) make any publication whereby the data furnished by any particular establishment or individual under this title can be identified; or (3) permit anyone other than the sworn officers and employees of the Department or bureau or agency thereof to examine the individual reports. No department, bureau, agency, officer, or employee of the Government, except the Secretary in carrying out the purposes of this title, shall require, for any reason, copies of census reports which have been retained by any such establishment or individual. Copies of census reports which have been so retained shall be immune from legal process, and shall not, without the consent of the individual or establishment concerned, be admitted as evidence or used for any purpose in any action, suit, or other judicial or administrative proceeding.

Similarly for the Internal Revenue Service, Section 6108(c) of the U.S. Internal Revenue Code of 1986 stipulates that

No publication or other disclosure of statistics or other information required or authorized by subsection (a) or special statistical study authorized by subsection (b) shall in any manner permit the statistics, study, or any information so published, furnished, or otherwise disclosed to be associated with, or otherwise identify, directly or indirectly, a particular taxpayer.

The U.S. Social Security Administration enjoys comparable legislative protection of its data through Section 1106 of the Social Security Act.

On the other hand, the Bureau of Labor Statistics has no specific statutory protection to preserve the confidentiality of identifiable information. Instead, the Bureau's confidentiality policy is established by Commissioner's Order 3-93, *Confidential Nature of BLS Records*, which in Section 7(a) states that data "...collected or maintained by, or under the auspices of, BLS under a pledge of confidentiality shall be treated in a manner that will ensure that individually identifiable data will be used only for statistical purposes and will be accessible only to authorized persons." (See de Wolf (1995) for discussion of BLS confidentiality policy.)

Chapter 5 of Duncan, Jabine, and de Wolf (1993) presents a comprehensive view of the legislative environment of federal statistical agencies. Under current legislation, the degree of data protection depends on the agency that holds it without regard to the sensitivity of the information. Also, data sharing among agencies is difficult because agencies with a high degree of legislative protection of their data are reluctant to share with those with a low degree of protection. For example, the National Agricultural Statistics Service (NASS) has had a complicated relationship involving the sharing of lists of farms for the Census of Agriculture, which is conducted every five years. The Census of Agriculture was officially moved from the Census Bureau to NASS on December 31, 1997. In conducting the 1997 Agriculture Census, the Census Bureaus provided NASS employees (many of whom were Census Bureau employees) with farm list information. To do this, they were made Census special sworn employees. Restricted access is provided through the Census Bureau's Bowie computer center to NASS headquarters and the regional centers. In 1992 the Census Bureau swore in a limited number of NASS employees to see data collected under the auspices of Title 13 but they were required to come to the Census Bureau's headquarters in Suitland, Maryland to see the data. The official transfer of the program was delayed until the end the 1997 so that the Census Bureau would continue to have the authority to get IRS tax return data to construct the list. (NASS had no such authority). Beginning in 2002, NASS will have to work with IRS to get access by amending the tax code or through proposed data sharing legislation if it becomes law.

In addition to this legislation, there are variety of other relevant laws and regulations at the federal level. They include, but are not limited to: Computer Security Act of 1987 (http://www.epic.org/crypto/csa/), Copyright Act of 1976 (http://www.law.cornell.edu/copyright/copyright.table.html), National Archives and Records Administration Regulations, Freedom of Information Act (http://www.aclu.org/library/foia.html), Information Technology Management Reform Act of 1996 (http://www.itpolicy.gsa.gov/mke/capplan/cohen.htm), Paperwork Reduction Act of 1995 (http://www.law.vill.edu/chron/articles/ombdon.htm), and the Privacy Act (http://www.eff.org/pub/Legislation/privacy_act_74_5usc_s552a.law). Discussion of each of these can be found on the Web at the indicated URLs.

What Principles Should Guide Data Stewardship?

The principles set forth here for data stewardship derive from Duncan, Jabine, and de Wolf (1993). The United States, and a growing list of other countries, embraces a freedom that recognizes pluralism, public decision making based on representative democracy, and a market-oriented economy. Consistent with this ethos an ethics of information can be built on three principles: democratic accountability, constitutional empowerment, and individual autonomy. These principles can provide a useful guide for assessing the societal impacts of information policies of any organization, whether in the public sector or not. They have particular interpretations for government agencies that are explored in Section 3.

Democratic accountability is the assurance through institutional mechanisms, culture, and practice that the public obtains comprehensive information on the effectiveness of government policies. Prewitt (1985) explored this concept. The technology of the web is the most exciting implement for fostering democratic accountability. A quick click to the Social Security Administration's web site at www.ssa.gov yields the SSA's Accountability Report for FY 1997. It provides full disclosure of SSA's financial and programmatic operations. This web presentation gave the agency the right to assert, "With its publication on November 21, 1997—less than two months after the close of the fiscal year—SSA became the first Federal agency to publish its FY 1997 Accountability Report. FY 1997 marks the eleventh year that SSA has published audited financial statements, the fourth year that SSA has received an unqualified opinion on its financial statements and the third year that SSA has been authorized by the Office of Management and Budget to streamline and consolidate statutorily required financial reporting into a single Accountability Report."

Constitutional empowerment is the capability of citizens to make informed decisions about political, economic, and social questions. Constitutional practice emphasizes restraints on executive excess and broad access to the political process through the direct election of representatives, as well as through separation and balance of power. Many government agencies have seized upon the web as a vehicle for providing information broadly to the citizenry. A prominent development in this regard is the plan announced on June 25, 1998 by Bruce A. Lehman, Commissioner of Patents and Trademarks, to create the largest Government database on the Internet. More than two million patents will be searchable by key word. Including trademark information, the database will comprise more than 21 million documents and require 1.3 terabytes of storage.

Individual autonomy is the capacity of the individual to function in society as an individual, uncoerced and cloaked by privacy. Individual autonomy is compromised by the excessive surveillance sometimes used to build databases (Flaherty 1989), unwitting dispersion of data, and a willingness by those who collect data for administrative purposes to make them available in personally identifiable form. Government agencies have both ethical and pragmatic reasons to be concerned about individual autonomy. Ethically, agencies ought to respect individual dignity and protect the personal information entrusted to them. Pragmatically, without attention to individual autonomy, agencies will find it difficult to enlist the voluntary cooperation that smoothes operations.

The Special Roles Of Government Agencies: *Functional Separation*

In implementing the three fundamental principles of democratic accountability, constitutional empowerment, and individual autonomy, a government agency should affirm a policy of *functional separation*. This policy makes a distinction between administrative data and statistical data. The distinction is on the basis of use:
- administrative data are used so that data on an individual has a direct impact on that individual
- statistical data are used to create aggregate measures that have an impact on individuals only through substantial group membership

Thus Joe Brown's liquor license application is initially part of administrative data since it is used to determine whether to issue Joe a license. When a database of such applications is used to determine whether females are issued liquor licenses as frequently as males, this constitutes a statistical use. Conceivably, such a study might affect administrative practice about license issuance in which case it might affect the chances of Joe Brown's subsequent application. This impact is due solely to Joe being male and is not determined by his particular data.

Agencies accept responsibility for protecting privacy and confidentiality for several ethical and pragmatic reasons. First, it is the right thing to do. Generally accepted ethical standards in the profession of data collection require attention to privacy and confidentiality (International Statistical Institute, 1986; American Statistical Association, 1989). Second, they get better data this way. Professionals believe that confidentiality pledges lower nonresponse rates and improve the quality of responses (Singer, 1993). Third, the law requires it. Privacy and confidentiality protection is often mandated by legislation or regulation (Duncan, Jabine, and de Wolf 1993).

The Privacy Protection Study Commission (1977, 574) proposed that:

"...the Congress provide by statute that no record or information contained therein collected for a research or statistical purpose under Federal authority or with Federal funds may be used in individually identifiable form to make any decision or take any action directly affecting the individual to whom the record pertains, except within the context of the research plan or protocol, or with the specific authorization of the individual."

The National Research Council sponsored the Panel on Confidentiality and Data Access. In its report, *Private Lives and Public Policies*, the Panel made the following recommendation (Duncan, Jabine, and de Wolf, 1993: Recommendation 5.1, p. 134):

Statistical records across all federal agencies should be governed by a consistent set of statutes and regulations meeting standards for the maintenance of such records, including the following features of fair statistical information practices:

(a) a definition of statistical data that incorporates the principle of functional separation as defined by the Privacy Protection Study Commission,
(b) a guarantee of confidentiality for the data,
(c) a requirement of informed consent or informed choice when participation in a survey is voluntary,
(d) a requirement of strict control on data dissemination,
(e) a requirement to follow careful rules on disclosure limitation,
(f) a provision that permits data sharing for statistical purposes under controlled conditions, and
(g) legal sanctions for those who violate confidentiality requirements.

This recommendation refers to federal agencies. The issues are similar for state agencies and for countries other than the United States. It is, therefore, maintained that these fair information practices are broadly applicable to government operations.

Problems and Opportunities in Ensuring Confidentiality and Data Access

The public sector faces a variety of predicaments as well as opportunities as it seeks to fulfill its responsibilities for both confidentiality and access to data. The problems and possibilities are accentuated by economic and cultural changes, and importantly by developments in information technology. This section will examine these factors as they affect the various stakeholders in the process—the data subjects, the data users, and the agencies that have stewardship of the data.

Data Subjects

Government agencies depend on individuals, firms, and organizations to provide data that accurately reflect some of the most personal and sensitive aspects of their lives and operations. Some of this data provision is mandated by legislation, as public corporations are required to provide the Securities and Exchange Commission with filing information, and individuals must file an income tax return with the Internal Revenue Service. Other data provision is voluntary, as when the Substance Abuse and Mental Health Services Administration interviews people at their residence about use of licit and illicit drugs.

Anecdotal evidence suggests that response rates of federally funded demographic surveys have been declining. To address this issue, the Federal Committee on Statistical Methodology formed a Subcommittee on Nonresponse that collected information on 26 federally-sponsored demographic surveys. Response and refusal rates remained relatively constant, but noncontacts fluctuated over the ten-year period from 1982 to 1991. They found a "core" proportion of the population that routinely refuses to participate in federally sponsored surveys.

The key ethical concepts related to data subjects are informed consent and notification. Informed consent is appropriate for truly voluntary surveys, while notification applies otherwise to data collection that is mandatory, such as the Decennial Census, or where benefits hinge on providing information, such as applications for welfare benefits. The Privacy Act requires that each person asked to supply information be informed of (1) the authority under which the information is requested, (2) the principal uses for the information, (3) the "routine uses" that may be made of the information, and (4) the implications, if any, of not providing the information. The National Research Council's Panel on Confidentiality and Data Access (Duncan, Jabine and de Wolf, 1993) made recommendations for strengthening these stipulations. Noteworthy among these are requirements that data providers be notified of (1) nonstatistical uses of their data, (2) any anticipated record linkages for statistical purposes, (3) the length of time the information will be retained in identifiable form.

Data Users

Data users span a diverse range of individuals and organizations. They include academic researchers at Cambridge University, policy analysts for the American Association for Retired Persons and the National Association of Home Builders, business economists for Wells Fargo bank, and statisticians for the Health Care Financing Administration. They include reporters for the *Toronto Star*, marketing analysts for L. L. Bean, advocates for the National Abortion Rights League, and medical insurance underwriters for Cigna. In general, data users employ the data they obtain for end uses such as policy analysis, commercial and academic research, advocacy, and education. The may also use data for various intermediate purposes such as the development of sampling frames for surveys and the evaluation of the quality of other data.

From a government agency's viewpoint, the primary concern of data users is obtaining access to data. Users desire data that are relevant, accurate, and complete. They also want a usable data format, easy accessibility (low price, little hassle, quick response), timeliness (automatic updates and corrections), and few limitations on use. All of these concerns are legitimate, and they are uncontroversial except for the last, which can raise serious confidentiality concerns.

Often unanticipated are data users who force access through legal action, often as part of a discovery process and involving a court-issued subpoena. As Duncan, Jabine and de Wolf (1993) note, many statistical agencies lack adequate legal authority to protect identifiable statistical records from mandatory disclosures for nonstatistical uses. An example of this was the ruling that Environmental Protection Agency could not protect company survey responses from the Department of Justice's Antitrust Division for use in compliance activities.

Many data users want to further disseminate the data to other users. This secondary data provision occurs in a variety of contexts, such as when a government agency sponsoring a survey may share the information with another agency, or a motor vehicle service may pass on licensed driver information to insurance companies for a fee. This data sharing requires careful managing of the advantages of more efficient data collection against the risks of confidentiality loss. Some laws governing confidentiality of data prohibit or severely limit interagency sharing of data, even for solely statistical purposes.

Organizations representing stakeholder interests

A number of organizations represent various configurations of the stakeholder interests described above.

- **Association of Public Data Users** (APDU; see http://www.apdu.org/) assists users in the identification and application of public data; establish linkages between data producers and users; and bring the perspectives and concerns of public data users to issues of government information and statistical policy.
- **Council of Professional Associations on Federal Statistics** (COPAFS; see http://members.aol.com/copafs/) represents academic/professional organizations interested in the production of federal statistical and research data. Member organizations include professional associations, businesses, research institutes, and others interested in Federal statistics. COPAFS seeks to:
    - ~ Increase the level and scope of knowledge about developments affecting Federal statistics
    - ~ Encourage discussion within member organizations to respond to important issues in Federal statistics
    - ~ Bring the views of professional associations to bear on decisions affecting Federal statistical programs.
- **Council for Marketing and Opinion Research** (CMOR; see http://www.cmor.org/) is a non-profit trade association formed to protect the interests of the marketing and opinion research industry. It encourages respondent cooperation and lobbies lawmakers to protect research from restrictive legislation.
- **American Civil Liberties Union** (ACLU; see http://www.aclu.org/) affirms both privacy rights and the public's right to know
- **Computer Professionals for Social Responsibility** (CPSR; see http://www.cpsr.org/) is a public-interest alliance of computer scientists and others concerned about the impact of computer technology on society.

Such organizations provide consequential input to government agencies in dealing with privacy and information issues.

Managing Confidentiality and Data Access Functions

General Issues

Wide-ranging mechanisms exist to deal with conflicts about the capture and dissemination of data. They span federal legislation, interorganizational contractual arrangements, intraorganizational administrative policies, and ethical codes. They also include technological remedies such as the release of masked data that may satisfy data users needs for statistical information while posing little risk of disclosure of personal information (Duncan and Pearson 1991). In managing confidentiality and data access functions, government agencies have two basic tools for responsible provision of information: restricted data and restricted access. As developed in Duncan, Jabine and de Wolf (1993), these concepts have the following interpretations:
- **Restricted data.** Data are transformed to lower disclosure risk. This is accomplished through disclosure limitation techniques such as (1) release of only a sample of the data, (2) including simulated data, (3) "blurring" of the data by grouping or adding random error, (4) excluding certain attributes, and (5)

swapping data by exchanging the values of just certain variables between data subjects.
- **Restricted access.** Administrative procedures imposing conditions on access to data. These conditions may depend on the type of data user; conditions may be different for interagency data sharing than for external data users. An example of an institutional arrangement for restricted access by external data users is the Census Research Data Center at Carnegie Mellon University (see http://www.heinz.cmu.edu/census/).

Various restricted access policies (Jabine 1993a,b) have been implemented in the last 20 years. Notable have been the fellowship programs run jointly by the American Statistical Association, the National Science Foundation together with four agencies, the Bureau of Labor Statistics, the Bureau of the Census, the U.S. Department of Agriculture, and the National Institute of Standards and Technology. The fellowship programs require that specific research projects and their data needs be evaluated. If approved, data users relocate to the agency to gain access to unrestricted data. In some cases of restricted access, for example, to the Panel Study of Income Dynamics and the National Longitudinal Survey of Youth (Jabine 1993b), the researcher must post bond. The money will be forfeited if the researcher fails to honor the release agreement, say by unauthorized sharing of the data or performing analyses not specified in the proposal.

The Bureau of the Census has long sought a mechanism by which it could make detailed Census information more readily available to researchers, as well as connect Census data to other important national datasets, such as those housed at the Environmental Protection Agency and the Department of Justice, while maintaining the integrity and confidentiality of that data. With this in mind, the Bureau recently granted Carnegie Mellon University's H. John Heinz III School of Public Policy and Management the only Census Center to be housed at a university. Through access to such valuable data, the Center has attracted nationally renowned scholars to engage in interdisciplinary, collaborative research on important policy issues.

Institutional Mechanisms
Privacy or Information Advocate

A *privacy or information advocate* is a one-sided intervenor (Kaufman & Duncan 1988) whose mandate is to counterbalance power and resource inequalities among parties to a data dispute. At the U. S. federal level, the Internal Revenue Service appointed Robert Veeder, a specialist in the Privacy Act and Freedom of Information Act at the Office of Management and Budget, to be the IRS's first privacy advocate. As an example of his activity, he presented a paper entitled, *Making Information Accessible while Protecting Privacy*, with Sara Hamer, Associate Commissioner of the Social Security Administration, to a seminar of the Federal Internet Institute in December 1997.

Privacy or information advocates act to right a power imbalance by championing the position of a weaker party. It is presumably difficult for an advocate to switch gears between privacy advocacy and data access advocacy. They are quite limited in their ability to address privacy and information disputes, as advocacy is their only tool. Access to advocates may be hindered if they are located within a bureaucracy, hence obstructing their visibility.

Privacy and Information Clearinghouse

A *privacy and information clearinghouse* provides a forum for intervention in disputes between information organizations and data providers as well as between information organizations and data users. It provides education and advice to those having questions and concerns about privacy and data access procedures.

An exemplar of such an institutional mechanism is the Privacy Rights Clearinghouse in California. It offers information on how consumers can protect their personal privacy. They provide a web site at http://www.privacyrights.org/ and also operate a telephone hotline for those who seek information about privacy issues. The Privacy Rights Clearinghouse was established with funding from the Telecommunications Education Trust, a program of the California Public Utilities Commission. Some of their materials were developed through the University of San Diego, Center for Public Interest Law, which administered the PRC from its inception in 1992 to October 1996. Given the need for such a clearinghouse to have a reliable source of funding and appropriate administrative support, its existence is contingent on highly specific circumstances. It may not be possible to replicate these conditions in other states.

Ombuds

Another intercessory mechanism with one-sided characteristics is an *ombuds*. An ombuds works within an agency to deal with complaints by data providers or data users.

The federal government has recently taken a step in the direction of using ombuds mechanisms for information and privacy disputes. Office of Management and Budget Circular A-130, that was revised February 9. 1996 (see http://www.whitehouse.gov/WH/EOP/OMB/html/circulars/a130/a130.html), provides uniform government-wide information resources management policies. In Section 9a(10) it provides that an ombuds(man) be designated by each agency. The ombuds(man) is to be a senior agency official charged "to investigate alleged instances of agency failure to adhere to the policies set forth in the Circular and to recommend corrective action as appropriate".

An ombuds provides an alternative and generally easily identifiable complaint route for those in dispute with an IO. This increases the power of data suppliers and data users. An ombuds can only be responsive to IO-specific disputes. This mechanism is limited in flexibility because the ombuds can only direct and articulate concerns. In particular, the ombuds typically does not have mediation or arbitration powers. Access may of course be limited if the ombuds is hidden within the bowels of an IO's bureaucracy. It is essential that an ombuds be granted the authority to act with some neutrality.

Internal Privacy Review Board

The function of *internal privacy review boards* is akin to that of institutional review boards (IRBs) in universities. In fact such IRBs could themselves provide "oversight mechanisms, with suitable definition of their scope to cover research uses of federal data sets, [to ensure that] adequate controls are in place to monitor compliance with data protection rules and regulations by users in the research community" (Duncan, Jabine, and de Wolf, 1993: 107).

The Bureau of the Census has a Microdata Review Panel that was formally chartered in 1981 (Cox, McDonald and Nelson, 1986). It is charged with reviewing policies for the dissemination of microdata files, especially public use data tapes and CD-ROM products. With a similar charge, the National Center for Education Statistics has a Disclosure Review Board which was created in 1989. It is staffed by NCES employees and a Census Bureau representative.

An internal privacy review board can vary in its influence on the balance of power in privacy and information disputes, depending on how it sees its mandate. Some such boards may see their role as simply ensuring that extant administrative rules and legislative requirements are met. Others may be more actively involved in disputes between an information organization and their data providers or their data users. An internal privacy review board can be quite responsive to specific disputes. If it is granted adequate authority, it can employ a wide range of mechanisms to resolve disputes. Unless the board is specially constituted for this purpose, access to an internal privacy review board by data providers and data users may be quite limited.

Administrative Review Agency

An *administrative review agency* would derive its mandate from legislative or executive authority. It would function like the OMB Statistical Policy Office. While not having direct administrative responsibility for federal statistical agencies, the Statistical Policy Office provides long-range planning for statistical programs and coordinates statistical policy within the federal government. The office reviews all data collection requests developed by the Census Bureau and the Bureau of Economic Analysis. Other federal agencies submit their data collection requests, including those for statistical purposes, to OMB clearance officers who are not part of the Statistical Policy Office.

An administrative review agency typically would have as part of its charge the responsibility to ensure an appropriate balance of power among agencies, data providers, and data users. As constrained by its legislative mandate and resources, it could have wide-ranging responsiveness to privacy and information disputes, high flexibility in dealing with them, and potentially high access by concerned parties.

Perhaps consistent with this notion is the announcement on July 31, 1998 by Vice President Gore that "OMB will be given responsibility for coordination of privacy issues, drawing on the expertise and resources of other government agencies. This will help improve the coordination of U.S. privacy policy, which cuts across the jurisdiction of many federal agencies."

Data and Access Protection Commission

Perhaps the most elaborate institutional mechanism is an independent *data and access protection commission*. It would have legislative authority to regulate all stages of the information gathering and dissemination process by promoting accountability and fair information practices. In various ways such commissions have been implemented in Canada and several European countries (see Flaherty, 1989) for a detailed discussion of their operation). Canada has institutionalized a balance between data protection and data access. They have both a privacy commissioner and an information commissioner. The province of British Columbia combines these functions in a privacy and information commissioner. Both Australia and New Zealand have Privacy Commissioners; the United Kingdom has a Data Protection Registrar; Switzerland has a Data Protection Authority; Norway has a Data Inspectorate; and Spain has a Privacy Authority.

In the United States, most drafts of the Privacy Act of 1974 provided for a permanent privacy protection commission, but this provision was deleted before final passage. Recently, interest in such a proposal has waxed and waned. In the House, Representative Wise introduced legislation in 1989 and 1991 to establish an independent data protection board. In 1995, Representative Collins introduced H.R.184 to amend the privacy provisions of the Privacy Act to improve the protection of individual information and to reestablish a permanent Privacy Protection Commission as an independent entity in the Federal Government. In the Senate, Paul Simon introduced Senate Bill 1735 in November of 1993 to establish a Privacy Protection Commission. The bill provided for an advisory and independent commission of five members to be appointed by the President, with the consent of the Senate, to serve staggered seven-year terms. As of July 1998, no such bill had passed. Nonetheless, the fact of repeated introduction of this provision and its support from various bodies, including the National Academy of Sciences Panel on Confidentiality and Data Access (Duncan, Jabine, and de Wolf 1993 Recommendation 8.5, p. 217). Although it does not appear on the current legislative agenda, there continues to be interest in the concept.

Data Protection Commissioners could also assist in reviewing data provider related disputes. The National Research Council's Panel on Confidentiality and Data Access recommended, "an independent federal advisory board charged with fostering a climate of enhanced protection for all federal data about persons and responsible data dissemination for research and statistical purposes." A data and access protection commission could have a legislative mandate, giving it wide-ranging authority. Such authority might charge it with the responsibility to provide for a balance of power among stakeholders, be broadly responsive to disputes about data, to be flexible in employing mechanisms to resolve disputes, and to provide easy access to all disputants. A commission could also serve as a liaison for the negotiation of international agreements regarding privacy and information issues.

Technical Procedures

Technical procedures for maintaining data confidentiality involve release of restricted data; techniques developed over the past t 20 years have been proposed in both the statistical and computer science literature (Duncan and Pearson, 1991; Fienberg 1994; Keller-McNulty and Unger, 1993). Unlike restricting access, restricting data is a technical device. It involves such methods as removing explicit identifiers and masking the sensitive data, e.g., grouping into categories or adding noise. By implementing data restrictions, agencies have operationalized statistical disclosure limitation practices. Some guidelines used by the European statistical system (Eurostat) are summarized in Manual on Disclosure Control Methods (1996).

Statistical disclosure limitation practices have allowed agencies to provide increasing amounts of data to the research community. Jabine (1993a) gives an excellent summary of statistical disclosure limiting practices for selected US agencies. The techniques proposed depend on the nature of the data, whether in tabular, microdata, or in on-line form.

Tabular Data

From demographic surveys frequency counts of variables such as age, sex, and race of responding individuals are tabled. Respondents can be identified, and so a disclosure occurs, with small counts in the cells of the table. If a table, for example, showed only one Asian female in a census tract and shows her as an orphan, then a disclosure has occurred. From establishment surveys variables such as Standard Industrial Classification Code and salary levels are used to create tables. For establishment data the disclosure issue is to avoid releasing information that will identify characteristics of particular establishments. As noted by Cox and Zayatz (1995), there are four principal methods for disclosure limitation of tabular data: cell suppression (Willenborg and de Waal, 1996), rounding (Cox, 1987), perturbation (Duncan and Fienberg, 1998), and modification of the underlying microdata (Griffin, Navarro and Flores-Baez, 1989).

Microdata

Microdata are records directly on the unit of analysis, so may involve data about specific individuals or establishments. Because of the demand for more information than can be obtained from tables, public-use microdata files have been developed by some agencies. A public-use microdata file provides unrestricted access to restricted data. Public-use microdata files have been limited to data concerning individuals. Data on organizations tend to be more highly skewed than for individuals. The skewed distributions coupled with the time series and longitudinal nature of organizational data make many data restriction techniques, including top-coding, difficult. Consequently, very few public-use microdata files for organizations have ever been released. An important exception to this is the U.S. Census of Agriculture, which beginning with the 1987 data has released microdata that has been disclosure limited through high levels of geographic aggregation and data categorization as well as being a 5 percent sample of farms (Kirkendall et al,. 1994).

Online Data

Technological advances in computers and communications offer both opportunities and threats: opportunities to capture, analyze, store, and disseminate large databases more efficiently and threats of unauthorized access to individually identifiable data. Full use of the capability of today's information technology involves data access through on-line data query systems (McNulty and Unger, 1989). The data user directly requests all statistical analyses of interest. Steel and Zayatz (1998) lay out the technical procedures for disclosure limitation that will be used for the 2000 Census. In order that the released data products may have both higher quality and lower disclosure risk, they propose data swapping procedures that will target the most risky records. To allow broader and easier access to data and to allow users to create their own data products, they are developing the Data Access and Dissemination System (DADS). Users would submit requests electronically. Because of the possibility of substantially increased detail in tabular data with DADS, new disclosure limitation techniques will need to be employed.

Conclusions

> Privacy is a basic American value — in the Information Age, and in every age. And it must be protected. We need an electronic bill of rights for this electronic age. You should have the right to choose whether your personal information is disclosed; you should have the right to know how, when, and how much of that information is being used; and you should have the right to see it yourself, to know if it's accurate.
> — Vice President Al Gore

Agencies in the public sector play a key role in responding to this challenge. They are central in collecting and disseminating data that bear on the most important issues in the public interest. Advances in information technology, particularly the Internet, have multiplied the tension between demands for ever more comprehensive databases and demands for the shelter of privacy. In mediating between these two conflicting demands, agencies must address a host of difficult problems. These include providing access to information while protecting confidentiality, coping with health information databases, and ensuring consistency with international standards. The policies of agencies are determined by what is right for them to do, what works for them, and what they are required to do by law. They must interpret and respect the ethical imperatives of democratic accountability, constitutional empowerment, and individual autonomy. They must keep pace with technological developments by developing effective measures for making information available to a broad range of users. They must both abide by the mandates of legislation and participate in the process of developing new legislation that is responsive to changes that affect their domain. In managing confidentiality and data access functions, agencies have two basic tools: techniques for disclosure limitation through restricted data and administrative procedures through restricted access. The administrative procedures can be implemented through a variety of institutional mechanisms, spanning privacy advocates, internal privacy review boards, and a data and access protection commission. The technical procedures for disclosure limitation involve a range of mathematical and statistical tools. The challenge developing and implementing these administrative and technical tools is great, and the value to society of the information that agencies can provide is hard to overestimate.

References

American Statistical Association, Committee on Professional Ethics (1989). Ethical Guidelines for Statistical Practice. Alexandria, VA: American Statistical Association.

Cox, L., McDonald, S.K, and Nelson, D. (1986). Confidentiality issues at the

United States Bureau of the Census. *Journal of Official Statistics*, 2, 135-160.

Cox, L. and Zayatz, L. (1995) An agenda for research in statistical disclosure limitation. Environmental Protection Agency.

Dalenius, T. (1993). Discussion: Informed consent and notification. *Journal of Official Statistics, 9*, 377-381.

Drucker, P. F. (1992). The new society of organizations. *Harvard Business Review*, September-October, 95-104.

Duncan, G. T. (1990a). Disclosure limitation research and practices: A commentary on two agencies' perspectives. *Proceedings of the Seminar on Quality of Federal Data Council of Professional Associations on Federal Statistics.*

Duncan, G. T. (1997) Data for health: Privacy and access standards for a health care information infrastructure. *Health Care and Information Ethics: Protecting Fundamental Human Rights* (Audrey R. Chapman, ed.), Sheed and Ward, 299-339.

Duncan, G. T., & Fienberg, S. E. (1998) Obtaining Information while Preserving Privacy: A Markov Perturbation Method for Tabular Data. Eurostat: Statistical Data Protection 98. Lisbon.

Duncan, G. T., Jabine, T., & de Wolf, V. (1993). *Private Lives and Public Policies: Confidentiality and Accessibility of Government Statistics.* Washington, D.C.: National Academy Press.

Duncan, G. T., & Lambert, D. (1986). Disclosure-limited data dissemination (with comments). *Journal of the American Statistical Association, 81*, 10-28.

Duncan, G. T., & Lambert, D. (1989). The risk of disclosure for microdata. *Journal of Business and Economic Statistics, 7*, 207-217.

Duncan, G. T., & Mukherjee, S. (1991). Microdata disclosure limitation in statistical databases: query size and random sample query control. *Proceedings of the 1991 IEEE Symposium on Research in Security and Privacy*, 20-22, Oakland, California.

Duncan, G. T., & Pearson, R. W. (1991). Enhancing access to data while protecting confidentiality: prospects for the future. *Statistical Science, 6*, 219-239.

Duncan, G. T., & de Wolf, V. A. (1990). Mediating confidentiality and data access. *Chance 3*, 45-48.

Duncan, G. T., de Wolf, V. A., Jabine, T. B., and Straf, M. L. (1993) Report of the panel on confidentiality and data access. *Journal of Official Statistics*, 9, 271-274.

Engelage, C. (1992). Statistical confidentiality in the context of community statistics: the legal framework. Eurostat report, Luxembourg. August 28.

Federal Committee on Statistical Methodology (1994). Statistical Policy Working Paper 22: Report on Statistical Disclosure limitation Methodology. Washington, DC: U. S. Office of Management and Budget.

Fienberg, S. E. (1994) Conflicts between the needs for access to statistical information and demands for confidentiality. *Journal of Official Statistics*, 10, 115-132.

Flaherty, D. H. (1989). *Protecting Privacy in Surveillance Societies.* Chapel Hill: University of North Carolina Press.

Griffin, R., Navarro, A.. and Flores-Baez, L. (1989) Disclosure avoidance for the 1990 Census. *Proceedings of the Section on Survey Research Methods, American Statistical Association*, 516-521.

International Statistical Institute (1986). Declaration of Professional Ethics. *International Statistical Review*, 54, 227-242.

Jabine, T. B. (1993a). Statistical Disclosure Limitation Practices of United States Statistical Agencies. *Journal of Official Statistics*, 9, 427-454.

Jabine, T. B. (1993b). Procedures for Restricted Data Access. *Journal of Official Statistics*, 9, 537-590.

Keller-McNulty, S. and Unger, E. A. (1993). Database Systems: Inferential Security. *Journal of Official Statistics*, 9, 475-500.

Kirkendall, N. J., Arends, W. L., Cox, L. H., de Wolf, V. A., Gilbert, A., Jabine and Zayatz, L. V. (1993). Report of the Subcommittee on Statistical Disclosure Limitation Methodology, Federal Committee on Statistical Methodology, Washington, D.C.

Lambert, D. (1993) Measures of disclosure risk and harm. *Journal of Official Statistics*, 9, 313-331.

Leftwich, W. (1993). How researchers can win friends and influence politicians. *American Demographics,* August: 9.

Manual on Disclosure Control Methods (1996). Eurostat. Luxembourg: Office for Official Publications of the European Communities.

National Science Foundation (1998) *Digital Government Program Announcement. Directorate for Computer and Information Science and Engineering.* Washington, D.C. March 15.

Norwood, J. (1990). Statistics and public policy: Reflections of a changing world. Presidential Address, *Journal of the American Statistical Association, 85*, 1-5.

Prewitt, K. (1985) Public statistics and democratic politics. In J. J. Smelser and D. R. Gerstein, eds. *Behavioral and Social Science: Fifty Years of Discovery.* Washington, D. C.: National Academy Press.

Regan, P. M. (1984). Personal information policies in the United States and Britain: The dilemma of implementation considerations. *Journal of Public Policy, 4*, 19-38.

Smith, J. P. (1991). *Data confidentiality: A researcher's perspective. Panel on Privacy and Confidentiality.* Annual Meeting of the American Statistical Association, Anaheim, CA.

Steel, P. and Zayatz, L. (1998) *Disclosure limitation for the 2000 Census of Population and Housing.* Annual Meeting of the American Statistical Association, Dallas, TX.

Willenborg, Leon and de Waal, Ton (1996) *Statistical Disclosure Control in Practice.* Lecture Notes in Statistics 111. Springer Verlag, New York.

de Wolf, V. A. (1995) *Procedures for researcher access to confidential microdata at the Bureau of Labor Statistics.* Office of Research and Evaluation, Bureau of Labor Statistics, Washington, D.C.

7

Electronic Governance on the Internet

by
Michael A. Warren
Electronic Archive Services
and
Louis F. Weschler
Arizona State University

Can Internet-based technologies deliver on the promise of making government more accessible? What tangible benefits can these technologies bring to the public manager? Computers are becoming smaller, yet more powerful and considerably less expensive. The power of the computer—a faster processor, more memory, and more storage capacity—is not as important as its network capability. How well does the computer connect to the Internet to send and retrieve needed information? Warren and Weschler examine how Internet-based technologies facilitate the two-way linkage of citizens, groups and government agencies. The authors address citizen access issues and the implications of Internet technologies for electronic governance.

Governmental institutions were transformed 100 years ago to recreate public order for an industrialized society. Today, the challenge is the transition from an industrial model of government—centralized, hierarchical, and operating in a spatially defined economy—to a new model of governance adaptive to a virtual, global, knowledge-based, digital economy, and fundamental societal shifts (Battelle, 1998). The shift from the Industrial Age to the Information Age requires us to take a hard, critical look at the basic interrelated functions and networks of governance.

Governance is the process of making collective, public decisions for the good of society. Governments in the United States are the principal, pub-

Copyright© 1999, Idea Group Publishing.

lic authorities of governance. Governments, however, interact with and depend on many other public, private and volunteer organizations in making, implementing and assessing public policies. Contemporary democratic governance consists of thousands of interacting networks. Good governance depends largely on the capacity of public administrators to effectively manage the public's affairs through networks. Likewise, effective democratic participation in governance depends on the capacity of ordinary citizens to communicate with those in power. Electronic networks hold great promise as tools for access to and management of the societal, political and organizational networks within which public managers operate.

In an information-rich society, issues about centralization, decentralization and autonomous decisionmaking in these social, political and organizational networks need serious reconsideration. How leaders, for example, define rules under which governance units may interact could facilitate growth of robust networks for information access and feedback among new systems to shape the future (Battelle, 1998). On the other hand, poor choices of new rules could retard the development and use of robust networks in governance.

Information technologies, especially those related to the Internet, promise to revolutionize conditions of participatory governance. Asymmetries in availability and use of information among various participants in governance—citizens, consumers, interest groups, lobbyists, legislators, administrators, judges and mass media—long have produced process and substantive political inequities. As technical information became an increasingly important resource in politics, those with expertise and access to expert information enhanced their domination of governance at all levels in the American political system. Widespread access to the voluminous information on the Internet, however, could support a more even distribution of usable information. This access may revolutionize capacity of all political actors including ordinary citizens to more fully participate in processes of governance. This outcome is not secure, but the promise is great.

Managers in the Midst of Networks

Public managers find themselves in the midst of a "strategic triangle" (Moore, 1995). The three corners of the triangle—substantive (client-centered outcome) values, operations, and politics—are three meta networks within which the manager works to create public good while managing public organizations. Managers must strategically manage their organizations to produce goods and services that are valuable to beneficiaries in an operationally feasible manner within the constraints of political legitimacy and support. The effective manager brings together and balances the demands and resources of each network in the process of leading public organizations.

Electronic information systems assist managers in tapping into and strategically interacting with each network. Electronic networks can enhance the capacity of public managers in making political strategies, operations decisions and value judgments in meeting citizen needs.

For example, electronic-based communication and commerce are at the core of competitive production and delivery of services. Operationally, public sector organizations continue to search for ways to get their goods and services to the consumer faster, at less cost, and with higher quality. Shortening cycle times, cutting out distribution obstacles, and applying technology solutions are some of the ways organizations have accomplished these objectives.

Public managers access two kinds of electronic networks in meeting public needs: (1) Intranets and (2) Internets. Intranets support the internal values and operations of the organization and internets support the external values and politics of the organizations. These networks, in fact, are not separable. They functionally overlap and interconnect, but treating them as distinctive nets will help us understand the potential and limits of electronic networks as resources for strategic management.

Intranets

Internal government/corporate Web sites, or intranets, give employees easy access to mountains of information. Integrating an organization's computing environment with Internet technology can help by:

- Simplifying internal information management and improve internal communication by applying page and link paradigms. Navigation and search paradigms pioneered on the Internet make it easier for users to find, create, and analyze information.
- Seamlessly integrate internal corporate networks with the Internet to enhance communication between an organization and its customers and partners.
- Integrate new products and Internet technologies with existing infrastructure and legacy systems to enable organizations to leverage their technology investment and evolve information technology systems smoothly.
- Simplify applications development, diffusion, and administration to help organizations streamline development life cycles (Microsoft, 1996).

As technology improves and is replaced with newer technology, organizations make decisions whether to acquire and implement the new technology. Hardware, software, and other technology change at an alarming rate. A poor choice can be a costly choice as direct and indirect costs add up. Costs include the new technology, as well as the retooling, (re)training, and organizational stress that accompanies the change. Intranet technology advances are helping government agencies control costs in numerous ways, most noticeably in the distribution/dissemination of information. On-line procedures, benefits information, and e-mail are just a few of the ways paper reduction and time efficiencies have been realized. Following is an illustration of an intranet prototype that government organizations might deploy.

The Internet

New and emerging technologies include client/server computing, object-oriented database technologies, data warehousing, global positioning systems, and new programming languages. However, none of the new technologies have captured the attention of the non-technical person as has the Internet, and, more specifically, the World Wide Web. Public, private and volunteer organizations increasingly use computers as a way to connect individuals and groups, selectively retrieve information, and manipulate data.

Figure 1. Architecture of an Intranet

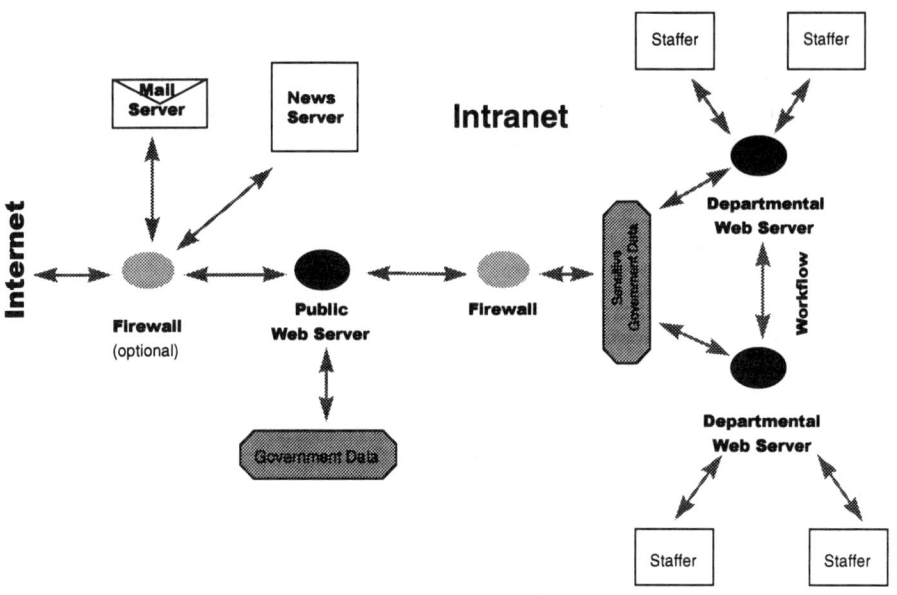

Figure 2. Architecture of the Internet

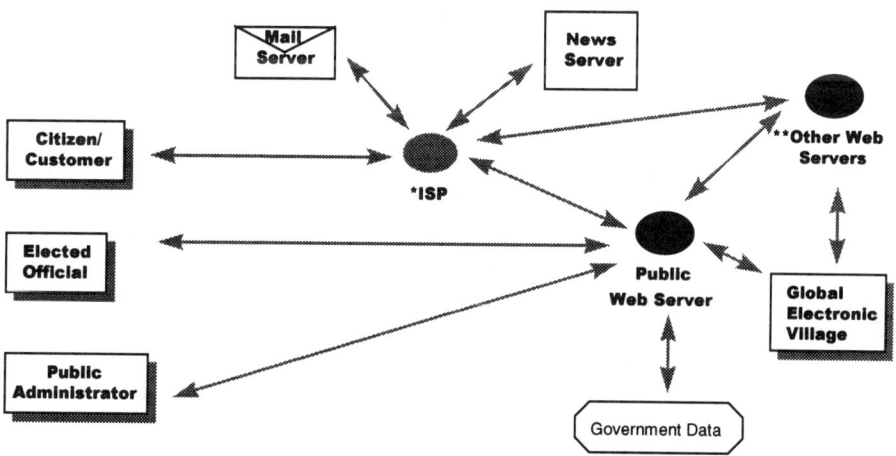

*ISP = Internet Service Provider

** Includes suppliers, partners, universities, hospitals, non-profits and other public and commercial organizations

The motives for implementing and promoting Internet technologies include:
- Increase productivity
- Improve customer service
- Reduce cycle times
- Decrease costs
- Increase revenue
- Create and improve external linkages with suppliers and customers
- Create and improve internal linkages with staff and management
- Reengineer business processes
- Improve management and control of information
- Exploit leading-edge technologies
- Enhance organizational flexibility
- Respond to competitive pressures
- Respond to the ever-increasing information avalanche

All of these motives are important in the decision making for implementing and deploying Internet technology. These motives would, however, apply to use of any kind of information technology. What makes the Internet and the web especially attractive to public organizations? Public organizations find Internet technology attractive for five major reasons: (1) size of the network, (2) fast access to data, (3) high quality interaction among staff, customers, and suppliers/partners, (4) improved efficiency of operations and (5) enhanced participation.

Size of the Internet

The Internet is a vast network of over 29 million host computers, most of them private, in more than 245 countries (Internet Domain Survey). As of early 1998, over 41.5 million U.S. adults actively used the Internet. This is an increase of 33 percent from the second quarter of 1997 (American Internet User Survey). As Internet usage continues to grow for the next few years, the implications for public-sector organizations are boundless. Most every federal agency has a Website. States, cities and towns are on-line as well. Information gathering and dissemination, service and product delivery, and interactive, direct communication between elected officials, administrators and citizens offer the most visible, direct benefit.

Fast access to data

BYTE Research conducted a survey of Fall Comdex (1997) attendees to gauge how important certain technologies will be in 1998. A total of 1,272 respondents rated various technologies on a scale of 1 to 5 (5 being the highest). These respondents also estimated the degree of deployment of these technologies within their organizations by mid-1998. The top technology in terms of overall rating by far is virus detection and elimination. Other top technologies include high-speed remote access, Windows 98/NT5, and next-generation internets. Those technologies scoring high for being deployed by mid-1998 are the anti-virus technology, directory services, Year 2000 projects, Java, remote access, and Windows 98/NT5 (Levkoff, 1998).

Persons working in public organizations need high-speed remote access to data. Although it takes time to use the Web and e-mail, use of personal computers, especially laptop models, greatly increase the capacity of persons to rapidly access data sets all over the world. Both synchronous and asynchronous communication over the web and e-mail radically altered the conditions of work in a short time. Users of computer networking are less hindered by temporal and spatial considerations than their network deprived counterparts.

High-speed remote access is a relative phrase, however. Some readers remember the acoustic coupler modems of yesteryear that operated at 300 bits per second. With current modem technology operating at 56,000 bits per second, most of us continue to beg for more speed. Access to large volumes of data, coupled with large storage capacities (hard disks) on personal computers, are inviting users to download the information to have readily available. Voice, video and text transmission is bogging down communication channels under strained, outdated wiring technology of today. New communication technologies are on their way. However, access to data is fast today, relatively speaking.

High quality interaction

The quality of interaction over the Internet varies. Fax, e-mail and other networks do enhance the communication capacity of both consumers and producers. Almost all private and public service providers have internal network mail. Many use external networks, mostly via the Internet, to connect with supplies and customers. Most private firms and governmental units have sites on the web. Customers and supplies that have access to the Internet may electronically interact with service providers. The quality of the technology continues to improve and the quality of electronic interaction is fairly high for those who know how to use the Internet effectively.

Everyone, however, does not have quality access to the Internet. For a variety of personal, professional, technical and economic reasons, many potential users lack full access to computer networking. Thus, access constrains the quality of interaction.

Efficiency of operations

Obviously, increased high-speed communication promotes higher production and delivery efficiency. The changes in relationships between a producer and a consumer may illustrate some potential savings. The Internet, for example, permits citizens to directly order services, pay bills, take part in a survey, ask a question, find a place, and make a demand on line. Its freedom from some constraints of space and its asynchronous communication mean that both parties do not have to be there to "talk." Thus, both citizen and agency can interact in their own space and time frame. The transaction costs of both parties are, potentially, reduced.

Enhanced participation

These rapidly changing technologies, especially those relating to the Internet and the World Wide Web, may radically alter conventional notions of participatory governance. "The Net changes the way we distribute information in a fundamental way that makes it highly participatory. One of the characteristics that are so important is that distribution costs fall almost to zero. For example, I put up the Center for Democracy and Technology web site and for a very low cost were in communication with potentially 40 million people out on the web. I didn't have to get a story in the Washington Post about the new organization. I could go directly to that constituency"

(Berman, 1998).

Governments, elected representatives and citizens are beginning to experiment in digital democracy with electronic town meetings, voting online, opinion polls, and direct communication with constituencies through Web sites, interactive Web events, and e-mail. Further, public administrators actively use the Internet for a variety of functions. They use it to communicate with each other and with legislative staff, citizen groups and clients. They conduct research via the Web. They use it, especially e-mail, as a routine means of exchanging data. "With the Internet, a lot more people potentially will get involved in decision making. Constituencies will have a lot more to say to institutions that they belong to" (Berman, 1998).

The Promise of Network Computing

A move is afoot . . . less is more. For many people, the personal computer is too much trouble. It remains too complex to master and fails often unexplainably. A new device is being developed that is purposely limited to only a few core tasks. Fewer features and easier to use are the design focus. These digital devices are more "appliance-like" taking a charge from televisions and telephones—working all the time, simplistically. Non-networked versions of the new digital information appliances, made primarily for home use, will allow the user to access the Internet. Its counterpart is an office version called a Network Computer (NC). The concept of the NC is based on the notion that an average worker linked to an office network does not need the power and complexity of a personal computer at her desk.

Network computing is a new architectural paradigm, a model that virtually any desktop device equipped with a Web browser, a modem or network adapter, and Internet/intranet access can support to help its user interact within the virtual realm. Relatively low hardware costs is one of the most important dimensions of network computing. A $500-to-$600 network computer can stretch a public access budget. For example, a library or community center might be able to get three NC's for the price of one 'traditional' personal computer. Three users can access the Internet simultaneously instead of one.

A New Governance Model

"The hand-off between government and governance is going to be one of the most delicate and demanding enterprises that the human species has ever had to take up, and I think that's where we are. And you are either at this point on the side of that change or you're trying to pretend it's not taking place" (Barlow, 1998).

Much of what drives the demand for technology in the United States is an emphasis on production efficiency, doing more with less. In some parts of the world, technology is primarily driven by information needs, how information is controlled and distributed. In this time of transition when governments do not know exactly what they should be doing, a focus on information is more valuable than a focus on efficiency. We can become highly efficient in doing the wrong things. Being efficient, therefore, should no longer be the dominate management objective. Public management should direct our attention more to ways to improve effective use of information technology (Thorson, 1998).

This does not mean that efficiency improvements should be abandoned. Increased focus on information technology and potential efficiency gains are not mutually exclusive. From a governance perspective, greater attention directed toward information technology must be done purposefully. It should improve service delivery, reduce staff resource needs, and improve information delivery. These figure into the efficiency equation.

The notion of governance through networks, however, causes one to rethink the interrelated nature of government. It is not only about being more efficient with technologies or simply moving existing systems from the national level to the state level or the local level. It is about defining government functions first, then building new systems around them that supports a truly distributed model of governance (Eisenach, 1998).

The future lies in networked government services with decision making resident at community levels wired to an intersectoral local, regional, national and international communication infrastructure. "As one example, let's take a look at the criminal justice/public safety area. Numerous agencies—courts, police, corrections, probation—that all share the same goal of creating safe communities. The government model of today has these groups separated out with cumbersome interfaces if they exist at all. If the public defender and the district attorney want to share briefs.... Here's my three inches of paper - you can scan it into your system if you want. But really the end product is safe communities" (Eisenach, 1998).

A Sampling of Electronically Enhanced Governance

Governments and other participants widely engage in "electronic commerce" and "electronic political communication" via the Internet. The numbers and scope of participants and communication expand daily. A sample of a few outstanding examples of electronic governance illustrates the rich opportunities the Internet and other electronic systems offer to officials, groups and citizens.

Smart States

The Smart States initiative spearheaded by the Western Governors' Association is good example of melding electronic communication with strategic management. The design is to create an electronic infrastructure to link education, institutions, and the public and private sectors to deliver services to citizens where they want it—at home, the workplace and school—as well as leverage the intellectual assets from various universities. The desired results include:
- Improving delivery of government services at all levels.
- Assisting economic growth through simplification of the regulatory process .
- Increasing citizen engagement in the process of governance.

Oregon created statewide benchmarks for delivery of services in the areas of child welfare, education, and work force training. Utah and Minnesota make information available to its citizens about the economy, children and families, government spending, and the environment. On the federal level, the acquisition rules on government purchases valued above $100,000 were rewritten via the Internet, gaining much larger participation in review and input.

Michigan, Virginia and Ohio are implementing systems that will improve program effectiveness for a variety of government social services. Such improvements will have a direct impact on at-risk children in these three states. Automating social service systems enables agencies to better supervise tasks such as child welfare, child care, child support enforcement, job placement, and child and adult protection.

The Michigan Family Independence Agency, formerly the state's Department of Social Services, will build a new Services Worker Support System (SWSS). SWSS is a comprehensive system designed to support caseworkers as they manage the business processes of children's protective services, foster care, adoption and delinquency programs as well as adult protective services, foster care and home-help programs. This system will allow robust statewide tracking on a country-by-country basis.

Virginia is developing a Statewide Automated Child Welfare System (SACWIS) and other social services programs. The agency plans to Web-enable its financial systems.

The agency is moving closer to a paperless environment by eliminating the need to send invoices throughout the state for employees who travel, as an example. And the production of federal reports, which has taken a week, now will be able to be done with the push of a button.

Minnesota

Minnesota utilizes the Internet in especially interesting, innovative ways. MN-POLITICS is the world's largest state-level political e-mail forum. This is the interactive public commons to discuss and follow Minnesota politics. MN-FORUM is a moderated e-mail forum for special events hosted by Minnesota E-Democracy and partner organizations. This e-mail list is only used for organized events, such as electronic debates between election candidates. Subscribers to this e-mail list catch ongoing and upcoming events. They can join MN-DEMOCRACY for announcements about future events as well.

Minnesota E-Democracy is a nonpartisan citizen-based project, whose mission is, "Improvement of participation in democracy in Minnesota through the use of information networks. Minnesota E-Democracy hosts quality online public spaces for citizen interaction on public issues."

Blacksburg, Virginia

The Blacksburg Electronic Village (BEV) is an outreach effort of Virginia Tech in partnership with the Town of Blacksburg, Virginia and Bell Atlantic. The BEV is based entirely on the Internet. The goals of the project are to:
- Continue to foster the virtual community that has been created to complement and enhance the physical community.
- Further refine the model for creating electronic communities in other towns.
- Investigate the factors that make community networks self-supporting and

responsive to user needs.
- Provide support and assistance to other communities that are trying to develop healthy community networks (Blacksburg, 1998).

The concept of the BEV came about in early 1991. At that time, Virginia Tech had a sophisticated campus-wide voice/data network, and began looking into ways to extend network access to faculty, staff, and students living in Blacksburg. A decision was made to join forces with the Town of Blacksburg and Bell Atlantic (the local telephone company) to offer Internet access to every citizen in town.

The next two years were spent readying the town's information infrastructure installing digital switching equipment and a fiber backbone. In the spring of 1993, a group of citizens beta tested the first distribution of the BEV software which included Internet e-mail and Gopher clients. The BEV officially opened its doors for business in October 1993. Initially, only dial-up access was offered; ISDN and Ethernet were made available in 1994. The software package was enlarged to include a full suite of Internet tools. Today, the BEV group works closely with the Town of Blacksburg, local civic groups, and individual citizens to ensure that these new communications tools are used to support the every day human activities of Blacksburg (Blacksburg, 1998).

By the summer of 1997, more than 60 percent of Blacksburg's 36,000 citizens were using the Internet on a regular basis. More than 250 local businesses advertise on-line or about 70 percent of all businesses in the Blacksburg area. Many office buildings in the area are completely wired for direct, high-speed access to the Internet. The ubiquitous network facilities in Blacksburg enable local businesses to conduct worldwide operations easily.

Just over half of the Internet users have dial-up (modem) access. Some connections are made using the public-access library computers. The remaining connections are made using Ethernet in offices, dorm rooms, and 600 apartment units (Blacksburg, 1998).

Chandler, Arizona

Chandler, Arizona residents have waged Web warfare on a proposed, nearby commercial and industrial development. Using the Internet, e-mail and fax machines, residents are signing opposition petitions. One resident developed a web site listing names and phone numbers of key contacts, dates and times when the plan will be heard by city officials. The web site links to Chandler's home page, with the names of City Council members and their City Hall addresses and phone numbers. It links to a second resident-developed web site that provides information about the preliminary development plan and rezoning application filed by the developer (Magruder, 1998).

The National Information Infrastructure

Although many localities began their own networks before the 1990s, the National Information Infrastructure initiative fostered additional and more inclusive efforts by state and local governments to join electronic governance. Access to public information and online services for all citizens is paramount to public-sector organizations utilizing the Internet. Consequently, many of these organizations have put Internet-accessible computers in libraries, community and senior centers. Much of this accessibility can be attributed to the National Information Infrastructure (NII), a Department of Commerce initiative.

The NII is a seamless web of communications networks, computers, databases, and consumer electronics that will put large amounts of information at citizens' fingertips. Beyond the physical components of the infrastructure, the value of the NII to citizens will depend in large part on the quality of its other elements: the information itself, which may be in the form of text, voice, video programming, scientific or business databases, images, sound recordings, library archives, and other media.

Applications and software, including web browsers, that allow citizens to access, manipulate and organize the growing mass of information. The network standards and transmission codes that facilitate interconnection and interoperation between networks, and insure the privacy of persons and the security of the information carried, as well as the security and reliability of the networks.

The people, who create the information, develop applications and services, construct the facilities, and train others to tap its potential. Many of these people will be vendors, operators, and service providers working for private industry (NII, 1998).

Democratic Governance via the Internet

These examples show the considerable promise of electronically based popular governance and enhanced administrator-client linkages. This potential, however, is limited by several constraints: (1) Lack of universal access, (2) Cyberspace demographics, (3) Electronic redlining, (4) Poorly developed and managed systems and (5) Inadequate training and knowledge.

Universal Access

The proliferation of personal computers, networked terminals, and powerful workstations throughout the public sector makes information systems and their information products readily accessible to most government workers. This holds true for private sector workers as well. In many cases, the use of information systems seems indispensable for public program success in service delivery, oversight, policy formulation, and accountability functions (Newcomer & Caudle, 1991). Today, unencumbered access to data for these workers is imperative to accomplish their jobs.

Universal access will continue as a social and moral debate as opportunity and commerce increasingly shifts to the Internet and technology. In households with income greater than $50,000, 52 have a computer in the home. In households reporting under $25,000 the rate of computers in homes drops to about 15 percent (Yankelovich, 1998). People who work with computers earn a substantial wage premium over those who do not and accounts for half of the increasing gap between the wages of college and high school graduates. As a society, we risk much if we leave many of our fellow Americans stalled on the entry ramp of the information highway.

Every American should have Internet access, and new taxes should foot the bill. So says the Rand Corporation, a non-profit think tank, in a proposal titled, "Universal Access to E-mail: Feasibility and Societal Implications." The proposal argues that the chasm between information age have and have-nots is ever widening, and concludes that universal Internet access is necessary to close the gap and foster a more inclusive society. Universal access will enable all Americans, rich and poor, to more easily contribute to democracy, communicate with government bodies, and partake in the "commercial and government transactions" that increasingly occur online (the net, 1996).

Not only does Rand propose that each U.S. citizen have his or her own e-mail address, it suggests installing computer kiosks in libraries, community centers, and other local venues to serve people who don't have computers at home. Rand states, "Although e-mail penetration is rapidly expanding, some program of economic assistance to marginal consumers maybe necessary. Any e-mail assistance will require public funding from an industry-wide tax or from general revenues. Subsidies will need to be narrowly targeted to reach consumers who would not otherwise subscribe."

Cyberspace Demographics

It has been estimated that by the year 2000, the number of individuals accessing the Internet will surpass 200 million worldwide. This is astonishing until one looks at the demographics. Sixty percent of cybercitizens are male. Fifty-two percent are between the ages of 30 and 49, with 31 percent under 30. Sixty-nine percent have education beyond high school. Seventy-six percent are employed. Seventy-six percent of the on-line users identify their race as white (Yankelovich, 1998).

At the end of 1997, 44 percent of households in the U.S. had a computer. About 22 percent were on-line (with Internet access). In the year 2000, household computers are expected to increase to almost 53 percent. Forty-one percent are expected to have on-line access (Jupiter, 1998). This information has far-reaching consequences for public and private sector organizations when coupled with access threats such as "electronic redlining."

Electronic Redlining

Internet connectivity will continue to be a thorn in the side of the Information Age in the foreseeable future. Fast access services, cable modems, digital subscriber lines will be available to millions. Unfortunately, tens of millions will have to wait.

According to Howard Bryant (1995) technology futurists expect that the high-speed communication links such as video telephones, movies-on-demand and the Internet will lead America into an all-inclusive information revolution. Such communications advances are a given to become a reality; however, the question is whether or not everyone will have equal access. Will the disadvantaged participate equally in the information revolution, or will they become victims of "electronic redlining"?

The question of which communities get wired for the new technology first has obvious major implications. The battle between telephone and cable companies rages as each fight to be the main architect for the information superhighway. That means building the infrastructure—replacing outdated copper coaxial cable with fiber optic cable to allow for more efficient voice, video and data transmission (Bryant, 1995).

In California, Pacific Telesis (PacTel) chose four affluent communities for the initial rewiring. The problem is that if disadvantaged communities receive access five to 10 years after the initial groundwork, an entire generation of lower income Americans will fall even further behind the general populace—hence, the phrase "electronic redlining" (Bryant, 1995).

Administration and Support of Networks

Numerous problems and obstacles may confront public organizations when implementing and deploying Internet technology. Local networks may be unreliable. The network managers may not be well trained and capable of communicating well with others. Potential internal users of the intranets and the Internet may lack usable knowledge of the systems, hardware, software and communication linkages. Potential external users also may lack technical knowledge and understanding of how to use citizen access sites. Further, the governmental sponsors and supporters may lack funding and other resources to operate and distribute the systems needed to promote full use of the Internet in governance.

Other problems and obstacles can occur. Should any of these problems and obstacles be deterrents? Probably not, given the enormous benefits public organizations can achieve. A review of the major reasons to implement Internet technology discussed above should be enough to strongly encourage all public organizations of the vast potential of being "plugged in."

Concluding Remarks: Electronic Democracy at the Crossroads

The key issues of electronic governance are not technology or Internet issues per se, but societal issues exacerbated by technology. With information access traveling at light speed, the network is [virtual] society and societal change is breathtakingly fast.

The issues of infrastructure and speed pose opportunities and threats depending on one's perspective. Wireless digital connectivity offers options that can significantly improved the communication channels of today. Unfortunately, regulatory, legal and technological problems come into play. These problems, coupled with the need to launch additional low earth orbit satellite systems, are cost factors that further cloudy the picture.

Future third-generation cellular systems are expected to connect large numbers of customers at 64,000 bits per second. Other wireless technologies are slated for much faster connections. Because it is much easier to point an antenna the size of a compact disc at a satellite than to dig a trench or string up cable, look for wireless technologies to grow. The cloudy picture will come into focus in the not-too-distant future.

One of the great dangers of this technological frontier is the disconnect factor. That is, the ease with which we can plug into the cyber universe and disconnect us from human interaction. The cold nature of e-mail when compared to voice communication is undeniable. An opportunity exists to connect visually and audibly. Video-conferencing and teleconferencing over the Internet has been steadily improving. Expect the interactivity among individuals and applications to improve significantly. The Internet has gone through a function shift in the last few years from its educational, nonprofit roots into a commercial entity. Inevitable growing pains have been the result. The fact that there is no central authority in charge of the Internet is certainly an opportunity. The Internet has always been run by consensus. The threat is that the ball game has changed, and consequently, so have the rules. Governments—American and foreign—try to determine their role in governing the Internet. Might this be the last vestige of a true democracy wherein governments become one vote in the consensus, no more powerful than the individual at home?

Representative democracy relies on the supposition that the best way for a nation to make political decisions is for all its citizens to process the information relevant to their lives. Further, the body politic is expected to express their conclusions in free speech and in votes to guide the polity. Computers coupled with the Internet, are providing individuals and groups all over the U.S. with the ability to receive and process information and to use their creativity to challenge the world around them in ways never before imagined.

Likewise, electronic governance permits administrators to more productively access the political, organizational and consumer networks so important to strategic management. Yet, the connections are limited. While on-line computers significantly aid in creating a more-inclusive society, only 41 percent of the households are expected on-line in the year 2000. This can hardly be construed as full participation. Costly hardware and software, hard to use, and the perceived lack of utility are some of the major factors stifling greater penetration into homes. This brings up a new set of questions—what is the "right" percentage of penetration? Should a 98 percent penetration into households matching telephones and televisions be the goal?

On-line access in public places such as libraries and community centers are, at least, part of the answer to the penetration question. When one looks at voter participation on local, state and national levels, the numbers are abysmal. The fact is that those so inclined to participate in the political system will continue to do so with or without computers and the Internet. Other avenues such as the print media, the electronic media (radio and television), town halls, community meetings and word of mouth will continue to exist.

Proliferation of computer and network technologies are not vehicles of exclusion or inclusion, per se. These technologies can provide more information, more timely information, as well as a forum for debate of the issues beyond current communication channels. The problem of equity, however, cannot be dismissed. The global village should not be built in such a way that cyber ghettos result. That is, affluent communities plugged in while bypassing neighborhoods of less economic means. All citizens should have equal access to public information. Wiring affluent sections of a city months or even years before wiring less affluent neighborhoods is discriminatory at best.

Leadership for successful transformation to more equitable, information rich governance through electronic networks is needed across executive, legislative and judicial branches of government at national, state, and local levels. Unfortunately, few legislators have enough basic understanding of the changing world to successfully lead in the Information Age. Conventional legislative responses, shaped by many years of reworking industrialization and a limited, internal view of the world, are counterproductive. Likewise, legislating for a new media, the Internet, without understanding its inherent characteristics, places any government at risk in the electronic frontier (Institute, 1998).

Glossary of Internet Terms

client/server - a type of network relationship in which a node runs "front-end" client software to access the software running on a server.

Ethernet - the first major local area network with nonproprietary communications interfaces and protocols.

firewall- A secured gateway placed at the perimeter of security domains. They are a computer version of a customs checkpoint, enforcing the site's security policy to control traffic into and out of the internal networks. Safe Internet connectivity is the major objective of firewalls.

Internet -The worldwide matrix of connecting computers using the TCP/IP protocols.

Intranet -Deployment models based on the adoption, adaptation, and integration of Internet-derived technologies and communications protocols for use in internal information systems.

ISDN - **I**ntegrated **S**ervices **D**igital **N**etwork. AT&T's high-speed network that features integrated voice and data transmission.

protocol- Defines how computers communicate; it is an agreement between different systems on how they will work together.

TCP/IP- The set of protocols that determine how data is transmitted on the Internet. **T**ransmission **C**ontrol **P**rotocol controls the transport of data, ensuring that it is delivered. **I**nternet **P**rotocol determines the packet structure of data and the addressing used to deliver data to its destination.

World Wide Web- A system that organizes Internet data through hypertext links, allowing you to explore resources from multiple entry points using a browser.

References

American Internet User Survey. (1998). Computer file, <http://www.cyberdialogue.com/marketing/releases/aius_study.html>.

And an URL In Every Pot . . . (1996). *the net,* March.

Barlow, J. (1998). Computer file, <http://www.ieg.ibm.com/20wht11.htm>.

Battelle, J. (1998). Computer file, <http://www.ieg.ibm.com/20wht11.htm>.

Berman, J. (1998). Computer file, <http://www.ieg.ibm.com/20wht11.htm>.

Blacksburg Electronic Village. (1998). Computer file, <http://www.bev.net/project/brochures/about.html#1>.

Bryant, H. (1995). Will there be redlining in cyberspace? *Black Enterprise.* July.

Eisenach, J. (1998). Computer file, <http://www.ieg.ibm.com/20wht11.htm>.

Internet Domain Survey. (1998). Computer file, <http://www.nw.com/zone/

WWW/report.html> (January 1998).

Institute for Electronic Government. (1998). Computer file, <http://www.ieg.ibm.com/20wht11.htm>.

Jupiter Communications. (1998). *PC and On-Line Households in the U.S., 1995-2000.*

Levkoff, K. (1998). Dual Modem Routers Double Your Bandwidth. BYTE, 23 (3), 32.

Magruder, J. (1998). Web warfare getting results. *The Arizona Republic.* March 18, 1998).

Microsoft. (1996). Microsoft's Intranet Strategy. Computer file, http://www.microsoft.com/intranet.

Moore, M. H. (1995). *Creating Public Value, Strategic Management in Government.* Cambridge, MA: Harvard University Press.

Mossberg, W. (1997). Technology and science. *The Wall Street Journal.*

National Information Infrastructure. (1998). Computer file, http://sunsite.unc.edu/nii/.

Newcomer, K. E. & Caudle, S. L. (1991). Evaluating Public Sector Information Systems: More Than Meets the Eye. *Public Administration Review,* 51, (5).

Thorson, S. (1998). Computer file, <http://www.ieg.ibm.com/20wht11.htm>.

Yankelovich Partners Inc. (1998). Demographic Characteristics of On-Line Users, or "Cybercitizens."

Part II

Computer Applications in Public Administration

8

Leading Edge Information Technologies and Their Adoption: Lessons from U. S. Cities

by
Donald F. Norris
Maryland Institute for Policy
Analysis and Research
University of Maryland,
Baltimore County

Based on a national study of the adoption of leading edge technologies, this essay surveys the range of information technology innovation in American cities and outlines the management and environmental characteristics associated with successful innovation diffusion and adoption.

In part because city governments believe that leading edge information technologies produce largely positive impacts, one obvious future trend will be that more city governments will adopt these technologies. Additionally, more leading edge technologies will be adopted by cities. A third trend is that leading edge information technologies will continue to penetrate cities more deeply, and as deeper penetration occurs, so will greater payoffs from use. A fourth trend is that as new and more sophisticated information technologies are adopted by city governments, integration of and support for them will become even more critical than is currently the case. Finally, although more of a finding than a trend, city population as a measure of city size will remain a key determinant in the number and type of leading edge information technologies adopted. While the overall extent of adoption of leading edge information technologies among city governments can be expected to increase, the greatest extent of adoption will be among larger jurisdictions.

Recent studies have shown that nearly all of American city governments use information technology routinely in their operations. For example, a 1993 information technology ICMA

Copyright© 1999, Idea Group Publishing.

survey found that 97 percent of all cities used computers, including: 100 percent of cities over 50,000 in population; 97 percent of those between 10,000 and 49,999, and 93 percent of those under 10,000 (Kraemer and Norris, 1994). A more recent ICMA survey, this one conducted in 1997, found a similar pattern of computer adoption among U. S. cities. Here again, 97 percent of all cities had adopted computers. This included 100 percent of cities over 50,000; 99 percent of cities between 10,000 and 49,999, and 95 percent of cities under 10,000 (Norris and Demeter, forthcoming 1999). These adoption data compare with figures from a 1975 survey which found that 98 percent of cities over 100,000 used computers as did 92 percent of those between 50,000 and 99,999, while only 42 percent of cities between 10,000 and 49,999 used computers (Kraemer and Norris, 1994).

These surveys show that information technology has thoroughly penetrated an entire organizational sector of the American society—municipal government. Computer technology is used by nearly all city governments, regardless of size. Only the very smallest cities do not use computers. Moreover, computers are deployed for a wide array of activities covering most, if not all, of the functional areas of city government -- literally from accounting to zoo operations.

However, penetration tells us very little about the innovativeness and sophistication of information technology applications and even less about nascent trends in information technology use in city governments. City governments may make extensive use of computers and information technology in their daily operations, but they may use the technology primarily in mundane ways. It may also be that only a relatively few cities have adopted more innovative information technologies that do more than automate routine activities. And, what does the future hold in store? In coming years, are city governments likely to adopt more advanced and sophisticated information technologies?

In the past, most payoffs from computing were attributed to more routine applications, especially those with substantial recordkeeping elements (Northrop, et al., 1990). Today, however, because of advances in hardware technology and in application software, it is conceivable that payoffs may occur as the result of technological sophistication and the use of more advanced and, hence, more innovative information technologies. Indeed, the use of more advanced and sophisticated or what might be called "leading edge" information technologies may well provide city governments with results that could not be obtainable from routine applications. One example that comes to mind is AFIS technology. Police departments that have adopted Automated Fingerprint Identification Systems (AFIS) report stunning improvements in clearing cases in which latent fingerprints were essentially the only evidence available. Without AFIS, most of these cases would never be solved. This is because it would not be feasible to staff a police department fingerprint section with a sufficient number of personnel to be able to sort and match latent prints manually against all fingerprints on file. In this case, an advanced information technology is a necessary prerequisite to getting the job done.

Additional evidence to suggest that greater sophistication may produce greater payoffs from use comes from a recent study that found a direct relationship between whether a city had a central computer system and the extent that it had adopted innovative applications (Norris and Kraemer, 1996). The authors found that:

[I]n cities with central systems, the technology is more sophisticated, is more widely diffused within the various functions of city government, and is used by a greater proportion of managers and professionals... (p. 574).

One of the reasons for this was that in cities with central systems, information technology had become more "institutionalized as a source of technical expertise and a provider of day-to-day computer services" than in cities that lacked central systems (Norris and Kraemer, 1996, p. 574). Hence, the technical and managerial capacity existed to foster and support more innovative and sophisticated applications. This, in turn, led to greater use and greater benefits from use.

Leading Edge Information Technologies

In this chapter, we examine leading-edge information technologies and their adoption by American city governments. Leading edge means information technologies that are currently on the vanguard (hence, "leading edge") of innovation adoption by municipal governments.[1] That is, to date, few of these technologies have been adopted by city governments. Indeed, the fact that these technologies have been adopted by relatively few cities strongly suggests that the act of adopting them is an act of innovation by those cities (Rogers, 1983).

Leading edge information technologies may also have a second important characteristic. Many of them are relatively more sophisticated technologically than information technologies used for more routine functions. These information technologies require more than just basic hardware and software, perform other than routine applications, involve both multiple departmental or functional area users, and require advanced knowledge and skills to operate. This characteristic is certainly observable in such leading edge information technologies as GIS, AFIS, interactive public access technologies, World Wide Web sites, and others. However, for some leading edge information technologies, adoption characteristics alone are sufficient for them to be considered leading edge. For example, a long range information technology plan is not a terribly sophisticated technology, nor is a CD-ROM drive, nor a fax modem. Nevertheless, as represented by the percent of cities adopting, even these technologies should be considered on the leading edge of adoption today. Therefore, in this chapter, adoption rates define leading edge information technologies – bearing in mind that at least some of them are also leading edge because of their technological sophistication.

Methodology

Following is a list of leading edge information technologies from three sources: two surveys conducted by the International City/County Management Association (ICMA, 1993 and 1997) and a series of case studies conducted by researchers at the University of Maryland, Baltimore County (UMBC) (Norris and Fletcher, 1998, in progress). Indeed, findings from these sources also provide the principal (though not sole) data to inform this chapter.

Table 1: Potential Leading Edge Information Technologies, 1993

Technology	% Adopted	% Considering
24 Hour City Hall	2.5	13.4
AFIS	7.3	12.6
Bar Code Technology	14.4	25.8
CD ROM	16.3	22.1
Electronic Mail	21.1	15.4
External Databases (Use of)	26.0	NA
Fax Modems	17.1	18.4
Fiber Optic Cable	7.9	9.2
GIS	16.5	26.0
Imaging	5.2	15.9
Interactive Video Training	5.7	7.3
Local Area Network	48.1	NA
Long Range IT Plan	13.1	NA
Multimedia	4.3	13.8
Optical Disk Storage	5.9	23.6
Portable Computers	30.7	17.3
Public Access Network to Query Jurisdiction's Databases	2.8	11.7
Scanners	24.0	19.1
Smart Traffic Monitoring Systems	4.4	2.9
Smart Public Buildings	1.3	3.7
Smart Highway	0.9	3.6
Smart-coded Toll Booths and Parking	0.7	1.0
Video Arraignments	1.7	3.5
Virtual Reality	0.4	2.6
Wide Area Network	5.6	7.6
Wireless LAN	2.0	8.8

Source: 1993 ICMA Information Technology Survey.

First are those information technologies listed in the 1993 information technology ICMA survey (Norris and Kraemer, 1994). This survey asked cities whether they had or were considering a number of potential leading edge information technologies (Table 1). An application was selected as being on the leading edge of municipal innovation from the 1993 survey if at least 10 percent but not more than 50 percent of responding cities had adopted it. The 10 percent base represented a minimum threshold of adoption. In essence, this meant that enough cities had adopted an information technology that it could be considered to be at the beginning of a trend toward broader adoption and, therefore, on the "leading edge" of adoption among all cities. At the level of adoption of 50 percent or greater, the information technology was no longer on the leading edge, but instead was verging on common rather than innovative usage. Using these criteria, an initial list of leading edge information technologies was developed from the 1993 survey. This list is found in Table 2.

A second source of information about leading edge information technologies comes from the UMBC case studies (Norris and Fletcher, 1998, in progress). This study involved in-depth examination of the adoption, uses and impacts of leading edge information technologies in 14 American cities. In this study, potential sites for case studies were initially identified using the 1993 ICMA database. In addition, cities that for other reasons (such as reputation) were considered innovative (e.g., Seattle, Washington, San Diego, California— neither of which had responded to the ICMA survey) were added to the list of potential case study sites.

A list of what were believed to include the most important leading edge information technologies, circa 1995, was developed, partly based on the 1993 ICMA survey list (Table 3). Next, the cities were screened via telephone to determine if, in fact, they had adopted these (or other) leading edge information technologies. As a result of the telephone interviews, several cities were eliminated because they failed to meet the criteria of adoption, and one city declined to participate in the study.[2] This left a final selection of 14 cities. Each of these cities had adopted at least 14 of these 18 technologies (Table 4).[3]

Table 2: Leading Edge Information Technologies, 1993

Technologies	% Adopted	Applications	% Adopted
Bar Coding	14.4		
CD ROM	16.3	AFIS	7.3
Fax Modems	17.1	Electronic Mail	21.1
Fiber Optic Cable	7.9	External Databases	26.0
Imaging	5.2	GIS	16.5
LAN	48.1		
Optical Disk Storage	5.9		
Scanners	24.0	Procedures	
WAN	5.6	Long Range IT Plan	13.1

Source: Norris and Kraemer, 1994.

Table 3: Leading Edge Information Technologies For Screening Potential Case Study Cities, 1995

AFIS
Central IT Department
CD ROM
Computer-based Training
Electronic Data Interchange
Electronic Mail
External Databases (use of)
Fax Modems
Fiber Optic Cable
GIS
GPS
Handheld Computers and PDAs

Imaging
Integrated Voice, Data and Video
Internet Access and Use
Long Range IT Plan
Multi-media
Public Access Technologies
   Kiosks
   Dial-up Access
   BBS
   ATM
   Public Use Terminals

Source: Norris and Fletcher, 1998, in progress.

Table 4: Cities in UMBC Leading Edge Information Technology Study

City	Population [a]	Region [b]	Form of Government
Boston, MA	547,000	NE	MC
Charlotte, NC	396,000	S	CM
Denver, CO	468,000	W	MC
Indianapolis, IN	731,000	NC	MC
Jacksonville, FL	635,000	S	MC
Mobile, AL	196,000	S	MC
New Orleans, LA	497,000	S	MC
Overland Park, KS	111,800	NC	CM
Philadelphia, PA	1,586,000	NE	MC
Richmond, VA	203,000	S	CM
San Diego, CA	1,110,500	W	CM
St. Paul, MN	272,000	NC	MC
Scottsdale, AZ	130,000	W	CM
Seattle, WA	516,000	W	MC

Source: Norris and Fletcher, 1998, in progress.
Notes: a. ICMA regions; b. population derived from 1990 Census.

Extent Of Adoption

Perhaps the first thing that should be noted is that overall American municipal governments are not especially innovative in their adoption of information technologies. The data from the 1993 ICMA survey, for example, show that only one of the leading edge information technologies listed had been adopted by something approaching half of all cities (the LAN or local area network), while one other (portable computers) had been adopted by nearly a third. Three (external database use, scanners and e-mail) had been adopted by between 20 and 30 percent of cities. Five others (CD-ROM, fax modems, Long range IT plan, and GIS) had been adopted by between 10 and 20 percent. The remaining 16 leading edge information technologies on the list had been adopted by fewer than 10 percent of cities. See Table 2.

In 1997, the ICMA conducted another survey of information technology in cities. This survey also contained questions about leading edge technologies (although unfortunately, the questions in the 1997 survey were not directly comparable to those in the 1993 survey). Table 5 contains the adoption rates of the leading edge information technologies listed in that survey.

The data in Table 5 reinforce the conclusion that American city governments are not in the forefront of innovation with information technology. Of the potential leading edge information technologies included in the 1997 ICMA survey, 10 of 18 had been adopted by fewer than 10 percent of U. S. cities. Four had been adopted by over a quarter of cities, including: Wireless services (49.5 percent); [4] WWW site on the Internet (37.5 percent); GIS (28.7 percent); and long range IT plan (26.8 percent). Two more have been adopted by between 15 and 25 percent of cities: CD-ROM (18.4 percent); and fiber optic cable (16.9 percent). And, two more between 10 and 15 percent: fax-back/reply service (14.5 percent) and Intranet server (10.7 percent).

Table 5: Adoption Rates of Leading Edge Information Technologies, 1997

Technology	% Adopted	% Considering
AFIS	7.9	12.0
CD ROM	18.4	27.1
Direct Broadcast Satellite	2.4	3.2
Fax-back/reply Service	14.5	1.8
Fiber Optics	16.9	14.2
GIS	28.7	27.1
GPS	7.7	15.0
Interactive Teleconferencing Facilities	2.7	10.1
Intranet Server [a]	10.7	22.5
Kiosk	2.5	14.0
Laptops (Use of)	51.2	13.2
Local Area Networks	69.9	NA
Long Range IT Plan	26.8	NA
Personal Digital Assistance [b]	2.6	4.6
Satellite Imagery/Data	2.1	4.0
Smart-coded Toll Booths	0.5	0.8
Video Arraignment	3.0	4.8
Virtual Reality Training	1.5	3.2
Wireless Services [c] (Mobile radios and cellular phones)	49.5	7.2
WWW Site On Internet [a]	37.5	30.1

Source: 1997 ICMA Information Technology Survey.
Notes: a. The survey asked "Does the city plan to have one?"
  b. Misprint in the survey; should be Assistant.
  c. The survey asked "Do plans exist to create a site?"

Even these data, however, may be somewhat misleading. As the UMBC case studies discovered, what cities report on surveys and what is actually in place are sometimes subtly or even dramatically different. For example, many GIS systems are that in name only. Some are little more than computer assisted drafting (CAD) systems. Still others are in the early phases of development and are not widely deployed or used. Another example is the use of fiber optic cable. Some cities have deployed fiber optic cable sparingly, to one or only a few governmental buildings. Their survey responses, however, place them in the same category as cities that have installed fiber optic cable extensively. Finally, one of the cities initially selected as a case study site was dropped after the initial site visit. This was because it had in place only a few of the technologies that had been indicated during the screening. Hence, caution should be exercised when interpreting these data.

A different sort of caution is also in order. Cities are adopting certain leading edge information technologies fairly rapidly. This has certainly been true of the LAN, which has been adopted by well over a majority of cities – increasing from 48 to 69 percent adoption in the four years between 1993 and 1997. Additionally, cities appear to be adopting a few other leading edge information technologies rapidly as well. These would include: home pages or web sites on the World Wide Web, long range information technology plans, wireless technologies (radios and cellular phones), and GIS.

Another observation that can be made from these data is that surveys may or may not be good predictors of actual adoption rates. The cities were asked in 1993 if they were considering adopting these technologies. In only a few cases was there a close relationship between the percent of cities considering a technology and the actual rate of adoption as reported in the 1997 survey. For example, there was virtually no increase in the adoption of AFIS and CD-ROM. The actual adoption rate in 1997 eclipsed by nearly 40 percent the combined and "considering" response to the 1993 survey. The actual adoption of GIS increased a respectable 11 percent, but not the 42 percent that "were considering." The 1993 survey responses more or less accurately predicted the adoption rates of fiber optic cable, portable computers, smart toll booths, video arraignment and virtual reality. (See Table 6.)

Finally, there is a direct relationship between city size and adoption of leading edge information technologies. For each of the leading edge information technologies in the 1997 ICMA survey, large cities were more likely than medium sized or small cities to have adopted (Table 7). Indeed, for some leading edge information technologies, such as AFIS, what constitutes full adoption among city governments may be achieved when all large cities and a sizeable fraction (say, 80 to 90 percent) of medium sized cities have adopted. This is because today AFIS technology is simply too costly for small cities – unless they are able to become remote users of regional or state AFIS systems.

Battling Technology Lists

The two ICMA surveys and the UMBC case studies have developed different lists of leading edge information technologies. This has the potential to lead to confusion. Consequently, this chapter has a comprehensive list of information technologies that should be considered leading edge among American local government in 1999 (Table 8). With the passage of time, this list will lose its validity. Some of the technologies on the list will be adopted beyond the point at which they can be considered on the leading edge of municipal innovation (at least among certain categories of cities). Other more innovative technologies will enter the marketplace.

Breadth and depth of Information Technology Penetration

The ICMA surveys also permit discussion of both the breadth and depth of penetration of information technology in American city governments. Not only are most cities computerized, but computers are used in most of the principal functions of city government. The 1993 ICMA survey found that nearly all of the routine administrative and housekeeping functions of city governments were automated. These included such functions as: word processing, budget development, budget analysis, database analysis, and use of spreadsheets; and automation in departments such as: finance, utilities, personnel, law enforcement, public works and governmental administration. In all of these cases, over 50 percent of cities reported automation

Table 6: Adoption Rates of Selected Leading Edge Information Technologies 1993 and 1997 [a]

	1993		1997	
Technology	**% Adopt**	**% Consider**	**% Adopt**	**% Consider**
AFIS	7.3	19.9	7.9	12.0
CD ROM	16.3	38.4	18.4	27.1
Electronic Mail	21.1	15.4	74.6 [b]	NA
Fiber Optic Cable	7.9	17.1	16.9	14.2
GIS	16.5	42.5	28.7	27.1
LANs	48.1	NA	69.9	NA
Long Range IT Plan[c]	13.1	NA	26.8	NA
Portable Computers[d]	30.7	48.0	51.2	NA
Smart-coded Toll Booths [e]	0.7	1.0	0.5	0.8
Video Arraignment	1.7	3.5	3.0	4.8
Virtual Reality	0.4	2.6	1.5	3.2

Source: 1993 and 1997 ICMA Information Technology Surveys.
Notes: a. Only those technologies that appeared on both surveys; b. The question was reworded for 1997 survey and asked % of employees connected to email: 48.4% said 1-10%, 17% said 11-50%, 8.3% said over 50%, 26.4 said none; c. Such an adoption rate means that LANs can no longer be considered a leading edge technology; d. 1993 survey asked about "portable" computers and 1997 survey asked about laptops; e. 1993 survey asked about smart-coded toll booths "and parking." NA means data not available.

Table 7: Adoption of Leading Edge Information Technologies by City Size, 1997

	Small City		Medium City		Large City		Total	
Technology	**No.**	**%**	**No.**	**%**	**No.**	**%**	**No.**	**%**
AFIS	148	5.0	121	17.5	23	56.1	292	7.9
CD ROM	352	12.0	292	42.3	30	73.2	674	18.4
Direct Broadcast Satellite	44	1.5	41	5.9	3	7.3	88	2.4
Fax-back/Reply Service	391	13.3	127	18.4	15	36.6	533	14.5
Fiber Optics	257	8.7	330	47.8	35	85.4	622	16.9
GIS	618	21.0	400	57.9	35	85.4	1053	28.7
GPS	145	4.9	123	17.8	14	34.1	282	7.7
Interactive Teleconferencing Facilities	58	2.0	35	5.1	6	14.6	99	2.7
Intranet Server	229	7.8	138	20.0	26	63.4	393	10.7
Kiosk	42	1.4	41	5.9	10	24.4	93	2.5
Laptops (Use)	1239	42.1	602	87.1	40	97.6	1881	51.2
Local Area Networks	1901	64.6	626	90.6	39	95.1	2566	69.9
Long Range IT Plan	571	19.4	386	55.9	29	70.7	986	26.8
Personal Digital Assistance[a]	43	1.5	43	6.2	9	22.0	95	2.6
Satellite Imagery/Data	39	1.3	33	4.8	5	12.2	77	2.1
Smart-coded Toll Booths	11	.4	6	.9	1	2.4	18	.5
Video Arraignments	48	1.6	50	7.2	11	26.8	109	3.0
Virtual Reality Training	29	1.0	22	3.2	3	7.3	54	1.5
Wireless Services (Mobile radios and cellular phones)	1315	44.7	463	67.0	39	95.1	1817	49.5
WWW Site on Internet	880	29.9	460	66.6	37	90.2	1377	37.5

Source: 1997 ICMA Information Technology Survey.
Notes: a: a misprint in the survey; should be Assistant.
Percentages are of total small, edium or large cities (i.e., AFIS has been adopted by 5.0 percent of small, 17.5 percent of medium, 56.1 percent of large, and 7.9 percent of all cities.

Table 8: Leading Edge Municipal Information Technologies, Circa 1998

Automated Fingerprint Identification Systems
Automated Traffic Control Systems
Automated Vehicle Locator
Bar Code Technology
CD ROM
Computer Based Training
Electronic Commerce
Electronic Data Interchange
Fax Modems / Fax Servers
Geographic Information Systems
Global Positioning
Hand-held Computers and PDAs
Imaging
Interactive Voice, Data and Video
Interactive Voice Response
Internet Access and Use
Intranets
Long Range IT Plan
Mobile Data Terminals
Multi-Media
Optical Disk Storage
Public Access Information Technologies, including:
    Automated Transaction Machines
    Bulletin Board Systems
    External Dial-up
    Kiosk
    Public Access Terminals
Remote Sensing Data
Scanners
Wide Area Networks
World Wide Web Applications (e. g., Home Page, Web Site)
Video Arraignment

Source: Norris and Fletcher, 1998 in progress.

with either PCs or central computer systems(Kraemer and Norris, 1994).[5]

This finding shows that a broad array of municipal functions are automated among a large fraction of city governments and speaks to *breadth* of penetration. Moreover, within each of these areas, a large number of activities is automated. This indicates *depth* of penetration. For example, in the area of finance, it is not unusual for even smaller cities to have fully integrated, automated financial management systems that include modules for such activities as budget preparation, budgetary analysis, budgetary accounting, payroll, purchasing, accounts payable, accounts receivable, and other related functions all of which operate using a standard chart of accounts and a single general ledger. This same type of computerized functionality can be found in myriad other areas of city government. Both breadth and depth of computing are produced by such systems.

To date, however, breadth and depth of penetration have occurred largely, although not exclusively, for *general governmental functions* in U. S. cities. The opposite is the case in terms of leading edge technologies. That is, most leading edge information technologies have not yet penetrated city governmental operations either broadly or deeply. This is, in part, a matter of definition. If, to qualify as leading edge, a technology cannot have been adopted by more than half of the potential adopting population, then it follows that the technology cannot have penetrated broadly into that population.

However, it is also possible that a leading edge information technology may have penetrated deeply into at least some of the units that have adopted it. For example, the court clerk's office in Jacksonville, FL, has implemented a document imaging system that captures, scans, indexes, and stores all documents that enter the court. Thus, this technology has penetrated the clerk's operation completely. It has also become routinized and institutionalized within that office. Additional examples might include such technologies as mobile data terminals in police cars and AFIS systems.

Nevertheless, depth of penetration does not seem to be the case with most of the leading edge technologies listed in Table 8. This is in part because the technologies are relatively new in municipal organizations. And, many are not fully developed or deployed. As indicated earlier, many of the self-reported GIS systems are not fully developed GIS systems, nor are they widely used within local governments. The same is true for other leading edge technologies as well. In fact, depth of penetration appears to occur incrementally for leading edge information technologies. In part, this is because these are more complex systems, and they require considerable time, funding and effort to become fully developed and deployed. As this occurs, these technologies also are more likely to become institutionalized within local governments. At the point of institutionalization, their use becomes more or less routine by appropriate classes of end-users. It is probably fair to say that at this point, these technologies are accepted and nearly taken for granted by their users.

The greatest payoffs from leading edge information technologies will occur after they are institutionalized in city governments. Take a fairly simple example like the use of mobile data terminals in parking enforcement vehicles in Denver, CO. These terminals are used to query (via satellite) a remote, commercially owned database system that contains information about vehicles with overdue parking tickets. Information obtained from the query tells parking enforcement personnel which vehicles should receive the famous "Denver boot." Not only has this system increased accuracy, but 25 percent more vehicles are booted by the same number of personnel in the same amount of time with mobile data terminals than without. Moreover, this increase has direct revenue implications for the city.

The converse of this example is GIS. GIS systems are, perhaps, the most complex, resource-intensive and leading-edge information technology in local government today. Nearly every expert in the field (and, of course, nearly every GIS vendor) contends that, ultimately, GIS will provide dramatic payoffs to local governments. Except in rare instances, these pay-offs are not yet occurring. This is because GIS systems, in many if not most cities that claim to have them, are not fully developed, are not widely deployed and used, and certainly are not institutionalized. Hence, cities are investing substantial amounts of scarce resources to implement GIS systems, hoping that institutionalization will produce payoffs sufficient to justify their costs. Indeed, this is an issue that should be the subject of future research: have GIS systems produced expected payoffs and what are the factors associated with these payoffs.

Why Adopt Leading Edge Information Technologies?

Something must be driving city governments to adopt leading edge information technologies. It cannot be just an effort to "keep up with the Joneses." Or can it? Clearly, cities are not unaware or unaffected by the behavior of their primary reference group – other cities. Earlier research into the diffusion of innovations among state and local governments has shown that policies and practices started by one or a few such governments can and often do spread to others (Walker, 1969; and Bingham, 1976).

The typical pattern of adoption of innovations over time for all classes of adopters – and this is certainly true for local government adoption of information technology— resembles an S curve. That is, relatively few units adopt an innovation in its early stages, but as the innovation becomes more well known and accepted within a class of adopters (perhaps because its effectiveness or because its benefit-costs ratio becomes clearer), the pace of adoption accelerates. Then, as the vast majority of potential adopters have adopted the innovation, the pace of adoption slows. Hence, the resemblance to an S curve (see Rogers, 1983).

A case in point is the PC or microcomputer. In 1982, six years after the beginning of the PC revolution and one year after the introduction of the IBM PC, ICMA conducted a survey of the adoption of PCs in U.S. cities. The survey found that only 13 percent of cities had PCs, although 35 percent said that they planned to purchase one (Norris and Webb, 1983). A 1983 survey of small local governments (counties under 100,000 and cities between 2,500 and 50,000) in the Great Plains and Midwest found that 22 percent had PCs (Norris, 1984).

Compare this with later surveys that found that nearly all cities have PCs. The 1993 ICMA survey found that overall 92 percent of cities had PCs. This included 100 percent of large cities, 94 percent of medium-sized cities, and 91 percent of small cities. The 1997 survey, although employing different questions, found that: 87 percent of cities used IBM PCs; 51 percent used laptops; 11 percent used Apple computers; and 49 percent used workstations. The pattern of larger cities exhibiting higher rates of adoption was present in the 1997 survey as well.

These data show that in the period between the early 1980s and the mid 1990s, the adoption of PCs by municipal governments followed the typical S curve pattern. Adoption of PCs increased from just over one in ten to greater than nine in ten cities in this period. The data also show that with nearly full adoption, the adoption rate (as indicated by the percent of additional governmental units adopting PCs) has slowed considerably.

Adoption rates, however, do not reveal much about the reasons that cities adopt leading edge information technologies. Data from the UMBC case studies and a review of literature in the field reveal two principal categories of reasons why local governments adopt leading edge information technologies. They are general reasons and reasons that are specific to functions and activities. General reasons are oft-cited reasons that include state and local government users' and officials' expectations or hopes concerning the outcomes of computer use. They include such things as: improving efficiency, effectiveness, and accuracy; saving money; increasing revenue; reducing the amount of time required to complete tasks; and reducing staff. Although these reasons are often stated quite generally, they nevertheless carry meaning. This is another way of saying that local governments do not adopt leading edge information technologies frivolously.

Additionally, even though the reasons may ring of generality, they can also be quite context specific. For example, in Charlotte, NC, officials reported that because of downsizing, city departments were losing personnel. In Jacksonville, FL, city departments found it difficult to get additional personnel positions approved. Hence, both cities used information technology to do the work that would otherwise require additional staff. As one respondent in Charlotte put it: "In a time of downsizing, we underspend our general fund budget. Information technology helps with this. We can lose positions and make up for it with information technology."

Also in Jacksonville, the electric utility reported that providing better service was a particularly salient reason for adopting the use of laptop computers in service vehicles. The utility was committed to providing same day power restoration after a customer's whose electricity had been turned off paid his or her bill. With laptops in the field that were linked via radio to the central computer system, technicians had up to date information about shut-offs and turn-ons literally at their fingertips.

Function or activity specific reasons, as might be expected, are tied to specific functions, and they can be as numerous and varied as the functions that are automated. Here are a few examples. Denver, CO, used its GIS system to address equity concerns and also to increase revenue generation from stormwater billing. In Denver, the city government bills property owners for the amount of impervious surface (which produces stormwater runoff that the city must manage) on their property. Manual methods of estimating the amounts of impervious surface had led to concerns about the fairness of the billing system. Using a GIS improved the accuracy of determining the amount of impervious surface. It also enabled the city to produce twice as much revenue from stormwater billing in the first full year of use of the GIS than previously ($10 million versus $5 million).

Denver also used video arraignment of suspected criminals. This system was implemented because of both cost and safety considerations. The jail is located 20 miles from the courts. This had meant that safety officers had to transport prisoners to and from the courts and guard them. Two-way, interactive video arraignment reduced the need for transport and simplified the task of guarding the prisoners. It also reduced the risk of harm to the safety officers.

New Orleans, LA, has a fully staffed, in-house computer-based training facility that provides training to all city staff. New Orleans has estimated that this facility has saved the city considerable money. On average, it costs $31.00 per pupil in-house versus $160.00 from a local university for the same training.

These are just a few of numerous examples from the UMBC case studies that confirm that local governments have both general and specific reasons for adopting leading edge information technologies. Although these governments do not often conduct elaborate analyses to justify the adoption of the technologies, they nevertheless approach them quite seriously and fully expect that the technologies will perform up to the cities' expectations. Whether they do is addressed in the following section on the impacts of leading edge information technologies.

In addition to reasons provided by managers and end-users of leading edge information technologies, several factors in city government tend to operate to either facilitate or hinder adoption.[6] Among the most important facilitating factors, as identified in the UMBC case studies were:

- *Support of top officials* —usually one or more of the following: the mayor, city manager, information technology director, key department heads, strategically placed (and technologically "smart") end-users.
- *Pressure from end users* – especially found in the more technically inclined departments such as engineering, planning and transportation. These are also departments in which personnel are likely to have been trained for their profession using computers and who use computers in their daily activities.
- *Positive organizational climate* – such things as support for innovation from top officials, support for risk-taking, the adoption of formal plans for adopting technology, a history of innovativeness and managerial proficiency.
- *Information technology champion* – often this was the information technology director, but it easily could be a mayor, city manager, or a key department head. Without a champion, information technology did not receive the type of support that enabled cities to be on the leading edge of innovation.
- *Slack budgetary resources* – having money makes buying and supporting innovative information technology much easier than not having money. Additionally, "special" sources of revenue were especially helpful (e.g., funds from the rate structure for utility departments and funds from RICO type statutes for police departments).[7]
- *Skilled personnel* – this speaks to the importance of having well-trained, capable technical personnel to assist with planning, acquiring, implementing and providing on-going support for leading edge information technologies.
- *Central information technology department* – cities with the most effective and most "user-friendly" central information technology departments were clearly the most innovative.

The case studies also found that there were several factors in city government that operated to hinder the adoption of leading edge information technologies. These included:

- *Lack of understanding of information technology by top officials* – this was often noted by respondents as they compared different city officials or administrations and noted which were or were not computer literate. In one city, when a new administration came into office, the mayor's staff wrestled not with ensconcing themselves in the best offices, but in finding outlets to connect their computers. According to respondents in this city, this signaled the arrival of top officials who understood information technology and for whom it would be a priority.
- *Lack of budgetary resources* - Several cities complained that tight budgets

meant that they could not do enough in the area of information technology. Having surplus funds was certainly better than not. (However, it was also clear that even in cities with tight budgets, if the top officials and administrators supported information technology, resources would be made available.)
- *Strategically placed individuals* – just as key individuals could be facilitators of the adoption of leading edge information technologies, strategically placed persons could also hinder it. These persons could include: department heads, an occasional information technology director, key end-users, and, in several cities, the budget office came in for particular criticism for "blocking" adoption of information technology.
- *Central information technology department* – just as the central information technology department could be a key facilitator, so it could also be seen as a negative factor in innovation. In a few of the cities, some respondents felt the department either remained a roadblock to innovation or had only recently "got religion." Getting religion generally meant that the department had abandoned what might be called the central DP shop mentality and had embraced the PC age and the age of decentralized computing.
- *Lack of inter-departmental coordination* – this was clearest in those cities which had the strongest tradition of departmental autonomy. And it showed up most obviously in GIS systems, with various departments developing their own (often incompatible) GIS systems.

Impacts of Adoption

Having discussed why cities adopt leading edge information technologies, it is fair to ask whether cities' expectations (or, perhaps, hopes) concerning the outcomes of using these technologies are met? Local governments in general and the case study cities in particular rarely perform formal studies, especially cost-benefit analyses, of the adoption of information technologies. Indeed, the absence of cost justifications for such technologies was a complaint made by many a city budget office. (On the other hand, line departments complain that budget offices made it far too difficult to acquire information technology by requiring cost justifications.) In any event, the absence of such studies means that analysis of the results of adopting leading edge information technologies have been and will largely be based on the perceptions of managers and end-users. Perceptions, however, especially those of managers and key end users, are valuable because they are based on what these individuals observe and experience concerning the performance of information technologies (see, for example, Northrop, et al., 1990).

The evidence from a variety of studies over the past two decades of research on information technology in local government points unambiguously to the following conclusion: the impacts of information technology in local governments are mostly positive, although the technologies are not without problems. Moreover, most local governmental officials and end users are quite satisfied with these technologies and believe that they have produced mainly positive results. (See Kling, 1978; Kraemer, Dutton and Northrop, 1981; Danziger and Kraemer, 1986; Norris, 1989; Northrop, et al., 1990; Kraemer and Norris, 1994; Norris and Kraemer, 1996; Kraemer and Dedrick, 1997.)

Among other things, these studies have found that information technology generally enhances rather than diminishes jobs and makes work easier and more enjoyable. At the same time, however, the technology can increase the pressure on employees and produce employee frustration. Information technology also improves efficiency and accuracy, provides more and better information for decision-makers, enables employees to provide better service to citizens, and improves speed and timeliness. Moreover, positive impacts are reported by managers and end users alike and also are reported regardless of gender or job category (Norris, 1992).

Yet, the use of information technology is not a one-sided coin. Among problems with information technologies, the following reported in the 1997 ICMA survey are fairly typical (Table 9). The major problems encountered by the reporting jurisdictions included: personnel training, underutilization of computer capacity, resistance to change, resistance to use, and vendor service—all reported by over a quarter of respondents. A similar question on the 1993 survey produced similar results for both central systems and PCs (Norris and Kraemer, 1996). Among other things, this data suggest that local governments believe that they do not do a good job training their employees to use information technology. Additionally, and perhaps as a result of inadequate training, nearly a third of cities believe that employees resist change, resist use, and do not use computers to their capacity. Finally, vendor service was reported by over a quarter of cities as a problem. In 1993, 26 percent of central system cities and 24 percent of PC only cities said that vendor service was a problem (Norris and Kraemer, 1996).

The UMBC case studies produced similar results. When asked about the impacts of leading edge information technologies, elected officials, managers and end users were nearly unanimous in their view that these technologies had produced mainly positive results – and positive results of the sort that have previously been reported in the literature. However, there was also somewhat of a "wait and see" attitude. That is, respondents in these cities felt that the leading edge information technologies had not yet lived up to their potential. This was because, for the most part, the technologies had not been fully developed and deployed within the cities.

Table 9: Problems With Computers

Problem	Percent
Personnel Training	46.3
Under utilization of computer capacity	37.2
Resistance to organizational change	31.0
Resistance to use	30.2
Vendor service	27.4
Equipment performance	19.0
Software availability	16.1
Integration of micros with mainframe/mini-computers	15.0
Equipment reliability	14.6
Equipment and quality	10.4

Source: 1997 ICMA Information Technology Survey.

One common negative impact that was reported by several of the case study cities concerned the start-up or initial implementation of leading edge information technologies. Start-up problems included technical difficulties with hardware and software and difficulties managing implementation. Here, respondents reported that implementation was always more difficult and took longer than initially estimated and was more frustrating. However, they also reported that after implementation was completed and a technology was in routine use that its impacts were nearly always positive.

The case study cities provided numerous examples of positive impacts.[8] Here are three that are typical. The electric utility in Jacksonville, FL, reported a 200 percent improvement in the productivity of technicians' handling of "trouble" calls in the field after they were equipped with laptop computers linked via radio to the central computer system. In Philadelphia, PA, the implementation of an automated mugshot system saved the city $600,000 annually. Finally, the finance department in Overland Park, KS, used the GIS system to identify cable TV customers located within the city on whom the cable company was not paying the city's franchise tax. This resulted in a net additional income to the city of $30,000 per year.

Future Trends

In part because city governments believe that leading edge information technologies produce largely positive impacts, one obvious future trend will be that more city governments will adopt these technologies. Additionally, more leading edge technologies will be adopted by cities. In other words, future surveys of information technology adoption among city governments will find that a larger fraction of cities have adopted leading edge technologies and that a larger number of such technologies have been adopted. These two trends are nearly inescapable. They clearly have been the case for at least the past five decades: more cities have adopted information technology and more technologies are being adopted each successive year. (And, each year, the sophistication of the technology increases.) Moreover, there is no evidence to suggest that these trends will stop. For the moment, Table 8 provides a handy guide to the most likely leading edge information technologies that cities will be adopting in the near future. However, the prudent reader will understand that this list is likely to have a short shelf life.

A third trend is that leading edge information technologies will continue to penetrate cities more deeply and, as deeper penetration occurs so will greater pay-offs from use. As more sophisticated technologies like GIS, document imaging, multimedia, and others become more well developed and deployed within city governments, as their use grows (especially as it grows across department and functional lines), they will become institutionalized and routinized. As this occurs, so too will a greater incidence of positive impacts.

A fourth trend is that as new and more sophisticated information technologies are adopted by city governments, integration of and support for them will become even more critical than is currently the case. One of the findings from the case studies is that "interoperability" is desired by nearly all cities with extensive information technology operations. In essence, interoperability means that any user can sit at any workstation and access any software or database (to which he or she has authorization) in the organization—regardless of platforms, operating systems or physical location in the organization. Today, however, because of the multiple and often incompatible platforms and operating systems that are often found in city governments, interoperability is an elusive goal. As cities add even more information technologies that themselves are quite sophisticated, there is little reason to think that this situation will change. Indeed, achieving interoperability may be the one of the biggest challenges city governments will face in the next several years in their quest for the most the effective and efficient use of information technology.

Finally, although more of a finding than a trend, city population as a measure of city size will remain a key determinant in the number and type of leading edge information technologies adopted. While the overall extent of adoption of leading edge information technologies among city governments can be expected to increase, the greatest extent of adoption will be among larger jurisdictions. Larger cities will adopt more leading edge information technologies than their smaller cousins. Larger cities will also adopt the more sophisticated and advanced information technologies as well. This will be due, in part, to the relatively greater budgetary resources possessed by larger cities. In part, it is due to need— a city of half a million has a far greater need for an AFIS than a city of 5,000. And, in part, it is due to the greater institutional ability of larger cities -- which are more likely than smaller ones to have central information technology departments—to plan, implement and support advanced information technologies (Norris and Kraemer, 1996).

End Notes

[1] It is useful to distinguish between being on the leading versus the bleeding edge. This difference has been brought to my attention numerous times by local government practitioners. Being on the *leading edge* means to be among the first wave of adopters of a *proven* technology. Innovation in the form of early adoption in such a case, while carrying some risk, is not inherently risky. Being on the *bleeding edge*, is much riskier (and, therefore, in the world of local government, is not often recommended) because it involves being among the first adopters of a technology that has not been tested and proven in the field. A good example of the latter would be a local government that purchased a complex computer system from a vendor to automate a critical function knowing that the vendor would have to write the software anew, test, debug, and install it for the very first time in the local government. Many a local government computer system has foundered in precisely this manner. Few local governments want to find themselves on the bleeding edge of technology innovation.

[2] This city had just completed an extensive long range planning process and did not want to "be studied" quite so soon again.

[3] The study also endeavored to provide balance in its selection of cities using the following additional criteria: region of the country, population and form of government. Cities in the Southeast were over-sampled somewhat, in part to meet an

objective of one of the project's funders. No cities smaller than 100,000 in population were included because the literature shows a direct relationship between adoption of information technology and city population. Finally, no cities over 1.5 million were included because of the amount of effort and time that would be required to conduct a case study in such a city.

[4] This adoption rate may be artificially inflated due to question wording. The question included radios and cellular phones to define wireless services. And, cities using radios but not cellular phones may have responded.

[5] Unfortunately, there was no comparable list of questions in the 1997 ICMA information technology survey.

[6] Most of these factors are not unique to the UMBC case studies, but have been observed repeatedly in the literatures on information technology in local governments and diffusion of innovations.

[7] The RICO, or anti-racketeering, statute, enables police departments to retain some or all of the funds derived from the sale of property in drug arrests.

[8] They provided very few examples of negative impacts even though researchers probed for them.

References

Bingham, Richard D. (1976). *The Adoption of Innovation by Local Government.* Lexington, MA: Lexington Books.

Danziger, James N., and Kenneth L. Kraemer. (1986). People and Computers: The Impact of Computing on End Users in Organizations. New York: Columbia University Press.

Kling, Rob (1978). *The Impacts of Computing on the Work of Managers, Data Analysts and Clerks.* Irvine, CA: Public Policy Research Organization, University of California-Irvine.

International City/County Management Associatio. (1993). *Information Technology Survey.* Washington, D.C.: Author. (Reported in Norris and Kraemer, 1994.)

International City/County Management Association (1997). *Information Technology Survey.* Washington, D.C.: Author. (Reported in Norris and Demeter, forthcoming 1999.)

Kraemer, Kenneth L., and Jason Dedrick (1997). "Computing in Public Organizations. *Journal of Public Administration Research and Theory.* Vol 7.

Kraemer, Kenneth L., William H. Dutton, and Alana Northrop (1981). *The Management of Information Systems.* New York: Columbia University Press.

Kraemer, Kenneth L., and Donald F. Norris (1994). "Computers in Local Government," in *1994 Municipal Yearbook.* Washington, DC: International City/County Management Association.

Norris, Donald F. (1984). Computers and Small Local Governments. *Public Administration Review.* Vol. 44, No. 1. (January/February).

Norris, Donald F. (1989). High Tech in City Hall: Uses and Effects of Microcomputers in United States Local Governments. *Social Science Computer Review.* Vol 7. No. 2. (Summer)

Norris, Donald F. (1992). Gender, Job, and the Effects of Microcomputers in Public Organizations. *State and Local Government Review.* Vol 24. No. 2 (Spring).

Norris, Donald F., and Lori Demeter. Forthcoming 1999. "Computers and Local Government." *(1999) Municipal Yearbook.* Washington, D.C.: International City/County Management Association.

Norris, Donald F., and Patricia D. Fletcher (1998). "Leading Edge Information Technology in American Cities: Adoption, Uses and Effects." Work in progress. Baltimore: Maryland Institute for Policy Analysis and Research, University of Maryland, Baltimore County.

Norris, Donald F., and Kenneth L. Kraemer (1994). "Leading Edge Computer Use in U. S. Municipalities." *Special Data Issue.* Washington, DC: International City/County Management Association.

Norris, Donald F., and Kenneth L. Kraemer (1996). "Mainframe and PC Computing in American Cities: Myths and Realities." *Public Administration Review.* Vol. 56, No. 6 (November/December 1996).

Norris, Donald F., and Vincent J. Webb (1982). *Microcomputers: Baseline Data Reports.* Vol. 15, No. 7. Washington, D. C.: International City/County Management Association.

Northrop, Alana, Kenneth L. Kraemer, Debora Dunkle, and John Leslie King. (1990). "Payoffs from Computerization: Lessons over Time." *Public Administration Review.* Vol 50. No 5 (September/October).

Rogers, Everett M. (1983). 3d. Ed. *Diffusion of Innovations.* New York: Free Press.

Walker, Jack L. (1969). "The Diffusion of Innovations Among the American States." *American Political Science Review.* Vol 63.

9

Management Information Systems in the Public Sector

by
Richard Heeks
Institute for Development Policy
and Management
University of Manchester
England

Management information systems (MIS) are fundamental for public sector organizations seeking to support the work of managers. Yet they are often ignored in the rush to focus on 'sexier' applications. This chapter aims to redress the balance by providing a detailed analysis of public sector MIS. It first locates MIS within the broader management monitoring and control systems that they support. Understanding the broader systems and the relationship to public sector inputs, processes, outputs and outcomes is essential to understanding MIS. The chapter details the different types of reports that MIS produce, and uses this as the basis for an MIS model and a description of the decision-making benefits that computerized MIS can bring. Finally, the chapter describes generic public sector MIS that address internal government transactions, public administration/regulation, and public service delivery. Real-world examples of all types are provided from the U.S., England, Africa, and Asia.

Introduction

Management information systems can be defined as information systems that provide reports which assist the managerial monitoring and control of organizational functions, resources or other responsibilities.

MIS were first developed during the 1950s and 1960s but came into the organizational mainstream somewhat later. There was a rich literature on MIS during the 1970s, continuing into

Figure 1: Monitoring and Control System Model

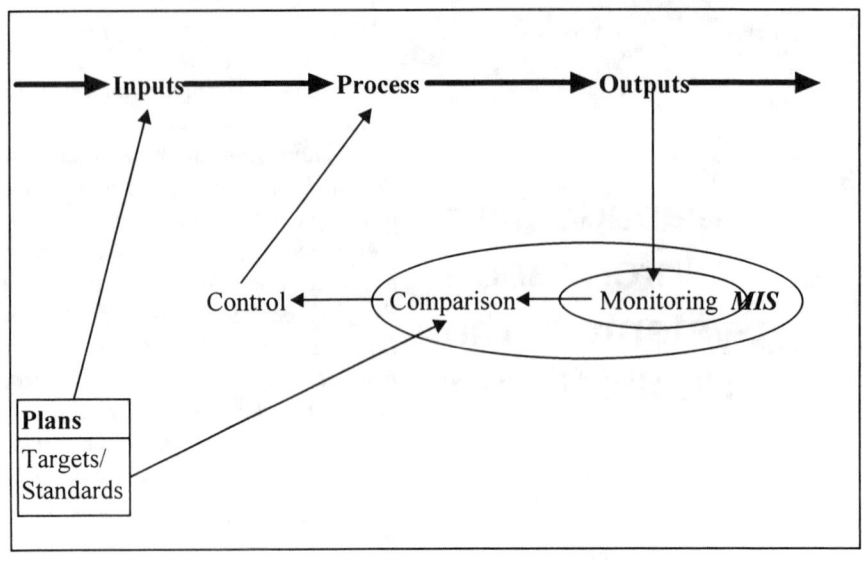

the 1980s (e.g. Davis, 1974; Davis & Olson, 1984). However, the explosion of other organizational applications of IT has led MIS – at least as defined above – to retain only a small foothold in many more recent publications. Despite their book titles, for example, Hicks (1993) devotes just one chapter to MIS, whilst Laudon & Laudon (1998) devote just a few pages. Nonetheless the fundamental importance of MIS has meant some writers continue to provide a broad and deep discussion of the topic (e.g. Zwass, 1992; Lucey, 1997).

Our discussion in this chapter begins with a deeper understanding of the managerial processes that management information systems support.

Management Monitoring and Control Systems

A generic model of a monitoring and control system is shown in Figure 1. This monitoring and control system consists of four main elements:

- *A process.* At the core of the system is some kind of process that turns inputs into outputs. Let us take the example of a public sector training project that seeks to provide new skills for the unemployed. This project turns inputs of money, equipment and staff labor into outputs of skilled people who are trained via processes of training delivery.
- *A monitoring mechanism.* This mechanism gathers information about the outputs from the process. For example, it would gather information about the number of people trained and the extent of their new skills in the training project.
- *A comparison mechanism.* This compares the information gathered about current performance with information on previously-set plans, benchmarks, targets, etc. These two types of information represent the information needs of the monitoring and control system. For example, this mechanism would

compare information on actual skills gained with skill gain targets. This part of the system is often known as the 'evaluation mechanism' (as in the phrase, 'monitoring and evaluation').
- *A control mechanism.* This decides upon and then ensures implementation of corrective action based on the output of the comparison. For example, where skill levels produced by training were lower than expected, changes to the method or location of training might be decided upon and implemented.

Monitoring and control therefore represents a *feedback loop*, in which information about a later stage is fed back into control of an earlier stage. Where all is well, the system's only function is to monitor and report. Where a problem—a shortfall between the actual and the desired situation—arises, the system's function is to assess the impact of that problem, and to decide on and then implement remedial action. Most organizational systems are intended to work on a *negative feedback* principle where corrective action is in the opposite direction to monitored deviations from norms. Take the case of a budget system. Where the monitoring mechanism indicated that more than budget was being spent, feedback should lead the control mechanism to correct this by starting to spend less.

Rationally, the system provides the mechanisms by which the organization a) knows if it is achieving its objectives, and b) achieves its objectives in the face of problems. In order for this to happen, all the following must be present:
- outputs that can be measured,
- a monitoring mechanism that does measure the outputs,
- a monitoring mechanism that produces information on the outputs that is accurate, timely, relevant, and complete,
- a comparison mechanism,
- targets against which to compare,
- a control and implementation mechanism, and
- an overall feedback loop that does not take too long to be effective.

The place of management information systems in the model is indicated in Figure 1. As shown, MIS can be of two different types:
- *Monitoring MIS*: these MIS merely gather information about output performance and present it to the manager, who will then do the comparison him/herself.
- *Monitoring and comparison MIS*: for these MIS, the preset standards for output performance have been entered onto the computer system. The MIS is therefore able to perform the comparisons itself. This forms the basis of exception reporting, discussed below.

Computers are not a necessary part of this or any other management system. There are many manual methods of monitoring and comparing, such as:
- tables of accounts and budgets,
- a chart of staff names and absence days, or
- a line on the wall, which when reached by a diminishing pile of stock items, indicates that they should be reordered.

However, computerization will be our focus in this chapter.

Complicating the Simple Picture

So far, a relatively simple picture has been presented of both management system and information system. However, there are four main ways in which these systems differ, as described next.

i. What is monitored: inputs, outputs and outcomes

The model above places a process at the center of the model. But, for many management information systems, the focus is on the measure being monitored and reported upon. In overall organizational terms, these measures are not always outputs, but can be divided into three categories:
- *Inputs*: the resources that are used by the organization.
- *Outputs*: the direct services (or products) produced by the organization.
- *Outcomes*: the wider impacts of organizational outputs.

To differentiate these, let us take the example of an enterprise development agency. Its inputs would include general financial expenditure and hours of staff time worked. Its outputs could include number of clients served, and number and size of loans provided or guaranteed. The outcomes could include number of new enterprises created, enterprise growth rates, number or proportion of people employed in enterprises, and average income per capita.

We can therefore redraw part of the system model, as shown in Figure 2, to show the different possible monitoring measures.

An MIS can monitor one or more of these measures. In the latter case, it will need some mechanism for integrating or at least coordinating the different measures.

ii. What is controlled: plans, inputs and processes

The control mechanism can focus on one or more different parts of the model:
- *Processes*. The training project example given above described control of processes.
- *Inputs*. Alternatively, information may be fed back further 'upstream' than processes, and affect the inputs to the process. For example, the information

Figure 2: Different Measures Monitored by Monitoring and Control Systems

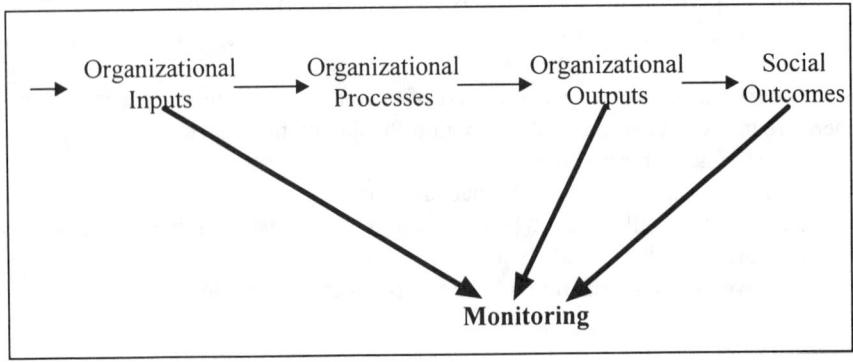

gathered on skill levels produced by the training project might indicate that, to generate the required outputs, altering the training method or location was not enough. Instead, more labor (e.g., a higher trainer:trainee ratio) or more investment (e.g., in better-paid, better-qualified trainers) was required.

- *Plans.* Moving even further 'upstream' in the model, information may be fed back to affect the original planning of the process. For example, the information gathered might indicate that no amount of 'tinkering' with inputs or methods can produce the originally-planned outputs. The plans themselves would therefore have to be amended. These changes could be directed at increasingly higher-order parts of planning:
  - *Amended targets.* For example, revised output targets on the number of skilled trainees or the depth of required skills to be produced.
  - *Amended immediate objectives.* For example, changing the project to produce a different set of skills.
  - *Amended intermediate objectives.* For example, changing the project type from increasing the employability of the jobless through training to provision of a direct employment subsidy.
  - *Amended overall objectives.* For example, changing from trying to raise employment levels in a poor rural district to encouraging relocation to areas of high employment demand.

We can therefore redraw part of the system model, as shown in Figure 3, to show the different focus of control mechanisms.

Figure 3: Different Control Focus in Monitoring and Control Systems

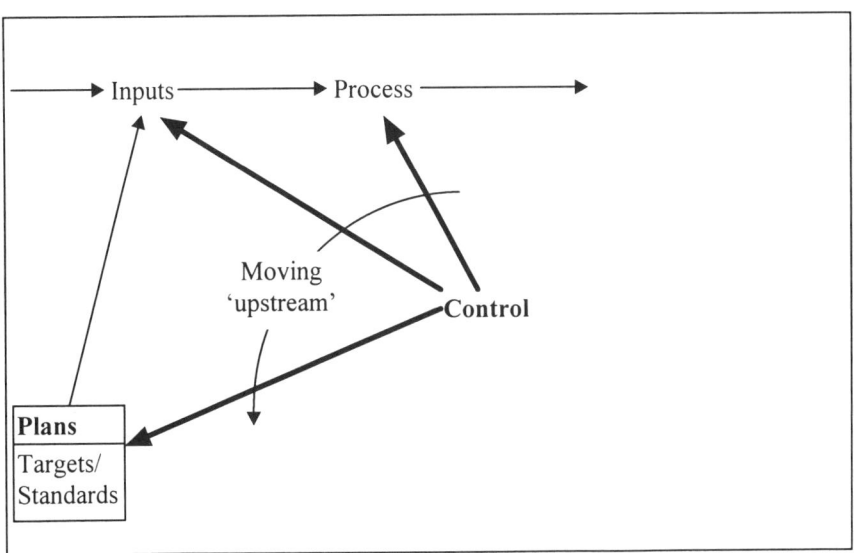

iii. Management role supported

Management information systems can support the different management roles of public administration:

- *Operational management.* This role is often largely supervisory in nature and so MIS for operational management may well be used to support day-to-day monitoring and control. Such MIS will not contain 'higher-order' feedback to plans. These MIS might involve any of the areas in which basic operational information systems function such as accounting and human resources. As described below, systems supporting this type of role may be particularly appropriate for automation of control and decision making because of the relatively narrow, structured nature of the role. Sea Lake County Welfare Department, for example, used an operational MIS to support the day-to-day monitoring and authorization of food stamps and other welfare payments (Schultheis & Sumner, 1995).
- *Tactical management.* MIS for this role operate in the same areas as for operational management, but take an organizationally-broader and longer-term perspective. There might be a greater emphasis on human decision making (because situations are less certain and structured) and on more 'upstream' control feedback. In the Sea Lake case, tactical MIS were used to monitor accumulated reasons for welfare denial, and for welfare case opening and closing.
- *Strategic management.* MIS can and do support strategic management. However, rational description of the strategic role places a particular emphasis on planning and, for more senior managers, on an integrated view of the organization. This is seen as being supported mainly by executive information systems. In the Sea Lake case, the executive information system incorporated both internal welfare data and external data on government regulations to assist strategic planning.

Figure 4: A Model of Automated Decision Making

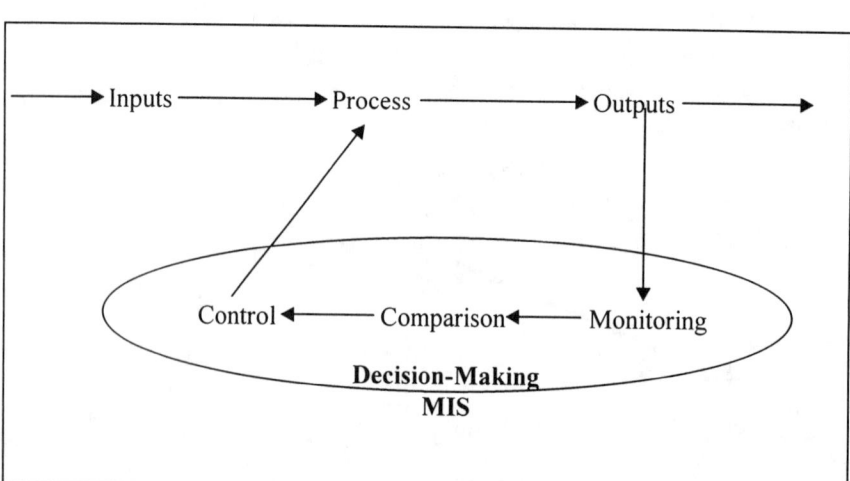

iv. Automation of control

In many management information systems, the output from the comparison stage forms an input to human decision making. However, in some information systems the process of decision making may be automated. For example, inventory information systems can gather data on the level of stocks and suggest the decision that particular items should be reordered if stocks fall below a certain level. Some such systems even create the order form and send it electronically to a supplier. Such automated decision-making systems are represented in Figure 4.

Features of Management Information Systems

You should by now understand the main rationale for a management information system. In order to draw up a model of an MIS, two further elements must be described: the link to data-gathering systems and the production of reports.

Link to Data-Gathering Systems

MIS often rely on monitoring data produced by a corporate database. In many cases, the division between the two systems is not obvious. For example, many users merely perceive that they have a payroll system that collects payroll data, produces both operational payroll information and management reports, and is used for both operation and monitoring/control of the payroll system.

Reports, Reports, Reports

Central to its monitoring and control roles, an MIS produces reports. This is mainly what managers perceive about an MIS since these are its tangible outputs. Reports come in many forms, as described below. They can be differentiated in two main ways: by content and by schedule.

i. Differentiation by content

MIS reports fall into three main categories of content:
- *Detail report.* This contains all relevant information on the report topic. For example, a detailed payroll report might give the following information for all staff: employee number, name, wage/salary rate, standard monthly earnings, standard tax payable, and each individual monthly payment for the year to-date.
- *Summary report.* This contains a summarization of information on the report topic. For example, the total number of staff in each unit, each unit's total payroll bill for this year and last year, and the percentage change between the two. Some summaries may be recognized performance indicators. For example, one measure of a unit's performance might be its total actual payroll bill as a proportion of the total budgeted payroll bill.
- *Exception report.* This filters out information to provide just that which is deemed to be most important, according to some pre-set criteria. It may be summarized or detailed. For example, a report could include employee name, total individual payroll payments this and last year, and percentage change between the two, only for those staff whose pay rose by more than ten per cent.

These reports may find themselves combined. For example, a report might:
- provide information on unit salary and income tax payment totals (summary),
- for only those units where the total was more than 5 per cent above last year's total (exception), and
- allow the manager to break this down into individual staff salaries and tax payments if required (detail).

ii. Differentiation by schedule

MIS reports fall into three main categories of schedule:
- *Periodic report*. This is produced at regular intervals: daily, weekly, monthly, quarterly, etc. For example, a report of organizational unit salary totals produced every month after staff have been paid.
- *Event-triggered report*. This is produced in response to a particular event or set of conditions. An example of the former might be a detailed payroll report, produced once the first tranche of federal government funding for a project was agreed. An example of the latter might be a detailed payroll report produced if the total payroll bill in a unit exceeded budget in any month by more than 3 per cent. In some cases, more than a report might be triggered. For instance, the last example could also trigger production of a pro forma memo to the head of unit warning them about their payroll expenditure situation.
- *Request report*. This is produced as and when required in response to an ad hoc request. For example, a payroll report on all staff in the top two salary grades could be produced in response to a politician's concern about increasing public vs. private sector pay differentials for top managers.

The Role of Reports

Periodic summary and detailed reports are the 'bread and butter' of management information systems. For certain older MIS, this might be all that they produced. However, it is the other forms of report that provide MIS with much of their organizational value. If they work correctly, for example, event-triggered reports can take a substantial monitoring workload from managers. Managers know that the computer system is 'watching out' for certain problems and will alert them if these problems arise. Examples could include alerting reports when:
- an unusually large amount of cash is involved in a transaction,
- there is a sudden increase in recorded imports, or
- more than three states report the incidence of Colorado beetle infestation.

Reports with just exception contents provide no redundant information, but just focus the manager on problem areas that require corrective action. This, therefore, helps managers cope with the problem of information overload. Exception reports have a wide variety of applications and can provide, for example:
- just the names of those staff who have been absent more than five times during the past month,
- details of only those loans which have received no repayment for more than eight weeks, or
- codes of only those budget heads which are more than 10 per cent over spent.

One exception report issue lies in the choice of exception condition on which to report. In the loan example, the eight week condition might be a bad choice. It could be that an eight week delay is perfectly normal. The report is therefore unnecessarily targeting many borrowers who are not in trouble. Alternatively, it could be that a default of only two weeks indicates that help is needed. By eight weeks, matters may have deteriorated too far for any outside assistance to be of value. There will have to be an input of both experience and analytical skills in the choice of exception condition.

A second exception report issue relates to data inputs: such reporting can only be relied upon if data inputs are being continuously and reliably gathered.

Request reports provide the manager with a great deal of power. They can produce information that more exactly matches the manager's particular needs at the moment of need. Request reports are often a response to the unexpected. Examples could include reports on:
- the finances of a project, for input to a meeting requested by the project manager,
- those clients who have been occupying a refuge bed for more than six months, in response to a shortage of beds for incoming homeless persons, or
- the past training of a staff member, in response to their request to go on a training course.

Figure 5: Management Information System Model

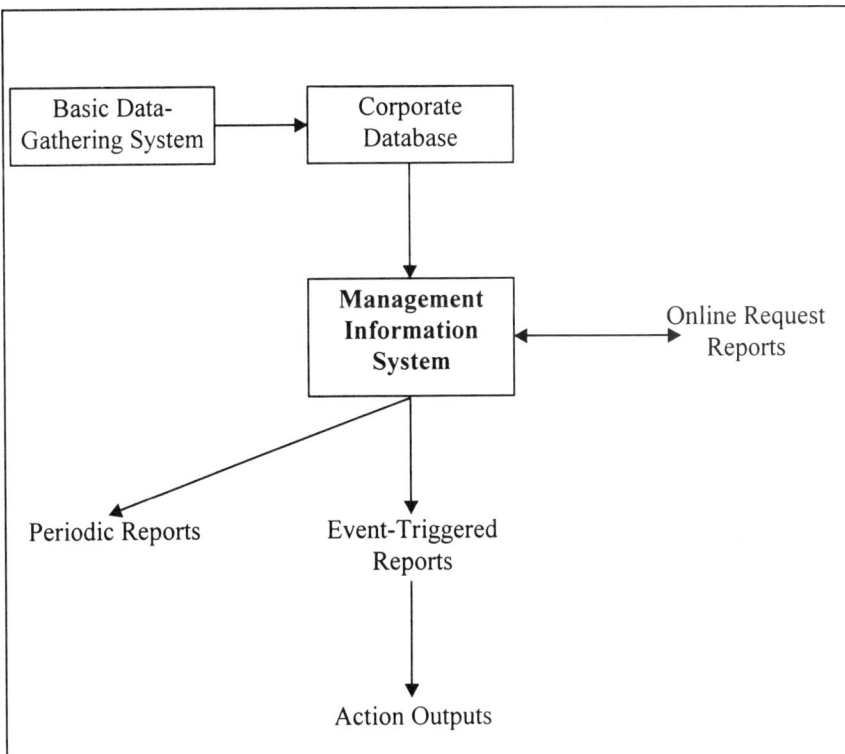

Typically these request reports are produced using search forms or search expressions. Many computerized management information systems allow this to be done online: the request is typed in and the report appears almost immediately on-screen. There will often be a choice of showing the report as a table of figures or, if appropriate, as a graph, or as both.

As with all information systems, the response to the request can only be as good as the data that has been put into the system. MIS data is often entered with the expected rather than the unexpected in mind, leading to the risk that unexpected requests cannot be answered. If, on the other hand, large swathes of data are entered into the MIS 'just in case they are needed', this runs the risk of substantial expenditure on gathering data that is never used. A balance should therefore be struck between the likelihood of needing data in a request plus the value of being able to respond to that request, and the cost of providing that data.

Management Information System Model

Using the further details described above, we can now draw an MIS model that builds on the organization's corporate database, as shown in Figure 5.

In some systems, the separation of basic data-gathering system and MIS would not be so clear cut as depicted here. Instead, they would merely be separate modules of the same overall information system. The data-gathering module would deal largely with data input and storage. The MIS module would deal largely with information retrieval and output.

Benefits of MIS Computerization

If it functions as anticipated, the creation of a monitoring and control system produces, by definition, greater understanding of the organization and a greater ability to manage organizational resources and their performance. Within these systems, and by comparison with manual systems, creation of a computerized, rationally-functioning MIS can produce a number of organizational benefits. These include:

- *Faster decision making and control* through provision of timely information. For example, the MIS described by Anthes (1993 cited in Laudon & Laudon, 1995) provided an early warning of performance problems in bulk buying of inputs by US public agencies. Faster decision making released time that would otherwise be tied up on monitoring. Tottle (1986) describes the introduction of an MIS to assist government agricultural extension workers in Malaysia. Time was released in this case thanks to upward reporting by the computer system and to exception reporting, which focused the extensionists on those farmers with immediate problems.

- *Better decision making and control* through provision of relevant information. The Malaysian government workers described by Tottle (1986) had a much better understanding of what was going on in their area thanks to the introduction of an MIS. They also had more detailed information which allowed them to provide farmers with a better service, and make better use of available resources. Similarly, in the Anthes (1993) example, the statistical analyses gave US state agencies a much better understanding of what was going on in contract bidding. Without the MIS, such an understanding would not have been possible.

In addition, MIS can improve job satisfaction for public servants and can reduce the number of paper records that have to be held.

Examples of Management Information Systems

Management information systems can be introduced to support a variety of public sector applications, as described below.

Internal Transaction-Based MIS

Three main types of management information system fall into this category: accounting, human resources, and 'other'.

i. Accounting MIS

Far more than anything else, the emphasis of public sector MIS has been on money: on monitoring how much has been spent; on comparing this with budget; and on controlling expenditure to bring it in as close as possible to budget at year-end. Examples of this type of computerization range from the Kenyan Ministry of Agriculture (Pinckney et al., 1987) to major U.S. regulatory agencies (Brown, 1999).

Typical reports include:
- Statements of account: month-end, year-end, year-to-date, etc.; these will generally have to be designed to fit with existing regulatory or legislative standards for public sector accounting.
- Warnings of budget head overspending or underspend against target; variance from planned budget can be shown either in absolute or in percentage terms.
- Statements of cash requirements in the month ahead based on payments still owed within accounts payable data.

Table 1: Accounting MIS Report Example

Accounting Report
Department of Land Management
Year-to-date, end September 1999

Expenditure Head	Budget (US$)	Actual (US$)	Variance (US$)	Variance (%)
Salaries	275,900	291,400	**15,500**	**5.6%**
Wages	241,200	248,000	6,800	2.8%
Office Equipment	113,600	141,600	**28,000**	**24.6%**
Utilities	88,500	84,500	-4,000	-4.5%
Transport	69,300	69,300	0	0%
Consumables	54,900	63,800	8,900	**16.2%**
Other	127,100	131,100	4,000	3.1%
TOTAL	970,500	1,029,700	59,200	6.1%

Payroll often represents the main cost for public sector organizations. It has therefore been a starting point for MIS in many organizations, looking to monitor and control salary and income tax payments, and also to issue payments. One focus for payroll MIS in some countries has been to identify and then eliminate 'ghost workers,' who do not exist but whose pay is fraudulently collected by other employees. Cain (1999) describes the importance of this approach in the creation of MIS for the governments of Ghana, Uganda and Zimbabwe. Examples of payroll reports were described above.

An example of a typical accounting MIS report is shown in Table 1.

The MIS reporting Table 1 has been instructed to highlight all variances greater than US$10,000 and all variances greater than five per cent. Rationally, in attempting to control the overspend indicated, management priority would be given to those items highlighted in both columns.

This form of accounting report, based on responsibility for particular budget heads, is widely used in the public sector. Some public sector organizations, especially those providing public services, have developed cost accounting MIS. These aggregate costs horizontally as they are incurred in the delivery of a service. They therefore require allocation of labor and other costs to particular services during the entire process of providing that service.

This is often difficult, but can provide very valuable information in helping to assign a value or cost to a public service, and in comparing costs between public service providers. The British public sector National Health Service, for example, has been creating management information systems that can report health care provision costs down to the level of individual patients. This allows better-informed decisions about prioritizing the use of scarce resources. It also allows health units to compare their costs with other units (HSMU, 1996).

Income-related MIS are the exception rather than the rule in the public sector. MIS are found, though, reporting on:
- Loans and loan repayment. For example, to report those applicants who have been waiting for more than one month to know if their loan application has been granted.
- Customer payments where cost recovery operates in health, education and other social welfare provision. For example, to report those public hospitals which have recovered most and least per patient treated.
- Customer payments to public sector utilities, transportation, rented housing, and enterprises. In these cases, the MIS are likely to be building upon some form of accounts receivable transaction processing system. For example, to report those customers whose accounts remain outstanding 60 days after bills for provision of utility services were issued.

ii. Human resources MIS

Management information systems are used in the entire human resource lifecycle from recruitment to termination or retirement. Reports include:
- *Vacancies*: for example, a detail report on all vacant posts in the organization.
- *Recruitment and selection*: for example, a summary report on the ethnic origin and sex of all job applicants and recruits for use in equal opportunities monitoring.

- *Staff performance*: for example, an exception report on only those secretarial staff who are able to take shorthand dictation and type at over 50 words per minute.
- *Payroll*: see previous page.
- *Training*: for example, an ad hoc report on all those staff who have received training in gender awareness.
- *Staff promotion*: for example, a detail report on all performance assessments for a potentially-promotable member of staff.
- *Staff departure*: for example, a comparative report on turnover rates and reason for departure in the information systems and accounting departments.
- *Pensions*: for example, a summary report on recent annual pension fund growth rates.
- *Other*: for example, a comparative report on workplace accident rates on different days of the week; this and other categories may relate to government reporting and compliance.

The State of Vermont developed a human resources management information system (albeit both over time and over budget) that covered a number of these reporting functions (Cats-Baril & Thompson, 1995). Similar experiences are reported in the development of a personnel information system with MIS capabilities for Northamptonshire County Council, a local government body in England (Palmer, 1993).

iii. Other MIS

Public sector inventory information systems tend to be relatively basic and/or automated. The aim of an inventory MIS is to monitor stock levels and to control stocks to ensure that all items are neither overstocked nor understocked.

MIS may also report on other entities such as fixed assets, financial investments and projects. One U.S. regulatory agency, for instance, set up an MIS covering its major facilities in order to monitor, control and then reduce expenditure on those facilities, as requested by Congress (Brown, 1999).

MIS may also combine the functional areas described above. The British Department of Social Security, for instance, has proceeded with development of an integrated MIS covering financial, personnel and resource management (Bellamy & Henderson, 1992).

Public Administration and Regulation MIS

Management information systems have been created to support the whole range of public administration and regulatory activities. In the U.S., for example, the National Drivers Register has MIS facilities to report on driver license details, such as all those within a given state whose license has been revoked or suspended (Danziger, 1991). Similarly, the US Environmental Protection Agency is pushing forward in use of MIS to help monitor and control environmental risks (Sparrow, 1992). Just a couple of other examples are provided here.

i. Buildings registration MIS

Based on data recorded about particular types of buildings, or buildings in a particular locality, this could monitor building ownership and use, and produce

reports on, for instance:
- all details of one individual building (building code, address, description, owner, floor space, utility connections, local tax liabilities, etc.),
- annual growth in the total number of small industrial units in major cities, or
- all buildings within one city block for which no ownership records were lodged.

Japan's registration MIS has these types of uses in mind. It was begun in earnest in 1988 as a 20-year project, and will eventually cover some 40 million buildings and 230 million parcels of land (Snellen, 1991).

ii. Taxation MIS

Based on data recorded about individual tax-paying entities (whether individuals or organizations), this could monitor the payment of taxation, and produce reports on, for instance:
- all details of an individual taxpayer (payer code, name, address, employment, employer, tax code, record of assets, record of recent tax payments and liabilities, etc.),
- a summary of sales tax receipts broken down by sector,
- patterns of non-payment in order to target enforcement efforts more effectively, or,
- the names and addresses of all those registered on public or private payrolls as taxpayers who are also claiming social welfare payments.

The State of New Jersey used the last of these report types to identify welfare cheats and to generate 'estimated savings of $45 million in the first two years of operation' (Danziger, 1991:175).

Public Service Delivery MIS

Many public service providers have developed management information systems to monitor and control the services that they provide. Both the US and UK Social Security agencies have developed MIS to report on the welfare payments and services that they provide (Danziger, 1991; Bellamy & Henderson, 1992). The

Table 2: Public Service MIS Report Example

Performance Report
Department of Education
Change in High School Examination Performance, 1998-99

School	1998 Average Exam Grade	1999 Average Exam Grade	Percentage Change
Jacobson	45.3	51.5	**13.7%**
Chaparral	63.7	66.9	5.0%
Tomoroon	58.8	61.7	4.9%
Beaunine	49.8	51.3	3.0%
Burndale	51.5	47.9	-7.0%
Cheyenne	56.2	46.2	**-17.8%**
AVERAGE	*54.2*	*54.2*	*0%*

British public healthcare system has also been a major investor in MIS as it tries to control healthcare costs and simultaneously improve delivery standards (HSMU, 1996; Ballantine & Cunningham, 1999). One further example is provided here.

i. Education sector MIS for schools

Based on data gathered from individual public schools and from other educational institutions such as exam boards and school inspectorates, this could monitor the provision of education and produce reports on, for instance:
- details of one individual school (school code, name, address, location, staff numbers, student enrollment by year, annual budgets, school facilities, examination grades, etc.),
- a summary of the average staff:student ratio for each state, or
- the name and location of all schools without on-site sports facilities.

An example of a typical school MIS report is shown in Table 2.

The MIS reporting Table 2 has been instructed to present the schools in decreasing order of percentage change and to highlight all percentage changes of more than ten percent. Those raising their average grades by more than ten percent might be the focus for special attention to learn how they achieved this (or to probe for exam fraud!). Those with averages falling by more than ten percent might be prioritized for external assistance or inspection.

Individual schools can also make use of MIS. Hobmoor Junior and Infant School, a public school in Birmingham, England, introduced a computerized attendance system to produce MIS reports that monitor pupil attendance. This improved the Principal's ability to understand and control absence patterns, resulting in a 2.5 percent increase in attendance rates (Capita, 1998).

Conclusion

Management information systems form a bedrock of IT use in the public sector. They are therefore found in all sections of the public sector and in all countries, as the examples cited in this chapter suggest.

Of course, different people use the term 'management information system' differently. The term should therefore not form the basis for arguments about what an MIS is and is not. So long as you and those with whom you work understand and agree on a definition, that is good enough. Similarly, when dealing with written material, you need to be able to understand and communicate, not get locked into doctrinal debate.

On the basis of our definition provided here, though, we can end by summarizing a few general points about MIS that differentiate them from other types of public sector information systems:
- Monitoring and control is central; the focus is therefore mainly on information about what has happened (or is happening) rather than, as with planning, what will happen.
- Reports are generally based on relatively simple analysis techniques.
- MIS normally feed into some human decision making, based on their reports; such decision making is usually structured or semi-structured.

- MIS are mainly targeted at operational and tactical management levels.
- Unless custom-written, MIS are often based on a database system, because of the superior query and reporting capabilities of database management systems.

References

Anthes, G.H. (1993). Stat tool weeds out bid-rigging companies, Computerworld, July 5.

Ballantine, J.A. & Cunningham, N. (1999). Strategic information systems planning: applying private sector frameworks in UK public healthcare, in R.B. Heeks (ed.), *Reinventing Government in the Information Age*. London: Routledge.

Bellamy, C. & Henderson, A. (1992). The UK Social Security Benefits Agency: a case study of the information polity?, *Informatization and the Public Sector*, 2(1), 1-26.

Brown, D.M. (1999). Information systems for improved performance management: development approaches in US public agencies, in R.B. Heeks (ed.), *Reinventing Government in the Information Age*. London: Routledge.

Cain, P. (1999). Automating personnel records for improved management of human resources: the experience of three African governments, in R.B. Heeks (ed.), *Reinventing Government in the Information Age*. London: Routledge.

Capita (1998). *Case Study: Attendance.* http://www.sims.co.uk/interest/CaseStudies/attendance.htm

Cats-Baril, W. & Thompson, R. (1995). Managing information technology projects in the public sector, *Public Administration Review*, 55(6), 559-66.

Danziger, J.N. (1991). Management information systems and interorganizational relations within the American governmental system, *Informatization and the Public Sector*, 1(3), 169-87.

Davis, G.B. (1974). *Management Information Systems*. New York: McGraw-Hill.

Davis, G.B. & Olson, M.H. (1984). *Management Information Systems (2nd edn.)*. New York: McGraw-Hill.

Hicks, J.O. (1993). *Management Information Systems* (3rd edn.). St. Paul, MN: West Publishing.

HSMU (1996). *The Evaluation of the NHS Resource Management Programme in England*. Manchester, England: Health Services Management Unit, University of Manchester.

Laudon, K.C. & Laudon, J.P. (1995). *Information Systems* (3rd edn.). Fort Worth, TX: Dryden Press.

Laudon, K.C. & Laudon, J.P. (1998). *Management Information Systems* (5th edn.). Upper Saddle River, NJ: Prentice Hall.

Lucey, T. (1997). *Management Information Systems* (8th edn.). London: Letts Educational.

Palmer, J. (1993). CPIS: three years on, in *Computers in Personnel*. London: Institute of Personnel Management.

Pinckney, T.C., Cohen, J.M. & Leonard, D.K. (1987). Kenya's introduction of microcomputers to improve budgeting and financial management in the Ministry of Agriculture, in S.R. Ruth & C.K. Mann (eds.), *Microcomputers in Public Policy.* Boulder, CO: Westview Press.

Schultheis, R. & Sumner, M. (1995). *Management Information Systems* (3rd edn.). Chicago: Irwin.

Snellen, I.Th.M. (1991). Informatization in Japanese public administration, *Informatization and the Public Sector,* 1(4), 247-67.

Sparrow, M.K. (1992). Informing enforcement, *Informatization and the Public Sector*, 2(3), 197-212.

Tottle, G. (1986). The use of computing techniques to support agricultural extension in rural development, *Information Technology for Development,* 1(3), 187-98.

Zwass, V. (1992). *Management Information Systems.* Dubuque, IA: WCB Publishers.

10

The Software Toolkit Approach for Public Administrators

by
Carl Grafton
and
Anne Permaloff
Auburn University at Montgomery

Almost any governmental task employing a computer can be accomplished more efficiently with a variety of tools rather than any single tool. Basic tools for inclusion in the software toolkit are word processing, spreadsheets, statistics, and database management programs. Beyond these, presentation graphics, optical character recognition (OCR), and scheduling software can be helpful depending upon the job at hand.

This chapter concerns computer applications and information technology in government. It could have been organized by public administration task such as human resource management or budgeting, but each governmental function uses several software tools that are not unique to that function. Thus a human resource manager uses word processing software and probably a spreadsheet and a database management program. The same could be said of someone involved in budgeting. This example suggests that a tool kit approach that concentrates on software type is a more useful way to organize this subject matter.

Topics covered in this chapter include: word processing and desktop publishing, spreadsheets, statistics packages, database management, presentation software, project planning software, graphics for illustrations, optical character recognition, network applications, and geographic information systems. Since most readers are likely to have substantial word processing experience, it would be unproductive to devote much space to word processing per se. The same applies to

Copyright© 1999, Idea Group Publishing.

searching the Web. At the opposite extreme, Web page creation programs are too complex to discuss here.[1]

The Document-centric Perspective

Microsoft president Bill Gates and others suggest that thinking in terms of such categories as word processing and spreadsheet software is obsolete. Gates prefers to focus on the document. For example, a memo would typically begin as text produced by word processing but added to it might be data and graphics from a spreadsheet and information from database management software. The authors do not believe that computing has reached the point of seamless integration of traditional software categories that Gates envisions. Word processing, spreadsheet, database management, and presentation software are still sold separately as well as together in suites, and the skills required to master each are substantially different. One Microsoft publication that attempts to explain the use of the Microsoft suite in a document-centric manner hops among traditional software categories, and explains none clearly or adequately (Microsoft, 1995).

A Complete Toolbox

Experience has taught us that to make the most of their time and talents, computer users in government or any other setting should have access to more than one tool for nearly any task that extends much beyond typing a short memo. Access to a variety of tools is usually of greater importance than having the latest version of one.

Word Processing and Desktop Publishing

Word processing software can produce anything from plain text little different in appearance from typewritten material to multi-column layouts with graphic images, photographs, data, and graphics pulled directly from spreadsheets, database management software, and other programs. Their strength lies in making typing and document production accurate and fast. The newer versions of the two major programs in use — Corel WordPerfect (1996) and Microsoft Word (1997) — allow for highlighting of mistyped words and permit the user to enable features that automatically capitalize the first word in a paragraph, place two spaces after a period, and even preset corrections for words frequently mistyped by the user. By marking text, tables of contents, indexes, lists, and the like may be generated automatically. Spelling checkers and a thesaurus are also built into the programs as are grammar checkers, but the latter are not reliable. Other useful tools include table creation with a variety of formatting options, the ability to convert columns to tables, and the ability to automatically shrink or expand a document to a specific page size by having the computer adjust margins, font size, and spacing.

Nonrelational flat file database capabilities are built into these programs. They allow the development of simple sets of data that may then be merged into a variety of documents, customizing them for a variety of purposes. Uses include mailing labels, addresses and salutations in mass mailed letters, simple membership lists, and elemental recordkeeping. Serious record keeping should be done through a relational database rather than word processing programs. Office suites (for example, Corel Office Suite, 1996; Microsoft Office Professional, 1995) contain both word processing programs and relational database management software. The separate programs may be linked together and updated information placed directly from a database (or spreadsheet) into a document.

Desktop Publishing

While relatively simple layouts can be easily produced with standard word processing software, complex designs may require the greater formatting power and flexibility of a desktop (DTP) publishing program such as Page Maker 6.0 (1996) or the bargain priced Serif Page Plus (1996). Basically, DTP programs allow page make-up and layout using objects from a wide variety of sources. These sources include word processor text material, pictures taken from paint and scanning programs, illustrations from drawing programs, clip art, lists and tables from spreadsheets, and more. The graphics produced are generally of much higher quality than those generated by word processing programs. The basic components of resulting publications (newsletters, cards, sales material, etc.) may be saved in template form for repeated use.

The Spreadsheet

No microcomputer tool is more widely used for numerical data storage and analysis than the spreadsheet. For example, among state governors' budget offices the microcomputer spreadsheet is the first choice for data storage, analysis, and graphics (Grafton and Permaloff, 1996). Despite its suitability to a variety of tasks, many public administration practitioners and students know little about spreadsheet operations even when a spreadsheet such as Excel (1996) resides on their hard disks as part of a suite of programs. The widespread unfamiliarity with this powerful and easy to use tool spans local, state, and federal governments and functional areas such as public health, justice and public safety, and the military.

A spreadsheet is a grid of columns labeled alphabetically and rows labeled numerically. The rectangular intersection of a column and row is a cell, and a cell's location is specified by its column letter and row number such as cell A1--the cell in the upper left corner. Four major kinds of information may be entered into a cell: text; numbers; formulas that perform calculations on the numbers or on other formulas; and macros (or parts of macros) which may be a series of stored key strokes to relieve the tedium of repetitive work or full programs with all the characteristics of any computer program including decision-making capability. In addition, a spreadsheet can produce graphs such as pie and bar charts based on selected data, and it can be used to query a database stored in the spreadsheet. Today's spreadsheets also create a variety of descriptive and inferential statistics.

Probably the spreadsheet's most common application is government revenue forecasting and budget formulation and presentation. Figure 1 displays state community college revenue sources for a number of years. It also presents spreadsheet column and row identifiers. The inclusion of column and row designations and/or the

Software Toolkit Approach 177

Figure 1: Spreadsheet financial data.

	A	B	C	D	E	F	G
1							
2		Significant Revenue Sources for Community Colleges					
3			State of C				
4							
5			(Dollars in Millions)				
6							
7	Source of Funds	1993-94	1994-95	1995-96	1996-97	1997-98	
8							
9	State General Fund	$1,631.5	$1,792.7	$1,799.5	$1,643.7	$1,021.1	
10	Lottery Fund	122.4	97.1	75.8	87.3	87.3	
11	Local Property Taxes	715.7	791.0	834.2	1,061.6	1,428.1	
12	Student Fees	67.2	72.0	82.3	126.1	138.8	
13	Other State Funds	14.1	6.5	5.2	6.4	5.5	
14	Federal Funds	119.8	126.4	120.0	120.0	120.0	
15	Local Miscellaneous	455.5	406.9	410.0	431.2	453.9	
16	Local Debt Service	9.3	6.7	5.0	9.3	9.3	
17	TOTAL REVENUE	$3,135.5	$3,299.3	$3,332.0	$3,485.6	=SUM(F9:F16)	
18							
19		(Percentage of Total Revenue)					
20							
21	Source of Funds	1993-94	1994-95	1995-96	1996-97	1997-98	
22							
23	State General Fund	52.03	54.34	54.01	47.16	=(F9/$F$17)*100	
24	Lottery Fund	3.90	2.94	2.27	2.50	=(F10/$F$17)*100	
25	Local Property Taxes	22.83	23.97	25.04	30.46	=(F11/$F$17)*100	
26	Student Fees	2.14	2.18	2.47	3.62	=(F12/$F$17)*100	
27	Other State Funds	0.45	0.20	0.16	0.18	=(F13/$F$17)*100	
28	Federal Funds	3.82	3.83	3.60	3.44	=(F14/$F$17)*100	
29	Local Miscellaneous	14.53	12.33	12.30	12.37	=(F15/$F$17)*100	
30	Local Debt Service	0.30	0.20	0.15	0.27	=(F16/$F$17)*100	

Percentage Revenue 1996-97

(Pie chart with segments: Local Debt Serv., Local Misc., Federal, Other State, Student, Property, Lottery, General Fund) columns and rows themselves in the printout is optional and ordinarily would not be done in presentation materials. They were included here to facilitate the discussion below. Once data and associated labels and formulas are keyed into a spreadsheet such as Figure 1, it is called a worksheet.

Several features of this worksheet are worth noting:

- The centered headings appearing in rows 2-5 were entered by highlighting cells A2 through F5 and then making menu choices that designated this rectangle an area in which text would be centered.
- All boldface type, italics type, and dollar figures were created by highlighting cells and selecting fonts and formats from icons or menu items.
- Total Revenue was calculated by entering the function (i.e., formula) in cell B17=SUM(B9:B16).[2] This added the figures in the block of cells designated inside the parentheses. This formula did not have to be retyped for the other columns. It was copied to the other cells in row 17. The formula in cell F17 was made to appear in this printout for purposes of illustration. In the course of copying the formula, it automatically adjusted to its new home in column F. Thus, the formula in cell B17 is a relative cell reference formula meaning that when it is copied it will automatically be rewritten to reflect its new location.
- The figures in the bottom half of Figure 1 were created by keying in formulas that referenced dollar amounts from the top half. For example, the formula in cell F23 takes the number in F9, divides it by the result of the calculation that occurs in F17 and multiplies by 100. This formula mixes relative and absolute cell reference characteristics. When it is copied downward, the F9 reference adjusts to its new location while $F$17 references only cell F17 no matter where it is copied.

Numeric data and text can be formatted to emphasize particular points or just to enhance the appearance of the worksheet.

The Figure 1 worksheet displays two dimensions--sources of funds and fiscal years. All spreadsheets possess a third dimension in the form of additional worksheets that can be thought of as a book or a third dimension extending outward (or inward) from the computer monitor. In this example, we might be interested in interstate comparisons in community college funding, so each of the other worksheets could represent a state. We could also have a summary worksheet that would add the dollar amounts in the other worksheets. If we are interested in analyzing differences between technical-vocational institutions and community colleges, this fourth dimension and more beyond that could be added with a device called a pivot table.[3]

We might also want to graph figures. A pie chart of FY1997 would display the percentage of total revenue coming from each source. A scatter plot would show either dollar amounts or percentages over time. These graphs can be printed to cover an entire page, share a page with worksheet data, be added to word processing pages, or be made part of an intranet (i.e., internal organizational network) or Internet Web page.

Little imagination is required to envision budget preparation, bookkeeping, cost accounting, and so forth using a spreadsheet.

Benefit-cost Analysis

Benefit-cost analysis compares the benefits and costs of choices and selects the

Software Toolkit Approach 179

choice that yields the highest net benefit (Stokey and Zeckhauser, 1978, pp. 134-76). In practice, most benefit-cost problems involve capital expenditures where benefits and costs are received and spent over a period of years. With data of this sort it is necessary to reduce the benefit and cost data to their present day equivalents or present value.

The formula for calculating present value for any benefit or cost stream is:
$PV = S_0/(1+r)^0 + S_1/(1+r)^1 + S_2/(1+r)^2 + \ldots + S_n/(1+r)^n$
where S_n is any sum of money (benefit or cost) in year n and r is the discount rate.

Performed on a hand calculator, the benefit-cost analysis of one or two streams of figures with the above formula is merely annoying. Done with present value tables found in some business administration books, it is considerably more convenient, but, either way, an actual benefit-cost analysis performed to aid decision-making (as opposed to providing decorative support for decisions already made) typically involves sensitivity analysis applied to combinations of benefits, costs, and discount rates. If the estimates for each of these are all calculated by hand, one is facing a considerable amount of work. With a spreadsheet such a prospect represents no problem.

Figure 2 shows a typical benefit-cost situation. In the first two years benefits are zero because the project in question (e.g., a building) is under design and construc-

Figure 2: Benefit-cost analysis example.

	A	B	C	D	E	F	G	H	I	J	K
1											
2											
3											
4					Benefit-Cost Estimates						
5					(millions of dollars)						
6					Year						
7			0	1	2	3	4	5	6		
8	Pessimistic Benefits		0	0	3	3	3	3	3		
9	Most Likely Benefits		0	0	3.5	3.5	3.5	3.5	3.5		
10	Optimistic Benefits		0	0	3.8	3.8	3.8	3.8	3.8		
11	Costs		1	12	0.1	0.1	0.1	0.1	0.1		
12											
13											
14					Discount Rate						
15	Present Value		3.0%	4.0%	5.0%	5.5%	6.0%	6.5%	7.0%	7.5%	8.0%
16	Pessimistic Benefits		13.3	12.8	12.4	12.1	11.9	11.7	11.5	11.3	11.1
17	Most Likely Benefits		15.6	15.0	14.4	14.2	13.9	13.7	13.4	13.2	12.9
18	Optimistic Benefits		16.9	16.3	15.7	15.4	15.1	14.8	14.6	14.3	14.0
19	Costs		13.1	13.0	12.8	12.8	12.7	12.7	12.6	12.5	12.5
20											
21	=NPV(D15,$D$11:$I$11)+$C$11 in Cell D19										
22											
23					Summary						
24											
25					Discount Rate						
26	Net Benefits		3.0%	4.0%	5.0%	5.5%	6.0%	6.5%	7.0%	7.5%	8.0%
27	Pessimistic		0.2	-0.1	-0.5	-0.6	-0.8	-1.0	-1.1	-1.2	-1.4
28	Most Likely		2.5	2.0	1.6	1.4	1.2	1.0	0.8	0.6	0.5
29	Optimistic		3.8	3.3	2.8	2.6	2.4	2.2	2.0	1.8	1.6

tion. The design and construction costs are relatively high compared to annual benefits. Because the high design and construction costs are incurred in the first few years, they are discounted relatively little by the present value formula. The smaller benefit figures are more and more heavily discounted as they extend further into the future. Thus, the higher the discount rate, which governs the severity of the discounting, the worse the project will look as calculated either by net benefits (benefit minus cost) or the benefit-cost ratio (benefit divided by cost). And results obviously also depend on cost and benefit estimates. Since cost estimates are likely to be relatively firm, they are held constant in this example, but discount rates and benefits are allowed to vary. The contents of all the cells in the middle table resemble the illustrated formula.

The syntax of the Net Present Value (NPV) formula is =NPV(rate,range) where *rate* is the discount rate and *range* is a range of cells.[4] As the spreadsheet's help utility notes, the NPV function begins discounting with the first cell in the range specified in the formula. Thus, if the formula in cell D19 began with C11 (or $C$11) instead of D11, it would have discounted the cost figure for year 0 which would have been a mistake. The cell address of the cost for year 0 is added separately.

Curve Smoothing and Forecasting

Although it is characterized by a serious theoretical weakness, the single moving average is one of the most common tools of applied time series analysis. Used both for simple curve smoothing and forecasting, the single moving average is easily calculated and plotted using a spreadsheet.

The time series in Figure 3 is relatively noisy. To highlight trends obscured by day to day fluctuations, it can be smoothed by a formula in which the

Figure 3: Moving averages for curve smoothing and forecasting.

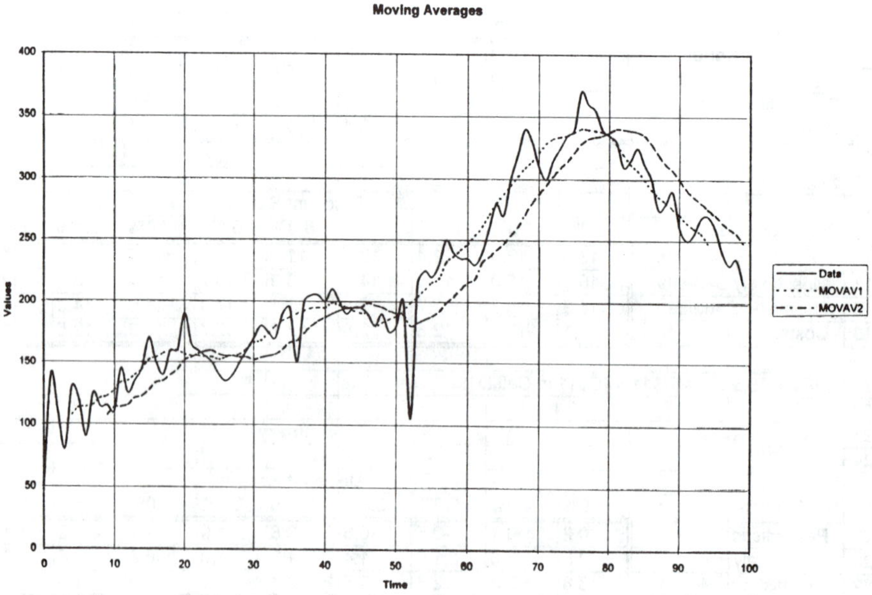

numerator, which contains the sum of data in a number of time periods, is divided by the number of time periods. Thus each point in the single moving average is the mean of part of the data set. When the moving average is centered on the raw data as is MOVAV1, the moving average smooths the raw data.

When the moving average is, in a sense, pushed forward, so that its last point coincides with the last raw data point, it becomes a predictive tool (see MOVAV2). The distance between the moving average in this form and the raw data is sensitive to changes in trend. Because each point in MOVAV2 represents the past, each point will be below raw data when the trend is up. However, when the rate of increase begins to diminish, the distance diminishes, and this change is regarded as significant by many financial analysts. Similarly, the moving average remains above raw data when the trend in the raw data is downward. A reduction in the rate of decrease of the raw data will also produce a reduction in the distance between the moving average and raw data.

In financial forecasting, moving averages of 30, 60, or even 90 days are common. In such calculations each day is treated as being equally important, i.e., data from a day 30, 60, or 90 days ago is accorded as much weight as yesterday's data. It seems likely that yesterday's data is in fact somewhat more important than data from a day before that, which in turn is more important than data from three days ago, and so forth. A family of curve smoothing techniques known as exponential smoothing takes this likely truth into account by systematically weighting more recent time periods more heavily than earlier ones (Fosback, 1987, ch. 41). Although some exponential smoothing calculations can be performed with a spreadsheet, they are more readily executed using statistics packages to be discussed below (Jarrett, 1987, pp. 24-37).

Regression analysis is another technique that can be implemented on a spreadsheet for forecasting as well as other purposes including policy analysis (Gaeng, 1993). Although regression analysis is not difficult to accomplish using a spreadsheet, a statistics package manages this task more easily and efficiently especially if many exploratory analyses are required.[5] Statistics packages also produce more detailed analyses and diagnoses of problems in the dataset. Regression analysis will be discussed below in the context of statistics packages.

Spreadsheets and Statistics

The above discussion regarding regression analysis also applies to other statistical functions built into spreadsheets. If a statistical analysis is to be confined to a few calculations of descriptive statistics, a spreadsheet is an adequate tool. However, statistical work often expands beyond what is initially expected as questions are asked, new data is added, and more analysis is done.

Spreadsheets are better tools than statistics packages for data entry, data editing, storage, and printing. If spreadsheet data entry follows simple rules specified by virtually all leading statistics package manufacturers, the data may be exported to the statistics package; leading statistics packages can read spreadsheet files almost as easily as their native format.

Data to be read by a statistics package should be arranged so that the top row is devoted to variable names and each subsequent row is an observation. For example, if the analyst is trying to understand the relationship between university funding and state economic performance, data would be arranged as follows:

	A	B	C
1	STATE	IN9490	ECAP9288
2	MAINE	492.85	.00742
3	NEWHAMP	-623.21	.00731
4	.	.	.
5	.	.	.

where STATE is a text variable, IN9490 is the change in per capita income in the years 1990-94, and ECAP9288 is the difference in university enrollment in the years 1988-92 as a fraction of a state's population. In this example, there would be 51 rows of data for the 50 states and the District of Columbia. Many statistics packages require that variable names be kept to eight characters or less, and the length of text variables must be held to specified limits. Elsewhere on the worksheet the definitions of the variables can be entered along with data sources and other critical information. Some statistics packages allow such notes to be added to a data set, but many do not.

If it is determined that a variable (column) is no longer needed, it can be easily eliminated in a spreadsheet. If a movement of variables (columns) can aid readability, this is much more easily done with a spreadsheet than statistics package. For example, in the above example, we might have data for two decades (enrollment, population, and income data for each year), and we may want to locate all per student expenditure variables in adjoining columns.

Data sets can easily number 50, 100, or more variables. To avoid mistakes, it is important that a key variable such as STATE, remain in view. With most, if not all, statistics package data entry screens, when more than approximately five variables have been added, the first column (variable) scrolls to the left out of sight. The invisibility of the STATE variable could easily result in the user entering data for Maryland when it should be in the Massachusetts row. With a spreadsheet, the STATE column may be frozen so that it is always in view. Similarly, with some statistics packages once data have been entered for roughly the first half of the states, variable names scroll away upward. In a spreadsheet they can also be frozen in place. At the same time, one can view two entirely different parts of the worksheet with a split window—a feature we have not seen in any statistics package data input screen.

Most statistics packages lack even elementary print formatting capabilities producing crude looking or confusing raw data printouts including data split between pages. The output may be saved in a format readable by a word processing program where the cleanup of layout and fonts may be (often laboriously) accomplished. A spreadsheet allows complete control over what appears on which printout page, and it is far superior to a statistics package in terms of the appearance of the printout.

Sampling

Worksheets can be designed to generate simple random samples and systematic samples with stratification. With the spreadsheet rows representing cases or subjects, each row may be numbered quickly and those numbers used with a formula to generate a simple random sample. The stratified systematic sample is first developed by sorting the data on one or more variables (for example, sex). Using a formula to generate a skip interval (population size divided by sample size), it is easy to generate another formula for sampling the list once a random start number is generated by simple random sampling within the first interval. If the data were sorted by sex, the resulting sample will have numbers of males and females proportionate to their numbers on the list.

Linear Programming

Linear programming is a technique for minimizing or maximizing a variable in the face of constraints. We might, for example, be attempting to minimize cost in a government printing shop by making the most efficient use of equipment and personnel. Spreadsheets can perform such calculations. Explaining how data for a particular situation are arranged for linear programming solution in a spreadsheet would require far more space than is available, but most texts on advanced spreadsheet usage provide guidance (Gips, 1997, ch. 8).

Database Applications

Everything regarding spreadsheet usage up to this point has concerned databases, but there are specific data storage and manipulation operations known collectively as database management. The traditional database structure is identical to the column (variable) and row (observation) arrangement discussed above except that in database management, columns are known as fields and rows as records. Inventories, mailing lists, and building room assignments are examples of the kind of information stored and processed as part of database management operations.

Spreadsheets can be used for this purpose if the number of records does not exceed the maximum number of rows in the spreadsheet. This amount varies depending on spreadsheet manufacturer and version, and it also may be limited by the amount of memory (RAM) in the computer. The practical maximum number of records is also governed by how the user plans to manipulate data; many operations can take additional space. Very roughly speaking, a database larger than 9,000 records (in many applications the maximum could be much smaller) should be processed using a database management program such as Access (1996) or Alpha-5 (1995). Such programs have much larger data handling capacities and other capabilities to be discussed below that often make them better database management tools than a spreadsheet. Statistics packages also have data handling capabilities that are much larger than spreadsheets, but statistics packages lack a full range of database manipulation capabilities as well as not having data entry features discussed above.

Sorting is a basic database management operation. Much can be learned from a dataset by sorting, and, assuming it has sufficient capacity, a spreadsheet is an effective tool for this purpose. Data may be sorted in ascending or descending order, alphabetically or numerically. Spreadsheets (and database management programs) also contain query functions that list records that fit user specified characteristics.

Statistics Packages

As noted above, spreadsheets can be made to perform statistical calculations, but if those operations are many in number and/or involve relatively sophisticated techniques, statistics packages such as SYSTAT 7.0 (1997), SPSS 7.5 (1997), or NCSS 97 (Hintze, 1997a) are far superior to spreadsheets or even the only tool that can be used.[6]

In public administration applications, a statistics package might be used for operations as elementary as producing descriptive statistics (even for this purpose a statistics package is better than a spreadsheet) or as advanced as leading edge statistical analysis.

Regression Analysis

Regression analysis can be employed to explain the relationships between and among variables, and it can be used alone or in concert with other techniques for forecasting.[7] An example of the first application of regression analysis concerns the relationship between the change in per capita income and the change in university enrollment for the states and Washington, D.C. This example is part of an actual test of a university lobbyist's claim that a state's economic well being was directly proportional to the number of people enrolled in universities. (Taken to its logical extreme, this claim suggests that a state would be best off if everyone is a college student.) Using the language of statistics, a state's economic health was the dependent variable being acted on by the independent variable, higher education enrollment. We discovered few direct relationships between higher education enrollment in a given year and measures of economic performance such as per capita income in

Figure 4: SYSTAT plot with regression line.

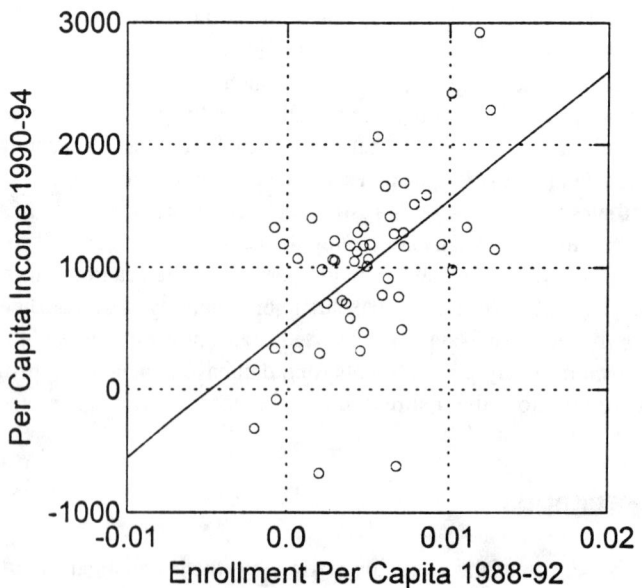

Figure 5: SYSTAT regression analysis

```
Dep Var: IN9490    N: 51   Multiple R: 0.561       Squared multiple R: 0.315

Adjusted squared multiple R: 0.301  Standard error of estimate: 569.629

Effect       Coefficient    Std Error  Std Coef  Tolerance      t      P(2 Tail)
CONSTANT         496.880      134.493    0.0         .         3.694    0.001
ECAP9288      105310.268    22194.796    0.561     1.000       4.745    0.000

                              Analysis of Variance

Source      Sum-of-Squares      df      Mean-Square    F-ratio   P

Regression    7305056.814        1       7305056.814    22.513
Residual      1.58994E+07       49        324477.403
```

that or subsequent years. However, we observed that there was a positive relationship between changes in enrollment (enrollment per capita) and per capita income as shown in the SYSTAT plot in Figure 4.

The straight line (called the regression line) running through the middle of the data set represents the middle of the data points. According to the regression analysis printout that accompanies the plot (see Figure 5), 31.5 percent of the variance of the dependent variable (change in per capita income 1990-94) can be explained by the independent variable (per capita university enrollment change 1988-1992). The 31.5 percent appears as Squared Multiple R known more commonly as r-squared. If the data points fell along a straight line instead of being scattered roughly along the regression line, the r-squared would be 1.0. If the data points were randomly scattered, r-squared would be zero.

The regression analysis warns that Case 2 is an outlier, meaning that it stands far apart from the other data points and has a disproportionate impact on the results. That data point (New Hampshire) appears on the plot as the second lowest (negative) per capita income change. Statistics packages permit the selective removal of outliers. Whether they should actually be removed is usually a matter of judgment. In this instance one could make the argument for removal of New Hampshire because it is a very small state. Its elimination produces an r-squared of .392.

The regression analysis printout has many other useful features, but we will focus on only one. The two figures in the column labeled Coefficient allow us to write the equation of the regression line. The equation is: IN9490 = 496.88 + 105310.268 * ECAP9288. The regression equation and the regression line are mathematically identical ways of expressing the relationship between the variables. The 496.88 is the point where the regression line hits the vertical axis at the zero point on the horizontal axis. The 105310.268 is the regression line's slope. One can read the likely per capita income change for any enrollment per capita change from the graph or calculate it from the regression equation. For example, if a state had experienced an increase of .02 in enrollment per capita the predicted per capita income change would be 496.88 + 105310.268*.02 or 496.88 + 2106.21 or 2603.09.

Regression analysis is used in the field of human resource administration to analyze whether discrimination based on race, sex, or other illegal factors is statistically likely. In this instance, regression analysis with several independent variables (multiple regression) is often the tool of choice (Berk, 1998, pp. 241-252). It can also be used for forecasting time series data, making time the independent variable (horizontal axis). The resulting regression line or the regression equation can be used to forecast the dependent variable which can be anything from tax revenues to jail inmate populations.

Interrupted Time Series Analysis

Interrupted time series analysis is an especially helpful analytical tool for policy analysis (Welch and Comer, 1988, pp. 289-295). The authors used it to test the claim that George Wallace's first term as governor had a positive effect on education spending in Alabama (Permaloff and Grafton, 1995, pp. 319-325), and it has been used in an unpublished evaluation of the effect of helmet laws on bicycle injury rates.

With interrupted time series analysis data are available for a number of time periods before and after an event such as the institution of bicycle helmet laws. This extremely useful technique measures whether the event has made a statistically significant difference and the nature of that difference (e.g., sudden or gradual decrease in bicycle injuries).

Time Series: Curve Smoothing

SYSTAT, NCSS, an SPSS component, and other statistics packages contain a wide variety of curve smoothing techniques which allow the user to vary the impact of data points in many ways (Wilkinson, Blank, and Gruber, 1996, pp. 583-594). One, called exponential smoothing, assumes that the most recent data point receives a weight w, the one before that is weighted $w(w-1)$, the one before that $w(w-1)^2$, and so forth where w is a "smoothing constant" set by the user with values between 0 and 1. By varying the smoothing constant, the user can modify the weight of the most recent data points (Berk, 1998, pp. 325-326). Although the formula appears complex, exponential smoothing is implemented in SYSTAT merely by accessing the time series menu, choosing exponential, keying in the desired smoothing constant, and naming a file in which the results will be stored. The process is no more difficult in NCSS and SPSS.

Complex Time Series Analysis

Time series data often contain several components. For example, monthly tax revenue data or daily jail inmate data might have a long term upward trend as well as seasonal and cyclical ups and downs. Sales tax revenues are likely to be above the yearly average every November and December and below average in January and February. A family of techniques called complex time series analysis permits forecasts that include trend, seasonal, and cyclical factors. In his text, Kenneth Berk (1998, pp. 330-343) concentrates only on trend and seasonality, and shows how the student version of SYSTAT can be used for forecasting. The NCSS statistics package contains perhaps the easiest to use and most sophisticated complex time series analysis module on the market as well as the clearest documentation (Hintze, 1997b, ch. 74-84; Jarrett, 1987, ch. 3, 7-9).

Database Management

Database management software such as Access, Approach (1995), Alpha-5, or Paradox (1995) is commonly used for personnel records, inventory management, or whenever large numbers of records will be stored, especially when those records include text numbering more than a few words.[8] Long text fields in a spreadsheet extend along a single row making the reading of a single record made up of several such fields very awkward as the user scrolls horizontally while reading a single line. Database management programs allow such records to be displayed in a more readable fashion somewhat in the form of text entered in a word processor.

Database management software is also ideal when data is to be entered by a computer novice. Data input screens can be designed that include instructions for the user to help insure that the correct types of information are keyed into particular fields. To some degree, each field can also be designed so that incorrect types of information will not be accepted.

We noted above that database management software is especially useful when large numbers of records must be stored. These records can be sorted and queried and particular records and particular fields can be printed or exported to other software (statistics, spreadsheet) for further processing. Database management software is also ideal for the generation of large numbers of mailing labels and form letters. Many database management programs also have modest graphing capabilities.

The programs listed above and many others are relational; they can link and draw information from two or more differently structured databases (as long as the databases have a common field) as if those databases were one (Grafton and Permaloff, 1993). This powerful feature is not shared with the other categories of software represented here.

Large scale organizations sometimes buy specialized relational database management programs set up for their specific applications. Such programs may cost thousands, if not hundreds of thousands, of dollars to buy, install, and maintain. Often a training component is included in the installation fees. Database management programs are frequently used to maintain personnel records. Another function is the maintenance of records of government regulatory agencies. For example, a state board may have multiple responsibilities: licensing applicants to a profession; disciplinary functions including the receipt of complaints and their investigation; monitoring of continuing education providers; and oversight of educational training programs. Each area would be served by different staff personnel with differing recordkeeping needs. As long as each area has at least one common field such as Social Security Number as an identifier linking the databases, one set of records could be queried for information needed by another area of the organization. For example, the licensing section may need to know the current status of disciplinary actions in order to determine if a renewal should be granted. With relationally linked databases, licensing personnel can query all of the databases as if they were a single database.

Project Planning and Management

Project planning and management programs are designed to assist in planning and managing complex projects in terms of time schedules as well as budgets, personnel, and other resources. This category of software can be used to schedule and estimate personnel requirements and budgets for construction jobs, landscape projects, conference planning, scheduling activities in a complex lawsuit, or any other enterprise with a clearly defined beginning and end. Over the years, the widely-used Primavera Project Planner and its sibling SureTrak Project Manager (1997) have probably received the most positive reviews, although Microsoft Project is also popular.[9]

Project planning requires that a project be broken down into building blocks called activities or tasks. An activity or task is defined as a job that involves one kind of work, can be reliably scheduled, uses the same resources from beginning to end, will probably not be interrupted, and is one person's or a single organization's responsibility (SureTrak, 1997, p.32).

Gantt charts represent one of two major graphical devices used by this family of programs. A Gantt chart is a bar graph with a horizontal bar representing each task in a project. Each bar's length is proportional to the time the task requires. The beginning of a bar is located at the start date of a task, and the end of the bar is located at the date the task should be complete.

The PERT (Project Evaluation Review Technique) chart is the other major graphical tool used by project planning and management programs. It is a better tool for highlighting relationships among tasks, but the Gantt chart is more space-efficient, allowing more tasks to be displayed on screen or on a single sheet of paper. Programs of this sort can also display bar charts and tables showing personnel plans and budgets.

Information is entered in these programs in forms. Task names and duration are keyed in by the user. Start and finish dates are calculated by the software based on a task's predecessor (or the project start date) and duration. Other forms are available in which the user enters resources required to perform a task, cost data, and other information.

Frequently, the first draft of a project plan results in an end date that is too late. These programs automatically highlight the longest path (the critical path) in a plan where a number of tasks are being executed simultaneously. By concentrating changes on the critical path an administrator can reduce the completion time of the overall project by focusing attention where it will do the most good.

Project planning and management programs are also used to monitor progress as a project is underway. Project-wide implications of early or late task completions are quickly observed.

Graphics for Illustrations

Illustrations often play an important part in reports, presentations, budgets, and other documents. Specialized software can be of great assistance augmenting the graphics features built into the software discussed above (Permaloff and Grafton, 1996).

Flow Charts and Organization Charts

A family of programs such as RFFlow (1994), Chartist (1995), and Visio 5.0 (1997) is used to create flow charts, organization charts, and similar diagrams featuring boxes (of all shapes) and lines (solid, dotted, with or without arrowheads). All can be helpful in creating illustrations.

Diagrams are created by the user selecting box shapes from menus, keying in labels (the boxes expand to fit labels), and connecting the boxes with lines also selected from menus. Once placed on the screen, boxes and lines can be rearranged as aesthetics and logic dictate. Some programs arrange boxes and route lines automatically.

We do not recommend that most public administrators attempt to employ a computer aided design (CAD) program for occasional diagram work unless the individual is already trained in its use. CAD programs can do far more than the programs mentioned above, but they exact a high price in terms of learning time, and they require many steps and much more time to complete tasks. (See Permaloff and Grafton, 1996.)

Scanned Graphics

Documents can also be improved with the inclusion of scanned material such as photographs. Scanners range in price from $100 to a little over $1,000, but even the least expensive are sufficient for many applications. Flatbed scanners are probably the easiest to use. The flatbed scanner resembles a small photocopy machine. The original image is placed in the scanner which generates a digitized version of the image that can be saved on disk and inserted into application programs including word processing, spreadsheet, database management, and project planning. In some cases, the image can be dragged directly from the scanning program into an application program without the need to save on disk.

Scanned Text and Optical Character Recognition

The scanned image of a printed page can be stored on disk for archiving purposes. This image is similar to that of a photograph of the original including hand written words such as signatures. Scanned text images archived on CD-R (compact disk-recordable) or CD-RW (compact disk-rewritable) consume relatively little storage space and are rated to last for 70 to 200 years if properly stored (Poor, 1998, April 21). However, it is doubtful whether in more than 15 years computers will be able to read the CD, since the CD format will almost certainly be replaced by some variant of the DVD format within five years. Most DVD drives can read CDs, but it is likely that within the time span over which we would want to access archived documents, the DVD format will be replaced by yet another format which will not read CDs. By comparison, consider how difficult it is becoming to find computers that accommodate 5 1/4-inch floppy disks. In normal office settings, the only computers that can read such disks are 386 and some 486 machines that are quickly disappearing. And how many offices can read the 8-inch floppy disks or the original Iomega Bernoulli cartridges that were in use less than two decades ago? The safest materials for long term archiving may still be paper (which is bulky) and microfilm or microfiche.

From the perspective of the computer, scanned text is no different than the scanned image of a photograph of an automobile. Both are pictures. Word processing software is incapable of recognizing the picture of a printed page as editable text. Optical character recognition (OCR) software that works with the scanner takes the scanned image and translates it into editable text. Once the page has been scanned, the OCR process requires only another mouse click to save results to disk in a format readable by any word processor. Accuracy depends on the quality and size of print of the original document, the complexity of the original document's layout, and the quality of the OCR software. Ordinary print found in newspapers, laser printed reports, or even photocopies of only moderate quality can be processed by OCR programs very successfully. Most scanners are sold bundled with OCR software.

OCR can be a very convenient tool. For an administrative task, the authors needed an editable version of a 24-page report written some years ago. The disk version had disappeared and might not have been saved in a format readable by our computer. The entire process of learning to use the scanner and the OCR software and generating files in the format we needed required less than one hour.

Presentation Programs

The use of computers and computer projection hardware or large monitors for presentations is rapidly increasing in popularity due to the improved quality of display or projection equipment and presentation software such as Power Point (1996) — probably the most widely used program because it is part of Microsoft Office. Presentations made with a computer and projector or monitor combination can appear more professional than what can be attained with an overhead projector or 35mm slide projector. The major limitation on the use of presentation software remains the cost of large monitors (approximately $2,200 for a 29-inch model) or computer projectors (the lowest is around $2,100). This compares unfavorably with the price of a simple overhead projector using transparencies which has the added advantage of greater portability (with some models) than a projector and a lap top computer (an additional expense). The 35mm slide projector is another relatively inexpensive and highly portable option. The biggest drawback with a slide projector is the necessity of having slides produced by a photo lab or copy center and the associated difficulty of making last minute changes that are easily accomplished using an overhead projector or computer.

Whether it is implemented with an overhead projector, a 35 mm projector, or a computer and monitor or projector, a presentation is built on slides. The slides in a computer presentation are virtual slides. A virtual slide may contain any combination of text and graphics including sound and motion. A single slide may contain elements from several sources. Menu choices or built in templates determine the background on which text and/or graphics will appear. That background can be any color or texture. Similarly, each slide's basic layout (whether there is a centered heading, bulleted text, a graphic, columns, etc.) is chosen from menus or templates. The content of a slide can be made to appear on screen all at once or a line at a time to maintain the audience's focus on each line.

Computer-generated virtual slides appear in the presentation in the order desired by the author, but that order can be changed on the fly during the presentation, and slides describing details can be included or skipped at will. On-screen time may even be preset by the user. The user can select from a number of visual and/or sound transition effects that occur as the presentation moves from one slide to the next. Presentation software can also handle the printing of all or parts of a presentation for distribution to the audience.

It is too easy to include so many clever graphics and sound effects in a computer presentation that the audience is distracted from content or even irritated by excesses. Good taste is important, and the user should err on the side of simplicity. The user should also be aware that the preparation of a computer presentation requires much more effort and time than a presentation based on overhead transparencies or printed handouts. Complete mastery of some presentation programs can also take many hours.

Group Work and Group Scheduling

Often the preparation of documents or worksheets involves the work of more than one author. Collaborative efforts can be developed via an organization's computer network. A document or worksheet can be distributed to everyone in a group simultaneously and then returned to the originator with each person's individual annotations or the document can be distributed to each person in the group in sequence with the resulting annotated document returned to the originator after each person has worked on it.

The manner in which a document is annotated can be tightly controlled by the originator. This is important because if a document can be freely changed, a subtle but important modification may be introduced by someone in the group (accidentally or not) without the originator's knowledge. The originator can protect a document from change but allow revisions that are clearly highlighted when the document returns to the originator. Or group members may just provide annotations separate from but connected to text. Group work on spreadsheets, databases, and project planning can also be shared on the network.

The wiring of a network and the installation of software to manage it is a highly specialized subject beyond the scope of this chapter.

Networks may, of course, be used to transmit e-mail and create Internet style web pages which serve as the equivalents of bulletin boards. They may also be used for electronic group discussions--what on the Internet are often called chat rooms (Alwang, 1998, February 24). These virtual conferences can adhere to either linear or threaded models. Linear discussions feature each individual's comments following one after the other in the order entered. The threaded model allows users to follow particular strands of parallel conversations rather than moving through comments that do not relate to their interests. Networks can also be used to schedule actual meetings. Those who are to attend the meetings enter days and times where they are committed to be elsewhere and desired days and times for the meeting. The software determines the best days and times for the meeting.

Geographical Information Systems

Geographical Information System (GIS) programs store and display data that are specific to geographical areas such as countries, states, counties, or zip codes. Data might include information regarding population, economics, numbers of users of government agency services, and crime rates. Data are typically displayed in the form of maps in which geographical areas are colored or patterned to represent various levels of whatever is being measured. Some GIS programs such as MapInfo (1997) are free standing while others are attached to software such as Lotus 1-2-3 or Visio. GIS packages vary widely in terms of file formats, data manipulation features, display capabilities, and price, so considerable research is required to make an informed purchasing decision.

Conclusions

It is difficult to imagine a job in government involving computer usage that would not benefit from the use of software tools beyond a word processing program and a Web browser. If highly complex page layouts are needed, a desktop publishing program can represent a substantial improvement over word processing software.

Those who work with numerical information for simple bookkeeping, work performance data, or virtually any other application, can improve the efficiency and effectiveness of their efforts with a spreadsheet. Statistical analysis can be performed on a spreadsheet, but a statistics package is a far more efficient and powerful analytical tool.

For large databases, multiple databases that must be linked, databases that include large amounts of text, and tailor made data input screens especially for use by computer novices, database management software is needed and often available as part of an office suite. If database management software is not already present on a computer, powerful programs may be purchased for as little as $50.

Word processing, desktop publishing, spreadsheet, statistics, and database management programs are the basic components of a government agency software toolkit. They are the equivalent of a hammer, drill, screwdriver set, saw, and pliers in a cabinet builder's tool kit. Beyond these basic tools are others such as presentation, graphics, scheduling, and OCR programs that are near necessities for particular individuals depending on the jobs at hand.

Almost any task employing a computer can be accomplished more efficiently with a variety of tools rather than any single tool, and those tools can often be had for very little expense. With two exceptions in each category we discussed above, very useful programs can be purchased that range in price between $50 and $125. One exception is project planning, where the minimum is approximately $380. The largest exception is full versions of statistics packages that can handle databases beyond 1000 observations and include advanced statistics. Such software is priced in the $700-$900 range.

Endnotes

¹ For an excellent introduction to the topic of Intranet and Internet Web page creation and administration see Ball (1997). This article concentrates on Microsoft's Front Page 97 for Web site authoring and management, Web scripting languages such as VBScript and JavaScript, and the three-dimensionally oriented Virtual Realty Modeling Language (VRML). Web page work is a large subject, and it would take someone with programming experience weeks to achieve even a minimal competence level in each of its many subdivisions.

² This is the Excel version. The Lotus formula would be @SUM(B9..B16).

³ A full explication of this subject would require more space than is available. See Gips (1997, chap. 16) for a clear description.

⁴ The Lotus syntax is the same except the equal sign is replaced by the @ symbol.

⁵ Making matters worse as far as the widely used spreadsheet Excel is concerned, some versions of Excel require extra installation steps before regression functions can be accessed, and if original disks and instructions are not available as is often the case in government settings we have observed, the analyst will not be able to proceed.

⁶ Student versions of SYSTAT and SPSS are available at bargain prices (well under $100) to anyone. However, those packages are limited in terms of the number of variables and observations they can handle. For a comparison of the full versions of SYSTAT and SPSS see Grafton and Permaloff (1998).

⁷ Our treatment of regression analysis is not intended to be in any sense exhaustive. Entire volumes have been written on this one subject such as Schroeder, Sjoquist, and Stephan (1986), Berk (1998, chap. 9-10), and Wilkinson, Blank, and Gruber (1996, chap. 4-7).

⁸ Approach and Access are part of the Lotus and Microsoft suites, respectively.

⁹ A student version of SureTrak may be obtained from the manufacturer for $35. The software is identical to the full $380 version except that its capacity has been reduced to 100 tasks. The manual that accompanies the student version is superb and unchanged from the standard manual. The student version represents an excellent opportunity for someone to try this product.

References

Access 7.0 [Computer software]. (1996). Redmond, WA: Microsoft.
Alpha 5 [Computer software]. (1995). Burlington, MA: ALPHA Software.
Alwang, G. (1998, February 24). Meeting of the minds. *PC Magazine,* 17(4), 179-192.
Approach [Computer software]. (1995).
Ball, W. J. (1997). Beyond the home page. Social Science Computer Review, Vol 15(4), 446-463.

Berk, K. N. (1998). *Introductory statistics with SYSTAT.* Upper Saddle River, NJ: Prentice-Hall.

Chartist [Computer software]. (1995). Richardson, TX: Novagraph.

Corel WordPerfect Suite 7 [Computer software] (1996). Ottawa, Canada: Corel Corporation.

Excel 7.0 [Computer software] (1998). Redmond, WA: Microsoft.

Fosback, N. (1987). *Stock market logic.* Fort Lauderdale: Institute for Econometric Research, chap. 41.

Gaeng, P. (1993). *Excel for science and technology.* Grand Rapids, MI: Abacus.

Gips, J. (1997). *Mastering Excel: A problem-solving approach.* New York: John Wiley, chap. 16.

Grafton, C. and Permaloff, A. (1993). Statistical analysis and data graphics. In G. D. Garson and S. S. Nagel (Eds.), *Advances in Social Science and Computers:* Vol. 3 (pp. 267-284). Greenwich, CN: JAI Press.

Grafton, C. and Permaloff, A. (1996). Use of analysis in governors' budget offices. *Southeastern Political Review,* 24(4), 675-698.

Grafton, C. and Permaloff, A. (1998). SYSTAT 7.0 and SPSS 7.5: A review essay with emphasis on SYSTAT. *Social Science Computer Review,* 16(1), 110-118.

Hintze, J. L. (1997a). NCSS 97 [Computer software] Kaysville, UT: Number Cruncher Statistical Systems.

Hintze, J. L. (1997b). [Computer manual] *NCSS 97 user's guide — II.* Kaysville, UT: Number Cruncher Statistical Systems.

Jarrett, J. (1987). *Business forecasting methods.* Cambridge, MA: Basil Blackwell.

MapInfo [Computer software] (1997). Troy, NY: MapInfo Corporation.

Microsoft. (1995). *Getting results with microsoft office for Windows 95.* Redmond, WA.

Microsoft Office Professional 7.0 [Computer software] (1995). Redmond, WA: Microsoft.

PageMaker 6.5 [Computer software]. (1997). San Jose, CA: Adobe.

Paradox 8.0 [Computer software]. (1996). Ottawa, Canada: Corel Corporation.

Permaloff, A. and Grafton, C. (1995). *Political power in alabama: The more things change . . . .* Athens, GA: University of Georgia Press, pp. 319-325.

Permaloff, A. and Grafton, C. (1996). Computer tools for crafting clear and attractive diagrams in social science. *Social Science Computer Review,* 14(3), 293-304.

Poor, A. (1998, April 21). The ravages of time. *PC Magazine,* 17(8), 234.

Power Point 7.0 [Computer software] (199). Redmond, WA: Microsoft.

Primavera Project Planner [Computer software] (1997). Bala Cynwyd, PA: Primavera, Inc.

RFFlow 3.0 (1994). [Computer software]. Loveland, CO: RFF Electronics.

Schroeder, L. D., Sjoquist, D. L., & Stephan, P. E. (1986). *Understanding regression analysis: An introductory guide.* Beverly Hills, CA.

Serif PagePlus 3.0 [Computer software] (1996). Nashua, NH: Serif, Inc.

SPSS 7.5 for Windows 95/NT [Computer software]. (1997). Chicago: SPSS, Inc.

Stokey, E. and Zeckhauser, R. (1978). *A primer for policy analysis.* New York: W. W. Norton & Company.

SureTrak Project Manager 2.0 [Software manual] (1997). Bala Cynwyd, PA: Primavera, Inc.

SYSTAT 7.0 [Computer software] (1997). Chicago: SPSS, Inc.

SYSTAT 6.0 for Windows Student Version [Computer software] (1997). Chicago: SPSS, Inc.

Visio 3.0 [Computer software] (1994). Seattle, WA: Shapeware Corporation.

Welch, S. and Comer, J. (1988). *Quantitative methods for public administration.* Pacific Grove, CA: Brooks/Cole.

Wilkinson, L., Blank, G., & Gruber, C. (1996). *Desktop data analysis with SYSTAT.* Upper Saddle River, NJ: Prentice-Hall.

Word 7.0 [Computer software]. (1996). Redmond, WA: Microsoft.

WordPerfect 7.0 [Computer software] (1996). Ottawa, Canada: Corel Corporation.

11

Computers, Survey Research, and Focus Groups in Public Administration Research and Practice

by
Michael L. Vasu
and
Ellen Storey Vasu
North Carolina State University

The integration of computing into survey research and focus groups in research and practice in public administration and related fields is the focus of this chapter. Coverage applies to other social science disciplines as well. This chapter reviews uses of computers in computer-assisted survey research (CASR), computer-assisted interviewing, computer-assisted telephone interviewing (CATI), computer-assisted personal interviewing (CAPI), and transferring survey research methods onto the Internet. A second portion of the chapter gives special attention to continuous audience response technology (CART). An example of a citizen survey focused on growth issues combined with a focus group dealing with the same topic in Cary, North Carolina, is also provided.

Survey research has been a pivotal methodology for academic social science research since World War II. Today, both survey research and focus groups are integral to research and practice in public administration and education (Floz, 1996; Miller & Miller, 1991; Morgan, 1998). Simply stated, both surveys and focus groups are forms of interviewing. Focus groups have been characterized as essentially group interviews (Morgan, 1998). Surveys are individual interviews typically targeted at a single respondent or unit of analysis. In the case of both focus groups and traditional survey research, the enterprise essentially involves the art of asking questions (Payne, 1951). The questions that are asked constitute variables in the language of research. The

Copyright© 1999, Idea Group Publishing.

purpose of asking these questions is to establish relationships between and among independent and dependent variables, and typically to test a series of hypotheses derived from some body of theory. The question and answer process integral to surveys and focus groups, is also a form of measurement and, as such, is subject to errors of measurement.

The types of questions asked in the fields of public administration and education are extensive. They may concern community aesthetics, growth management issues, budget priorities, dimensions of program effectiveness, and feedback from citizens, constituents, or customers. The questions may involve the attempt to measure some theoretical construct, for example, job satisfaction (Folz, 1996; Rea & Parker, 1991). The traditional approach to capturing the data via the question and answer interviewing process previously described, typically involved paper and a pencil, and hence was called Paper and Pencil Interviewing (PAPI) (Dufour, Kaushal, & Michaud, 1997). The advent of computers promised advantages over the paper and pencil approach that included decreased cost, and increased convenience and quality. It also promised ways to reduce some of the errors of measurement inherent in the survey research process. Many of these promises have been realized.

This chapter focuses on ways in which computers can enhance the survey research and focus groups processes, and looks at this topic through the lens of research and practice in public administration and related fields. It contains a broad discussion of software applications, rather than specific reviews of selected software applications as they relate to survey research. For more extensive software reviews that are typically discussed down to the keystroke level, the reader is advised to consult, for example, *Social Science Computer Review* (http://www.sagepub.com). This chapter specifically reviews uses of computers in computer-assisted survey research (CASR), computer-assisted telephone interviewing (CATI), computer-assisted personal interviewing (CAPI), and survey research on the Internet. A second portion of the chapter gives special attention to continuous audience response technology (CART). Finally, an example of a citizen survey focused on growth issues combined with a focus group dealing with the same topic in Cary, North Carolina, is also provided. We begin by discussing the survey research process.

The Survey Research Process

Survey research has been central to social science research since World War II. Currently, technological changes are giving new strength to an old workhorse. In order to understand both the real and potential impact of computers on the survey process, it is necessary to understand that process. Subsequently, we start by outlining the stages of the survey process and identify potential sources of measurement error inherent in survey research.

All methodological techniques seek to minimize the total error of measurement in an attempt to gain some understanding about the relationship between and among variables. All fail in some important respects. Even in experimental research, relationships between variables need to be replicated many times prior to being accepted. In ex post facto research, where both the independent and dependent variables have already occurred in time, (survey research is one type of ex post facto research) the measurement problems are significantly greater (Bradburn & Sudman, 1991; Lyberg, et al., 1997). Typically, in surveys we seek to reduce total survey error in search of meaningful relationships. This total survey error is *all the error* that can seep into a study that affects that survey's accuracy, and the ability of the survey to mirror something in the real world. This total survey error is the result of a variety of factors: sampling error, non-response problems, interviewer bias, biased questions, non-sampling error, and other general errors of measurement. Moreover, even well constructed, valid and reliable survey questions offer very little depth or ability to probe when compared, for example, to a focus group (Folz, 1996; Lyberg, et al, 1997; Rea & Parker, 1991; Sudman & Bradburn, 1982). Moreover, what is typically reported as error in scientific surveys is sampling error (e.g. plus or minus 3%) which is actually only one source of error, and not necessarily the largest type of error found in many surveys (Converse & Traugott, 1986). However, scientific surveys provide breadth across a number of variables that allow generalizations from a sample to a population as a result of using a sampling design based on probability theory.

The steps or stages in the survey research process provide a framework for understanding the degree to which the computer can enhance the survey process. Specifically, computing can cut costs, improve quality, and minimize some errors of measurement. These stages of the survey process are presented in various forms in survey textbooks (e.g., Babbie, 1990; Folz, 1996; O'Sullivan & Rassel, 1995; Rea & Parker, 1991; Rossie, Wright & Anderson, 1983). In the next section, we provide our own summary of these steps.

Conceptualization and Planning and Management

This is the stage in which the purposes and methods of the survey research design are defined and established, the variables are conceptualized, operational definitions are developed, scale and indexes are created, the literature is reviewed, the theoretical constructs are established, hypotheses are developed, and statistical procedures are selected. During this stage, the purposes of the research (exploration, description, and explanation) are defined. The types of information required is determined (attitudinal, behavioral, demographic, etc.). Who will be surveyed and by what method (telephone, mail, or in person) is decided. Moreover, a variety of logistical issues are addressed, for example, what personnel are required (field staff, technical staff, senior professional staff), and what financial resources are required.

Arguably, the most important stage in the survey research process, is at this stage in which various management decisions are made. All surveys require good management. The larger the survey, the more complex the management system. Failures in survey management affect total survey error. The management complexity involved in dealing with people and data in a large survey project is very well summarized in the following quote (Rossi, Wright, & Anderson, 1983):

> Not only people have to be managed. There are also tasks of managing schedules, deliverables, final products, and of course, budgets. But much of what is interesting about the management of schedules, products, and budgets concerns people management. For example, because surveys are labor intensive, schedules generally can be accelerated only by adding more staff labor. Budgets, as we have already observed, are based mostly on project payrolls. To monitor the budget is largely to attend to how much labor is going into different

tasks. Seldom will cost overruns be the result of faulty estimates of non-labor costs; they frequently will result from underestimates of the staff effort required to administer a complex questionnaire or trace respondents or code open ended answers. Poor management of staff labor will directly affect schedules and budgets more than anywhere else in the survey process. Of course, deliverables and products, whether scholarly monographs policy evaluations, or simply clean data, depend upon assigning the right people to the correct task with appropriate resources and creating the incentives that motivate performance (p. 134).

Sampling

The basis of scientific survey research is probability theory which includes the concept of random selection. Random selection is typically defined as a process in which every element (typically a person in a survey) has and equal or known probability of inclusion in the sample. The ultimate goal of sampling is to secure a representative sample, ideally one that includes every important variable in the same proportion that would be in present in the total population. A specific goal of a representative sample is to acquire a sample in which no group is systematically under or over represented.

Since researchers seldom have exact information about population parameters, they use the logic of probability theory to make statistical inferences about larger populations predicated on a single sample, the one that they have selected for a given research project (Deming, 1950; Kish, 1965; Lyberg, et al, 1997). Each sample statistic (e.g., the mean age of 1,140 members of a sample selected from the roster of the American Institute of Planners) becomes an estimate of a population parameter (e.g., the mean age of all the members of the American Institute of Planners).

The difference between a sample statistic and a population parameter is known as sampling error. The degree of precision, essentially a statistical statement about how close our estimate (sample mean age) is to the real population parameter (population mean age), can be determined using probability theory. Usually expressed as plus or minus 3, 4, or 5%, precision is a measure of how much error the researcher is willing to tolerate.

In addition to tolerated error, the researcher is also interested in a statement of confidence that a given population parameter really lies within the plus or minus error range specified around the sample estimate. This is stated as the degree to which we are confident that a confidence interval (e.g,. the interval on the number line from 15 to 35) actually captures the population parameter. Confidence coefficients are usually expressed as 95% or 99%; or in terms of 95 or 99 samples in 100. Sampling designs (e.g., simple random, systematic, stratified, cluster and multistage) specify methods for selecting cases from a sampling frame in a manner that insures that the random selection required for the application of probability theory is achieved. Finally, some sampling designs require disproportionate sampling and weighting of cases (Kish, 1965).

Designing the Survey Instrument

The essential objective in designing questions for survey research is to elicit valid and reliable responses from respondents. In other words, questions that measure what you want them to measure and, questions that produce results that are consistent over time. Failure to produce valid and reliable responses constitutes another potential source of error in surveys. In effect, in seeking valid and reliable responses we seek to avoid the inherent bias evident in the answer to the question "Have you stopped beating your wife?" This question illustrates one common feature of a biased question, since it channels the answer in a specific direction. In this example, the respondent incriminates himself with either a "yes" or a "no" answer.

In addition to this type of outright bias, there are other potential errors in the survey process that are more subtle. These errors confound the ability of the researcher to interpret the response to a question by potentially changing response patterns because of the form of the question, rather than its context. According to Folz (1996), this bias may be the result of "instructions, question wording, question order, response choices, or the format of the instrument" (p. 87). We will briefly review the major categories of such errors.

Outside of sampling error, question order effects have been identified as the most frequently cited explanation for errors in surveys (Schuman & Presser, 1981). Question order is a general term used to describe the extent to which answers to a given question are influenced by the questions that precede them in a survey. The question order effect is typically explained as the contextual effect that can be produced by asking a series of questions that produces a frame of reference for the respondent (Bradburn & Sudman, 1991). For example, asking a series of general questions about the commitment to free speech would potentially influence responses to a question that directly followed asking whether a known communist should be allowed to speak in the public schools. Question order effects are real and have been documented empirically to affect response outcomes (Schuman & Presser, 1981). An analogous problem to that of response order is the primacy or recency effect — the tendency of the respondent to choose the first or last alternative in a response set (Lyberg, et al., 1997; Schuman & Presser, 1981; Schwarz & Hippler, 1991; Sudman & Bradburn, 1982;).

The two major types of questions typically employed in surveys are closed versus open. A closed question, sometimes referred to as a fixed-choice or precoded question (Schuman & Preser, 1981), provides a list of mutually exclusive and exhaustive categories to the respondent. An open question, as implied, offers the respondent the opportunity for an extended narrative.

Closed questions are subject to a response set bias, an example of which is a long series of agree or disagree questions in which the respondent initially tries earnestly to answer the questions, but who because of boredom or fatigue speeds through the rest of the questions by marking all agree or disagree.

Social desirability is another response bias that affects responses to questions that have strong social norms for compliance associated with a given response, for example, answers to questions about voting. Finally, there are the very important concerns related to "non-attitudes." One empirical study found that the absence of the "Don't Know" or DK option produced attitudes about non-existent laws (Schuman & Presser, 1981):

> Our analysis of questions about two issues unknown to the American public leads to several important conclusions. First, a substantial minority of the public - in the neighborhood of 30%—will provide an opinion on a proposed law that

they know nothing about if the question is asked without the DK option. This figure is certainly lower than the "majority" sometimes bruited about, but it is obviously large enough to trouble those assessing attitudes or beliefs concerning public issues (p. 158).

The fact that respondents will express *attitudes about issues about which they have no knowledge* has lead many researchers to use screening or filter questions that determine if the respondent has any knowledge about the subject before responses about his or her attitude are solicited.

Pre-Testing the Instrument

One practical way to insure that many potential factors that ultimately can influence total survey error are minimized prior to the start of a survey is to pretest the questionnaire on a sub-sample of the population of interest. This allows the researcher to determine if there are any general problems in the instructions, wording of questions, the order of questions in terms of context effect, response set bias, or the general design or the format of the questionnaire. It is tempting to assume that these factors can be discovered without a dry run. However, experience shows that this is not so. Rarely, does a pre-test not result in some modification that ultimately reduces total survey error.

Data Entry Creating the Codebook

Data are the information gathered during the survey. The case or the unit of analysis for most surveys is typically the individual respondent. The questions that constitute the survey questionnaire are variables that are usually labeled (Folz, 1996; Vasu & Palmer, 1977). Creating the codebook is the process of assigning a unique variable name, variable description, variable width, valid values, value label, and identifying codes for both valid values and missing data. The variables have values that are measured at a given level of measurement (nominal, ordinal, interval or ratio). These variables usually have names, descriptions, and the valid values (codes) allowed for the variable. An example of one line from a codebook is displayed for the variable gender (see Table 1).

Coding decisions also potentially affect total survey error and should be made before the survey is implemented (Folz, 1996). Both open and closed questions need a coding scheme that will provide a framework for statistical and conceptual analysis.

Data Analysis and Report Writing

The final stage in the survey process is the analysis of data and the writing of

Table 1: Example Of One Line Of A Codebook For The Variable Gender

Field	Variable Name	Variable Description	Value	Value Label
1	Gender	Respondent's Gender	0	0 = Male
			1	1 = Female
			.	. = Missing

a report. Typically, the analysis process begins with getting a univariate breakdown for each variable in the survey. Each univariate breakdown usually displays a frequency distribution for the variable which includes the variable's name, description, values, value labels, and missing data. This is usually referred to as the machine codebook and typically breaks down the variables by valid percentages, cumulative percentages, and percentage of missing data.

Bivariate analysis compares an independent variable with a dependent variable. Multivariate analysis involves more than two variables and usually employs the concept of statistical control. Finally, the inclusion of tables, bar charts, histograms, and figures when appropriate are important elements of the final report.

Computer Assisted Survey Research (CASR)

In outlining the stages in the survey research process in the previous section, we attempted to provide a framework for understanding how computers can enhance the survey process. Specifically, how computing potentially cuts costs, improves quality, and minimizes some errors of measurement. By far, the most significant single influence on the practice of survey research to occur in the 1990's is the development of the powerful personal computer (PC) at an affordable cost. Today most researchers and practitioners who have access to a Pentium II machine with sufficient RAM and a large enough disk drive can perform almost any analysis on their desktop without being tied to a large mainframe computer. Moreover, as we shall subsequently discuss, while the *collection of* primary or original data for most surveys still typically requires more infrastructure than a single PC, the *analysis* of primary or secondary data — data previously collected and, for example, available via the Internet — is revolutionized by the current power of desktop PCs and available software (Clark & Maynard, 1998; Folz, 1996). Finally, by using today's PCs, a thoroughly professional final report complete with first rate graphics and tabular materials, is possible using readily available software like Microsoft Office (1994) and SPSS for Windows (1997) (http://www.spss.com) or SAS for Windows (1994) (http://www.sas.com).

Computer Assisted Survey Research (CASR) is a general term for the integration of the computer into different levels of the survey process. CASR was first established at larger university survey research programs (Skronski, 1990). Computer assisted surveys have numerous advantages. In addition to automating the large amount of drudge-work associated with manual implementation of surveys, CASR techniques can help to reduce total survey error. First of all, CASR helps eliminate interviewer bias since the computer provides exactly the same instrument in exactly the same way each time. If desired, however, the computer can also randomly administer two ostensibly similar but differently worded instruments to test instrument validity by the split-halves method. This has both basic research and practical applications. On the one hand, it allows researchers to test empirically hypotheses about, for example, the inclusion or omission of a "Don't know" response, or the inclusion of a middle position (neutral) between two polar anchor points (strongly agree, strongly disagree). As a practical matter, this feature can given the survey researcher certain control over question order and response set bias. Computer-assisted interviews allow automatic branching to further questions contingent upon the respondent's earlier answers, helping to make interviews not only more efficient but also more conversational in tone. Given that the computer does not suffer from fatigue and can search through a complex questionnaire very fast, this can reduce errors in complex branching structures common to some survey designs. While most research shows no difference in responses received for computerized versus pencil and paper instruments, some research has noted more extreme responses to some items with computer surveys than with paper and pencil surveys (Synodinos, Papacostas & Okimoto, 1994).

Electronic data collection exhibits more stability across levels of methodological variables (Helgeson & Ursic, 1989). Kiesler & Sproull (1986), in an experimental comparison of electronic surveys compared to traditional paper and pencil mail surveys, found that the computer method led to more honest and detailed results. Researchers found that response set patterns to closed questions in electronic surveys when compared to response set patterns in paper and pencil surveys were less likely to invoke socially desirable responses. The respondents tended to choose more extreme positions, possibly suggesting greater respondent honesty.

Research has also shown open questions that allow answers that can be edited by respondents are relatively long and disclosing (Kiesler & Sproull, 1986). Moreover, the recent development of computer software that creates category systems extracted from textual materials holds enormous promise for using open questions. The traditional way to analyze open ended responses in survey research is content analysis. Content analysis seeks categories of meaning from, for example, verbatim interviews of respondents. This process is complex, subjective, and can add to total survey error by producing errors related to interrater reliability. New software based on formal linguistic processes for analyzing categorical systems, holds great promise for formalizing the analysis of textual responses to open questions. This software requires adherence to category development principles that have been developed over time and are based on research in grammar and semantics. This software offers an empirical foundation for what has traditionally been a qualitative process. This will clearly reduce total survey error by increasing validity and reliability in the development of response sets for open questions (Litkowski, 1997).

Computerized versions of standard psychological tests have been in use for several years and are now widely accepted as equivalent to paper and pencil instruments (e.g., Nurius, 1990). Researchers who have compared computer administered surveys with other methods of survey administration to determine if differences exist in respondents' assessment of survey mode or in responses have found very few differences. Most research concludes response rates were very similar by mode (Synodinos, Papacostos, & Okimoto, 1994). Fully computerized surveys eliminate coding errors that often plague manual survey research (Folz, 1996). The computerization of survey research functions preserves anonymity, thereby improving veracity of results. It appears less threatening and more neutral to the subject. CASR provides more timely feedback to subjects and research sponsors alike, helps prevent interviewer bias and subject intimidation (e.g., when subjects are the sponsor's employees or students), and reduces overall costs of the information gathering process. Finally, it is possible with computerized surveys to measure response delay intervals, which have been shown to be correlated with faking of responses. CASR software may thus record response latency times, compare them with norms, and branch to probe questions when latency times are outside the normalized range (George & Skinner, 1990; Synodinos, Papacostos, & Okimoto, 1994).

CASR is currently evolving computer based management systems that assist in the survey research project. Statistics Canada, for example, has developed a computer based case management system (CMS) that performs three main functions: (1) it routes cases for analysis during the survey process from interviewer to the head office, (2) it tracks the status of a survey at a given point in time including describing the status of interviews, (3) it gives options to interviewers to make appointments and records specialized notes (Defour, Kaushal, & Michaud, 1997). CASR has evolved to such a point that on-line codebook browsing and conversational survey analysis is now possible. The University of California at Berkeley (He & Gey, 1995) has developed a system to encourage undergraduate research. Using their codebook browser with its point and click features, the student can click on a particular variable such as "Catholic" and the question text window will jump to the first question with that text. The student can then select a second variable and do a crosstabulation. This technology is presently restricted to rectangular data formats.

Computer-assisted Personal Interviewing (CAPI)

CAPI is computer-assisted personal interviewing, a term for methods under which the interviewer brings a portable computer on which CAPI software has been loaded to the interview site. Typically, the interviewer reads questions from it, and enters responses directly. CAPI allows the respondent to be interviewed in their home, place of business, at the mall, etc. Completed interviews are then sent to the central office via disk or via modem for processing. Pioneered in Europe by Statistics Sweden (Lyberg, 1989) and the Netherlands Central Bureau of Statistics (Van Bastalaer et al., 1987), CAPI has been used in this country for the Nationwide Food Consumption Survey (Rothschild & Wilson, 1988).

Statistics Canada has recently perfected a CAPI system that involves an initial in-person interview, in which over 1,000 interviewers are equipped with portable computers and conduct a Labor Force Survey at the household level. This CAPI interview is then followed by five telephone interviews (Dufour, Kaushal, & Michaud, 1997). Research shows CAPI is accepted by both interviewers and respondents and increases data quality. It appears, however, that CAPI is initially more expensive than traditional paper and pencil interviewing (Baker, 1990; Baker, 1992). Virtually every major American survey organization has, or is developing, a CAPI system. CAPI is currently a well established computer application with a number of specific advantages that impact data quality, and the reduction of total survey error, CAPI is used (Baker, 1992):

- To reduce the time needed to collect and process survey data. Computers can help us perform all the steps to collect and process data faster. The capacity to integrate several of these steps—for example, editing, coding, data entry, cleaning, and in some cases receipt and low level sample management—into a single process reduces the elapsed time between survey design and analysis

help of the respondent.
- To exert greater control over the survey process and therefore improve the quality of the information collected. Errors, both by interviewers and respondents, can be detected more quickly and resolved, often with the help of the respondent.
- To reduce survey costs. The efficiency created by integrating formerly discrete tasks into the single step.
- To implement more complex questionnaire designs than are possible with paper and pencil. Computers can deal with can deal with much more complex skip patterns and use previously collected information more effectively than can human beings working only with paper and pencil. (p. 146).

As of this writing, multimedia applications are making their appearance in the area of computerized survey research including CAPI. These multimedia applications have both practical and measurement implications. Research Triangle Institute for example (Cooley, et al., 1996), has experimented with adding audio to the interviewing process. The process works as follows, the respondent listens to a digitally recorded version of questions and answer choices through headphones. The respondent subsequently records his or her answer directly into the computer essentially making the process a self-interview. This technology allows maximum privacy. It has a number of applications in areas where the answers required are highly sensitive, for example, sexual behavior. It also has a number of advantages that potentially reduce total survey error. First of all, it does not require the respondent to be literate, only that they can hear. It allows multilingual interviewing without requiring multilingual interviewers. It allows the type of controlled branching previously mentioned, automatic range checking, and the automated production of data files for analysis. Finally, this system (hardware and software) always produces a standardized questionnaire in all languages in which it is administered (Cooley, et al., 1996). This use of audio is not only innovative, but has a number of potential uses that will proliferate as the technology decreases in cost and increases in quality.

Computer Assisted Telephone Interviewing (CATI)

Computer-assisted telephone interviewing (CATI) is a hardware and software technology that has become sufficiently inexpensive and convenient so that it will no doubt grow substantially in the next decade. Though CATI has been available since the early 1970's (Fink, 1983), it now provides a convenient and cost effective method of obtaining interview data. Once used on minicomputers like the VAX, CATI today is implemented on microcomputers with support provided by database and statistical tools for related analyses (Crispell, 1989).

The advantages of CATI are several, after the initial investment in computing hardware, software, and telephone lines. Much of this infrastructure may be used for other purposes and, therefore, may not represent additional costs. CATI allows projects to be completed faster and at a lower cost, particularly in terms of labor costs. It also can deal with complex questionnaires with branching formats. Since it permits only the entry of valid codes, it reduces total survey error. It also lets the researcher immediately track the respondent's profile (Anderson & Magnan, 1995; Folz, 1996). Also, if respondents are properly familiarized with the method, CATI is perceived as more anonymous in nature and hence is better suited for obtaining candid responses. This is even more true of another form of computer-assisted survey, in which respondents enter information in voting booth style using a computerized survey which never asks identifying information.

CATI varies substantially with the specific software used, and can be differentiated broadly between two forms: partial and full. Partial CATI still requires human telephone interviewers, but the interviewers are prompted on the computer screen with the questions to ask. They enter data directly into the survey database thereby eliminating an extra coding step. Full CATI eliminates human interviewers altogether. This technology is sometimes called TDE (touchtone dial entry), or ATI (automated telephone interviewing). The computer poses the questions to the respondent using either voice emulation or recordings, and the respondent answers by pressing buttons on a touch-tone phone. These tones are translated by the software and the corresponding responses are entered directly into the survey database (Werking, Tupek & Clayton, 1988). TDE has been used by the Bureau of Labor Statistics to collect some of its Current Employment Statistics data.

Some advantages cited for CATI are simplification of interviewer training, closer interviewer supervision in partial CATI designs, more rapid changing of survey instruments, easier use of multiple forms, more rapid availability of data, and improved cost control and recordkeeping. More sophisticated uses of CATI also allow branching within a questionnaire contingent on an interviewee's responses; re-presentation of past responses to assist in recall; on-line calculations using prior responses to change content of items currently being posed; and availability of standardized help screens and prompts where explication of items is desired. Other features of CATI software are sample generation from telephone databases, call scheduling (e.g., handling time zones; making call-back appointments), accepting incoming call-backs, management reports (e.g., on interviewer productivity or refusal rates), quota control in stratified designs, menu-driven questionnaire authoring systems, pretest administration and analysis, question order randomization, text insertion (e.g., or the respondent's name) in item text, dynamic generation of choices (respondent-supplied information from prior items appears as choices in subsequent items), revision editing (users can back up), and handling of respondent skips and qualifiers. For a discussion of advanced CATI techniques see Groves (1988). For a discussion of optimal call scheduling with CATI see Weeks, Kulka, and Pierson, (1987), Weeks (1988), and Greenberg and Stokes (1989). Finally, The Questionnaire Programming Language (QPL) a public domain software developed by the U.S. General Accounting Office is accessible to public administrators and educators and is extremely useful in conducting CATI surveys (Anderson & Magnan, 1995).

In addition to all the foregoing advantages, CATI systems can be used in conjunction with random digit dialing (RDD) for sampling purposes. RDD is far superior to relying on available lists such as outdated phone directories that, obviously, do not contain unlisted numbers. Recall, probability sampling requires that all sampling elements have an equal or known probability of inclusion. This assumption along with that of adequate response rate are assumptions that underlie many commonly employed statistical tests. RDD is one way to reduce sampling error and increase precision because it increases the probability that every household with a phone (regardless if it is a listed phone number) can be sampled. RDD typically begins by establishing all sampling prefixes that are isomorphic with a given geographical area (for example, 380, 467, 319, etc. for Cary, North Carolina) and then uses some randomized process to select the other four digits. As a practical matter, a number of commercial sampling services exist that will draw RDD samples for specified localities. These companies typically use an algorithm that produces sample lists of phone numbers in proportion to the number of lines in each of the prefixes in the telephone companies jurisdiction.

CATI is enhanced by the appearance of massive databases of phone numbers, such as the CD-ROM products *Disc America*, with 100 million residential and business names, addresses, and phone numbers; and *Disc America - Business*[2], a CD-ROM with 10 million U.S. business names, addresses, and phone numbers with SIC codes and Boolean searching. A similar resource is the *Associations CD*[3], a CD-ROM version of the 18-volume *Encyclopedia of Associations*, comprehending 90,000 associations worldwide, 22,600 U.S. associations, 8,200 international associations, 60,000 U.S. subnational organizations, and 11,000 association periodicals. It comes with software for producing mailing labels for survey research or marketing purposes, and has a built-in autodialer for computer-assisted telephone interviewing.

In addition to CD-ROM databases of telephone numbers, similar data are available on-line. For instance, researchers in non-profits may be interested to know that the *Encyclopedia of Associations* is also on-line on DIALOG (http://www.dialog.com), a leading information vendor (File 114). For survey research purposes, this file can be used to identify groups offering computerized membership lists.

The Internet

As of this writing, a few highly innovative *academic* survey research applications exist that use the Internet. These innovations exist both for the collection of original data and in the secondary analysis of survey research data. Collecting survey data on the Internet is currently evolving, and, we believe, will develop at breakneck speeds in the next five years. Our focus in this chapter will be restricted to attempts to collect data for social science versus commercial purposes (Comer, 1997).

The Munich Public Health Service in Germany reports its experience in collecting data by direct mailing on the Internet using features of the World Wide Web (Swoboda, et al., 1997). The World Wide Web (WWW) is an Internet service that organizes information using hypermedia that effectively links geographically dispersed people by linking their computers and by providing access to multimedia capabilities. The Munich Public Health Service has experimented with transferring traditional survey research methodology onto the Internet. They have conducted a direct mail world wide survey using the Internet. The focus of the survey was future risks to the world and to mankind (Swoboda, et al., 1997). A random sampling procedure was employed in which two hundred newsgroups were randomly selected by the news server of the Technical University of Munich (http://news.iunformatik.tu-muenchen.de). A parsing program was employed to scan all newsgroup messages for e-mail addresses and to store those messages on a file. In this way, the researchers were able to overcome the fact that there is no complete e-mail directory of users on the Internet. All returned questionnaires were stored in a single concatenated file. Data was then converted to a SAS file for analysis.

While the substantive findings of the survey are beyond the scope of this chapter, the authors conclusions about the experiment are worthy of comment (Swoboda, et al., 1997). There are between 20 and 50 million users on the Internet and, while this sampling frame of Internet users is biased toward well educated, upper-class, males, this is changing daily. Data collection on the Internet is fast, inexpensive, capable of utilizing the multimedia capabilities of computing, and allows for the immediate processing of data. Many of the technical problems of survey research on the Internet are being streamlined as we speak. The Internet also has one additional feature. It provides the researcher with *access to a world wide group of respondents, a sampling frame that is growing daily* (Swoboda, et al., 1997). Clearly, we are only seeing the beginning of the direct mail using the Internet.

A second major impact on survey research using the Internet is in the analysis of secondary data. Secondary data are data that were collected for a purpose other than that for which the data are currently being analyzed. This secondary analysis generally has as its purpose the presenting of new findings — findings different from those contained in the original final report. Given the costs of collecting primary data, the analysis of secondary data can be very important to public administration and educational researchers and practitioners. The ability of researchers and practitioners with a PC and a connection to the Internet, to analyze large data collected according to the strictures of a well-executed sampling design and using questions that have been constructed and pre-tested for the types of errors discussed in this chapter, is an exciting development. Moreover, access to these data sources are moving toward the point-and-click technology found in the Windows and Macintosh environments (Clark & Maynard, 1998).

Public opinion archives worldwide are in the process of making access to end-users more user-friendly, by using tools like Java programming. Using common gateway interface (CGI) and Web browsers, the user can request pages and basic statistical analysis of archived survey data. Having data on-line makes it possible to pursue multiple databases from one's own PC. In addition, a variety of search engines are available to assist the researcher in locating the data they need by entering keywords and subject headings related to the research endeavor.

Many data archives, such as the Roper Center, currently provided datasets to users over the Internet using FTP (file transfer protocol). Increasingly, these on-line data sets can be searched at the question level, which greatly facilitates topic searches and longitudinal analysis (Clark & Maynard, 1998). Among the major data producers and data archives are the Gallup Organization (http://www.gallup.com), the National Opinion Research Center (NORC) (http://www.norc.ucchicago.edu), and the Institute for Social Research (ISR) at the University of Michigan (http://www.isr.unmich.edu).

Continuous Audience Response Technology (CART)

Survey research is firmly established as a major tool of social scientists. Now the focus group is coming of age. Focus groups are currently used by, academics, pollsters, market researchers, and educators, as well as federal, state, and local governments (Morgan, 1998). The format of a focus group involves a moderator, a group of 6 to 14 subjects who may be compensated for their time, and an organized theme or objective about which the group is gathered. For example, one of the authors of this paper recently moderated a focus group called "Growth Issues in Cary, North Carolina."

Focus groups are regarded as forms of qualitative research in which the principal mode of analysis is carefully listening to what the focus group conveys to the moderator (Krueger, 1998). When done well, qualitative focus groups involve "a disciplined process, systematic steps, a defined protocol, verifiable results and multiple feedback loops (Krueger, 1998, p. 5). Focus groups are predicated on open questions and an interactive process that allows respondents to change their position in response to the dialog in which they are participating.

The analysis of responses in traditional qualitative focus groups requires great skill in semantics and an understanding of the dimension of the problem that is being considered. A new form of instant polling for focus groups has evolved, first labeled "continuous audience response technology" (CART) by Vasu, Long, & Hughes (1990). Also called "real time research," the emergence of CART technology and its impact on focus group methodology is the focus of this portion of the chapter.

One important distinction between research methodologies is the dimension of time and the degree of control that the experimenter has over the independent variable (Cook & Campbell, 1979). All quantitative research designs can be considered ex post facto or quasi-experimental, except a true experimental design in which the researcher manipulates an independent variable and measures a dependent variable under conditions of physical control. Ex post facto research underscores the inability of the researcher to manipulate the independent variable and the inability to randomly assign subjects to treatment groups. It also suggests that the independent and dependent variable have already occurred in time (Cook & Campbell, 1979; Lyberg, et al., 1997). Traditionally, in survey research the inability to achieve the control to manipulate the independent variable has been seen as a necessary tradeoff, thereby gaining statistical generalization to a larger population by employing a large random sample of subjects.

Stated simply, CART technologies offer a potential bridge between the best aspects of experimental and quasi-experimental design. CART also gives new life to the time tested qualitative focus group methodology (Krueger, 1998). CART technology is a merger of microcomputer and video technology that allows subjects to respond to a variety of continuous stimuli. CART also creates methodological options which can overcome some of the limitations inherent in many quasi-experimental studies. A discussion of the mechanics of CART follows.

Continuous audience response systems enable subjects in a traditional focus group setting to respond to continuous stimuli (e.g., political commercial, political speeches, statements rolling up the screen with voice overlays, etc.) by turning a dial on a handheld keypad, moving a slide, or pressing a button on their individual response devices. The responses are captured at intervals as frequently as 1/5th of a second and fed into a microcomputer with customized software designed to analyze and output the responses. The data are saved in some file format.

The sophistication of the output is a function of the sophistication of the software. The more advanced systems provide a combination of continuous curves and digital averages for demographic breakouts, and immediately superimposes these data summaries on video (stimulus) tape for playback and response in a debriefing with the subjects of the focus group. A few systems offer concurrent printouts and graphics of the demographic tabulations and the subjects continuous responses. One example would be a simulated jury responding to output from a videotaped segment of a defense attorney's opening argument in a jury simulation conducted by one of the authors of this paper. Only the high-end of CART technology allows for the continuous measurement and screen display of responses in both the aggregate (all subjects), as well as for subgroups (men and women, liberals, moderates and conservatives, etc.). This technology can be conceptualized as a form of instant feedback analysis. In other words, the focus group members can have replayed back to them their own responses (in quantitative format) to any stimulus, and then be probed as to why as a group (or as individuals) they responded as they did. This feature of CART allows the researcher to explore qualitatively issues which are presented in the stimulus tape. However, this quantitative probing can be based on the qualitative knowledge of the group and individual responses to the stimulus.

Some CART systems allow for a smooth, continuous response dial and a two-line screen so subjects can confirm their input with feedback in numbers and words. The response dials are calibrated for a variety of metrics (e.g., 1 to 100, 1 through 7, etc.). The keypad can be used for precise responses to demographic questions that are recorded and become the basis for the moving breakdowns that the subjects subsequently see in debriefing.

A typical CART session takes place in a focus group facility or pre-wired conference room. The technology is now portable enough so that one can "parachute in" with a CART system into virtually any location, or use such facilities as U.S. Sprint rooms located all over the country, that allow groups to be gathered throughout the nation for simulcasts. In addition, a moderator in one time zone can run CART sessions using the video teleconferencing features of U.S. Sprint with subjects from multiple time zones. Subjects typically sit around a table or in a theater configuration, depending on the size of the group, and are directed by a moderator (Krueger, 1998). They are given ten minutes of training on their response tasks. Demographic questions that have been typed into the computer are sent to the subjects television monitor. The subjects respond with their handheld input devices. Their responses become a part of overlay tape that is created while they dial. As we mentioned previously, this overlay tape is available for immediate playback to the group. Typically, the stimulus tape has a "warm-up" tape and a "benchmark tape," as well as the stimulus tape containing the dependent variable concepts of interest.

Subjects' explanations in their own words are an important part of this research technique. Clearly, the reaction of subjects to their own responses, allows for more depth in probing issues than is afforded by traditional qualitative methodologies. In addition, a CART session may produce a third tape which is an instantly edited combination of key sections of the overlay tape and a camera view of the moderator and group discussion sessions.

The combination of quantitative and qualitative approaches to measurement produces a variety of validity and reliability implications worth briefly exploring. One of the reasons for the popularity of the focus group with certain researchers is the ability of a focus group to provide qualitative responses of greater depth about a variety of stimuli. The deficiency of the traditional focus group is its susceptibility to group effects such as being dominated by opinion leaders. The CART handheld keypad gives the focus group member anonymity and allows the moderator, who is frequently linked to the control room by remote microphone, the information necessary to minimize the effects of the strident but unrepresentative opinion leader.

CART technology gives the researcher a great deal of knowledge with which to mitigate many of the negative aspects of group dynamics. For example, in the playback portion or debriefing of a CART session the focus group sees for itself, its group mean superimposed on the stimuli, as well as a moving histogram (if available) that underscores demographic differences in responses to the stimuli. The moderator knows the group and individual responses and can use such information to direct the flow of debriefing. For example, if a gender difference is evident with respect to a segment of a commercial, it can be brought to the forefront of discussion by the moderator. In traditional focus groups, the moderator would not even know of such a difference and, in fact, such a difference might be subsumed by a group consensus. Moreover, an experienced researcher behind the scenes can feed questions to pose to the group based upon his or her review of the continuous data output provided by the microcomputer. This last technique allows for the discovery and probing of issues not initially in the research design.

Most sophisticated CART systems provide all data outputs in at least ASCII format and some produce SPSS or SAS file formats. These files typically include the independent variables (focus group demographics) with the continuous responses of the subjects to the stimuli for post-session analysis. CART technology can easily accommodate 30 to 60 subjects per session/ per room with either multiple sequenced sessions or multiple simultaneous sessions using U.S. Sprint rooms. These options can generate adequate sample sizes for most research designs. Finally, the permanent record provided by the videotape with the quantitative overlays provides an enduring record of the session. This feature of the technology greatly enhances many aspects of the reliability of measurement in that it allows for multiple independent judgments of the same event and variables. The development of content analysis software previously mentioned is another important analysis tool that can be used in conjunction with CART.

The availability and cost of the technology is a consideration to those in public administration and education. The technology, while becoming less costly, is still moderately expensive. Consequently, its uses tend to be in the arenas of corporate and campaign research. However, the essential elements of CART involve non-proprietary technology (microcomputers and videotape record and playback systems).

CART systems are proliferating and their cost will continue to decrease. Some universities are currently purchasing CART systems. A list of the major commercial and research vendors of this technology include: *OR/ED LABS*[4], *The Perception Analyzer*[5], and *ViewFacts*[6].

The cost of using CART technology alone adds approximately $1,000 - $4,000 per focus group session. Where one falls in this range of pricing depends on the sophistication of the hardware/software configuration. This pricing may or may not include any analytical report on the session. The more sophisticated users of CART technology realize that the technology without an accompanying research design is of limited utility. CART is best conceptualized as a technology and a methodology. However, the vendors of some systems will sell or rent them to researchers devoid of any methodological assistance.

The handheld control units that the respondents use come in variety of forms and are in constant evolution. This is also a factor in the pricing of the system. One current variety of handheld device is a combination of a dial and alphanumeric keypad. The keypad is employed to respond to demographic questions that appear on the monitor such as "indicate your gender, A (male) or B (female)." The top portion of the device is turned in response to the stimulus. Some CART systems have only keypads. Such keypads require the user to move his attention from the stimulus in order to focus on the correct position on the keypad and pose some reliability problems. The newest version of the technology will include remote hand held devices.

Many CART systems must deal with electronic interference such as that found near Airports. An other important difference in CART systems that is reflected in the price is how often the system samples the session (e.g,. 1/5 of a second versus every 2 seconds).

The software that runs CART is generally proprietary and determines the quality of graphic and statistical output available at the end of the session. Some systems have a software component that will allow presentation graphics on any segment of the videotape.

A Research Application: Growth Issues in Cary, North Carolina

Overview of the Study

After reviewing some of the ways in which computers can be integrated into survey research and focus group processes, it is appropriate to provide an illustration of a citizen survey that uses some of the applications we have discussed in this chapter. We will briefly outline the implementation of a study designed to report to the city council on public concerns about growth issues in the community. The complete scope of the research project is beyond the scope of this article. Rather, we want to focus on the fact that this particular citizen survey was a combination of quantitative (survey research) and qualitative approaches (focus groups), and used a number of computer applications discussed in this chapter in the process.

Cary, North Carolina, a city in the Research Triangle, has experienced explosive growth in the last two decades. For years, this growth was welcomed. In recent years, the costs of growth have become a major public issue. In the public debate evidenced in the media and in contentious council meetings, the community appeared polarized. Recent local elections resulted in the defeat of two long-time city council members who were considered "business as usual." In their place, candidates who were perceived as favoring controlled growth were elected. The city council and a non-partisan group commissioned one of the author's of this chapter to conduct a poll and focus groups about growth issues in Cary and to report back the results to them (Vasu, 1998).

The study developed as follows. First of all, an on-line DIALOG search was conducted of a number of data sets that contained research relevant to growth issues. From this, a number of conceptual categories were developed and a first draft questionnaire completed. A pre-test was conducted and it became clear that a major issue in the community, urban sprawl, lacked conceptual clarity among the respondents. It was clear that people needed a visual referent and that this would not be possible on a telephone poll.

It was decided that both a telephone poll and a focus group would be conducted. The telephone poll gave us the advantage of being able to generalize the findings, however, at the cost of any significant depth of analysis. The combination of a telephone poll along with the inclusion of a focus group compensated for many of deficiencies of both techniques when they are used independently. The telephone poll preceded and directed the *content* of the focus group discussion.

The Telephone Poll

The sampling frame for the telephone poll was a list of valid telephone numbers for the municipality of Cary, North Carolina. From this list, a random digit dialing (RDD) sample was drawn. The number of valid respondents for the survey was 454. The degree of precision for the sample is as follows. The sampling error was approximately plus or minus 5%. The confidence coefficient was 95%, or 95 samples in 100. A comparison of the demographics of the sample with the U.S. Census Block figures indicated that the sample was representative of the known demographic profile of the community.

The questionnaire employed in the telephone poll was designed to define current attitudes toward a variety of social, political, and economic issues inherent in the urban growth of Cary, North Carolina. The data were collected by a private firm in West Virginia using a proprietary CATI system which produced an ASCII file that was readable using SPSS for Windows, the program that produced the analyses. The final report was written using Microsoft Word (1994) and relevant tabular and graphic output from SPSS (1997) and Adobe PageMaker (1996) was included.

The questionnaire was designed to analyze the image of the Cary city government as a steward of that growth through its land use growth controls. Results of research in other communities resulted in a number of findings that formed a conceptual framework relating to how citizens perceived the issues and actors relevant to high growth. The questionnaire also was designed to target issues that were identified in the public debate as both problems and good things associated with Cary's growth. Specific questions about the desirability of Cary imposing growth controls that would limit the building of houses and business in undeveloped areas were included. The respondents were also asked to rate the importance of certain factors in choosing a community to live in. A variety of transportation questions and the willingness to pay a tax increase were asked of the respondents. Finally, an overall satisfaction with the way Cary has managed its growth over the last few years was included in the questionnaire. The telephone poll was completed one week prior to the focus groups.

Focus Groups

Subjects for the focus group (N = 30) were residents of Cary of voting age who were identified by their positive response to a question asked during the interview that related to their willingness to participate in a focus group. They were chosen according to specific demographic criteria designed to achieve a representative socioeconomic mix of Cary residents. The subjects were combined into two focus groups of 15 each. Since the focus groups do not represent a true probability sample, we did not employ inferential statistics or tests of statistical significance for the focus groups as we did for the poll. We employed a content analysis methodology of the recorded audio portion of the focus group in conjunction with statistical analysis of the data provided by the telephone interview to reach the conclusions presented subsequently in our findings (Morgan & Krueger, 1998).

The two focus groups were presented a series of visual representations of the way Cary has developed and the way Cary might develop in the future — specifically a more compact development profile. The visual representations were done by an architect on Adobe PageMaker and sent to the author as an attachment to e-mail. These visual representations were the reason that Continuous Audience Response Technology (CART) could not be employed. The static visual forms did not lend themselves to this form of continuous sampling.

The focus groups were shown architectural drawings of different forms of urban development. Form 1 characterized Cary as it is now. Among the perspectives shown were the a shopping mall now and in the future. The graphic of the future of the shopping center was done by computer enhancement of development currently consistent with zoning and development policy. In addition, a number of aerial shots of suburban developments with cul-de-sacs were shown. Form 2 illustrated a more dense development pattern similar to that evident in the old downtown Cary area, as well as residential development patterns that were more mixed use with a higher residential density.

The focus groups were split about their individual preferences between Form 1 and Form 2, however, the overwhelming majority of citizens in the focus groups supported the idea of the city of Cary using developmental controls (zoning, subdivision regulations, and Planned Unit Developments [PUD], etc.) to implement Form 2. The focus group participants were able to recognize that certain features of Cary's current development pattern — large lots, cul-de-sacs, and very low densities — were likely to lead to a development pattern known as urban sprawl.

Both the poll and focus groups underscored the fact that urban growth is an issue that resonates with the citizens of Cary. This issue is clearly on the forefront of the minds of the citizens. Citizens are clearly aware that rapid growth has tangible costs as well as benefits. Currently, the costs of rapid growth is seen through the lens of traffic congestion, overcrowded schools, and the loss of natural areas primarily. While Cary was perceived as a clean and well-planned community, an emerging recognition that some of these features are in jeopardy of being eroded by rapid growth was discovered. The final report was presented to the Cary City council as both a printed document and as an oral report to an open city council meeting in April, 1998.

Conclusion

Computer-assisted survey research (CASR), computer assisted personal interviewing (CAPI), and continuous audience response technology (CART) are exciting because they are available today, evolving as we speak, and are only beginning to be exploited by public administrators. While use of the Internet and the World Wide Web is still in its experimental stage, it is clear that as significant as the developments are that were outlined above, more is yet to come. Because of computing and related developments in telecommunications and multimedia processing, the old approaches to survey research (and how professors teach survey research) need reexamination. Most of the developments make collection and secondary use of survey data more accessible to end users. However, with all this technology, as grand as it is, we need to keep in mind that good survey research is as much an art as a science. Specifically, it is the art of asking questions.

Endnotes

[1] We will not discuss a number of additional potential errors in questionnaire design due to space limitations. Some of more important omissions include: avoiding double-barreled questions, avoiding double negatives, use of biased terminology like "socialized medicine" or "bureaucrats," measuring the middle position, balance and imbalance in question design, issue intensity, centrality, crystallization, specifics of formatting mail questionnaires, and "Don't know" filters. All of these issues are richly elaborated in the references provided.

[2] *Disc America,* SilverPlatter Directories, 20 Edenville Road, Warwick, NY 10990; 914-986-2649.

[3] *Associations CD,* Gale Research Inc., Book Tower, Dept. 77748, Detroit, MI 48277-0748; 800-223-GALE.

[4] *OR/ED LABS,* 652 Swan Point Road, Bayboro, NC 28515, (919) 745-5544.

[5] *The Perception Analyzer,* Columbia Information Systems, 333 SW 5th Avenue, Suite 200, Portland, Oregon 97204 (503)-225-0112.

[6] *ViewFacts,* 150 N. Michigan Ave., Suite 1000, Chicago, Illinois 60601, (312) 781-1259.

References

Adobe PageMaker [Computer software]. (1995). Adobe Systems.

Allen, D. (1987). Computers versus scanners: An experiment in non-traditional forms of survey administration. *Journal of College Student Personnel*, 28(3), 266-73.

Anderson, R. & Magnan, S. (1995). The questionnaire programming language

(QPL): An overview with examples of call management. *Social Science Computer Review,* 13(3), 291-303.

Babbie, E. (1990). *Survey research methods* (2nd ed.). Belmont, CA: Wadsworth.

Baker, R. (1990, April). Applications of new computer technology in survey research: An overview. *Proceedings, Conference on Advanced Social Science Computing.* Conducted at Williamsburg, VA.

Baker, R. (1992). New technology in survey research: Computer assisted personal interviewing (CAPI). *Social Science Computer Review,* 10(2), 145-157.

Baum, M. & Rowe, B. (1989). Uses of CATI at NNCHS. National Field Technologies Conference. St. Petersburg, FL.

Bradburn, N., & Sudman, S. (1991). The current status of Questionnaire design. In P. Biemer, R. Groves, L. Lyberg, N. Mathiowetz, & S. Sudman (Eds.), *Measurement errors in surveys* (pp. 29-40). New York: John Wiley.

Clark, R., & Maynard, M. (1998). Using online technology for secondary analysis of survey research data. *Social Science Computer Review,* 16(1), 58-71.

Code of professional ethics and practices. (1986). Ann Arbor, MI: American Association for Public Opinion Research.

Comer, D. (1997). *The Internet book.* Upper Saddle River, NJ: Prentice Hall Inc.

Converse, J., & Presser, S. (1986). *Survey questions: Handcrafting the standardized questionnaire.* Beverly Hills, CA.: Sage.

Converse, P. & Traugott, M. (1986). Assessing the accuracy of polls and surveys. *Science,* 234, 1094-1098.

Cook, T., & Campbell, D. (1979). *Quasi-experimentation: Design and analysis issue for filed studies.* Boston, MA: Houghton Mifflin.

Cooley, P., Turner, C., O'Reilly, J., Allen, D., Hammill, D. & Paddock, R. (1996). Audio-CASI: Hardware and software considerations in adding sound to a computer assisted interviewing system. *Social Science Computer Review,* 14(2), 197-204.

Crispell, D. (1989). People talk computers listen (Using Computer Assisted Interviewing). *American Demographics,* 11(8), 1.

Deming, W. (1950). *Some theory of sampling.* NY: John Wiley & Sons.

Dillman, D. (1978). Mail and telephone surveys: The total design method. New York: John Wiley.

Dufour, J., Kaushal, R., & Michaud, S. (1997). Computer-assisted interviewing in a decentralised environment: The case of household surveys at Statistics Canada. *Survey methodology,* 23(2), 147-156.

Eiler, J., Nelson, W., Jensen, C. & Johnson S. (1989). Automated data collection using bar code. *Behavior Research Methods, Instruments, and Computers,* 21(1), 53-8.

Fink, J. (1983). CATI's first decade: The Chilton experience. *Sociological Methods and Research,* 12(2), 153-168.

Floz, D. (1996). *Survey research for public administration.* Thousand Oaks, CA: SAGE Publications Inc..

George, M. & Skinner, H. (1990). Using response latency to detect inaccurate responses in a computerized lifestyle assessment. *Computers in Human Behavior,* 6(2), 167-175.

Gilliland, J. & Kinchen, S. (1987). Microcomputers for survey data-entry and analysis. *Population Index*, 53(3), 374.

Greenberg, B., & Stokes, S. (1989). Developing an optimal call scheduling strategy for a telephone survey. *National Field Technologies Conference*, St. Petersburg, FL.

Groves, R. (Ed.). (1988). *Telephone survey methodology*. NY: Wiley Interscience.

Groves, R., & Mathiowetz, N. (1984). Computer assisted telephone interviewing: Effects on interviewers and respondents. *Public Opinion Quarterly*, 48(1B), 356-369.

He, J. & Gey, F. (1996). Online codebook browsing and conversational survey analysis. *Social Science Computer Review*, 14(2), 181-186.

Helgeson, J. & Ursic, M. (1989). The decision process equivalency of electronic versus pencil-and-paper data collection methods. *Social Science Computer Review*, 7(3), 296-310.

Holden, R. & Hickman, D. (1987). Computerized versus standard administration of the Jenkins-Activity-survey (form-T). *Journal of Human Stress*, 13(4), 175-179.

Horton, L. (1990). Disk-based surveys: New way to pick your brain. *Software Magazine*, 10(2), 76-66.

(1990). Face-to-face with computers. Hypotenuse (Research Triangle Park, NC: RTI), Jan/March, 8-9.

Ingels, J. (1989). Microcomputers and field management at NORD. *National Field Technologies Conference*, St. Petersburg, FL.

Kiesler, S. & Sproull, L. (1986). Response effects in the electronic survey. the *Public Opinion Quarterly*, 50(3), 402-413.

Kimmel, A. (1988). *Ethics and values in applied social research*. Newbury Park, CA: Sage.

Kish, L. (1965). *Survey sampling*. NY: John Wiley & Sons.

Krueger, R. (1998). *Analyzing and reporting focus group results*. Thousand Oaks, CA: SAGE Publications Inc..

Litkowski, K. (1997). Category development based on semantic principles. *Social Science Computer Review*, 15(4), 394-409.

Long, L., & Vasu, M. (1988). *Public Issues in 1988*. NY: Independent Insurance Agents of America.

Lucas, R., Mullen, P., Luna, C., & McInroy, D. (1977). Psychiatrist and computer interrogators of patients with alcohol-related illnesses: A comparison. *British Journal of Psychiatry*, 131, 160-167.

Lyberg, L. (1989). Topic 18.2. *Proceedings of the 45th Session*, International Statistics Institute, Book III.

Lyberg, L., Biemer, P., Collins, M., deLeeuw, E., Dippo, C., Schwarz, N., & Trewin, D. (1997). *Survey measurement and process quality*. NY: John Wiley & Sons.

Malcolm, R., Sturgis, E., Anton, R., & Williams, L. (1989). Computer-assisted diagnosis of alcoholism. *Computers in Human Services*, 5(3-4), 163-170.

Microsoft Office [Computer software]. (1995). Microsoft Corporation.

Microsoft Word [Computer software]. (1994). Microsoft Corporation.

Miller, T., & Miller, M. (1991). *Citizen Surveys: How to do them, how to use them, what they mean.* Washington, DC: ICMA.

Morgan, D. (1998). *The focus group guidebook.* Thousand Oaks, CA: SAGE Publications Inc.

Nicholls, W. (1988). Computer-assisted telephone interviewing: A general introduction. In R. Groves et al. (Ed.), *Telephone survey methodology* (pp. 377-385). NY: Wiley and Sons.

Nurius, P. (1990). A review of automated assessment. *Computers in Human Services,* 6(4), 265-281.

Optical mark reader software and hardware. (1987). *T.H.E. Journal,* June, 76-77.

O'Sullivan, E., & Rassel, G. (1995). *Research methods for public administrators.* New York: Longman.

Payne, S. (1951). *The art of asking questions.* Princeton, NJ: Princeton University Press.

Rea, L., & Parker, R. (1992). *Designing and conducting survey research.* San Francisco: Jossey - Bass Inc.

Rossi, P., Wright, J., & Anderson, A. (1983). *Handbook of Survey Research.* San Diego, CA: Harcourt, Brace, Jovanovich.

Rothschild, B. & Wilson, L. (1988). National Food Consumption Survey 1987. *Proceedings of the 4th Annual Research Conference.* Conducted at U.S. Bureau of Census, Washington D.C., 347-356.

Schuman, H., & Presser, S. (1981). *Questions and answers in attitude surveys: Experiments on question form, wording, and context.* New York: Academic Press.

SAS® for Windows (Statistical Analysis System), Release 6.10) [Computer software]. (1996). Cary, NC: SAS Inc.

Schwarz, N., & Hippler, H. (1991). Response alternatives; The impact of their choice and presentation order.. In Biemer, P., Groves, M., Lyberg, L, Mathiowetz, N., & Sudman, S. (Eds.), *Measurement errors in surveys* (pp. 41-56). New York: John Wiley.

Skronski, M. (1990). Computer-assisted survey methods has a new data collection facility. *Berkeley Computing Quarterly,* 2(2), 4-5.

SPSS® for Windows (Statistical Package for the Social Sciences) (version 8) [Computer software]. (1997). SPSS Inc.

Sudman, S., & Bradburn, N. (1982). *Asking questions: A practical guide to questionnaire design.* San Francisco: Jossey-Bass.

Swoboda, W., Muhlberger, N., Weitkunat, R., & Schneeweib, S. (1997). Internet surveys by direct mail. *Social Science Computer Review,* 15(3), 242-253.

Synodinos, N., Papacostas, C., & Okimoto, G. (1994). Computer-administered versus paper and pencil surveys and the effect of sample selection. *Behavior Research Methods, Instruments and Computers,* 26(4), 395-401.

Van Bastelaer, A., Kerssemakers, F., & Sikkel, D. (1987). A test of the Continuous Labour Force Survey with hand-held computers: Interviewer behavior and data quality. In bill (Ed.), *CBS Select 4: Automation in Survey Processing* (pp. 33-35). Voorburg, Netherlands: Netherlands Central Bureau of Statistics.

Vasu, E,. & Palmer, R. (1977). *Introduction to research and the computer: A self-instructional package.* Chapel Hill, NC: Institute for Research in Social Science.

Vasu, M. (1998). *Cary growth strategies project.* Raleigh, NC: Triangle Growth Strategies Inc.

Vasu, M., Long, L., and Hughes, D. (1990). Continuous audience response technology combined with survey methods in field research: A description and application. *Advances in Social Science and Computers,* Volume III. Thousand Oaks: Ca, Sage Publications.

Waksberg, J. (1978). Sampling methods for random digit dialing. *Journal of the American Statistical Association* , 73(361), 40-46.

Weeks, M. (1988). Call scheduling with CATI: Current capabilities and methods. In R. M. Groves et al. (Ed.), *Telephone survey methodology* (pp. 403-420). NY: Wiley and Sons.

Weeks, M., Kulka, R., and Pierson, S. (1987). Optimal call scheduling for a telephone survey. *Public Opinion Quarterly,* 51, 540-549.

Werking, G., Tupek, A. & Clayton, R. (1988). CATI and touchtone self-response applications for establishment surveys. *Journal of Official Statistics,* 4(4), 349-362.

12
Managing Geographic Information Systems in the Public Sector

by
T. R. Carr
Southern Illinois University
Edwardsville

Geographic information systems emerged in the 1970s and have become significant decision-making tools as their capabilities have been enhanced. This chapter includes a brief discussion of various GIS applications and a more detailed discussion of issues that public managers should consider when evaluating implementation of a geographic information system. GIS applications provide benefits at the basic level in terms of producing maps efficiently, at the planning level through the use of database applications, and at the management decision-making level through an ability to access relational databases for policy level decisions. Issues impacting GIS implementation include: needs assessment, project planning, access to public records, liability issues, public and private partnerships, dissemination of information and privacy issues. Public managers should be aware of difficulties associated with justification of costs associated with GIS implementation and that a hesitancy exists on the part of GIS program managers to share missteps and implementation failures.

The term "geographic information system" (GIS) was first used in the 1970s to describe a variety of techniques that could be used to create maps as an aid in the analysis of data for public agencies. This application was an outgrowth of the development of tools such as computer-aided mapping (CAM) and computer-aided design (CAD) systems used primarily by cartographers, draftsmen and engineers to produce very detailed and accurate maps and drawings in an efficient manner. With the application of CAM and CAD programs, very precise maps could be drawn and updated quickly and efficiently to reflect changes in infrastructure, political boundaries and topography. Surveyors and cartographers found these new techniques to be an especially efficient addition to their craft. As the use and availability of these techniques increased, other disciplines found new applications for the technology. Urban planners and economic development directors found that CAM and CAD applications provided the foundation for spatial analysis of geographic data stored in large databases. This application of spatial (location) analysis allowed policy analysts to display economic, demographic, and other data in graphic or map form which enhanced their ability to understand and communicate complex relationships (Huxhold, 1991).

GIS techniques differ somewhat from CAM and CAD type applications in that the spatial analysis of data for decision makers can be effectively conducted with a tolerance for lower levels of accuracy than can the work of surveyors and draftsmen. An error of a few feet or a few yards usually has little impact on decisions relating to demographic characteristics, land use or economic development issues. But an error of even a few feet in a map indicating the path of a water main, a sewer line, or a property boundary can have significant impacts for construction and maintenance purposes. Errors in property boundary lines have the potential for significant legal consequences arising from litigation. This means that the ultimate purpose for creating a GIS should serve as a guide for selecting hardware, software and implementation strategies.

The foundation of a geographic information system involves both the creation and maintenance of an extensive relational database. Relational databases are characterized by the ability to integrate information from one function, such as a street network, with information from a variety of other functions, such as utility services, property assessments, zoning codes, property ownership and demographic data. A true GIS has the ability to access a large relational database and create a graphic display for almost any combination of data. This might include a map of blighted or substandard housing, attendance zones for elementary schools, land use patterns, residential income levels or any of a multitude of other factors. The utility of a GIS for decisionmaking is directly related to the level of current information contained in the database. Obsolete information in the database will produce obsolete maps. This means that a geographic information systems involves a commitment to direct sufficient resources for database development and revision.

GIS Applications

The literature concerning GIS contains an expansive array of public sector applications. This is due to the fact that geography (physical, social and political) has a profound impact on the activities of government agencies. Diverse activities such as establihsing bus transportation routes, school attendance zones, election precincts, police station siting, and infrastructure construction and maintenance have all been performed with the aid of geographic information systems. The following examples of public sector GIS applications illustrate the utility, adaptability, and flexibility of this technique for public managers.

Emergency Dispatch

Minimizing dispatch and arrival time is a crucial element for emergency services such as ambulance, fire and police units. GIS has proven to be an important tool for public agencies in improving response times (Mitchell, 1997). Such a system might typically include a relational database consisting of several different files containing telephone numbers and street addresses; property lot size and location; street and road networks; and locations of emergency service stations, such as hospitals and police and fire stations. With a GIS system in place, the emergency dispatcher with a few keystrokes or mouse clicks can identify the exact location needing service, produce a map with the shortest distance for the emergency response team and provide that information while the team is in route. For small cities, this type of system can be implemented on today's desktop computers.

Land Use Planning

The use of GIS has been used to provide decision-makers with high quality information for making decisions relating to land use and zoning (Aronoff, 1988). Typically data files containing such information as geology, topography, ownership, population density, transportation networks and commercial activity are linked to produce a variety of derived maps for analysis purposes. This spatial analysis enhances the ability of decision-makers to visualize the potential impact of zoning and other land use decisions.

Healthcare Planning

Geographic information systems have demonstrated considerable utility for healthcare planners (Birkin, Clarke, Clarke and Wilson, 1996). "Medical geography" is a term that reflects this application of GIS. Epidemiology, linkages between poverty and disease, and the impact of access to service on utilization are three major areas in which GIS has been used to support healthcare planning activities. Geographic patterns reflecting demand for services, costs associated with service delivery and allocation of financial and personnel resources are important elements in healthcare planning.

Infrastructure Planning

GIS has been used as a tool for debt management associated with infrastructure planning (Hokanson, 1994). Through an extensive database of current and proposed infrastructure and other capital improvement projects containing items such as cost, projected timelines, types of improvement or construction, location and funding mechanism, decision-makers can access multi-year maps and assess the impact of growth on debt. With the inclusion of property assessment data, decision-makers can evaluate the potential impact of development on tax revenues.

Political Campaigns

Novotny and Jacobs (1997) document the increasing importance of GIS in election campaigns at all levels of government. The Clinton presidential campaigns of 1992 and 1996 were heavily influenced by maps containing demographic and attitudinal data. Campaign strategy, media advertisements and resource allocation decisions were all heavily influenced by analysis produced by geographic information systems. Political campaigns at all levels of government will be increasingly influenced by this technology. Public managers at the local level will be presented with requests for "public domain" data that will be used for explicitly partisan political purposes.

Reapportionment

The ability of GIS to integrate population data with detailed maps, allows decision-makers the ability to examine a variety of plans for revising political boundaries mandated by demographic changes. GIS technology allows the creation of a variety of redistricting plans for consideration in an efficient manner. While the technology facilitates the development of numerous potential political boundaries, the ultimate decision will be made in the context of political realities.

Private Sector Applications

GIS has been used extensively by the private sector to increase operating effectiveness and efficiency. Marketing research applications allow business enterprises to map customer behaviors such as shopping frequency, residence, household income and driving distances (Ross, 1998; Pack, 1997). This type of information enhances marketing strategies, advertising campaigns and planning for future growth and expansion (Harder, 1997). Some examples of other applications include: realignment of sales territories based on demand, employee workload and competition; real estate acquisition and management; transportation routing; and use of interactive maps on the World Wide Web for marketing purposes.

Continued GIS Development

Both public and private sector applications of GIS continue to expand due to the utility of this management tool. Today's faster processing speed and data access when combined with software improvements create an environment in which more governmental units are able to consider adoption of GIS as an aid in their decision-making process. When reviewing the literature surrounding GIS, multiple examples of successful applications are documented while examples of unsuccessful implementation efforts are somewhat rare (Ventura, 1995). There is some indication in the literature that GIS has not completely lived up to its advertised potential and in the words of some critics "GIS is an unfortunate diversion in our journey towards truth" (Pickles, 1995; Worral and Bond, 1997). In this chapter, attention will be given to issues for public managers to consider when faced with the tasks associated with developing, maintaining and expanding a geographic information system.

Issues for Public Managers

Geographic information systems have the potential to serve managers on several different levels:
- Basic Level: as a mechanism for producing maps for record keeping, reflecting such variables as street networks, utility networks, and land use patterns.
- Planning Level: using database information to produce maps that enhance the capability of governmental units to engage in planning.

- Management Decisionmaking Level: accessing information contained in large relational databases to facilitate decision-making at the operational, strategic and policy levels.

The implementation and utilization of a GIS as an aid to the decision-making process is influenced by a variety of technical, legal, ethical and managerial issues (Somers, 1998; Johnson, 1996 and Worral, 1994).

Needs Assessment

An adequate needs assessment process is a time and resource consuming activity that, when conducted completely, can provide the foundation for implementation of an effective geographic information system. Information concerning system requirements for hardware, software, database requirements, human resources and provisions for future system expansion are identified during this process. An inadequate needs assessment has the potential to create a number of problems at the implementation stage. If an emphasis is placed primarily on meeting immediate or short-term needs, inadequate hardware or software may be acquired which severely limits system ability to meet future needs.

GIS systems have an expansive appetite for data. The needs assessment process is the point at which the time and costs associated with creating the necessary databases are established. Most governmental units find that their current databases require significant cleaning, modification and a commitment to continuous updating if the databases are to serve as the foundation for a quality geographic information system. Since data acquisition and maintenance activities consume considerable financial and personnel resources, GIS implementation is heavily influenced by resource allocation decisions based on the needs assessment.

Project Planning

A geographic information system must be integrated into the operations and functions of the organization if it is to serve its intended purposes. It is at this phase that the implications concerning the impact of the system on agency procedures and functions can be assessed. Effective project planning incorporates a "top-down" view of the design and implementation process (Somers, 1998). The long-term impact of the system on routine functions, resource allocation, and agency mission should be clearly identified and the necessary commitments to accept changes in procedures and allocate support to the system be obtained.

Implementation of any system can produce unintended and unanticipated impacts on agency operations and resource consumption patterns. For example, public access to GIS output on planned capital spending for infrastructure development can impact the behaviors of real estate developers and fuel speculative land purchases. Creating and maintaining GIS databases is an expensive endeavor. Since these databases are created by public agencies, are they in the public domain and how are they to be treated in terms of access by other public, private and not-for-profit agencies? Effective project planning activities afford the opportunity to investigate the experiences of other agencies with GIS implementation and to establish strategies for dealing with those consequences.

Effective project planning recognizes that both the literature concerning GIS as well as GIS vendors tend to report only successful applications and experiences. Both vendors and public agencies find their interests to be better served by minimizing dissemination of information about mistakes, shortfalls, and disappointments with geographic information systems. Public managers and GIS vendors are not rewarded for implementing systems that fail to meet expectations, hence, there is a natural tendency to emphasize and report only successes. This means that an agency considering adopting a GIS will be advised to expend significant effort to identify missteps taken by other public agencies relating to GIS, as well as other management innovations.

Access to "Public Records"

Policy concerning access to GIS data is largely governed by legislation dealing with access to public records in general (Johnson, 1996). Effective GIS systems are supported by extensive databases that are often created from public records that were gathered for purposes originally unrelated to the objectives and needs of the GIS system. For example, property ownership records, property assessment data, property surveys and zoning data were traditionally collected and maintained for different purposes and any linkages between the records was incidental. With the implementation of a geographic information system, these files may be computerized and linked for spatial analysis purposes. The extent to which an agency has an obligation to make these new databases available to citizens and private groups continues to be an issue of concern.

One approach used by public agencies is to sell GIS data on a cost-recovery basis. This allows public agencies to recover a portion of the costs associated with data collection and database creation activities. One problem with this approach involves secondary and tertiary dissemination of GIS data after it has been obtained from the public agency. In some instances contracts and licenses have been used in an effort to regulate such activities, enforcement of any contract involving public information between a government agency and a citizen is somewhat problematic.

Liability Issues

Liability issues are related to public access in that public agencies may be required to assume some responsibility for the accuracy and quality of the data provided to secondary users. This issue of liability is increased when the agency vends the data to others even on a cost-recovery basis. Attempts to restrict access to GIS data to "qualified" users may, in turn, raise additional liability issues. Given the litigious nature of society today, a high probability exists that public agencies will be held liable for erroneous decisions made by consumers, if those decisions were partly the product of inaccurate data.

Public and Private Partnerships

In an effort to reduce the financial burden on public agencies associated with creating and maintaining GIS databases, partnerships with the private sector have been proposed as a viable mechanism for cost sharing (Skurznski, 1998). Public agencies have access to an extensive array of data but tend to operate in an environment of limited financial resources and other budgetary constraints. The private sector tends to have access to venture and investment capital, but lack the ability to access the data available to public agencies.

Proponents of partnerships between public and private agencies argue that the access to data by the public agency and the access to venture capital by the private sector provides an irresistible solution to the financial burden associated with creation of a GIS. Such partnerships are not without risks. Negotiating contracts for such a partnership can be a lengthy and expensive process. Parties may possess a range of unrealistic expectations concerning both the process and the ultimate GIS product into the partnership. Elected and other officials may mistakenly view the income from the partnership as "new revenues" suitable for any number of uses unrelated to GIS. These revenues require protection and should be allocated to the GIS project for both development and maintenance purposes.

Expectations concerning dissemination and ownership of GIS data may not be realistic. Private sector organizations may confuse the right to possess and use data with data ownership. Due to legal constraints much of this data, even that contributed by the private partner, may ultimately be considered as in the public domain and accessible by their competitors.

Dissemination Issues

Attempts to achieve a degree of cost recovery for GIS development conflict with policies promoting open access to public information. There is little uniformity between governmental units in terms of their own policies. Some agencies are committed to open access while others have moved to implement cost recovery policies and procedures (Johnson, 1996). Considerable variation exists between local governments across the U.S. One consequence of this variability in policy is that private sector consumers will continue to seek open access to GIS data rather than engage in cost sharing partnerships whenever possible.

Differences in dissemination policy increase the difficulty in sharing data across governmental units. A city or county committed to cost recovery is understandably hesitant to share data with another governmental agency committed to open access. Prior to, and after GIS implementation, attention to dissemination issues will remain on the policy agenda of the governmental unit.

Privacy Issues

Geographic information systems do raise significant issues relating to the right to privacy (Dodson, 1998). The threat to individual privacy is created by the nature of the relational databases used by GIS systems. It is not necessary for a GIS to gather new information about an individual to create a relatively accurate personal profile for any given individual. For example property records, tax assessment data, credit card purchase information, and other demographic data can be combined to describe the behavioral patterns of neighborhoods as well as for individuals. The issue of privacy becomes increasingly important when partnerships between public agencies and private sector companies facilitate the combination of extensive records of both a consumer related (private) and citizen related (public) nature.

While GIS may be viewed as a potential threat to privacy, "social surveillance" unrelated to GIS continues to expand. Video cameras are widely used for security and law enforcement purposes and satellite photography allows detailed monitoring of a range of daily activities by nations and by individuals. Even though other threats to privacy may be largely ignored there remains considerable concern with the impact of GIS systems on this basic right.

System Requirements and Design

Development and implementation of an effective GIS requires incorporating the perspectives drawn from all levels within an agency. In the design process, the technical, legal, managerial and conceptual perspectives are utilized to create a system capable of providing the type of analysis necessary to support the decision-making process. A preferred sequence of events would flow as follows: GIS analysis objectives would govern selection of software, software selection would govern selection of both hardware and personnel training. An inherent risk that public managers face is that a persuasive representative from a software vendor will influence the purchase of a less than adequate or inappropriate GIS software package and be unable to deliver the desired type of analysis.

Alternatively, public managers may be drawn to the acquisition of an alternative non-GIS program, such as a computer-aided drafting or computer aided mapping program due to financial and other pressures. While these types of programs can provide very accurate graphs and maps, they do not have the ability to support spatial analysis that is integral to a true geographic information system.

System design also incorporates human resource requirements. A true GIS requires significant maintenance in terms of data entry, data cleaning and verification, and data revision. In order to achieve an acceptable return on the investment in a GIS, personnel training and retention costs should be factored into the implementation. Individuals with highly developed GIS skills tend to be very marketable and capable of demanding competitive salary packages. One aspect of the system design should involve a strategy to retain skilled employees that have been trained by the agency. Failure to adequately address this personnel issue has the potential to create an ongoing training problem for either the private sector or other governmental bodies.

Organizational Issues

Many of the elements associated with successful GIS implementation can be traced to the human factor—employee attitudes and values (Nedovic-Budic and Godschalk, 1996; Ventura, 1995). Bureaucratic resistance to new procedures and techniques can be attributed to a variety of factors. These include fear of change, requirements to learn potentially difficult skills, questions about procedure growing out of administrative control and authority, fear that new procedures and techniques may expose weakness and inadequacies in current operations, and concern about budgetary impacts of new projects on personnel positions.

Accordingly, effective GIS implementation strategies would be enhanced by providing some combination of the following to employees: emphasizing personal benefits which can be derived from the change; selecting or incorporating individuals with strong computer skills for the implementation; maximizing employee exposure to GIS operations before, during and after implementation; and provision of reassurances concerning potential impacts on personnel assignments, duties and employment status.

Institutional Issues

Implementation of a GIS has the potential to impact the existing external relationships of an agency. Existing intergovernmental relationships may be changed or altered due to changes in the flow of information. These changes may be either vertical in nature (between local, state and federal bodies) or horizontal in nature (between departments with the same governmental unit). As stated in the previous section, fear of change has the potential to be a significant factor in resisting implementation of innovative technologies. Effective implementation strategies require public managers to examine potential changes in external and internal relationships.

Communication patterns within departments may be significantly altered with the implementation of a geographic information system. Such change is the product of data being shared with diverse departments within the agency and potentially to external entities as well. As communication patterns change, informal power structures are created, eliminated or changed. Changes in the flow of information has potentially significant impacts on the institutional environment.

Political Support

Implementation of a geographic information system typically involves building an internal and sometimes an external political base (Budic, 1994). Securing the support of upper level management and elected officials is typically a prerequisite in the development of a GIS. Political support ranges from the allocation of budgetary resources necessary for funding to organizational and institutional support associated with changes in the flow of information within and from the agency. Political support is necessary to overcome hesitancy in sharing information between departments and with external consumers, whether they are governmental or private sector.

Even though GIS represents a potentially valuable advancement in technology, successful implementation requires that public managers exercise considerable political skill.

GIS Prospects For The Public Manager

Public managers interested in developing a geographic information system should carefully evaluate the claims for benefits associated with GIS implementation. Enthusiastic supporters of GIS claim that the technology affords managers with the capacity to "reinvent local government" due to its capability to conduct spatial analysis of data (Wilson, 1995). Without challenging the utility and potential of GIS applications, two cautionary notes should be sounded.

First the ability to justify costs associated with GIS applications for local governments can be a difficult and daunting task (Worrall, 1994). Costs associated with GIS implementation tend to be highest during development and then continue at a reduced level over the life of the system. These costs are relatively easy to assess and document. Benefits, on the other hand tend to be more difficult to quantify and typically are produced over the life of the system after implementation. The patterns of benefits produced may be difficult to document, since GIS applications are designed to impact private sector operations as well as those of government. Managers should enter into the process with an understanding that hard data justifying implementation may be somewhat elusive.

Second, GIS evaluation efforts should be conducted with a sensitivity to benefits that can be measured such as: cost savings associated with records maintenance; cost savings produced by automation of previously labor intensive mapping procedures; productivity gains associated with the adoption of new procedures; improved regulatory functions; and income generation through enhanced management of infrastructure resources. Specific benefits can be identified and procedures can be established at the point of implementation to begin the process of documenting benefits.

GIS project managers seem to be unwilling to provide detailed cost-benefit data associated with implementation for some very understandable reasons. First, there may be some level of discomfort or embarrassment that the databases that support the system may be inadequate to support all of the capabilities of the system. Second, there is a hesitance to acknowledge what may be six or seven figure costs associated with consultant fees associated with implementation. And third, there may be a desire to use the information provided by the availability of GIS to generate revenues from other governmental units (Worrall, 1994).

With these cautionary notes in mind, there is little doubt that geographic information systems do have significant potential to improve the operations of governmental agencies. The literature and promotional data contain a seemingly endless record of GIS success stories and this trend is expected to continue.

Bibliography

Ammerman, P. (1998) Turnkey solutions cut GIS timeline. *The American City and County,* 113, 12-13.

Armstrong, M.P. (1994) Requirements for the development of GIS based group decision-support systems. *Journal of the American Society for Information Science,* 45, 669-674.

Aronoff, S. (1989). *Geographic Information Systems: A Management Perspective.* Ottawa, Ontario: WDL Publications

Birkin M., Clarke G., Clarke, M., and Wilson, A. (1996) *Intelligent GIS: Location Decisions and Strategic Planning.* New York: John Wiley & Sons, Inc.

Briggs, D.J. and Elliot, P. (1995) The use of geographical information systems in studies on environment and health, *World Health Statistics Quarterly,* 48, 85-90.

Budic, Z.D. (1994) Effectiveness of geographic information systems in local planning. *Journal of the American Planning Association,* 60, 244-254.

Dobson, J. (1998) Is GIS a privacy threat?, *GIS World,* 11, 20-21.

Harder, C. (1997) *GIS Means Business.* Redlands, CA: Environmental Systems Research Institute.

Hokanson, J.B. (1994) Planning and financing infrastructure using GIS technology. *Government Finance Review,* 19-21.

Huxhold, W.E. (1991). *An Introduction to Urban Geographic Systems.* New

York: Oxford University Press

Johnson, J.P. (1996) Case Studies of Dissemination Policy in Local Government GIS Agencies. *Computers, Environment and Urban Systems,* 19, 373-389.

Longley, P. and Clarke, G. (1995) *GIS for Business and Service Planning.* New York: John Wiley & Sons, Inc.

Mitchell, A. (1997) *Zeroing In: Geographic Information Systems at Work in the Community.* Redlands, CA: Environmental Systems Research Institute, Inc.

Nedovic-Budic, Z. and Godschalk, D.R. (1996) Human factors in adoption of geographic information systems: a local government case study, *Public Administration Review,* 56, 554-567.

Novotny, P. and Jacobs, R.H.(1997) Geographical information systems and the new landscape of political technologies. *Social Science Computer Review* 15, 264-285.

O'Looney, J. Garson, D.G. (1998) *Beyond maps: GIS and decision-making in local government.* Washington, DC, ICMA.

Pack, T. (1997) Mapping a path to success, *Database,* 20, 31-35.

Pickles, J. (1995) *Ground truth: the social implications of geographic information systems.* New York: Guildford Press.

Ross, J.R. (1998) Geography lessons: why you should teach customers about GIS, *Reseller Management,* 21, 84-88.

Somers, R. (1998) Building your GIS from the ground up. *American City and County,* 113, 14-41.

Skurzynski, J. (1998) Public/private partnerships hurdle data costs, *GIS World,* 11, 12-18.

Ventura, S. J. (1995) The us of geographic systems in local government. *Public Administration Review,* 55, 461-471.

Wilson, J.P. (1995) Reinventing local government with GIS, *Public Works,* 126, 38-39,83.

Worrall, L. (1994) Incorporating GIS into strategic management in local government. *Local Government Policy Making,* 21, 15-24.

Worrall, L. (1994) Justifying investment in GIS: a local government perspective. *International Journal of Geographic Information Systems,* 8, 545-565.

Worrall, L. and Bond, D. (1997) Geographical information systems, spatial analysis and public policy: the British experience, *International Statistical Review* ,65, 365-379.

13

Legal Aspects of Electronic Mail in Public Organizations

by
Charles Prysby
University of North Carolina at Greensboro
and
Nicole Prysby
Attorney at Law, Charlottesville, VA

The increasing use of electronic mail in the workplace has generated important legal questions, especially for public organizations. The legal questions concerning e-mail in public institutions and agencies fall into two basic categories: (a) issues of employee privacy regarding e-mail messages; and (b) public access to e-mail under applicable freedom of information legislation. While employees might believe that their e-mail messages are private, the employer has broad legal grounds for reading workplace e-mail. In particular, when the employer owns the e-mail system, which almost always is the case, the employer has considerable latitude to access and read stored e-mail messages, at least if there is some legitimate business reason for doing so. Government organizations also must treat at least some of their e-mail as part of the public record, making it open to public access. State laws vary considerably in terms of how they define the types of e-mail messages that are part of the public record, some being far more inclusive than others. Given the uncertainty and confusion that frequently exists among employees regarding these legal questions, it is essential that public organizations develop and publicize an e-mail policy that both clarifies what privacy expectations employees should have regarding their e-mail and specifies what recording keeping requirements for e-mail should be followed to appropriately retain public records.

Electronic mail (e-mail) has become increasingly important in the

Copyright© 1999, Idea Group Publishing.

workplace. The growth of this new medium of communication has generated important legal questions, so much so that most experts strongly recommend that organizations adopt explicit policies about e-mail. Public organizations in particular must be concerned about the legal ramifications of e-mail. The legal questions concerning e-mail in public institutions and agencies fall into two basic categories: (a) issues of employee privacy regarding e-mail messages; and (b) public access to e-mail under applicable freedom of information legislation. We discuss both of these topics in this article, attempting not only to outline current legal thinking in the area, but also to raise questions that public managers and policy makers should consider.

It is worth noting at the start that many of the legal issues surrounding the use of e-mail are direct extensions of principles that apply to other forms of communications. Indeed, much of the law that governs e-mail is not legislation that was written explicitly to cover this particular form of communication. Issues of the privacy of employee e-mail messages, for example, are directly analogous to issues of the privacy of employee phone calls or written correspondence. Similarly, the right of the public to have access to governmental e-mail messages is a direct extension of the right to have access to written documents. To be sure, there are questions about exactly how legal principles that were established for older communication technologies should be applied to a new one, and perhaps not all of these questions are fully settled at this point in time. But our understanding of this topic is broadened if we appreciate the application of legal principles across communication media.

Privacy Issues

Many employees, whether in the public or private sector, probably believe that it would be highly inappropriate for supervisors to listen to their phone conversations at work--except perhaps for the monitoring of employees who primarily handle public phone calls, such as tax department workers responding to taxpayer questions. Most employees undoubtedly feel the same way about their employer opening and reading their personal correspondence. By extension, these employees may also feel that e-mail falls into the same category and that supervisors should not be reading their e-mail without permission, except in certain narrowly defined cases. Many employees undoubtedly use their work e-mail system to send personal messages, both internally and externally, or they may mix personal and professional items in the same message, in much the same way that both may be mixed together in a phone conversation with a colleague. Employees may believe that they are entitled to privacy in these matters, and the fact that a password is required to access their computer account, and thus their e-mail, may be considered confirmation of this belief (Greengard, 1996).

Regardless of what many employees might believe should be the case, their legal right to privacy is quite limited when it comes to e-mail messages. The possible basis for a right to privacy of e-mail messages from the scrutiny of the employer might come from several sources. First of all, the Fourth Amendment prohibits the government from unreasonable searches and seizures, and this restricts public (but not private) sector employers. Second, federal legislation, most notably the Federal Electronic Communications Privacy Act of 1986, provides some protection for communications. Third, many states may have their own constitutional and legislative provisions, which may even go beyond what the U.S. Constitution or federal laws stipulate. Finally, under common law an individual may assert a tort claim for invasion of privacy. However, the application of the above legal and constitutional principles to workplace e-mail is extremely limited, as we shall see.

The various legal protections of an individual's privacy stem from general societal beliefs that individuals are entitled to privacy. Unwanted intrusion into an individual's personal affairs violates the respect and dignity to which an individual is entitled (Adelman and Kennedy, 1995: xiii). The concept of privacy is a complex one that is not easily captured with a simple definition. Doss and Loui (1995) argue that privacy has at least three distinct meanings: confidentiality, anonymity, and solitude. The first two are highly relevant for communications, including e-mail. Confidentiality refers to the right to keep personal information private. Anonymity refers to the absence of unwanted attention. Individuals frequently send communications (via e-mail, telephone calls, or surface mail) that are for the intended recipient only. When a third party intercepts such a communication without permission, one or both individuals suffer a loss of confidentiality, because personal or private information is divulged to others, and both suffer a loss of anonymity, as they now are the subject of undesired attention (Doss and Loui, 1995). Of course, putting these general philosophical principles into a workable legal framework can be difficult.

Fourth Amendment Protections

The Fourth Amendment protects citizens against unreasonable searches by government officials, a protection that extends to unreasonable searches of public employees by their employers. An important legal principle is that an employee has no valid objection to a search by the employer unless the employee has a reasonable expectation of privacy in the situation (White, 1997). This legal principle applies not just to e-mail, but to other aspects of the workplace. For example, the employee may or may not have a reasonable expectation of privacy regarding his or her desk drawers or file cabinets. In one case, the U.S. Supreme Court ruled that a public hospital employee did have a reasonable expectation of privacy regarding the desk and file cabinets in his office *(O'Conner v. Ortega,* 1987). The Court also said, however, that such expectations would have to be determined on a case-by-case basis, depending on the particular facts of each case (Cole, 1997).

The determination of whether a reasonable expectation of privacy exists would depend on a variety of factors, including the context of the search, the uses to which the searched area is put, and the societal expectation of the extent to which the area deserves protection from governmental intrusion. For example, an expectation of privacy in an office might be reduced by actual office practices, including broad access to co-workers (Jenero and Mapes-Riordan, 1992). In one case, *Simmons v. Southwestern Bell Telephone Company* (1978), a deskman at a phone company's test center was subject to monitoring of all calls he made from the testboard telephones. The employee was aware that the telephones were monitored and that other telephones were available for personal calls and were not monitored. Although the court dismissed the Fourth Amendment claim because the telephone company was a private employer, the court did note *in dicta* that under the circumstances, the employee would have no reasonable expectation of privacy in the calls made from the testboard telephone. The court did state, however, that it would have found a violation of the Fourth Amendment if the company had been a public employer and had monitored the employee's calls from the telephones designated for personal calls (Jenero and Mapes-Riordan, 1992).

One commentator suggests that an employee would have no reasonable expectation of privacy in e-mail messages because most people would realize that the system administrator has access to individual employees' e-mail messages (Lee, 1994). In addition, if governmental employers have publicized a policy providing that e-mail may be subject to monitoring, the employee will have assumed the risk that his e-mails are subject to searching. Furthermore, even if a password is required to log on to a computer, if the employee's supervisor or the network administrator knows the password, the employee would not have a reasonable expectation of privacy, even for files that were stored in a location requiring the password (Dawes and Dallas, 1997). Therefore, it is possible that in many situations, there would be no reasonable expectation of privacy.

Even if the employee is able to assert a reasonable expectation of privacy, the employer may still have a right to read the employee's e-mail messages, as the Fourth Amendment only prohibits unreasonable searches. The Supreme Court ruled in *O'Conner* that even though the employee had a reasonable expectation of privacy regarding his file cabinets and desk drawers, the employer nevertheless had a right to search these locations because the search was not unreasonable (Cole, 1997; Cozzetto and Pedeliski, 1997). The general rule is that a search must be reasonable both at its inception and in its scope. A search is reasonable at its inception if there are reasonable grounds to suspect that it would turn up evidence of work-related misconduct or if it is necessary for a noninvestigatory work-related purpose. A search is reasonable in its scope if the extent of the search is reasonably related to the accomplishment of the objectives of the search (Jenero and Mapes-Riordan 1992).

While the *O'Conner* case did not involve e-mail, the principles are clearly extendable. An employer's search of an employee's files is reasonable if the employer has a necessity or valid business reason to conduct the search (Cole, 1997; White, 1997). This necessity would be indicated in a variety of circumstances. One situation would be where the employer needs to retrieve information to conduct business, such as if an important message must be obtained from an absent employee's electronic mailbox. Another possibility would be a situation where an employee was suspected of violating organizational policies or otherwise engaging in inappropriate or even illegal conduct, and where searching the individual's e-mail might reasonably provide the employer with evidence pertaining to the suspected activity. In order for the search to be reasonable, the employer must also conduct the search in a fashion that is designed to obtain the information without unnecessarily intruding into the individual's privacy (Cole, 1997).

State Protections

Public employees also can claim privacy rights under applicable state constitutional provisions or state statutes, which also might apply to private sector employees. Some states have privacy clauses in their constitutions, and most states have statutes that protect privacy in personal communications (Fitzpatrick, 1997; White, 1997). In recent years, some states have added legislation to deal specifically with electronic communications and/or unauthorized access to computer systems, both of which are relevant to the privacy of e-mail (see Perritt, 1996: 117-121, for a state-by-state summary of such legislation).

Several states have legislation prohibiting unauthorized access to computer systems or data, which presumably would cover e-mail. (Cal. Penal Code § 502, Conn. Gen. Stat. Ann. § 53a-251, Iowa Code Ann. § 716A.2, S.C. Code Ann. § 16-16-20). However, these statutes are not specifically written for the protection of employees, and it is unclear if they could even be enforced against an employer. The statutes generally refer to the owner of the system as the enforcer of the law; because the employer is almost certain to be the system owner, employees would probably not be able to use these statutes.

Nebraska, however, does have a specific employer-employee monitoring statute. Under the Nebraska statute, an employer, on the business premises, may intercept, disclose, or use electronic monitoring in the normal course of employment. The employer may not randomly monitor employees unless notice of the policy is given to the employees (Neb. Rev. Stat. § 86-702). One other state has taken specific steps to address this issue specifically for public employees. As of July 1, 1997, public employers in Colorado who maintain an e-mail system are required to adopt a policy on the monitoring of e-mail, including the circumstances under which monitoring may take place (Dawes and Dallas, 1997: Col. Rev. Stat. Ann. § 24-72-204.5). About 20 percent of states have a right to privacy as part of the state constitution (see Lee, 1994, for citations). Of these, only California's constitutional provision has been extended to private employees; for the other states, only public employees would be protected under the provisions.

Tort Law Protections

Finally, employees, public or private, may be able to assert a violation of privacy under common law if their e-mail is monitored by their employer. Tort law varies from state to state, but in most states it is now recognized that violation of privacy torts do apply to employment situations (Fitpatrick, 1997). Invasion of privacy is a tort with four possible causes of action, two of which might apply to e-mail. The first would be an intrusion into affairs that an individual has a right to keep private, by a method objectionable to the reasonable person; the second would be a public disclosure of private matters, where the disclosure is highly offensive and not of public concern (Perritt, 1996: 93).

The reasonable expectation of privacy is an essential element in common law tort claims, just as it is in cases asserting constitutional (federal or state) protections. An employee cannot claim that his or her privacy has been invaded if there was no reasonable expectation of privacy in the employment situation. With regard to e-mail at work, privacy expectations have been very narrowly defined by the courts. First of all, if the employer has a written statement that e-mail messages may be monitored, which many employers do have, the employee probably will find it very difficult to claim an expectation of privacy. Even in the absence of a written statement, it may still be difficult for an employee to assert a reasonable expectation. In fact, in one case involving a private company, *Smyth v. Pillsbury Co.* (1996), the court ruled against an employee who sued his employer for wrongful discharge following his firing, which was based on information gathered by the employer through reading his e-mail. The court's decision was that the employee had no reasonable expectation of privacy despite the fact that the employer had assured employees that their e-mail messages were considered confidential items (Farber, 1997; White, 1997).

However, it should be noted that in many of these types of cases, the employee is engaging in some sort of inappropriate or illegal behavior and is simply not a very sympathetic character. For example, the *Smyth* employee had communicated unprofessional comments over the company e-mail system, and the court noted that the comments were voluntarily communicated (as opposed to a forced disclosure, such as a property search) and that the employer's interest in preventing inappropriate or illegal activity over its e-mail system outweighed any privacy rights the employee may have had in the messages.

Relevant Recent Cases

Several important cases have reaffirmed the employer's right to inspect employee e-mail. In a well-known case, *Shoars v. Epson* (1992), an employee claimed that her employer wrongfully terminated her after she complained that her supervisor was reading employee e-mail (Adelman and Kennedy, 1995: 310-315). Her attorney also filed a companion class action invasion of privacy lawsuit, *Flanigan v. Epson* (1992). The California Superior Court rejected the invasion of privacy claim, stating that the California statute protecting privacy of communications did not extend to e-mail at work (Adelman and Kennedy, 1995: 315). In *Bourke v. Nissan Motor Co.* (1991), two employees sued their employer because they were terminated after their supervisor read their e-mail message and found that they had been making fun of him, but the court rejected their argument that the company had violated their privacy (Cozzetto and Pedeliski, 1997).

While the above cases involved private employers, the principles appear to apply equally to public sector employers. For example, in *Bohach v. City of Reno* (1996), the court rejected any claim of a reasonable expectation of privacy on the part of police personnel using the departmental computer system (Bramsco, 1997). Similarly, in *Jandak v. Village of Brookfield* (1981), the court ruled that a police officer implicitly consented to monitoring of his personal phone calls because he used a line that he knew was regularly monitored (Fitzpatrick, 1997).

From the limited number of cases that have been decided, it appears that employees may have fewer privacy rights for e-mail than for other forms of communications. This difference may be explained in part by the fact that the employee is using the employer's computer system, and therefore, the employer may be regarded as having a right to monitor what is transmitted on the system. The argument is that if the employer owns the computer, then the employer should be able to read what is stored on the computer. In most cases, the employer can do so very easily and surreptitiously, making the action perhaps seem less intrusive than opening personal mail, for example. Moreover, since the e-mail messages generally are stored in a common location, such as on a network server, the employee cannot regard them in the same light as personal items stored in a desk drawer in one's office.

It also may be that the relatively newness of e-mail means that social conventions have not firmly developed in this area. While most people would regard listening in on another person's phone conversation as very impolite, perhaps the same social stigma is not attached to the reading of someone else's e-mail (Doss and Loui, 1995). However, for recovery under most privacy common law, even if regarded as outside usual social norms, an intrusion must usually be shown to be "highly offensive" to a reasonable person.

The Electronic Communications Privacy Act

The Federal Electronic Communications Privacy Act (ECPA), enacted by Congress in 1986, does not appear to provide employees with much protection of their workplace e-mail communications. The ECPA attempted to extend the legal restrictions on wiretapping of phone conversations to electronic communications, providing both criminal and civil penalties for illegal interception and disclosure of protected communications (Perritt, 1996). However, the legislative history of the ECPA suggests that Congress did not intend to restrict employers from reading the e-mail of employees (Cole, 1997; Cozzetto and Pedeliski, 1997).

First of all, ECPA does not prohibit the monitoring of communications in situations where one of the parties consents (Cole, 1997; White, 1997). Thus, if an employer has a policy stating that e-mail will be monitored, which employees were aware of and at least implicitly agreed to, that alone would appear to provide legal justification for reading of employee e-mail. However, there are employment situations where the implied consent might be questioned. For example, in a case involving telephone monitoring (*Watkins v. L. M. Berry & Co.*, 1983), the court ruled that the employee had not given consent for the monitoring of personal calls. The employer could intercept the calls to determine if they were personal or business calls, but once it was determined that they were personal, monitoring was no longer permitted (Cole, 1997; Cozzetto and Pedeliski, 1997; White, 1997).

Similarly, another court found that an employer violated the ECPA by listening to all of the personal calls of an employee that were tape recorded by the employer, even though the employee was suspected of theft and the employer therefore had a legitimate reason for monitoring (Greenberg, 1994, citing *Deal v. Spears*, 1992). Still, even the absence of clear consent on the part of the employee does not guarantee e-mail privacy, as other provisions of the ECPA may provide employers with broad rights in this area.

The ECPA includes a business exemption, which essentially states that the provider of the communications system being used by employees in the ordinary course of business, which almost always will be the employer in the case of e-mail systems, has a right to intercept messages, at least if there is a legitimate business purpose for doing so (Cole, 1997; White, 1997). Moreover, the ECPA also distinguishes between intercepting a communication and accessing a stored communication, providing more latitude for the latter. This is particularly applicable to e-mail, which almost always would be accessed by the employer from stored files, rather than during transmission. Specifically, the ECPA states that restrictions on the reading of stored files do not apply to the provider of the electronic communications service (Bramesco, 1997; Cole, 1997; Perritt, 1996: 109-110). Thus, any government organization or agency which owns the computer network in which the employee e-mail messages reside could cite both the general employer-owned system exemption and the stored communications provision. The combination of these would appear to confer a very broad right to read stored e-mail, at least as far as federal law is concerned.

While internal e-mail messages usually travel and are stored on the organization's own computer system, external messages might be in a different category. An external e-mail message traveling over the Internet would appear to fall under the jurisdiction of the ECPA, which prohibits third party interception of electronic communications traveling over public networks. Whether the employer could intercept the message after it arrived on the local system (presumably owned by the employer) without violating the ECPA, is unclear. One possibility is that connecting a local e-mail system to the Internet makes the local system part of a public system, and thus messages traveling over the Internet are protected by the ECPA even if intercepted on the local system. In fact, it might be argued that making the local system part of a public network extends ECPA protection to all messages on the system, including purely local ones (Perritt, 1996: 110). However, if the employer accesses the message after it has been stored on the local system, the "stored communications" principle, discussed above, might apply, thus permitting employer reading of employee e-mail, even that which came from external sources over public lines. At this point, the law appears unclear on this matter (Perritt, 1996: 110).

While the employer may be able to read the employee's e-mail, the ECPA clearly prohibits outside third parties from doing so. The same rule generally applies to state wiretap statutes. A private third party who surreptitiously accessed an e-mail conversation between two individuals would be guilty of criminal conduct, just as if that person tapped the phone conversation between two individuals. However, many experts feel that even in these cases the ECPA provides little real protection against such actions. Computer hackers are capable of breaking into the computer network of an organization and accessing stored files, including stored e-mail, perhaps far more so than people suspect (Behar, 1997). Many individuals undoubtedly feel that such a threat is extremely remote, in large part because they have nothing in their stored e-mail files that would be of interest to an outside individual. But as one expert puts it, a hacker "has to learn how to hack, and will start off by breaking into a computer system that is relatively easy to break into" (Garcia, 1996). Organizations often feel that e-mail messages do not contain the kind of sensitive information that requires elaborate security measures, so e-mail files may be left more vulnerable to external hackers than other computer files (Garcia, 1996). Hackers may often operate without great fear, either because they believe there is little chance that they will be caught, or because they do not believe that they will be severely penalized if apprehended.

Other Privacy Considerations

It should, of course, be understood that nothing prevents the recipient of an e-mail communication from divulging its contents. An individual has no reasonable expectation of privacy regarding information communicated to another person, except in some narrowly defined situations of "privileged" communications, such as between an individual and his or her attorney (Garcia, 1996). The recipient of the message is free to tell anyone, including law enforcement officials, about its contents. In the case of e-mail, this could include forwarding the message to others, a common practice. All of our discussion of possible privacy rights concerns the situation where the employer or supervisor accesses an employee's e-mail message to someone else without the permission of one of the two parties directly involved in the communication.

Under some circumstances, the employer may have not only the right but also the responsibility to monitor e-mail communications. When one employee is suspected or accused of harassment by sending offensive e-mail messages to another employee, the employer's obligation to ensure that employees do not have to work in a hostile environment may require the monitoring of the employee's e-mail. If, for example, an employee is known to have sent harassing e-mail to a co-worker previously, some monitoring might be considered necessary to shield the employer from further liability.

While recent court cases involving the monitoring of workplace e-mail have almost always upheld the right of the employer to engage in such monitoring, it would be a mistake to conclude that there are no restrictions on the extent and nature of this monitoring. The cases that have been decided have usually involved monitoring that was in some way job-related. The employer was capable of making an argument that the monitoring was necessary for business purposes. It is not at all clear that the courts would rule that an employer had the right to routinely read the personal e-mail messages of an individual when there was no good reason to believe that the contents of the messages were in any way job-related (Cozzetto and Pedeliski, 1997).

In sum, managers and supervisors in public agencies and organizations have broad power to read the e-mail of their employees. Their legal situation effectively does not differ greatly from that of managers and supervisors in the private sector. However, while they may have broad legal rights in this area, the political situation is not the same. There may be more concern on the part of the public, or the media, or elected officials, to the monitoring of e-mail in public agencies. What might be tolerated if carried out in a private company could be seen as objectionable if it occurred in a public organization. Public universities in particular tend to stress the privacy of individual e-mail (Doss and Loui, 1995). All of this points to the need for a carefully thought out, explicit, and disseminated e-mail policy, a topic we address in the last section.

Public Access

Public organizations have to contend with one important problem involving e-mail that their private sector counterparts do not have to face. The public has some right to see the e-mail messages in a public agency. At the federal level, the 1982 Freedom of Information Act (FOIA) outlines the public's right to access written materials and documents, and e-mail communications are included in this category (Garson, 1995: 77-79). At the state level, public access will depend on the specifics of state legislation. Many states have freedom of information acts that provide for even more public access to e-mail than does the federal FOIA.

The Federal Freedom of Information Act

The FOIA stipulates that federal agencies must make public records available when requested. Government reports, notices, bulletins, newsletters, publications, and policy statements would be considered public documents. Exemptions are made for information defined as private or confidential, which would include certain aspects of personnel records, proprietary data contained in government contracts or proposals, certain criminal records, and so on. Most of the exemptions are the usual and familiar ones. Also included in the exemptions are internal communications prior to a policy decision (Garson, 1995: 78). Thus, while a policy is being discussed within an agency, the employees are free to send messages to each other, either written or via e-mail, expressing thoughts about various aspects or implications of some possible policy, and those messages are not considered part of the public record. The exemption is designed to protect only those materials bearing on the formulation or exercise of policy-oriented judgment; peripheral documents are not protected (*Ethyl Corporation v. U.S. E.P.A.,* 1994). To meet the exemption, the agency would need to show that the document in question is (1) predecisional and (2) deliberative (*City of Virginia Beach v. U.S. Department of Commerce,* 1993).

Depending on how strictly this exemption is interpreted, it potentially could exclude a considerable amount of e-mail communication. However, in one case, *Armstrong v. Executive Office of the President* (1993), the court ruled that the National Archive could not refuse to provide a computer tape of certain e-mail created during the Reagan administration, as these e-mail messages could qualify as public records (Hunter, 1995). Furthermore, the court ruled that the e-mail messages had to be retained in electronic form; printing and saving the hard copies was not equivalent to saving the electronic versions. The court explained that the printed version might not contain all of the information found in an electronic file, such as the headers stating who sent the message, the recipients, and any attachments.

The FOIA provides that individuals requesting information must be specific about the content of the information being requested. The request must "reasonably describe" the records sought (5 U.S.C. § 552(a)(3)(A)). Little guidance is provided as to any more exacting requirements. However, case law indicates that although the size of the request is not the test for specificity, blanket requests for all of a certain type of record are generally considered not to be sufficiently descriptive and that broad requests that would require unreasonably burdensome searches need not be fulfilled (*Sears v. Gottschalk,* 1973).

The agency may charge for providing such information, although if the information is provided to news media, only the actual duplication costs may be charged. Other organizations or individuals can be charged for the costs involved in searching for and reviewing the information that has been requested.

State Freedom of Information Laws

State laws often provide for far more public access than does the FOIA. For example, the North Carolina Public Records Act defines public records far more broadly. Included in the definition of public records are internal memos and messages, electronic or otherwise, that are part of the consideration of policies or actions, not just the statements of the policies and actions (Capone, 1998). A considerable amount of e-mail might fall into this category. Colorado's open public records law contains a similar provision, including electronic mail as "correspondence" subject to the law. The Colorado law also states that e-mail is included under the law whether transmitted locally or globally and whether read, printed, or stored (Colo. Rev. Stat. Ann. § 24-72-202). Therefore, as in North Carolina, it would appear that e-mail in Colorado could be broadly accessed. On the other hand, Michigan law under certain conditions, discussed below, exempts communications that are of an advisory nature and are preliminary to a final policy decision (Hunter, 1995).

California law specifically provides that "writings" subject to the state inspection of public records act includes any means of recording information, including material on a disk, but also contains an exemption for preliminary drafts, notes, etc. of a public agency (Cal. Gov't. Code §§ 6252, 6254).

The question of whether e-mail messages that are preliminary discussions of possible policies or actions qualify as public records seems especially important. E-mail frequently substitutes for the type of conversation that individuals often have in person or by telephone. Various ideas or thoughts may be put forth just to stimulate thought or explore various possibilities. In some cases, the messages may be little more than "thinking out loud." There is a valid interest in encouraging open and honest discussions of various decision options, and e-mail often is a convenient way of doing so. If government employees fear that all their e-mail messages dealing with some topic may be publicly disclosed, open and honest discussions may be discouraged, at least through e-mail. In fact, Michigan law recognizes this fact, as advisory or preliminary discussions are exempt from public disclosure if the public agency shows that the public interest in encouraging frank communications outweighs the public interest in disclosure (Hunter, 1997). Connecticut law contains a similar exception (Conn. Gen. Stat. Ann. § 1-19). Other states, however, may not contain such exemptions. The Virginia Freedom of Information Act does not contain an exclusion for such preliminary types of documents and the Colorado law contains an exemption only for the work product of an elected official (Va. Code Ann. §§ 2.1-340 *et seq.*, Colo. Rev. Stat. Ann. § 24-72-202).

State law routinely excludes a variety of government records from public disclosure. Commonly excluded information includes individual tax records, certain law enforcement and criminal justice records, personnel information of a confidential nature, and communications made within the scope of the attorney-client relationship. Regarding e-mail, it is worth noting that in most cases a government agency could not refuse to publicly disclose e-mail communications on the grounds that personal and confidential information is commingled with the requested information. The agency would have to separate the confidential information from the public information. Moreover, if the agency has a policy that the e-mail system is to be used for business purposes, an employee may not have a valid objection to the release of his or her e-mail messages, if they fall within the scope of a public record, even if personal information is contained in some of the communications. From this perspective, a public employee may have less of a privacy right regarding his or her e-mail than a private sector employee.

As is the case with federal law, state laws generally restrict the charges that can be imposed on those who request public records. Under North Carolina law, the government agency cannot charge more than the actual cost of providing the information, regardless of whether or not the request is made by a news organization, a provision that is more generous than the federal FOIA (N.C. Gen. Stat. § 132-6.2). This cost cannot include the time involved in complying, since that is considered part of the job definition of state employees (Capone, 1998). The agency also must supply the information in the medium chosen by the requestor, if the agency is reasonably capable of providing the records in that format (N.C. Gen. Stat. § 132-6.2). If an individual requested e-mail messages in an electronic format, then presumably the only cost that could be charged would be for the diskettes given to the individual.

If state law regards public records as the property of the people, it logically follows that state and local government agencies have certain obligations to retain these records, including electronic ones. This does not mean that every e-mail message must be retained. For example, North Carolina guidelines distinguish between transitory messages and those of lasting value (State Public Records Cataloging Service, 1998). A message setting up or confirming a meeting time is clearly transitory and can be deleted after the meeting has been held. A message of lasting value must be retained for a longer period of time. Moreover, it should not be retained as an e-mail message. Rather, it either should be printed out and the hard copy filed, or it should be stored in an electronic database, but filed with other related documents (State Public Records Cataloging Service, 1998). In either case, the files can be reviewed periodically, and out-of-date information discarded. The responsibility for retaining these messages rests with the recipient of the message.

By contrast, Michigan law is far less specific regarding e-mail, and it appears that very little of the e-mail communications in a government agency would have to be retained (Hunter, 1997). It should be noted that the Michigan freedom of information act does not impose an obligation to keep records, only an obligation to make public records that have been retained; the management and budget act specifies recordkeeping requirements. Thus, if e-mail communications are retained, they must be provided on request, unless they fit into one of the specifically exempted categories. However, if the communications are not required to be retained, they can be destroyed and therefore made unavailable for public access (Hunter, 1997).

Toward a Model E-mail Policy

We conclude this discussion with an examination of possible components of an e-mail policy for a public organization. All authorities in this field recommend that public organizations (and private ones also) develop clear policies regarding e-mail and communicate those policies to their employees. Differences of opinion exist on what features an e-mail policy should have, however, and we attempt to outline some of the thinking in this area.

A number of attorneys recommend that employers tell their employees that the workplace e-mail system is for business use only, that e-mail can and will be monitored, and that employees should not expect any privacy regarding their e-mail (Fitzpatrick, 1997; White, 1997). Some even recommend that the policy appear on the computer monitor screen every time the user logs on and that the user be required to acknowledge consent in order to proceed. As earlier discussions made clear, such a policy provides the employer with the most protection in the event employee e-mail is monitored. Of course, many of those who recommend a policy of this nature would not recommend that employee e-mail be regularly monitored; they simply are recommending a course of action that is likely to minimize potential legal problems for an employer.

Another opinion is that employees should be given some privacy rights regarding their e-mail (Doss and Loui, 1995). First of all, limiting the workplace e-mail system to business use only is a substantial restriction. Many employees find it extremely convenient to use their e-mail for personal use, just as they use their workplace telephone for personal calls. A stronger argument can be made for permitting personal telephone calls at work—urgent or even emergency calls might be necessary, for example. On the other hand, prohibiting personal e-mail would be a significant inconvenience that would raise several questions. What happens if an employee receives an external e-mail message of a personal nature? What if a communication between two colleagues contains both business and personal items, just as the two can easily be contained in one phone call? Rather than completely prohibiting personal e-mail, public employers might consider appropriate guidelines for allowable personal messages. For example, personal e-mail might be permitted if it: (1) is not excessive in amount and/or does not overburden the e-mail system; (2) is not used for private business (i.e., profit-making) purposes; and (3) is not in violation of agency policies or federal or state laws.

It also may be desirable to provide employees with some privacy rights regarding their e-mail, especially if personal communications are allowed. Rather than stating that all e-mail is subject to monitoring, possible conditions for monitoring could be spelled out. Monitoring naturally would be conducted when there was some legitimate business reason for doing so, such as a situation in which there was reason to believe that the employee was violating organizational policies. In such cases, however, monitoring of e-mail should be limited in duration and scope (Fitzpatrick, 1997). Moreover, the results of the monitoring should be kept confidential. Thus, employees should expect that their e-mail communications would not be randomly monitored without cause, but that they could be monitored under appropriate situations.

There are possible benefits from a policy that provides employees with some privacy expectations, as opposed to a policy that provides maximum legal protection for the employer. First of all, employee morale is likely to be higher. Employees do not like being distrusted. They are likely to resent monitoring of their e-mail, even if perfectly legal, just as they would object to their employer routinely searching their office. Recognizing and respecting these privacy desires undoubtedly contributes to a healthier atmosphere in the organization (Doss and Loui, 1995). Second, employees may feel freer to use e-mail for honest and open discussions when they have some privacy expectation. Encouraging such interchange is desirable, especially for public organizations. A free flow of ideas should contribute to better decisions and policies. Thus, establishing an e-mail policy that provides employees with some privacy rights can be defended on pragmatic as well as ethical grounds, and these considerations might outweigh the desire to have maximum legal protection.

There is almost universal agreement that an e-mail policy should contain a prohibition of obscene, hostile, threatening, or harassing communications (Cozzetto and Pedeliski, 1997; Fitzpatrick, 1997). An employee should not have any expectation of privacy for communications that contain offensive language. As we discussed earlier, the employer has certain responsibilities to maintain a workplace that is free of harassing or hostile behavior, which mandates that certain language be restricted. Suspicion of violating this policy naturally would be a valid reason for monitoring an employee's e-mail. Some authorities go as far as recommending a "zero tolerance" policy regarding this behavior (Cozzetto and Pedeliski, 1997).

Another important part of the e-mail policy for a public organization is a clear statement of what types of e-mail messages qualify as public records and what requirements exist to save qualifying e-mail communications. As we have noted above, there are two competing public interests here--the desire to encourage open discussion of alternatives and the desire to inform the public. Of course, government organizations must operate within established legal parameters, which may not allow much flexibility on the part of the organization. To the extent that flexibility in interpreting and implementing the laws exists, the agency or organization has to decide what the proper balance is between keeping e-mail private, especially communications that are advisory or preliminary to an action or decision, and providing the public with the information that legitimately should be available for scrutiny. No matter how this is decided, an important part of the policy is to communicate to employees what the legal requirements are and what constitutes acceptable implementation of the legislation. What employees need are clear guidelines that allow them to make appropriate decisions regarding the retention of their e-mail. Given the lack of long-standing conventions in this area, there is considerable potential for confusion over how to treat e-mail communications.

To conclude, there are important legal questions surrounding e-mail in public organizations. These questions involve issues that are not unique to e-mail, such as questions of employee privacy rights or public access to information. It is useful for public managers to understand current legal thinking and to consider the issues involved in order to develop an appropriate and useful e-mail policy.

References

Adelman, Ellen, and Caroline Kennedy. (1995). *The Right to Privacy*. New York: Knopf.

Behar, Richard. (1997). Who's Reading Your E-mail? *Fortune* 135:56-61 (Feb. 3).

Bramsco, Julienne W. (1997). Employee Privacy: Avoiding Liability in the Electronic Age. *Litigation and Administrative Practice Course Handbook Series*. Number H-562. New York: Practising Law Institute.

Capone, Lucien. (1998). UNCG Counsel. Personal interview. April 9.

Cole, W. Scott. (1997). E-Mail: Public Records and Privacy Issues. Paper presented at the Annual Meeting of the National Association of College and University Attorneys.

Cozzetto, Don A., and Theodore B. Pedeliski. (1997). Privacy and the Workplace: Technology and Public Employment. *Public Personnel Management* 26:515-527.

Dawes, Steven J., and Susan E. Dallas. (1997). Privacy Issues in the Workplace for Public Employees, Parts I and II. *Colorado Lawyer* 26:61-85.

Doss, Erini, and Michael C. Loui. (1995). Ethics and the Privacy of Electronic Mail. *The Information Society* 11:223-235.

Farber, Mark. (1997). Employee Privacy and E-Mail. http://wings.buffalo.edu/academic/... /Complaw/CompLawPapers/farber.html.

Fitzpatrick, Robert B. (1997). Technology Advances in the Information Age: Effects on Workplace Privacy Issues. Current Developments in Employment Law. ALI-ABA Course of Study, Sante Fe, NM (June 17-19). Washington, DC: Fitzpatrick and Associates.

Garcia, Erik C. (1996). E-Mail and Privacy Rights. http://wings.buffalo.edu/academic/... /Complaw/CompLawPapers/garcia.html.

Garson, G. David. (1995). *Computer Technology and Social Issues*. Harrisburg, PA: Idea Group Publishing.

Greenberg, Thomas R. (1994). E-mail and Voice Mail: Employee Privacy and the Federal Wiretap Statute. *American University Law Review* 44:219-253.

Greengard, Samuel. (1996). Privacy: Entitlement or Illusion? *Personnel Journal* 75:74-88.

Hunter, Daniel F. (1995). Electronic Mail and Michigan's Public Disclosure Laws: The Argument for Public Access to Governmental Electronic Mail. *University of Michigan Journal of Law Reform* 29:977-1013.

Jenero, Kenneth A. and Lynne D. Mapes-Riordan. (1992). Electronic Monitoring of Employees and the Elusive "Right to Privacy." *Employee Relations Law Journal* 18:71-102.

Lee, Laurie Thomas. (1994). Watch Your E-mail! Employee E-mail Monitoring and Privacy Law in the Age of the "Electronic Sweatshop." *John Marshall Law Review* 28:139-177.

Perritt, Henry H., Jr. (1996). *Law and the Information Superhighway*. New York: John Wiley.

State Public Records Cataloging Service. (1998). Frequently Asked Questions About Public Electronic Records. North Carolina Division of Archives and History. http://www.spr.dcr.state.nc.us/faq.

White, Jarrod J. (1997). E-Mail@Work.Com: Employer Monitoring of Employee E-Mail. *Alabama Law Review* 48:1079-1104.

Court Cases

Armstrong v. Executive Office of the President, 877 F.Supp. 690 (D.D.C. 1993).

Bohach v. City of Reno, 932 F.Supp. 1232 (D.Nev. 1996).

Bourke v. Nissan Motor Co., No. YC 00379 (Cal. Sup. Ct., Los Angeles 1991).

City of Virginia Beach v. U.S. Department of Commerce, 995 F.2d 1247 (4th Cir. 1993).

Ethyl Corporation v. U.S. E.P.A., 25 F.3d 1241 (4th Cir. 1994).

Flanigan v. Epson, No. BC 007036 (Cal. Sup. Ct., Los Angeles 1992).

Jandack v. Village of Brookfield, 520 F.Supp. 815 (N.D.Ill. 1981).

O'Conner v. Ortega, 480 U.S. 709 (1987).

Sears v. Gottschalk, 357 F.Supp. 1327 (E.D.Va. 1973), *aff'd* 502 F.2d 122 (4th Cir. 1974).

Shoars v. Epson, No. SWC 112749 (Cal. Sup. Ct., Los Angeles 1992).

Simmons v. Southwestern Bell Telephone Co., 452 F.Supp. 392 (W.D.Okla. 1998).

Smyth v. Pillsbury Co., 914 F.Supp. 97 (E.D.Pa. 1996).

Watkins v. L.M. Berry & Co., 704 F.2d 577 (11th Cir. 1983).

14

World Wide Web Site Design and Use in Public Management

by
Carmine Scavo
and
Yuhang Shi
East Carolina University

The Word Wide Web (WWW) represents a major opportunity for local government to better the ways by which it interacts with local residents. The promise and reality of WWW applications are explored in this chapter. Four types of WWW applications are analyzed–bulletin board applications, promotion applications, service delivery applications, and citizen input applications. A survey of 145 municipality and county government web sites was conducted and the data is used to examine how local governments are actually using the WWW. The chapter concludes that the promise of the WWW has not yet been realized. Local government, while doing a fairly good job of implementing the less sophisticated uses of the WWW, must rethink the ways that it interacts with the citizenry in order to fully utilize WWW technologies.

Not long ago, a group of "netizens"–permanent residents of cyberspace–posed a question for themselves, Technology, Yea or Nay? In a self-congratulating tone, one of them responded, "Technology is wonderfully liberating. I don't need my stockbroker or travel agent anymore. I may choose to use them for a variety of reasons, but I don't NEED them anymore. Multiply that by millions of people and you have an entire industry that could be irrelevant in the Information Age.... Take this even further–maybe technology at some point will make government irrelevant..." (Technology, yea or nay, 1998).

Copyright© 1999, Idea Group Publishing.

For those of us who visit cyberspace only occasionally, a scenario like this is hardly cheerful and conceivable. But the irony is that if there is any truth to the prediction about the fate of government, it is government itself now poised to embrace the new technologies in the Information Age, most notably, the World Wide Web (WWW). A growing number of governments across the country, following a similar trend in the private sector, have moved into cyberspace and begun to disseminate information and to interact with citizens they serve through this new communication venue (Sprecher, Talcove & Bowen, 1996; Nunn & Rubleske, 1998). In some cases, a viewer (you can be one without relocating to cyberspace) can find a wide range of information about government services presented in a fairly elaborate and graphic format. In others, a viewer can get government services without taking a trip to downtown during the business hours, a blessing for those living in an area with high traffic volume or a government located a hundred miles away (Milward & Snyder, 1996). The dynamics behind this wave of WWW adoption and diffusion is the desire to capitalize on the so-called information revolution to allow citizens to obtain up-to-date government information and use government services more cheaply, quickly and conveniently.

Fortunately, our own experience with these developments has not suggested even a slightest possibility that technological innovation will ultimately lead to the demise of government. If there is any problem, it is the sluggish pace by which the new technologies come into the public sector. Despite great efforts, much of the governmental presence in cyberspace is still in the early stage, not counting the federal and some state governments (Nunn & Rubleske, 1998). It is not uncommon, for example, that one finds nothing more than an expanded version of the telephone directory in a government's Web site. Public administrators face some daunting challenges if they want to jump on the sensational information superhighway bandwagon and be a comfortable rider.

This paper intends to explore the potential of the WWW as a way of information and service delivery for local governments, an area that has been largely unaffected by the new computer technology. We will first describe briefly what the WWW is and what a government agency can do with the technology. We will then survey a large sample of Web sites maintained by city and county governments to find what information and services they are providing on the WWW. Based on the results of that survey, we will discuss some major issues involved in the WWW application: how to identify government services that can be provided online via the WWW, how to establish and maintain a service delivery system on the WWW, and what impacts such a system would have on the personnel and structure of a government organization and its users. The future public managers must be equipped with certain strategic perspective if we expect them to make intelligent decisions concerning the use of information technology. We will conclude this paper with a discussion on key issues for the future research.

What Is the WWW?

The WWW is an Internet tool introduced in 1991 by Tim Berners-Lee, a computer engineer associated with the CERN, the European Particle Physics Labo-

Figure 1: U.S. Census Bureau Web Page

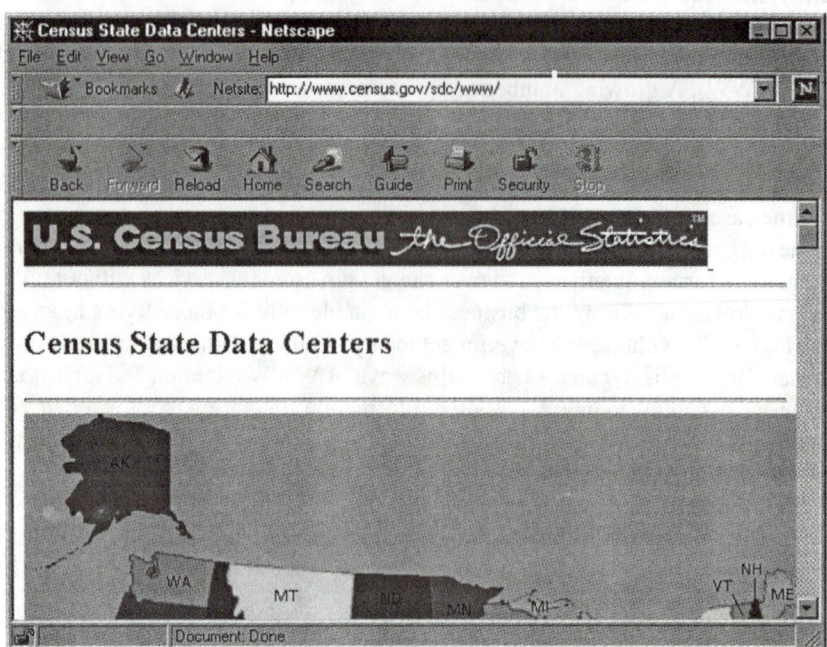

ratory in Geneva, Switzerland. It was designed to allow people all over the world to work together by combining their knowledge in a web of documents formatted in a non-sequential manner known as hypertext. Like its older Internet siblings, such as Telnet, File Transfer Protocol and Gopher, the WWW involves at least two wired computers, one serving as a Web site or server (we will use the terms interchangeably unless specified otherwise) and the other, a Web client. A Web server stores many computer files (called web pages) and is equipped with software that allows an Internet user to download those files. A web client, on the other hand, is installed with software that allows a viewer to connect to a Web server through the Internet and to download Web pages from there. The software on a client is called Web browser and the most popular ones nowadays are Netscape Navigator and Microsoft Internet Explorer, two head-to-head rivals. Figure 1 illustrates a typical Web page displayed on Netscape Navigator. The web site in this example is the one maintained by the U.S. Census Bureau.

The potential of the WWW as an information and service delivery system depends primarily on the contents of Web pages we put on a Web server. Put simply, a Web page is a plain-text (also known as ASCII) computer file that can be created with any editor or word processor. Figure 2 shows the file for the Web page we saw in Figure 1. The italic texts are what everyone can read when the page is displayed in a Web browser like Netscape Navigator. The texts enclosed in brackets are known as Hypertext Markup Language (HTML) tags, which are invisible to viewers. HTML tags can be divided into two groups depending on their functions, one for formatting and the other for everything else. In Figure 2, the tag associated with *Census State Data Centers*, <h2> ... </h2>, is a formatting tag instructing a Web browser to display

Figure 2: HTML Source Code for US Census Bureau Web Page

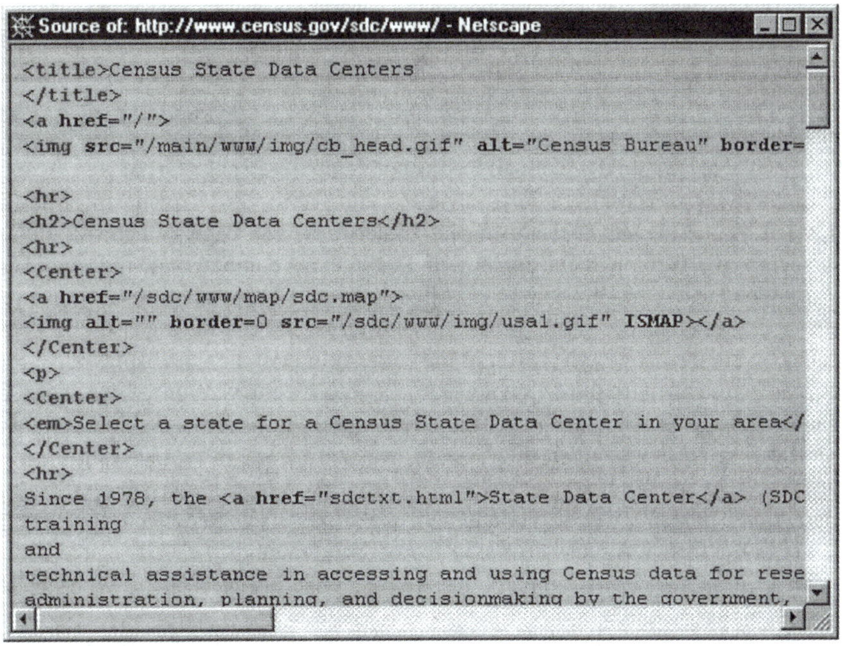

```
Source of: http://www.census.gov/sdc/www/ - Netscape
<title>Census State Data Centers
</title>
<a href="/">
<img src="/main/www/img/cb_head.gif" alt="Census Bureau" border=

<hr>
<h2>Census State Data Centers</h2>
<hr>
<Center>
<a href="/sdc/www/map/sdc.map">
<img alt="" border=0 src="/sdc/www/img/usa1.gif" ISMAP></a>
</Center>
<p>
<Center>
<em>Select a state for a Census State Data Center in your area</
</Center>
<hr>
Since 1978, the <a href="sdctxt.html">State Data Center</a> (SDC
training
and
technical assistance in accessing and using Census data for rese
administration, planning, and decisionmaking by the government,
```

the phrase in bold and large size as a second-level heading. <hr> creates a horizontal line. <p> creates a paragraph.
 breaks a line. <center> ... </center> centers everything in between. In this example, HTML tags for non-formatting purposes include <html>, <img src="...">, and <a href="..."> ... </a>. <html> tells a Web browser that this document is an HTML document. <img src="..."> brings a graphic image in a Web page when displayed in a Web browser. <a href="..."> ... </a> is the quintessential of WWW technology. It "anchors" a link to another Web page or a non-HTML computer file, whose address and filename are specified within quotation marks. This tag can be associated with a word, a sentence, a graph or any other element in a Web page as specified between <a href="..."> and </a>. In general, the more elaborate a Web page is, the more HTML tags one has to use. But not all Web viewers have graphical clients or multimedia capabilities on their computers and the most important thing for a Web page is not the format but the contents.

The potential of a Web server can be enhanced significantly in at least two ways. The first is to connect a web page to an external application following a standard known as Common Gateway Interface (CGI). Let's say that we want to set up a web server to let people from all over the world find some specific information about our community. Since the database is so large, we cannot put everything in a few Web pages. To overcome this problem, we can create a CGI program and put it on the Web server along with the database. Once a viewer connects to the Web server and decides the item he or she needs, the server will execute the CGI program to search the database for the information requested. Once the search is completed, the server sends the results back to the viewer. A CGI program is executed in real-time, so that it can output dynamic information. Since a process like this can be repeated as many times as it is needed, we can make Web browsing a two-way street and solicit input from a viewer.

The second approach to increasing the capacity of a Web server is to include Java applets in Web pages. A Java applet comprises a series of Java codes intended to accomplish a particular task and executed on a viewer's computer. It works like this: Suppose that we want to let citizens know the tax they have to pay for the motor vehicles they own. Since the tax schedule varies from one type of vehicle to another, it will cause confusion if we put all the tax codes on a Web page. What we can do is write a Java applet that can calculate a viewer's tax liability based on the information supplied by the viewer, and attach that applet to a Web page. When the viewer connects to the Web page, the applet will be sent to his computer and then executed by the Web browser on his computer. After the viewer supplies necessary information about the make, model, and year of the motor vehicle he or she owns, the program will calculate the tax and the result of the calculation will then be displayed. While such an application requires a viewer to have a recent version of Netscape or Microsoft Web browser, it has several advantages. First, since Java codes are not specific to a particular operating system, we don't need to worry what kind of computer a viewer uses. Second, like a CGI program, a Java applet can increase the interaction between a web server and a viewer. It allows us to collect input from a viewer in the form of mouse clicks, keystrokes and the like. Third, because a Java applet is run on a viewer's computer, it can save time, especially when a Web site has a large amount of hits.

The WWW has only a short history, but since it was made available to the Internet community, it has proven to be the most powerful and exciting innovation in the information technology. Although the description above is rather simple, we can conclude that the WWW offers a promising future for local governments to deliver its services more quickly and conveniently. First, as a menu-driven Internet tool, the WWW is easy to use, even for a person with little computer background. By clicking the mouse on some elements in a Web page, a viewer can jump from one document to another without knowing where the next document is located and in an order that makes most sense for him or her. Second, the information distributed on the WWW can be accessed at anytime and from anywhere. Third, with the assistance of other software on a computer (called plugs-in or application helpers), information transmitted via the WWW can be displayed in the form of text, graphics, audio and video. Fourth, a web browser such as Netscape Navigator or Microsoft Internet Explorer has incorporated all other Internet tools, including electronic mail, remote operation (Telnet), file transfers (FTP), and document inspection (Gopher). Such incorporation has facilitated a simple straightforward access to all on-line information, not merely WWW documents. Finally, with the CGI and Java technologies, the WWW has been equipped with the interactive capacity, allowing a person browsing a web page to interact with the person who authors the web page.

The WWW and Public Management

For a long time, the dominant philosophy in public management has centered on the notion of efficiency, where public managers are disposed to raise the productivity within the organization and reduce the cost of operation. This has compelled public managers to seek new technologies that can help them increase managerial control and productivity of individual employees. Studies show that as the computer is penetrating into every area of government operation ranging from accounting to personnel, it has been utilized to beef up office automation and data processing. This includes word processing, spreadsheet, recordkeeping and retrieval, graphics, scheduling, financial calculation, statistics, engineering design, expert systems, and geographic information system (Hurley & Wallace, 1986; Hadden, 1986; McGowan & Lombardo, 1986; Kraemer & Northrop, 1989; Lan & Cayer, 1994). The computer has become indispensable to any public agency seeking a high level of efficiency.

The advent of the WWW, however, has added a completely new dimension to computer applications in the public sector. In our view, this technology's most important potential is that it gives public managers an opportunity to practice a management philosophy that emphasizes more the quality of service than efficiency. Such a philosophy, introduced under names like Total Quality Management (TQM), entrepreneurial government and customer-driven government, considers customer satisfaction rather than productivity as the top priority of good management and encourages public managers and employees to find the ways to achieve this goal (Osborne & Gaebler, 1992). The computer-based communication such as the WWW holds great promise for this new preaching for at least two reasons. The first is that it permits a public agency to deliver its services more quickly and conveniently. The second is that it gives customers the opportunity to evaluate the services and input their opinions back into some monitoring mechanism. As many scholars in public administration have long recognized, by improving government communication with the public, computer networks will help government become more open and responsive (Kraemer & King, 1986; Gorr, 1986; Vasu, 1988). As far as the WWW is concerned, there are at least four specific areas of application:

Bulletin Board

This type of utilization refers to the case where a government agency maintains a web site to publish online the information regarding the services it provides, the programs it runs, the policies or regulations it enforces, the names, telephone numbers, and e-mail addresses of its key personnel, job opportunities, the important events associated with the organization, etc. The information posted on the bulletin board can be used by both the agency's employees and citizens.

Promotion

This type of utilization refers to the case where a government agency maintains a web site to offer a wide range of information about the city, county or region in which it is located. This includes population, economy, education, recreation, history, tourist attraction, business opportunity, and cultural events in the community. The purpose of such application is to raise the profile of the area, increase the spirit of community, and attract outsiders. Regional economic development is often the most important aspect of this use of the WWW. Another important part of promotional web site is a linkage to many public and private organizations–library, schools, hospitals, etc.–located in the area. Still another feature is an application of

Geographic Information System (GIS) software which allows data to be overlaid on maps of the community.

Service Delivery

This type of utilization represents a new direction in WWW application. Both bulletin board and promotion are information dissemination. Service delivery means that a government agency maintains a web site to provide services to citizens online, for example, specific information on local taxes and payment for local taxes, application for city permits and licenses. This utilization requires that the Web site be interactive–the viewer must be able both to view information on the computer screen and to input information to the Web site.

Citizen Input

This type of utilization refers to the case where a government Web site allows citizens to communicate with local government officials and personnel directly. This often reflects the degree of willingness on the part of government personnel to tailor the services to the needs of citizens. The highest form of such solicitation will be some kind of public forum in which citizens can express their opinions on various policy issues. Today, local governments have to decide a wide range of controversial issues concerning community development, environment protection, local taxes, cable television rates, traffic management, public health, zoning regulations, etc. Like many private companies soliciting consumers' preferences via the WWW, government agencies can also use the WWW to invite citizens to contribute their opinions on policy issues facing the community. However, unlike private companies (whose primary goal is to increase sales no matter to whom they are made), government *needs to be* concerned about the representativeness of those who use a WWW page. We will take this point up later in this chapter.

Survey Results

To investigate the four areas of WWW application described above, we conducted a survey of local government Web sites listed on the Web page (http://www.pti.nw.dc.us/)[1]. A one-fifth stratified sample of local governments in each state was identified and the Web sites of those governments were coded to ascertain the extent that the each Web site used components of the four areas of WWW application (see the Information Gathering Sheets in the appendix to this chapter) identified above. The resulting sample of 145 local governments contained 117 (81%) municipalities and 28 (19%) counties. There were no statistically significant differences between cities and counties in the overall web site score or the scores on any of the four application scales, so we combine the scores of the two forms of local government in the discussion below.

There were 38 separate indicators in the four areas of application we sought to code in the local government web sites. No local government received a perfect score of 38; the highest score of 26 was achieved by two cities–Roanoke, VA and Annapolis, MD. Other highly ranked local governments were Cape Girardeau, MO (25); Renton, WA (24); Des Moines (24); Virginia Beach (24); College Station, TX

(24); Santa Barbara (24); San Bernardino County, CA (24). Low ranking local governments were Riverton, WY (0); Stillwater, MN (1); and Wakefield, MA (3).

There were 13 indicators of the bulletin board type application; the highest score that any local government attained was 11. Highly ranked governments on the bulletin board application were Tumwater, WA (11); St. Charles County, MO (10); and seven municipalities tied at 9. There were 18 indicators of the promotion type application; the highest score that any local government attained was 16. This was attained by Roanoke which was followed by Annapolis; Littleton, CO; Cape Girardeau; and Aurora, NE with scores of 15. There were six indicators of the service delivery type application; no government web site attained a score higher than three on this scale. Roanoke, VA; College Station, TX; Renton, WA; and Norristown, PA all attained that score. And last, there were three indicators of the feedback solicitation application–San Bernardino County, CA; Manhattan Beach, CA; and Roswell, NM all scored at this highest level of feedback solicitation.

More interesting than the absolute scores of the local governments on these four scales is the interrelationship of the scales themselves. The scales were interrelated with low to moderate correlations. The bulletin board application was significantly correlated with all three other scales (Pearson's $r = .35$ with promotion; .36 with service delivery; and .24 with feedback solicitation), supporting the argument made above that bulletin board applications are the baseline of WWW applications. Promotion was moderately correlated with service delivery (.29) and insignificantly related to feedback solicitation (.16). Feedback solicitation was insignificantly correlated with service delivery (.07) and so was *only* significantly correlated with the bulletin board application. The hypothesized structure in the four areas of Web page design is therefore somewhat supported by empirical observation–bulletin board uses appear to be both the most common and to be at the base of any hierarchy of uses that web pages show. The above bulletin board uses would be promotion, then service delivery. Feedback solicitation would be at the top of the hierarchy, being the least common and most specialized of any of the four uses.

It should also be apparent that this survey shows that local government web sites are not nearly as sophisticated as they could be. While only some 4.1% (n = 6) of local governments scored a zero on the bulletin board scale and only 1.4% (n = 2) scored a zero on the promotion scale, 63.4% (n = 92) scored a zero on the service delivery scale and 20.7% (n = 30) scored a zero on the feedback scale. Thus, the two more technologically sophisticated web site uses are also the ones that large numbers of local governments do not utilize at all. In our estimation, improving the capacity of local government to use the potential of the WWW more fully will require higher level management to be more intimately involved in WWW design and management issues.

Designing and Managing a Web Site

Like any other technology introduced to the public sector, the WWW raises a series of challenges to public managers and employees alike. The subsequent discussion addresses two major issues facing those in the decision-making position: first, how to set up a Web site, and second, how to utilize the technology to its full potential.

Building Blocks

Certain resources must be committed in order to establish and maintain a Web site in cyberspace. Much of the investment at the initial stage is related to the purchase of hardware and software. The first is a computer system. The choice can be any type of computer as long as it is equipped with a large hard disk, a large memory (RAM), a quick processor (CPU), and a device called a network card. Most of the mainframe and minicomputers used by local governments today are certainly up to this task. For those agencies that do not have a mainframe or minicomputer, a powerful personal computer, either IBM PC or Macintosh, should serve the purpose. With the rapidly declining price in the computer market, any government agency today should be able to afford to buy a state-of-art model, if not the most powerful one.

The second is an Internet connection. A computer designated as a Web server should be attached to a network through cables. In addition, the computer should have a unique address and be able to run a program called TCP/IP. The address of a computer, assigned by the Internet naming authority following some conventions, is a numeric value translated into alphabetic form. www.ecu.edu, for example, is the address for the web site of East Carolina University and its numeric equivalent is 150.216.15. The last suffix, edu, known as domain, indicates the nature of the host organization–.gov is the domain for all governmental agencies. TCP/IP, which stands for Transmission Control Protocol and Internet Protocol, represents two pieces of software. IP is responsible for receiving and sending digitized information through the Internet, and TCP helps solve various problems arising from the process of data communication (for a brief introduction for non-professional readers, see Comer, 1995).

Finally, a computer designated as a Web server should be installed with a piece of software that runs the computer as a Web server. Typically, such software (also

Figure 3: Selected Web Servers

Web Server	Applicable Operating System	Company
Lotus Domino Go Webserver 4.6.1	Windows 95 Windows NT Unix	IBM
Oracle Web Application Server 3.01	Windows 95 Windows NT	Oracle
Netscape Enterprise Server 3.5.1	Windows NT Unix	Netscape
Internet Information Server 4.0	Windows NT	Microsoft

called Web server) consists of the functions for Web page authoring, launching and logging, image and map handling, security, archiving, searching, and site maintenance. There are numerous choices out there, especially for computers that run on a popular operating system like Windows NT, Windows 95, or Unix. Some of these servers are free and others charge a nominal fee. A company named Mecklermedia Corporation provides on-line information about the features of various software for web servers (http://webcompare.internet.com). Figure 3 lists the most comprehensive web servers for computers running on Windows NT, Windows 95, and Unix.

Planning

Past research on computer application in public and private organizations has demonstrated that simply focusing on the technical aspect of a new technology will not achieve the results as expected (Davenport, 1993; Hammer & Champy,1993; Cats-Baril & Thompson, 1995; Overman & Loraine, 1994). Any gains from investment in computer technology depend on (1) management decisions that shape the path of technology diffusion, (2) the resources that are available, (3) government employees who use computers, (4) the population that is served by the organization, and (5) past computer use in the organization (Caudle, 1987; King & Kraemer, 1988; Martin & Overman, 1988; Northrop et al., 1990; Brudney & Selden, 1995). In what follows, we will talk about each of these elements for WWW application except the last one.

Let us start with management decisions. When a government agency decides to go online and use the WWW for information and service delivery, the first and foremost question is what information and what services are to be posted online? This is a difficult question and the answer will certainly vary from case to case. We suggest two common rules. First, all the information that can be made public and of importance to the public can be put online. This includes the information on the agency's services, programs, policies or regulations, the names, telephone numbers, and e-mail addresses of its key personnel, job opportunities, important events associated with the organization, etc.[2] A Web site can also link to other Web sites that provide information about the local community such as school, hospital, news media, recreation, business, demographics, environment, etc. Second, all the services that only involve paperwork can be delivered through the WWW. An example will be an application for a home business license. In most communities, the process will start with a visit by an applicant to their city hall to obtain all the application forms and instructions from city clerks or the department granting the license. But such a trip can be saved if the forms and instructions are put on a Web server for anyone to download.

If a government agency has the necessary technical expertise and its Web server is equipped with interactive capability, more can be done with the WWW. Again, take the application for a home business license, for example. Typically, after getting the application forms and instructions, an applicant must fill the forms and mail them to the licensing agency. But in the city of Santa Monica, not only is there no need to visit city hall for the forms or instructions, an applicant doesn't need to send the forms back via the mail at all. He or she can supply all the information on the city's web server and send it to the relevant city office by simply clicking a "submit" button (http://pen.ci.santa-monica.ca.us/finance/homeocc.htm). Residents of Santa Monica can also request other services as well via the WWW. They can complain about shady businesses, airport noise, traffic conditions, discrimination, or the state of the city in general. They can request graffiti removal, street maintenance, bus itineraries, or library cards; and they can report petty thefts, sign up recreation classes, register for volunteer activities, and pay some taxes or fees.

A common error in many WWW applications is the overemphasis on formats. The WWW is attractive in a large part as a result of its multimedia interface, which has offered a variety of means for data presentation and service delivery. A creative use of multimedia enhances the functionality of Web pages and reduces the boredom. It brings attention to important information conveyed via the WWW. However, overuse of multimedia can be counterproductive. A Web page garnished with elegant graphics or "toys" (animated pictures, etc.), for instance, often takes a long time to be loaded on a viewer's computer, forcing the viewer to stare at his or her computer monitor waiting for something to happen. In the case of audio and video, not only does transferring files take a long time, but additional software is often required for the program to display its full effect. Designers must be aware that long waiting time and frequent technical troubles can easily turn away the browsing public.

There is no universal rule as to what and how much multimedia should be used in a particular case. The rule of thumb is that if a format does not serve any functional purpose, then it should not be used. A government Web site is not for entertainment purposes. Another point to bear in mind is that a functional Web site should have a clean and short front page that provides a general overview of the information available on the web site. In our view, the front page of the U.S. Census Bureau web site (www.census.gov) exemplifies this. The requirement of being short is also applied to other components of a Web site. A Web page that forces a viewer to scroll down and up or left and right many times will turn away many people. A CGI or Java program that takes a long time to execute can also be frustrating. The solution is to break a long document or program into small and sequentially related segments.

Funding

While the initial investment for a web site is manageable for most government agencies, the cost of maintenance could be a serious problem. If the past experience tells anything about the future, we can expect that government agencies will have to devote a lot of resources to network or WWW specialists (Sprecher, Talcove & Bowen, 1996). This is because, as we will explain shortly, running a Web site requires a level of technical expertise often beyond what most government employees can do. Given the current state of the job market, the cost of hiring computer specialists can be an extremely difficult problem for some local governments. According to the research on technological adoption in the public sector, government units of small size or located in the less developed areas tend to lag behind large governments in keeping with technological innovation because they are either constrained by their limited resources or by the small returns from investment in technology (Walker, 1969; Agnew, Brown & Herr, 1978; Smith & Taebel, 1985; Brudney & Selden, 1995).

From our survey, we have found two possible solutions to this problem. The first is to solicit donations from the private sector in exchange for advertisement space on an agency's Web pages. The city government of Greenville, North Carolina, exemplifies this approach as its Web site is financially sponsored in part by Pepsi Cola, Inc. The second solution is a kind of cost-sharing arrangement among several government units. In the San Francisco Bay area of California, local governments share the cost of one Web site where each contributor has the access to its share of space. Milward and Snyder (1996) have made a convincing case for cost sharing from service perspective. They argue that a cooperative arrangement will help integrate clients with the services they need. A homeless mentally ill person, for example, will need food and shelter from the social service department and a medical evaluation and care from the mental health unit. While Milward and Snyder's interest is mainly in computer networking, the argument they make offers a useful insight into the funding problem of a WWW application.

Personnel

The third aspect of WWW application concerns government personnel who use the technology. A successful WWW application must involve employees in every functional department of a government from the very beginning, especially those who have direct contacts with the public. This is because these employees know more about what information and service ought to be posted online than do computer technicians. Another benefit of increasing employee participation is to boost the level of responsiveness to citizens requesting information and services. There is evidence that in public organizations employees in functional departments are more interested in new technologies than computer specialists and top managers (Bugler & Bretschneider, 1993; Caudle, 1990). According to Kraemer and Dedrick (1997), this is because program and middle-level managers are more likely to be engaged with people outside the organizations and understand the problems and challenges facing the organizations.

Nevertheless, in the case of WWW application, a centralized coordination must be maintained as to who has access to a Web site (access here means that a person can alter the contents of a Web page, enter, and delete Web pages) and how the web pages are connected. While much of the centralization-decentralization debate in computer technology has centered on questions of economies of scale (Danziger et al., 1993; Reschenthaler & Thompson, 1996), we find such questions to be virtually moot in this case. The technology of computer design has changed enough that a decentralized computing environment can now show the same kinds of economies that a centralized, mainframe system showed in the past. Thus we support a balanced control model of computer management. This is based on the recognition that a government agency must present a unified image to the browsing public and that the data on a Web server need to be updated, integrated and safe-guarded. What is more, managing a Web site involves some difficult technical problems that require a certain degree technical expertise. In general, designing and writing a Web page is a very simple task. Anyone who can do word processing on computer can master the vocabulary and grammar of HTML language with some basic training. Both Netscape and Microsoft have incorporated the element in their latest versions of their web browsers, enabling a user to compose a Web page directly while some newer versions of popular word processing programs such as WordPerfect and Word have the ability to design web pages directly. But a simple HTML document can create only a static Web page. When the application moves towards a higher level–

involving database searches, interactive citizen input, and service delivery–Web pages must be integrated with some database, CGI programs and Java applets. Such integration, along with security and other networking needs, would require a certain degree of technical expertise in database management, programming and network engineering. Unless we want to increase anxiety among employees, the job of managing a web site should be left to a network specialist.

From the management point of view, a balanced model is more difficult to manage than a purely decentralized or purely centralized model. The first problem is how to cultivate a cooperative relationship between network specialists and other employees when a Web site is run in-house. A number of surveys have found that computer technicians in the public sector tend to attribute problems in computer application to employees who they believe lack a good understanding of the role of information technology, don't like using computers, and don't have the skills or training to utilize computing resources (Caudle, Gorr & Newcomer, 1991; Swain, White & Hubbert, 1995). Conversely (but not surprisingly), non-technical employees tend to put the blame squarely on computer technicians (Danziger et al., 1993). Based on the research done on this issue, we suggest that a public agency moving online set up a protocol that specifies who provides the leadership in WWW adoption, who is responsible for developing plans, directions, and priorities for WWW application, and who determines how computer technicians and other employees interact with one another. An interdepartmental steering or review committee may help solve the conflicts between the technical and non-technical employees.

The second problem is how to minimize any undesirable impact WWW adoption may have on employees. Researchers in public management have noticed for some time that computer technology can sometimes cause anxiety or even resentment among employees because of the worry about job displacement and additional work requirements (Kraemer & King, 1986). Employees who can adapt themselves quickly to a new technology tend to feel better and more receptive, while those who are less technically sophisticated may experience some decline in productivity and job satisfaction. In the case of WWW adoption, the pressure on employees may not be as large as that in other computer adoptions. However, an active involvement of all employees is critical. To ease anxiety, public managers should recognize which groups of employees are most likely to be affected by WWW adoption, and try to provide training opportunities for those employees so that they will acquire new skills and be prepared for any change in their work as a result of new technologies.

Outreach

Finally, we want to address the access problem. Citing some online estimates, Novak and Hoffman (1998) report that somewhere between 60 to 75 million adults in the United States have access to the WWW. And the number would certainly keep growing in the years to come, although there is evidence that the rate of growth has begun to slow down somewhat (Martin, 1997). This suggests that online government services would have great potential in meeting public demand. But how can a government agency inform those customers who are equipped with WWW access of the services provided online? There are two approaches to this. One approach, targeted mainly at local residents, is to utilize all the local media, such as newspaper, radio, and television, to bring about some publicity for a government Web site. Internet service providers in the local community can also provide information about local WWW access. The other approach, targeted at the general online public, is to have a government web site catalogued by such on-line search engines as Yahoo, Excite, Infoseek, Lycos, etc.

A more important question for a public agency is how to reach those customers who have no online access. The data on Internet use show that WWW access is not randomly distributed, but rather correlated with socioeconomic and demographic differences. Those who have lagged behind in catching the new technology tend to be minorities and have a low level of socioeconomic status (Novak & Hoffman, 1998; Cyberatlas, 1997). The implication of this is both ethical and technical. On the ethical side, with the different levels of the WWW, on-line government services would benefit the affluent more than the poor, thus reinforcing the socioeconomic divide in the information era between the haves and the have-nots. On the technical side, the cost-benefit ratio in setting up and maintaining a government web site may vary from one community to another. If the residents of a community have little WWW access, the benefits may not justify the cost. We don't have any readily available solution to this issue. However, the government in a community like this should take a more prudent approach to WWW adoption. It should put education on information technology as a key priority in its strategy for overall socioeconomic development.

Conclusion

The WWW represents a major new technology for local government. The potential for the WWW to reduce the costs of service delivery, promote civic pride, increase awareness of the types of programs local governments offer, etc. cannot be doubted by even the most casual observers of Internet operations. However, this potential is far from being realized by current local government use of the WWW. The survey summarized in this chapter shows that for a large percentage of local governments, the WWW is no more than an elaborated telephone directory–allowing those who access the Web page to see an on-line listing of city officials, along with titles, addresses (perhaps e-mail addresses), and telephone numbers. Far fewer local governments have taken the additional steps to take fuller advantage of WWW technology, by making their Web pages interactive, for example.

Our observations on the findings from the survey and our review of the literature on both WWW adoption and technology diffusion are that this situation will continue as long as those in charge of WWW technology at the local government level persist in thinking of the WWW in the same terms as they think of more traditional avenues of service delivery, citizen input, and local promotion. When the WWW was first introduced, several observers noted that it had the potential to remake virtually every type of human interaction. The anecdote related in the introduction to this chapter is one example of this type of thinking. Several years of experience with the WWW has caused somewhat of a backlash to this position. Many users of the WWW who may refuse to be seduced by the promises of entirely new modes of interpersonal and intergovernmental exchanges may instead not recognize that the WWW *can* fundamentally change *some* of the ways people interact with each other and with government. While the exaggerated claims of developers and pundits on the introduction of virtually any new technology should be treated with caution, one should also not under-estimate the change that new technology can cause in an existing system. Local government's tendency to try to fit WWW technology into its pre-existing notion of what the relationship between itself and the population is can result in under-use of the capabilities of the WWW. As more and more people become accustomed to going online to conduct such things as their personal correspondence, their banking, their travel plans, etc., local government cannot afford to be left behind. As one observer put it, "One-hundred years ago, a town without a railroad stop was condemned to a lingering death. Thirty years ago, interstate interchanges helped communities prosper, while towns on the back roads deteriorated. Now the 'information superhighway' is coming. Will your town be ready?" (Bowser, 1998: 32).

Appendix

Information Gathering Sheets

0. General
1. Date of Recording _____
2. Name of City or County _____
3. Web Site URL _____
4. Who administers the web site?
    a. Government agency _____
    b. Chamber of Commerce _____
    c. University or College _____
    d. Single Sponsor _____
    e. Joint Sponsor _____
5. Date of the last update in the web site _____

I. Bulletin Board

1. Does the Web site contain an organization chart for the agency?
    Yes ____
    No _____
    Note _____

2. Does the Web site contain the information about the services the agency provides?
    Yes ____
    No _____
    Note _____

3. Does the Web site profile the key government officials?
    a. Name: Yes ____   No ____
    b. Telephone number: Yes ____   No ____
    c. Mailing addresses: Yes ____   No ____
    d. Others _____
    Note: _____

4. Does the Web site contain the information about job opportunity with the agency?
    Yes _____
    No _____
    Note _____

5. Does the Web site contain the information on important events?
    a. Council meeting: Yes _____   No _____
    b. Public hearing: Yes _____   No _____
    c. Voting / elections: Yes _____   No _____
    d. Budgets: Yes _____   No _____
    e. Others: _____
    Note: _____

II. Promotion

1. Does the Web site contain or provide the links to the information about the area?

    a. Population   Yes _____   No _____
    b. Economy   Yes _____   No _____
    c. Business opportunity   Yes _____   No _____
    d. Transportation   Yes _____   No _____
    e. Recreation facilities   Yes _____   No _____
    f. Public health care   Yes _____   No _____
    g. Schools   Yes _____   No _____
    h. Libraries   Yes _____   No _____
    i. Community   Yes _____   No _____
    j. Entertainment   Yes _____   No _____
    k. Tourist facilities   Yes _____   No _____
    l. Others _____
    Note: _____

2. Does the Web site have connection to other institutions serving the public?
    Yes _____
    No _____
    If yes, what are those institutions?
    _____
    Note _____

3. Does the Web site use Geographic Information System to provide any spatial or demographic information?
    Yes _____
    No _____
    Note _____

III. Service delivery

1. Does the Web site contain the information on local taxes, fees, etc.?
    Yes _____
    No _____
    Note _____

2. Does the Web site allow a user to pay local taxes, fees or other charges?

Yes _____
No _____
Note _____

3. Does the Web site allow a resident to place an order for services?
   Yes _____
   No _____
   If yes, what are those services?
   _____
   Note _____

4. Does the Web site contain the information on government procurement?
   Yes _____
   No _____
   Note _____

5. Does the Web site contain the information on government contract?
   Yes _____
   No _____
   Note _____

6. Does the Web site allow a resident to apply for licenses and permits?
   Yes _____
   No _____
   Note _____

IV. Feedback solicitation

1. Does the Web site invite any feedback?
   Yes _____
   No _____
   Note _____

2. Does the Web site ask a user to supply any information about him- or herself?
   Yes _____
   No _____
   Note _____

3. Does the Web site contain or provide a link to some kind of discussion groups?
   Yes _____
   No _____
   Note _____

Glossary

Bulletin Board: A way of utilizing the WWW to publish on-line information regarding the services government provides, the programs it runs, the policies or regulations it enforces, the names, telephone numbers and email addresses of its personnel, and other vital information.

Citizen Input (Feedback Solicitation): A way of utilizing the WWW to allow citizens to communicate their concerns about local government directly to governmental personnel. This information is used as feedback to redesign local government programs to better service clientele.

Common Gateway Interface (CGI): A standard computer interface for connecting a single computer to an external application in the WWW.

Cyberspace: Reality as it exists inside of a computer network.

Geographical Information System (GIS): Computer software and hardware which combines mapping applications with the ability to overlay the maps generated with data drawn from a variety of sources (U.S. Census, survey data, etc.).

Hypertext Markup Language (HTML): A plain text set of instructions for formatting (tags) a set of data for a web page.

Java applet: A computer program (developed by Sun Computers, Inc) intended to accomplish a specific task which is downloaded automatically to a viewer's computer when he or she accesses a Web page.

Promotion: A way of utilizing the WWW to offer a wide range of information about the city, county, or region in which a government is located. Such information can include data on the population, economy, education, recreation, history, tourist attractions, business opportunities, and cultural events in the community. The purpose of this type of application is to raise the profile of an area, increase community spirit, and attract outsiders.

Service Delivery: A way of utilizing the WWW to provide governmental services to citizens online. An example is the ability to pay local property taxes through a city or county Web site.

TCP/IP (Transmission Control Protocol and Internet Protocol): Two separate pieces of software. IP sends and receives digitized information through the Internet while TCP helps solves problems arising from the process of data communication.

Total Quality Management (TQM): A management philosophy, developed by W. Edwards Deming, which, when applied to government, emphasizes the entrepreneurial nature of governmental programs.

Web Page: The basic organizing block of the WWW. A Web page is composed of computer files stored on a computer server.

World Wide Web (WWW): A network of computers joined together by hyperlinks which emphasizes graphical display of data.

Endnotes

[1] PTI, Inc. is "the non-profit technology research, development and commercialization organization for all cities and counties in the United States. The National League of Cities (NLC), the National Association of Counties (NACo), and the International City/County Management Association (ICMA) provide PTI with its policy direction, while a select group of city and county members conduct applied R&D and technology transfer functions" (www.pti.nw.dc.us).

[2] The choice of exactly what information to place online is, of course, a much more complicated matter than stated here. Only a large group of decision-makers can

develop a comprehensive list of such information; leaving the decision to one person (or a small group of people) risks omitting key pieces of information in which the public may be interested. Most importantly, however, it is *not* necessary to decide once-and-for-all what information to put online. Web sites can be designed to solicit feedback for users as to what information *they* would like to see on the Web site that is currently not provided. At the current time, very few, if any local government Web sites solicit such feedback.

References

Agnew, J. A., Brown, L. A., & Herr, P. (1978). The community innovation process: A conceptualization and empirical analysis. *Urban Affairs Quarterly,* 14, 3-30.

Bowser, B. (1998, January), WWW.localgovernment.com: Opening the window to on-line democracy," *The American City and County,* 113 (1) 32-41.

Bozeman, B., & Bretschneider, S. (1986). Public management information system: Theory and prescription. *Public Administration Review,* 46, 475-487.

Brudney, J. & Selden, S. (1995). The adoption of innovation by smaller local governments: the case of computer technology. *American Review of Public Administration,* 25, 71-86.

Bugler, D. & Bretschneider, S. (1993). Technology push or program pull: Interest in new information technologies within public organizations. In B. Bozeman, (Ed.), *Public management: The state of the art.* (pp. 275-293). San Francisco: Jossey-Bass.

Cats-Baril, W. & Thompson, R. (1995). Managing information technology projects in the public sector. *Public Administration Review,* 55, 559-566.

Caudle, S. (1980). Managing information in state government. *Public Administration Review.* 50, 515-524.

Caudle, S. (1987). High tech to better effect. *The bureaucrat.* Spring: 47-52.

Caudle, S., Wilpen, G., & Newcomer, K. (1991). Key information systems issues for the public sector. *MIS Quarterly.* 15, 171-188.

Comer, D. (1995). *The Internet book.* New Jersey: Prentice Hall.

Cyberatlas (1997). Who's on the net in the U.S.? paper at http://www.cyberatlas.com/market/ demographics/index.html.

Danziger, J., Kraemer, K., Dunkle, D. & King, J. (1993). Enhancing the quality of computing service: Technology, structure, and people. *Public Administration Review.* 53, 161-169.

Davenport, T. (1993). *Process innovation: Reengineering work through information technology.* Boston: Harvard Business School Press.

Gorr, W. (1986). Use of Special Event Data in Government Information System. *Public Administration Review.* 46, 532-539.

Hadden, S. (1986). Intelligent advisory systems for managing and disseminating information. *Public Administration Review.* 46, 572-578.

Hammer, M. & Champy, J. (1993). *Reengineering the corporation: A manifesto for business revolution.* New York: Harper Business.

Hurley, M. & Wallace, W. (1986). Expert systems as decision aids for public managers: An assessment of the technology and prototyping as a design strategy. *Public Administration Review.* 46, 563-571.

King, J. L. & Kraemer, K. (1988). Information resource management: Is it sensible and can it work? *Information & Management: The International Journal of Information Systems Management.* 15, 7-14.

Kraemer, K. & Dedrick, J. (1997). Computing and public organizations. *Journal of Public Administration Research and Theory.* 7, 89-112.

Kraemer, K. & King, J. L. (1986). Computing and public organizations. Public Administration Review. 488-496.

Kraemer, K. & Northrop, A. (1989). Curriculum recommendations for public management education in computing: An update. *Public Administration Review.* 49, 447-453.

Lan, Z. & Cayer, J. (1994). The challenges of teaching information technology use and management in a time of information revolution. *American Review of Public Administration.* 24, 207-222.

Martin, J. (1997). Is the web explosion fizzling? *Governing.* 54

Martin, J. & Overman, S. (1988). Management and cognitive hierarchies: What is the role of management information systems? *Public Productivity Review.* 11, 69-84.

McGowan, R. & Lombardo, G. (1986). Decision support systems in state government: Promises and pitfalls. *Public Administration Review.* 46, 579-83.

Milward, B. & Snyder, L. (1996). Electronic government: Linking citizens to public organizations through technology. *Journal of Public Administration Research and Theory.* 6. 261-275.

Northrop, A., Kraemer, K., Dunkle, D., & King, J. L. (1990). Payoffs from computerization: Lessons over time. *Public Administration Review.* 50, 505-514.

Novak, T. & Hoffman, D. (1998, April 17). Bridging the digital divide: The impact of race on computer access and internet use. *Science.*

Nunn, S. & Rubleske, J. (1998). 'Webbed' cities and development of the national information highway: The creation of world wide web sites by city governments. http://www.spea.iupui.edu/cupe/news/rpt-cvr.htm.

Osborne, D. & Gaebler, T. (1992). *Reinventing Government.* New York: Addison-Wesley.

Overman, S. & Loraine, D. (1994). Information for control: Another management proverb? *Public Administration Review.* 54, 193-196.

Reschenthaler, G. B. & Thompson, F. (1996). The information revolution and the new public management. *Journal of Public Administration Research and Theory.* 6, 125-143.

Smith, A. C. & Taebel, D. A. (1985). Administrative innovation in municipal government. *International Journal of Public Administration.* 7, 149-177.

Sprecher, M., Talcove, H., & Bowen, D. (1996). Local government technology survey release. *Government Technology.* 9 (1).

Swain, J., White, J., & Hubbert, E. (1995). Issues in public management information system. *American Review of Public Administration.* 25, 279-296.

Technology, yea or nay? (1998, May 13). Web culture. Available: http://

form.netscape.com/ directory/community/html/pc_unreg_mian.ht

Vasu, M. (1988). Information Utilities and Telecommunications Networks for Public administration. *Public Productivity Review*. 11, 219-227.

Walker, J. (1969). The diffusion of innovations among the American states. *American Political Science Review*. 63, 880-899.

15

On-line Research for Public Administration

by
G. David Garson
North Carolina State University

This paper presents an overview of on-line research tools for public-sector practitioners and researchers. Sections cover generic searching on the World Wide Web, common governmental website destinations, academic Web sites in public administration, non-governmental organization Web sites, public policy Web sites, data-related Web sites, the exploration of data from the U. S. Census, legislative and legal research on-line, news research online, on-line geographic data, public-sector labor research, researching bibliography online, and keeping up with the changing online environment.

Today it is increasingly recognized that developing competencies in on-line research is a requirement for the training of professionals (Barry, 1997). Nowhere is this more true than in public administration research because the federal and other levels of government have taken the lead in on-line access to public records (Taylor, 1991; Stowers, 1996; Milward and Snyder, 1996; Reschenthaler and Thompson, 1996). As Roberta Balstad Miller has observed, information technology is providing unprecedented access to data as well as to the ability to analyze it (Miller, 1995). Traditional modes of data collection are destined to be replaced by electronic access to metadata and databases. Researchers will spend less time on data collection itself and will spend more time on analysis and interpretation. As electronic access reduces the cost of research, the scope of research is expanding, as is on-line research collaboration.

Copyright© 1999, Idea Group Publishing.

In fact, so swift has been the rise in the significance of online research and the volume of use that by the mid-1990s, significant problems had arisen related to the scalability of existing research discovery tools. The Internet Research Task Force was established to study problems associated with the continued growth of data volume and data diversity. The Task Force has recommended ways to improve data retrieval, improve data servers, and upgrade searching algorithms (Bowman et al., 1994). Several government and corporate initiatives, including the National Information Infrastructure (NII) and Internet II, are now directed at assuring the viability of on-line access as a research tool. It is no exaggeration to say that national corporate and political leaders now see massive investment in the infrastructure for on-line research as the key to American research, development, and productivity competitiveness in the twenty-first century.

Generic Searching on the Web

GPO (Government Printing Office) access is available through many libraries (ex., http://www.lib.ncsu.edu/stacks/gpo/), providing on-line access to a wide variety of govenment documents, including but not limited to:
Blue Book (Overview and Compilation of U.S. Trade Statutes)
Budget of the United States
Code of Federal Regulations
Commerce Business Daily
Congressional Bills
Congressional Directory
Congressional Documents
Congressional Record
Congressional Record Index
Congressional Reports
Department of the Interior Inspector General Reports
Economic Indicators
Economic Report of the President
Federal Register
General Accounting Office (GAO) Reports
General Accounting Office (GAO) Comptroller General Decisions
History of Bills and Resolutions
Public Laws
Supreme Court Decisions
U.S. Government Manual
United States Code
Weekly Compilation of Presidential Documents

Apart from the GPO, numerous web sites specialize in providing gateways to federal government information:

http://www.whitehouse.gov/WH/Cabinet/html/cabinet_links.html, The Cabinet Departments
http://www.catalaw.com, CataLaw Legislation Locator
http://www.access.gpo.gov/nara/cfr/cfr-table-search.html, Code of Federal Regulations, National Archives and Records Administration
http://www.house.gov/govsites.html, Federal Government Resources, U. S. House
http://www.lib.lsu.edu/gov/fedgov.html, Federal Government Websites, LSU
http://www.whitehouse.gov/WH/Independent_Agencies/html/independent_links.html, Federal Independent Agencies and Commissions
http://fic.info.gov/, Federal Information Center
http://thomas.loc.gov/, Federal Legislation from the U.S. Congress Library
http://www.access.gpo.gov/su_docs/aces/aces140.html, Federal Register
http://medoc.gdb.org/best/fed-fund.html, Federal Research Info Online
http://www.law.vill.edu/fed-agency/fedwebloc.html, Federal Web Locator
http://www.fie.com/www/us_gov.htm, Federal Web Servers
http://www.fedworld.gov/, FedWorld
http://cobar.cs.umass.edu/ciirdemo/Govbot/, Govbot Keyword Search
http://www.yahoo.com/Government/Indices/, Government Indices, Yahoo
http://www.nara.gov/gils/gils.html, Government Information Locator Service
http://www.info.gov/, Government Information XChange

Another set of web sites specialize in providing gateways to state-level governmental information:

http://www.csg.org, The Council of State Governments
http://web.fie.com/index.htm, FEDIX
http://www.governing.com/, Governing (State and Local Government)
http://www.gol.org, Government Online
http://ksgwww.harvard.edu/~library/states.htm, Harvard's Kennedy School of Government, State and Local Page
http://www.ncsl.org, National Conference of State Legislatures (NCSL)
http://www.ncsl.org/public/sitesgov.htm, NCSL Policy Sites Page
http://libertynet.org/community/phila/natl.html, Neighborhoods Online
http://www.statelocal.gov/, State and Local Gateway
http://www.piperinfo.com/state/states.html, State and Local Government on the Web
http://www.law.indiana.edu/law/v-lib/states.html, State Government Web Sites
http://www.nasire.org, StateSearch
http://oyez.at.nwu.edu/cases/subject-index.html#federalism, Supreme Court Cases on Federalism
http://sunsite.unc.edu/usa/usahome.html, The USA Home Page

In addition, generic on-line searching in public administration can be accomplished through any of the large number of web search engines. AltaVista (http://www.altavista.com) is perhaps the leading such engine, and others include Yahoo (http://www.yahoo.com), Excite (http://www.excite.com), Lycos (http://www.lycos.com), and WebCrawler (http://www.webcrawler.com). All accept keyword searching and some, such as Yahoo, actively organize pages of web links on selected topics, some of which are related to public administration concerns.

Besides web sites, there are also thousands of electronic discussion groups, often called listservs or just lists, many on topics of interest to public administration. One may search for these discussion groups through Liszt (http://www.liszt.com/), or search by keyword the contents of any and all discussion groups through DejaNews (http://www.dejanews.com/).

Common Governmental Web Site Destinations

Of course, the federal agencies themselves all have Web sites providing a wealth of research information. Among the most common governmental Web site destinations are these:

http://www.uscourts.gov/, Administrative Office of the U.S. Courts
http://www.ojp.usdoj.gov/bjs/, Bureau of Justice Statistics
http://stats.bls.gov/blshome.html, Bureau of Labor Statistics
http://www.odci.gov/cia/, Central Intelligence Agency
http://www.census.gov, Census Bureau
http://www.doc.gov/, Commerce Department
http://www.senate.gov/~budget/republican/, Committee on the Budget, U. S. Senate
http://www.doe.gov, Energy, Department of
http://www.epa.gov, Environmental Protection Agency
http://www.access.gpo.gov/su_docs/budget/index.html, The Federal Budget
http://www.fbi.gov, Federal Bureau of Investigation
http://www.fcc.gov/, Federal Communications Commission
http://www.fdic.gov/, Federal Deposit Insurance Corporation
http://www.fec.gov, Federal Election Commission
http://www.fjc.gov/, Federal Judicial Center
http://www.ftc.gov/, Federal Trade Commission
http://www.financenet.gov/, FinanceNet
http://www.gsa.gov, General Services Administration
http://www.access.gpo.gov/su_docs/, Government Printing Office
http://ssdc.ucsd.edu/gpo/, Government Printing Office Access, Including Federal Register
http://www.os.dhhs.gov, Health and Human Services, Department of
http://www.hud.gov/, Housing and Urban Development, Department of
http://amcom.aspensys.com/huduser/, HUD User Databases
http://www.huduser.org/, HUD User
http://www.usdoj.gov/, Justice Department

http://www.fpmi.com/MSPB/MSPBhomepage.html, Merit Systems Protection Board
http://www.hq.nasa.gov/, National Aeronautics and Space Administration
http://www.nara.gov, National Archives and Records Administration
http://www.nlrb.gov/, National Labor Relations Board
http://www.npr.gov/, National Performance Review ("Reinventing Government")
http://www.nsf.gov, National Science Foundation
http://www.nsa.gov:8080, National Security Administration
http://www.osha.gov/, Occupational Safety and Health Administration
http://www.whitehouse.gov/WH/EOP/omb, Office of Management and Budget
http://www.opm.gov/, Office of Personnel Management
http://adams.patriot.net/~permail/, Public Employees Roundtable
http://www.state.gov/, State Department
http://www.ustreas.gov/, Treasury Department
http://www.gpo.ucop.edu/search/govman.html, U. S. Government Manual Search
http://www.usia.gov, U. S. Information Agency
http://www.usoge.gov/, U. S. Office of Government Ethics
http://www.usps.gov/, U.S.Postal Service
http://www.ussc.gov/, U. S. Sentencing Commission

Academic Web Sites in Public Administration

In addition to agency Web sites, academia provides its own array of destinations valuable for public administration research, including these common destinations:
http://www.aom.pace.edu/websites/index.html, Academy of Management
http://www.apsanet.org/, American Political Science Association
http://www.fsu.edu/~spap/orgs/apsa.html, American Political Science Association Policy Section
http://www.aspanet.org/, American Society for Public Administration (ASPA)
http://qsilver.queensu.ca/~appamwww/index.html, Association for Public Policy Analysis and Management
http://www.wvu.edu/~socialwk/A/arnova.html, Association for Research on Nonprofit Organizations and Voluntary Action
http://www.nmc.csulb.edu/users/publicadmin/, Charting a Course in Public Administration
http://www.cox.smu.edu/mis/cases/home.html, Cases in MIS: Edwin L. Cox School
http://www.hallway.org, Electronic Hallway: Cases and Teaching Resources for Public Policy and Management (Univ. of Washington)
http://cid.unomaha.edu/~wwwpa/fsite.html, Finance Administration Web Sites
http://sfswww.georgetown.edu/sfs/programs/isd/files/pub.htm, Georgetown University's Case Collection

http://english.hss.cmu.edu/Govt/, Government, Law, and Society Server, Carnegie-Mellon University
http://www.hbsp.harvard.edu/homepage.html, Harvard Business School Publishing
http://ksgwww.harvard.edu/~innovat/, Innovations in American Government
http://www.willamette.org/ipmn/, International Public Management Network
http://www.uakron.edu/paus/africa.html, Journal of African Public Policy
http://www.uakron.edu/paus/pae.html, Journal of Public Administration Education
http://ksgwww.harvard.edu/caseweb/, Kennedy School of Government Case Studies
http://www.unomaha.edu/~wwwpa/parost.html, MPA Program Web Sites
http://www.unomaha.edu/~wwwpa/nashome.html, National Association of Schools of Public Affairs and Administration
http://garnet.berkeley.edu:3333/budget/budget.html, National Budget Simulation
http://www.hbg.psu.edu/Faculty/jxr11/, Public Administration and Management: An Interactive Journal
http://www.niu.edu/ext/par/, Public Administration Review
http://deming.eng.clemson.edu/pub/psci/, Public Sector Network
http://unicron.unomaha.edu/faculty/cbayer/web/npomarks.htm, Web Sites for Nonprofit Managers
http://www.yale.edu/isps/ponpo/pubs/casesnpg.html, Yale: Cases in Nonprofit Governance
http://www.gol.org/bestof.html, Best of Practice Government Solutions
http://www.brook.edu/, Brookings Institution
http://www.capaccess.org/, CapAccess, the National Capital Area Public Access Network
http://www.civiced.org, Center for Civic Education
http://www.civic.net:2401/, Center for Civic Networking (related to the emerging National Information Infrastructure)

NGO Web Sites

Non-governmental organizations provide yet more Web sites useful for public administration research, beyond those from federal agencies and from universities. Leading NGO sites include the following:
http://www.city.net, City Net
http://comm-dev.org, Community Development Society
http://www.compa.org, Conference of Minority Public Administrators
http://medoc.gdb.org/best/fed-fund.html, Federally Funded Research
http://www.govtech.net, Government Technology Homepage
http://www.ipma-hr.org/, International Personnel Management Association
http://www.ncl.org/ncl/, National Civic League
http://www.urban.org/, The Urban Institute

Public Policy Sites

Each public policy arena has a large set of Web sites, too numerous to list here. However, common public policy gateway sites for the researcher include the following.
http://www.fsu.edu/~spap/orgs/apsa.html, American Political Science Association, Policy Section
http://www.brook.edu, Brookings Institution
http://www.cato.org/, CATO Institute
http://www.epn.org/, Electronic Policy Network
http://essential.org/, Essential Information
http://www.fedworld.gov/, FedWorld
http://www.igc.org/an/, Institute for Alternative Journalism
http://www.ipi.org/, Institute for Policy Innovation
http://ksgwww.harvard.edu/~ksgpress/opinhome.htm, Kennedy School of Government

Economic Policy

http://www.cyberpoint.co.uk/asi/, Adam Smith Institute (UK)
http://www.cbo.gov/index.cfm, Budgetary Policy: The Congressional Budget Office
http://www.whitehouse.gov/WH/EOP/OMB/html/ombhome.html, Budgetary Policy: The Office of Management and Budget
http://domino.stat-usa.gov/, Commerce Dept. Stat-USA
http://www.inficad.com/~cbolton/econ.html, Economic Policy - A Libertarian Viewpoint
http://ecolan.sbs.ohio-state.edu/links.html, Economics Information Center, Ohio State University
http://econwpa.wustl.edu/Welcome.html, Economics Working Paper Archive</A>
http://www.bog.frb.fed.us/, Federal Reserve Board
http://www2.tax.org/taxhistory/Documents/Fiscal/fiscal.htm, Fiscal Policy, Tax History Project
http://weber.u.washington.edu/~fpcweb/, Fiscal Policy Center, University of Washington
http://www.cato.org/research/fiscal.html, Fiscal Policy Studies, Cato Institute
http://epn.org/idea/economy.html, Idea Central: Economics and Politics
http://www.ita.doc.gov, International Trade Administration
http://woodrow.mpls.frb.fed.us/info/policy/, Monetary Policy, Federal Reserve Bank
http://www.financenet.gov/financenet/start/topic/private.htm, Privatization Resources, FinanceNet
http://www.eden.com/~reporter/, The Progressive Populist

http://www.regpolicy.com/, Regulatory Policy Center (focus on property rights)
http://www.worldbank.org, World Bank
http://www.worldbank.org/html/prddr/prdhome/prddr.htm, World Bank Policy Research Department
http://www.yahoo.com/Social_Science/Economics/, Yahoo Economics Links

Education Policy

http://www.aasa.org/index.html, American Association of School Administrators Home Page
http://www.aft.org/index.htm, American Federation of Teachers
http://www.coe.memphis.edu/coe/CREP/crep.html, Center for Research in Educational Policy
http://csr.syr.edu/, Charter School Research
http://www.whitehouse.gov/WH/New/html/educationfact.html, Clinton National Testing Standards Proposal FAQ
http://www.collegeboard.org/index_this/grn/html/lcposits.html, College Board's Legislative Priorities
http://csl.wednet.edu/, Commission on Student Learning
http://olam.ed.asu.edu/epaa/, Educational Policy Analysis Archives
http://home.aisr.brown.edu/ces/publicat/horace/v06n02.htm, Educational Policy and the Essential School, HORACE, Brown University
http://www.nassp.org/, National Association of Secondary School Principals' Home Page
http://www.nea.org/, National Education Association
http://www.colostate.edu/Orgs/NREA/, National Rural Education Association
http://www.nsba.org/, National School Boards Association
http://www.cel.mcgill.ca/orep/default.html, Office of Research on Educational Policy
http://www.ncrel.org/sdrs/pathwayg.htm, Pathways to School Improvement, North Central Regional Educational Laboratory

Health Policy

http://www.aarp.org, American Association of Retired Persons
news:bit.listserv.ada-law, Americans with Disabilities News Server
http://www.ama-assn.org/, American Medical Association
http://lhcwww.soph.uab.edu/, Center for Health Policy, University of Alabama-Birmingham
http://www.whitehouse.gov/WH/Publications/html/WH-Major-Docs.html, Clinton Health Security Act
http://epn.org/idea/health1.html, IdeaCentral, Health Policy Page
http://www.cdc.gov/nchswww/index.htm, National Center for Health Statistics
http://www.uab.edu/pedinfo/Government.html, Pedinfo: Government Agencies and Policy for Children's Health

Tax Policy

http://www.irs.ustreas.gov/prod/cover.html, IRS Digital Daily
http://www.taxsites.com/policy.html, Links to Tax Policy Groups
http://omer.actg.uic.edu/, Tax World
http://omer.actg.uic.edu/othersites/stateinfo.html, States' Tax Policies
http://www.taxhistory.org/, Tax History Project
http://www.accf.org/TaxPolAn.htm, Tax Policy Analysis, American Council for Capital Formation
http://www.ustreas.gov/treasury/browse/tax.htm, Tax Policy Page, Dept. of the Treasury
http://shell5.ba.best.com/~ftmexpat/html/taxsites/proposed.html, Tax Policy Sites

Welfare Policy

http://www.apwa.org/index.htm, American Public Welfare Association
http://stats.bls.gov/news.release/empsit.toc.htm, Bureau of Labor Statistics News Releases
http://www.afj.org/mem/welflaw.html, Center for Social Welfare Policy and Law
http://aspe.os.dhhs.gov/hsp/isphome.htm, Department of Health and Human Services, Economic Support for Families Page
http://www.handsnet.org/handsnet2/welfare.reform/, Handsnet Welfare Reform Watch
http://www.acf.dhhs.gov/programs/hsb/index.htm, Head Start
http://epn.org/idea/welf-bkm.html, Idea Central, Welfare Reform Links
http://nch.ari.net/, National Coalition for the Homeless
http://www.census.gov/hhes/www/poverty.html, Poverty Statistics, U. S. Census
http://www.ssa.gov, Social Security Administration
http://thomas.loc.gov/cgi-bin/bdquery/z?d104:HR00004:, Welfare Reform Legislation (1996)

Data-related Sites

In terms of generic searching for data on the Internet, there are a large number of Web sites which are pertinent to data-oriented public administration research:
Statistical data:
http://www.census.gov, Bureau of the Census
http://www.icpsr.umich.edu/gss/,General Social Survey (GSS) Home Page at the ICPSR
http://www.icpsr.umich.edu/gss/search.htm,Search the General Social Survey
http://www.lib.umich.edu/libhome/Documents.center/stats.html, University of Michigan Statistics Page
http://www.lib.virginia.edu/socsci/, Social Sciences Data Center
http://www.ntu.edu.sg/library/statdata.htm, Statistical Data Locators
http://odwin.ucsd.edu/jj/idata/index.html, UCSD Searchable Listing of Social

Science Data Sources
http://www.stat-usa.gov/, Stat-USA (Commerce Dept)
http://www.cudenver.edu/psrp/psrp.html, Political Science Research Page
Poll data:
http://www.gallup.com/,Gallup Organization
http://www.unc.edu/depts/irss/, IRSS Home Page
http://www.irss.unc.edu:80/data_archive/, IRSS Data Archive
http://www.irss.unc.edu:80/data_archive/pollsearch.html, Search
http://www.louisharris.com/home_content.html, Louis Harris and Associates
http://www.isr.umich.edu/src/, University of Michigan Survey Research Center
http://www.lib.umich.edu/libhome/Documents.center/opinion.html, University of Michigan Library: Public Opinion
http://www.princeton.edu/~abelson/index.html, Princeton Survey Research Center
http://www.ropercenter.uconn.edu/, Roper Center for Public Opinion Research, including POLL (also available in Dialog, discussed below)
http://www.nsd.uib.no/cessda/namer.html,Social Science Data Archives-North America
http://ssdc.ucsd.edu/ssdc/pubopin.html, Social Science Data Collection, from UCSD
http://polecat.iupui.edu/pol/links/links.html, More Polling Links

Exploring Census Data

Census Access

A very wide and changing variety of data pertinent to public administration are available online through the Census.

Approximately 300 Census CD-ROMs are available online at http://cedr.lbl.gov/cdrom/doc/cdrom.html, by arrangement with the University of California. Once Census data has been downloaded, the problem becomes one of putting it in a format which is useful. The Census provides free, downloadable software for this purpose. Extract, located at http://www.census.gov/main/www/epcd/www/extract.html, is the general purpose PC-based data display and extraction tool that works with Census Bureau CD-ROMs recorded in dBASE format.

Integrated Public Use Microdata Series (IPUMS) data, the richest source of time series census data, is made available through the University of Minnesota at http://www.ipums.umn.edu/ (IPUMS-98 home page) and http://www.ipums.umn.edu/~ipums/index1.html (IPUMS-95 home page). IPUMS was created at the University 13 federal censuses from 1850 to 1990, using uniform codes across all the samples and providing documentation. It includes nearly everything originally recorded, with the principal exception is that confidentiality laws apply to years from 1940 on. No names, addresses or other identifying information are included. Moreover, samples from 1940 on include only geographic areas with 100,000 inhabitants or more (250,000 in 1960 and 1970). The 1850 and 1860 samples exclude the slave population. The pre-1890 samples exclude "Indians not taxed." The pre-1960 samples, except 1900 and 1910, exclude Alaska and Hawaii. Samples since 1970 include unoccupied housing units. Variables include fertility, nuptiality, life-course transitions, immigration, internal migration, labor-force participation, occupational structure, education, ethnicity, and household composition. Since 1960, detailed housing characteristics are also included. Extract software, referenced above, is used in conjuction with IPUMS data.

SIPP, the Survey of Income and Program Participation, is made available online through the ACCESS project, described by Robbin (1992).

The Government Information Sharing Project, discussed below, provides links to a variety of Census resources at http://govinfo.kerr.orst.edu/. At the time of this writing, links included USA Counties 1996 (including GIS choropleth maps for selected variables), 1992 Economic Census, U S. Import-Export History, Regional Economic Information System, Consolidated Federal Funds Report, Earnings by Education and Occupation, Population Estimates by Age, Sex, and Race, and more.

The 1990 Census Lookup allows the user to create his or her own extract files, located at http://venus.census.gov/cdrom/lookup.

The Ferret Data Extraction and Review Tool provides another method of obtaining Census data extracts, located at http://ferret.bls.census.gov/cgi-bin/ferret.

The Data Extraction System (DES), also known as Surveys-on-Call, also creates custom data extracts at MABLE/GeoCorr is the Census's Geographic Correspondence Engine, located at http://www.census.gov/main/www/DES/www/welcome.html.

MapStats is an online guide to data profiling the states and counties, located at http://www.census.gov/main/www/datamap/www/index.html.

The Tiger Map Server allows the user to fenerate detailed maps on-the-fly, located at http://tiger.census.gov/cgi-bin/mapsurfer. The Tiger Map Server requires Netscape 2.0 or higher.

Direct file access to Census files is available using file transfer protocol at ftp://ftp.census.gov/pub/.

MABLE/GeoCorr is the Census's Geographic Correspondence Engine, located at http://www.census.gov/main/www/plue .

The U.S. Gazetteer provides place name and ZIP code searches, located at http://www.census.gov/cgi-bin/gazetteer.

State Data Center (SDC) and Business and Industry Data Center (BIDC) Programs

The Bureau of the Census's State Data Center (SDC) Program was established in 1978 to provide training and technical assistance in use of Census materials by educators, researchers, business, and government. Later, in 1988, the Business and Industry Data Center (BIDC) Program was added to provide specific support for the business community, but it is also useful for academic and other researches engaged in business-related work. Both SDC and BIDC web sites contain a wide variety of general and state-specific data resources, with emphasis on Census materials.

Following are the Web sites of SDC/BIDC programs:

Alabama
http://www.cba.ua.edu/~cber/asdc.html, Alabama State Data Center

http://www.cba.ua.edu/~cber/, Center For Business & Economic Research
Arkansas
http://www.aiea.ualr.edu/depts/csdc/about.html, Arkansas State Data Center
California
http://www.dof.ca.gov/html/Demograp/druhpar.htm, California Department of Finance (State Data Center)
http://www.abag.ca.gov, Association of Bay Area Governments
http://www.sacog.org, Sacramento Area Council of Governments
http://www.sandag.cog.ca.us, San Diego Association of Governments
http://ucdata.berkeley.edu, University of California Data Archive & Technical Assistance—UC Berkeley
http://www.sonnet.com:80/usr/saag, Stanislaus Area Association of Governments
Colorado
http://www.dlg.oem2.state.co.us/demog/demog.htm, Colorado State Data Center
Delaware
http://www.state.de.us/dedo/index.htm, Delaware State Data Center
Georgia
http://www.gatech.edu/sdrc, Georgia State Data and Research Center
Hawaii
http://www.hawaii.gov/dbedt/stats.html, Hawaii State Data Center
http://www.hawaii.gov, Information and Communication Services Division
http://www.lava.net/~plnr, Office of Hawaiian Affairs
Illinois
http://www.cgs.niu.edu/, Center for Governmental Studies
http://www.cagis.uic.edu/, Chicago Area Geographic Information Study
http://www.nipc.cog.il.us, Northeastern Illinois Planning Commission
Indiana
http://www.statelib.lib.in.us/www/RL/SDCMENU.HTML, Indiana State Data Center
http://www.iupui.edu/it/ibrc, Indiana Business Research Center (BIDC)
Iowa
http://socserver.soc.iastate.edu/census, Iowa State University
Kansas
http://kufacts.cc.ukans.edu/cwis/units/IPPBR/IPPBR_main.html, Kansas State Data Center
Kentucky
http://www.louisville.edu/cbpa/sdc, Kentucky State Data Center
Louisiana
http://www.state.la.us/state/census/census.htm, Louisiana State Data Center
http://leap.nlu.edu, Louisiana Electronic Assistance Program
http://www.lapop.lsu.edu, The Louisiana Population Data Center
Massachusetts
http://www.umass.edu/miser/sdc/datacnt.htm, Massachusetts State Data Center

http://www-unix.oit.umass.edu/~miser, Massachusetts Institute for Social and Economic Research
Michigan
http://www.state.mi.us/dmb/mic, Michigan Information Center
http://www.cus.wayne.edu/mimic/mimhome.htm, MIMIC/Center for Urban Studies
http://www.libofmich.lib.mi.us/, Library of Michigan
http://asa.ugl.lib.umich.edu:80/libhome/Documents.center, University of MI Graduate Library
http://www.semcog.org/, SE Michigan Council of Govts. (SEMCOG)
http://www.flint.lib.mi.us/fpl.html, Flint Public Library
http://www.iserv.net:80/grpl, Grand Rapids Public Library
http://www.libofmich.lib.mi.us/, Library of Michigan
http://monroe.lib.mi.us, Monroe County Library
http://metronet.lib.mi.us/SFLD/south1.html, Southfield Public Library
http://www.nwm.cog.mi.us, Northwest MI Council of Governments
http://www.nmc.edu, NW Michigan College, Osterlin Library
Minnesota
http://www.mnplan.state.mn.us/demography/demog_01.html, Minnesota
Missouri
http://www.oseda.missouri.edu/mscdc, Missouri State Census Data Center
http://www.oseda.missouri.edu/mosl/libser.html, Missouri State Library
http://www.missouri.edu/~sbdwww/, Missouri Small Business Development Centers
http://www.state.mo.us/oa/bp/plngrsrc.htm, Office of Administration
http://www.oseda.missouri.edu/uic/, University of Missouri-St. Louis
http://www.oseda.missouri.edu/, University of Missouri-Columbia
http://msdis.missouri.edu/, University of Missouri-Columbia
http://cei.haag.umkc.edu, University of Missouri-Kansas City
Montana
http://commerce.mt.gov/ceic/, Census and Economic Information Center
http://msl.mt.gov/, Montana State Library
http://nris.mt.gov/, Natural Resource Information System
http://jsd.dli.mt.gov/lmi/lmi.htm, Research & Analysis Bureau
Nebraska
http://www.nrc.state.ne.us, Nebraska Natural Resources Commission
Nevada
http://www.clan.lib.nv.us/docs/NSLA/SDC/sdc.htm, Nevada
New Jersey
http://www.state.nj.us/labor/lra/njsdc.html, New Jersey
New Mexico
http://www.unm.edu/~bber, Bureau of Business and Economic Research
http://www.edd.state.nm.us, New Mexico Economic Development Department
New York
http://205.232.252.23/nysdc/, New York:
http://www.marist.edu/management/bureau.html, Bureau of Economic Re-

search, Marist College
http://www.cdrpc.org, Capital District Regional Planning Commission
http://www.ciser.cornell.edu, Cornell Institute for Social and Economic Research
http://www.dutchessny.gov, Dutchess County Department of Planning
http://www.erie.gov/environ/planning/div_plan.htm, Erie County Department of Environment and Planning
http://www.gflrpc.org, Genesee/Finger Lakes Regional Planning Council
http://www.albany.net/~rpb/, Lake Champlain-Lake George Regional Planning Board
http://rockinst.org, The Nelson A. Rockefeller Institute of Government
http://www.ci.nyc.ny.us/html/dcp/home.html, New York City Department of City Planning
http://www.labor.state.ny.us, New York State Department of Labor
http://www.nysl.nysed.gov, New York State Library
http://www.orps.state.ny.us, New York State Office of Real Property Services
http://www.plattsburgh.edu/qmib, Quebec-Mexico Information Bank (QMIB)
http://www.albany.edu/csda/csda.html, State University of New York at Albany
http://www.binghamton.edu, State University of New York at Binghamton
http://ublib.buffalo.edu/libraries/units/lml/Government_Doc, State University of New York at Buffalo
http://www.plattsburgh.edu/tac, State University of New York at Plattsburgh, Technical Assistance Center,
http://www.cny.com, Syracuse Chamber of Commerce
http://www.co.westchester.ny.us, Westchester County

North Carolina
http://www.ospl.state.nc.us/OSPL/, North Carolina Office of State Planning
http://www.dcr.state.nc.us/ncslhome.htm, State Library of North Carolina
http://www.unc.edu/depts/irss, Institute for Research in Social Science
http://www.cgia.state.nc.us, Center for Geographic Information and Analysis

North Dakota
http://www.sdc.ag.ndsu.nodak.edu, North Dakota

Ohio
http://www.odod.ohio.gov/osr/, Ohio:
http://www.ipr.uc.edu/sordc/index.htm, Southwest Ohio Regional Data Center
http://www.oki.org, Ohio-Kentucky-Indiana Regional Council of Governments
http://www.ag.ohio-state.edu/~dataunit/index.html, OSU Extension Data Center
http://winslo.ohio.gov, WINSLO - State Library of Ohio
http://cua6.csuohio.edu/~ucweb/nodis/nodis.htm, Northern Ohio Data And Information Service

Oklahoma
http://www.odoc.state.ok.us/osdc.htm, Oklahoma State Data Center
http://origins.ou.edu, The University of Oklahoma: CEMR - ORIGINS

Oregon
http://www.upa.pdx.edu/CPRC/, Oregon

Pennsylvania
http://www.hbg.psu.edu/, Pennsylvania
Rhode Island
http://www.riedc.com, Rhode Island Economic Development Corporation
http://www.visitrhodeisland.com, Visit Rhode Island
South Carolina
http://www.state.sc.us/drss, Office of Research and Statistics
Tennessee
http://www.people.memphis.edu/~bberlib, The University of Memphis, Bureau of Business and Economic Research
Texas
http://www-txsdc.tamu.edu/, Texas
Utah
http://www.governor.state.ut.us/dea/sdc/census.html-ssi, Utah
Vermont
http://www.uvm.edu/~cdae/crs, Vermont
Virginia
http://www.arch.vt.edu/vchr/.html, The Virginia Center for Housing Research
http://www.virginia.edu/~cpserv/, Weldon Cooper Center for Public Service
West Virginia
http://www.wvdo.org/research/stdata.htm, West Virginia
Wisconsin
http://www.doa.state.wi.us/deir/boi.htm, Department of Administration
http://www.ssc.wisc.edu/poplab, Applied Population Laboratory

Legislative and Legal On-line Research

Legislative and legal research has been dominated by electronic modalities since the 1980s (Hubbard, 1982; Maclay, 1989). As in the area of bibliographic searching, some legislative and legal research may be done for free on the Web, but recurrent use will warrant subscription to an on-line service. The leading example of such a general service is Lexis-Nexis, whose home page is http://www.lexis.com/. In the more specific area of citation research, the leading service, also fee-based, is West (Beckman and Hirsch, 1997). West Publishing Group's electronic research system, KeyCite, is only available online to maintain its currency, reflecting a sea-change in research as in one area after another, on-line access is becoming the modality of choice. KeyCite's graphical interface supports hypertext links to cases, case histories, precedent cases, and other authorities. From a cost viewpoint, even a modest research program could easily spend thousands of dollars a year for either the West or Lexis/Nexis service, but some law schools and bar associations will arrange for access to databases on a fee-for-use basis, and some research university libraries make them available for fee or free to faculty and graduate students.

Although fee-based services provide the best and most comprehensive access for legislative and legal research, a variety of free on-line research tools also exist, such as FindLaw (Quinn, 1997; Healey, 1997).

The U. S. Code itself is available online from Cornell University, at http://www.law.cornell.edu/uscode/.

The U. S. Congress "Thomas" website, at http://thomas.loc.gov/, supports keyword searching for bills, laws, the Congressional Record, committee documents, U. S. government links, and more.

NCJRS is the National Institute of Justice's National Criminal Justice Reference Service. Its purpose is to share information about criminal justice research and evaluation, work, statistical analysis, policy, and programs.

UNOJUST is the United Nations On-line Crime and Justice Clearinghouse. Supported by the NCJRS, which has had extensive relationships with the international community, the United Nations Crime Prevention and Criminal Justice Branch asked NIJ to assist in designing the prototype of an Internet-based system of information exchange (Lively, 1995). The outcome, UNOJUST, is based on a structured approach intended to link each of its 13 institutes via the Internet in order to support research on crime and justice.

News Research Online

Computer-assisted reporting has become an important tool for newspaper reporters in the 1990s. A University of Miami study revealed that such usage at newspapers from 1995 to 1996 was most pervasive in areas of interest to public administration, including local government, politics and election, and policy areas such as education (Garrison, 1997). In fact, government information was among the most common subject of on-line searches by newspaper reporters.

Many newspapers have their own online access services, some free, some not. Also, database vending services such as Dialog (discussed below) provide another avenue for news clipping searching. If one can be satisfied with shorter articles and limited, but still very extensive, general news coverage, Pointcast (http://www.pointcast.com) provides a free service through which one can access both general news sources (ex., *Washington Post*, *New York Times*, CNN, *Time*) and specialized ones, including a range of governmental sources (ex., Congressional committee materials, *Federal Register*).

Geographic Data Online

Most agencies now use mapping in one form or another. Fortunately, on-line access to geographic data has expanded as has online access of text or statistics. Some leading web sites are listed below:

Government sites:
http://www.dma.gov/, Defense Mapping Agency
http://www-nmd.usgs.gov/www/gnis/, Geographic Names Information System, USGS
http://images.jsc.nasa.gov/, National Aeronautics and Space Administration Digital Image Collection (NASA)

http://164.214.2.59/index.html, National Imaging and Mapping Agency (NIMA)
http://www.noaa.gov/, National Oceanic and Atmospheric Administration (NOAA)
http://www.bts.gov/gis/links/links.html, Transportation Department GIS Links
http://www.census.gov/main/www/access.html, U.S. Census Online Mapping Tools
http://info.er.usgs.gov/, U.S. Geological Survey (USGS)
http://www.govtech.net/services/connections/gis.shtm, State GIS Programs and Other GIS Resources
Educational and professional sites:
http://www.aag.org/, Association of American Geographers (AAG)
http://wings.buffalo.edu/geoweb/services.html, GeoWeb GIS Links
http://geog.gmu.edu/gess/jwc/cart2.html, Index of Cartographic Resources
http://www.urisa.org/, Urban and Regional Information Systems Association (URISA)
Vendor sites:
http://www.esri.com/, ArcView at ESRI
http://campus.esri.com/campus/home/home.cfm, ESRI Virtual Campus
http://www.esri.com/base/data/catalog/type.html, ArcView-Format Data Vendors

Public-sector Labor Research

Most public-sector unions have extensive Web sites, which can be a valuable aid in labor relations research:
http://www.unionpride.com/afgeWWWnetwork.shtml, American Federation of Government Employees
http://www.afge.org/history/history.htm, A History of American Federation of Government Employees
http://www.afscme.org, American Federation of State, County, & Municipal Employees (AFL-CIO)
http://www.apwu.org, American Postal Workers Union (AFL-CIO)
http://www.mailhandlers.org, National Postal Mail Handlers Union
http://www.nalc.org, National Association of Letter Carriers (AFL-CIO)
http://www.natca.org, National Air Traffic Controllers Association
http://www.natcavoice.org/, National Air Traffic Controllers Assn. Newsletter
http://www.nteu.org, National Treasury Employees Union

Bibliographic Research Online

In addition to online data-oriented research, public administrationists, like other scholars, often need to engage in bibliographic research to determine what other work and analysis has been done in a given area. Although a limited amount of bibliographic searching may be done free on the Web, agencies and educational institutions which have a recurrent need in this area will almost certainly find it cost beneficial to subscribe to a fee-based online service such as Dialog, the nation's leading vendor of bibliographic and full-text databases. This is also true when searching for national, regional, and local news clippings on a given topic.

If bibliographic research is to be undertaken on a regular basis, a preliminary step is arming oneself with bibliographic data management software. ProCite and its companion products, BiblioLinks, and BookWhere?, are leading examples that complement searching on the Web or on Dialog. ProCite stores citations in a database and can print them out in any format. BiblioLinks automatically takes Dialog and other downloaded information and puts citations in a ProCite database. BookWhere? automatically goes out over the Internet to download citations from college libraries and the Library of Congress, and puts the finds in a ProCite database. ProCite also installs itself as a tool in WordPerfect or Word so you can "cite while you write," adding the references for any author or subject you highlight, based on searching the ProCite bibliographic database.

Searching with Dialog

Dialog makes available several hundred databases, many of them bibliographic in nature. These include Public Affairs Information Service (PAIS), the leading general-purpose public administration bibliographic resource. Others include Sociological Abstracts, Criminal Justice Abstracts, Dissertation Abstracts, Books in Print, and most bibliographic reference sources one would encounter in the reference section of a university library. One may also access leading national and regional newspapers, trade journals, and a limited amount of numeric data (CenData, with Census data; and POLL, the Roper Center's database of almost every survey item ever published, not only by Roper, but also by Gallup, NYT, ABC, and many others). Details on each database are found in "Dialog Bluesheets," which are available online at http://www.krinfo.com/dialog/krinfo/bluesheets.html. To get to Dialog itself, one uses telnet to the address telnet://dialog.com. Telnet will require one has first obtained an account number and password from the Knight-Ridder Corporation, the owners of Dialog. Help in using the Dialog system is available online at http://www.krinfo.com/search/dir_search.html.

The first step in Dialog searching is selecting the databases you want from among the several hundred available. Though there are certain pre-selected groups of databases, such as the GOVT government databases list or the PUBAFF public affairs list, use of these is very apt to be inefficient, including many databases of marginal interest. Instead, one will usually be better off by investigating the available databases through one of two paths. The Dialong "Blue Sheets" are available free online and contain descriptions of the features of each database, along with a sample record. Alternatively, one can invoke the "DialIndex" database, which contains metadata on all the others. After entering keywords into DialIndex, the researcher will be presented with the number of hits (matches) available in each database, ranked by frequency, thereby enabling the researcher to select the databases which are likely to be closest to his or her interests.

Commonly selected data files on Dialog include those listed below. In each case there is an associated file number (ex., 1 for the ERIC database). These file numbers are used to actually invoke a database in an on-line session. DialIndex, mentioned above, is file number 411, and Dialog Blue Sheets is file 415.

File No.   Name
1   ERIC, educational and general coverage
11   PsychInfo, the leading bibliographic source in psychology
21   NCJRS, leading criminal justice source
22   Employee Benefits Infosource, on personnel
35   Dissertation Abstracts Online
37   Sociological Abstracts, the leading sociology source
38   America: History and Life
39   Historical Abstracts, the leading history source
40   Enviroline, one of several environmental databases
41   Pollution Abstracts
47   Magazine Index, general coverage
64   Child Abuse, Neglect, & Family Violence
68   Environmental Bibliography
75   Management Contents
86   Mental Health Abstracts
93   Public Affairs Information Service, the leading public administration source
122   Harvard Business Review
135   Congressional Record Abstracts
137   Book Review Index
139   Economic Literature Index
150   Legal Resource Index, for law articles (not citations)
163   Ageline, covering human services for the elderly
166   GPO Publications Reference Index
171   Criminal Justice Periodical Index
202   Information Science Abstracts
291   Family Resources
415   Dialog Bluesheets
468   Public Opinion Online (POLL), from the Roper Center, covering not only Roper but also Gallup, Yankelovich, and most other opinion polls (frequency data, no crosstabulations)
470   Books in Print
580   CENDATA, providing Census data in tabular form

Numerous other databases are available, including some of interest to public administration, such as the National Technical Information Service (NTIS), which covers all federally-funded research.

To go online with Dialog, one must prearrange an account number and password, since this is a fee service. One can connect to Dialog (as of 1998) by using Telnet software to go to the address dialog.com. After entering the account number and password, the research can choose between a menu mode and a command mode. Typing /MENU at command mode "?" prompt invokes the menu system. Typing /NOMENU at a menu system ? prompt returns one to the command mode.

The command mode can be executed successfully with a half dozen commands. There are five basic steps:

1. First, the researcher invokes the desired databases with the "B" (Begin)

command, as for example, "B 1,35,37" (but without the quote marks) to invoke ERIC, Dissertation Abstracts, and Sociological Abstracts simultaneously. Predefined sets can also be invoked in the same way, for example, B GOVT. Other predefined sets include BOOKS, BUSECON, BUSSTAT, EDUCAT, ENERGY, ENVIRON, HUMANIT, INFOSCI, LABOR, LAW, MANAGE, NEWSWIRE, PAPERS, PSYCH, PUBAFF, and SOCSCI.

2. Second, one enters one's keywords. A common strategy is to define each dimension separately, generating a set for each dimension, then asking for the intersection of the sets. For instance, a "government" dimension might include terms like government, public, federal, city, state, municipal, and so on. A "management" dimension might include terms like management, administration, and supervision. There may be several such dimensions. Root terms can be entered with a question mark wildcard: supervis? will get supervise, supervision, supervisor, etc. Phrases can be entered with the "w" operator: public(w1)policy, for instance, gets hits in which the two words are within one word of each other. One can also enter predefined descriptor terms found in the database's dictionary, or found in the descriptor portion of previous hits which have been displayed or printed. The actual request for the keywords is implemented with the "S" search command: S manage? or administ? or supervis?, to get the management dimension. Dialog will list the number of matching hits and assign a set number. Once all the dimensions have been created, one can request the intersection: S S1 and S5 and S8, for instance, gets the intersection of sets 1, 5, and 8. The Dialog command DS displays set numbers if the researcher forgets.

3. The third step is usually to filter the large number of hits one is apt to receive. For instance, one may limit hits to keywords appearing in the article titles. If S15 is the desired intersection, then the command "S S15 and public/TI" (without quotes) would give only the intersection hits in which the term "public" appears in the title. One can also limit by publication year: "S S15 and PY=1995:PY=1999" (without quotes) gets only hits between 1995 and 1999.

4. The fourth step is to print out one's hits. Each version of Telnet differs somewhat, but there is always a menu choice along the lines of "Start logging." This choice will allow the researcher to specify a directory and file name under which to save the hits one is about to list. After logging is turned on, everything that appears on the screen will also go into the file, which will be a plain ASCII text file. If the final set is S17, then it can be listed by the "T" type command: "T S15/5/all" (no quotes). There are three parameters: the set number, S15; the format, described on the Blue Sheets (5 is almost always "full format" and gives the most information; other formats may leave out the abstract, the descriptors, or other elements; KWIC can also be used in place of the 5 to get keyword-in-context listings); "all" specifies which records should be printed (one may also enter a numeric range, such as 1-25 for the first 25 records, which tend to be the 25 matching records most recently entered into the database). If a bibliographic database manager such as ProCite is used, the type command may also need the added term "TAG" at the end of the line. This adds tags such as "AU=" for the author component of the record, helping the database manager read in the

downloaded records.
5. The fifth step is to log off. It is important that the researcher select "Stop Logging" or equivalent from his or her Telnet software, to close the logging file. In Dialog one then simply enters the command term LOGOFF.

There are, of course, numerous other options in the Dialog system. For instance, one can get an online explanation of any command by typing the command "HELP" followed by the command word of interest (e.g.: HELP TYPE). RANK DE will give a ranked list of descriptor terms for the current set of hits. The command EXPAND can be used with descriptor terms to generate additional potential keywords. EXPAND ROBBERY, for instance, will generate a list of keywords related to "robbery," assuming "robbery" is a descriptor for the current database. RD will remove duplicates prior to using the "T" command to display the records.

Other Paths to Online Bibliographic Research

ERIC. Perhaps the leading free online bibliographic resource is ERIC, the Educational Resources Information Clearinghouse. Though funded by the U.S. Department of Education and having some focus in this area, ERIC is a general-purpose bibliographic search engine with broad coverage of current events and social sciences topics. The ERIC search engine works like most others, accepting keywords and returning citations. It is located at the web address http://ericir.syr.edu/Eric/. Documentation is located at http://ericir.syr.edu/Eric/plweb_faq.html.

LOC. The Library of Congress Search System gives access to citations on nearly every book ever published in the United States, and to many foreign works. It is located at the URL http://lcweb2.loc.gov/ammem/booksquery.html. Once there, one searches for books in the usual keyword manner, but a useful feature is that after finding a "hit," there is a "Browse the Shelf" button that gives access to adjacent titles in Dewey Decimal System library order so that one may seek additional titles much as many researchers do in manual library research.

Amazon.com is a good source for online searching of books in print, available at http://www.amazon.com/. In some cases, reviews are also available.

Bartlett's Quotations is searchable online at http://www.columbia.edu/acis/bartleby/bartlett/.

City Net provides a wide variety of general information about major metropolitan areas, including maps, located at http://www.city.net.

The Electronic Newsstand, at http://www.enews.com/, links to over 2,000 online periodical sites. See also the Electronic Newspapers and Media page of the Yahoo search service, at http://www.yahoo.com/news_and_media/.

The Federal Web Locator is a major search service for federal governmental web sites, located at http://www.law.vill.edu/fed-agency/fedwebloc.html.

The Internet Public Library, run by the University of Michigan, is at http://ipl.sils.umich.edu/ref/. Here one may pose questions to a virtual librarian as well as browse the Ready Reference Collection.

Leading Political Science Sites is an extensive collection of website links, maintained by the author. It is located at http://hcl.chass.ncsu.edu/garson/burns/leading.htm. Click on "Bureaucracy", "Public Policy", and "Federalism" chapters for public administration, public policy, and state government topics respectively.

Research-it at http://www.itools.com/research-it/research-it.html contains a general-purpose collection including a dictionary, thesaurus, translators, language tools, biographical dictionary, Bartlett's Quotations, maps, CIA Factbook, telephone directories, financial tools, zip codes, listservs lists, and more.

Time-Warner Pathfinder at http://pathfinder.com provides searching for CNN, AllPolitics, Time, Life, Money, Fortune, and more.

U. S. Government Information Resources is an on-line collection of Web links located at http://www.nttc.edu/gov_res.html.

How to Cite Documents Found on the Web

There are a variety of suggested citation styles for Internet information. One is found at the Library of Congress web site at http://lcweb2.loc.gov/ammem/ndlpedu/cite.html. Another is found at the Internet Law web site at http://www.ipl.org/ref/QUE/FARQ/netciteFARQ.html. Specifically for users of public administration materials, the Bureau of the Census has provided one widely-used format, which is recommended below.

For Web pages, including ASCII text or PostScript document format (PDF) files, the Census recommended format is as follows:

Author (last name, first name)—if applicable, followed by "U.S. Census Bureau;"

Within quotation marks, title of agency source or output/work, and/or html title (if different from the previous title); if available, the publication/issue/release (or "last revised") date, e.g., "published 27 December 1996;" universal resource locator (URL) of the tile page, if applicable, or the page where cited material appears, set off by angle brackets (); if there is no visible publication date, one may note the date, within parenthesis, when the data were accessed, e.g., "(accessed: 7 January 1997)." Semicolons are used to separate elements.

Examples:

Citing a Web page: U.S. Census Bureau; "Advance Data from the Quarterly Financial Report for Manufacturing, Mining, and Trade Corporations—First Quarter 1993;" published June 1993, <http://www.census.gov/agfs/qfr/view/qfr931mg.txt>.

Citing a specific table: U.S. Census Bureau; "The Foreign-Born Population, (Table) 1. Selected Characteristics of the Population by Citizenship: 1994;" published 4 October 1996; <http://www.census.gov/population/www/socdemo/foreign.html>

Citing a .pdf file: U.S. Census Bureau; Population Projections of the United States by Age, Sex, and Hispanic Origin: 1995 to 2050; <http://www.census.gov/prod/www/titles.html#popest>; (accessed: 10 January 1997)

On the Web, there is a difference between static pages discussed above and dynamically generated pages. Dynamically generated tables and files do not exist as a specific URL address, but are created "on the fly" in response to a user completing a Web-based form. For dynamic pages, the Census-recommended format is as follows:

Name of agency; name of the database or other data repository/source (e.g., Data Access and Dissemination System [DADS], Survey of Income and Program Participation [SIPP], TIGER Mapping Service, etc.), set off by quotation marks, or follow publication citation style; the name of the person who generates the extraction, tabulation, etc., e.g., "generated by John Smith;" the name of the software package used to generate the extract, tabulation, etc., if known, e.g., "using Data Extraction System;" the URL of the application software's main or first page set off by angle brackets, e.g., <http://www.census.gov/des/p1>; the date, within parenthesis, when the user generated the extract, tabulation, etc., e.g., (7 January 1997). Again, semicolons are used to separate elements.

Examples:
U.S. Census Bureau; 1990 Census of Population and Housing, Summary Tape File 3A;" generated by John Smith; using 1990 Census Lookup; <http://venus.census.gov/cdrom/lookup>; (12 February 1997).

A third type of citation is represented by file transfer protocol (FTP) files, which are simply files residing on a remote computer, such as a file server belonging to the Census Bureau. These files are normally downloaded to the user's computer and may not be viewed with a Web browser at all. This is the recommended format for FTP files.

U.S. Census Bureau; filename, e.g., "stp222.06;" file date, if available, e.g., "published 10 January 1997;" universal resource locator (URL), set off by angle brackets (), of page where cited material appears, e.g., <ftp://ftp.census.gov/housing>; if no file date found, the date, within parenthesis, when the user accessed the data, e.g.: (accessed: 7 January 1997). Semicolons separate elements.

Examples:
U.S. Census Bureau; stp222.06; <ftp://ftp.census.gov/housing>; (accessed: 7 January 1997).

U.S. Census Bureau; M20a9611.wk1; published 7 January 1997; <ftp://www.census.gov/pub/industry/M20a9611.txt>.

E-mail is a fourth and final type of citation, where the format is:

Message author's name (last name, first name, middle initial), e.g., "Smith, John T.; words "personal e-mail"; name of agency; subject from subject line of e-mail message, e.g., subject: fertility statistics;" date e-mail sent, e.g., "7 January 1997." Semicolons separate elements.

Example:
Smith, John T.; personal e-mail; U.S. Census Bureau; subject: fertility statistics; 7 January 1997.

Keeping Up

Although this chapter seeks to constitute an overview of on-line research in public administration, providing good beginning points, the online world is constantly changing an expanding. Fortunately, there are a variety of ways of continuously updating one's on-line research skills.

The Government Information Sharing Project is an electronic mailing list sponsored by Oregon State University Information Services. It specializes in providing users with links and information on updates and additions related to public administration data. The list includes notices of what is listed in its "What's New" page, and only includes informat sent to the list by the staff of the Government Information Sharing Project. That is, it is an open list for purposes of announcement list, but it is not an open discussion list. One joins the list in the conventional way: send e-mail to listserv@mail.orst.edu with nothing in the "Subject:" line and in the body of the message put GOVINFO firstname lastname.

Government-oriented publications which specialize in information technology are another way of staying current with what is new online. Two leading examples are *Government Computer News* (http://www.gcn.com/) and *Government Technology* (http://www.govtech.net/).

References

Barry, Christine A. (1997). Information skills for an electronic world: training: Doctoral research students. *Journal of Information Science*. 23(3): 225-38.

Beckman, David and David Hirsch, David (1997). New approach to cite-seeing: West/Thompson merger yields all-electronic method of researching cases. *ABA Journal*, 83(1): 85.

Bowman, C. M., Peter B. Danzig, Udi Manber, and Michael F. Schwartz (1994). Scalable Internet resource discovery: Research problems and approaches. *Communications of the ACM,* 37(8): 98-107. (Special Issue: Internet Technology).

Garrison, Bruce (1997). Computer-assisted reporting. *Editor & Publisher ,* 130(25)(June 21): 40 - 43.

Healey, Brian W. (1997). How to use the Internet for legal research. *Trial,* 33(5): 84.

Hubbard, Abigail (1981). Online research for a state legislature. *Online,* 6(4): 27-41.

Lively, G. M. (1995). United Nations On-Line Crime and Justice Clearinghouse (UNOJUST). Presented at the Workshop on International Cooperation and Assistance in the Management of the Criminal Justice System: Computerization of Criminal Justice Operations and the Development, Analysis, and Policy Use of Criminal Justice Information, Cairo, Egypt, May 2, 1995.

Maclay, Veronica (1989). Selected sources of United States agency decisions. *Government Publications Review,* 16(3): 271-301.

Miller, Roberta Balstad (1995). The information society: O brave new world. *Social Science Computer Review,* 13(2): 163-170.

Milward, H. Brinton and Louise O. Snyder (1996). Electronic government: Linking citizens to public organizations through technology. *Journal of Public Administration Research and Theory,* 6(2): 261-75.

Quinn, Peter C. (1997). Research sites on the World Wide Web. *Trial,* 33 (4): 84-92.

Reschenthaler, G. B. and Fred Thompson (1996). The information revolution and the new public management. *Journal of Public Administration Research and Theory,* 6(1): 125-43.

Robbin, Alice (1992). Social scientists at work on electronic research networks. *Electronic Networking: Research, Applications and Policy,* 2(2): 6-30.

Stowers, Genie N.L. (1996). Moving governments on-line: implementation and policy issues. Public Administration Review, 56(1): 121-125.

Taylor, John A. (1991). Public administration and the information polity. *Public Administration,* 69(2): 171-90.

Weiskel, Timothy C. (1991). Environmental information resources and electronic research systems, *Library Hi Tech,* 9(2): 7-19.

About the Authors

About the Authors

T. R. Carr is Associate Professor and Chair of the Department of Public Administration and Policy Analysis at Southern Illinois University Edwardsville. He served on the faculty at Texas Tech University and at the University of Arkansas at Fayetteville prior to moving to SIUE. He holds a Ph.D. in political science, a Master of Public Administration degree from the University of Oklahoma, and a B.A. from Minot State College. He has published in the International Journal of Public Administration, the Labor Law Review, the Brock Review, and has co-authored the text *American Public Policy* published by St. Martin's Press. His teaching interests are in the areas of quantitative methods and public policy analysis.

George T. Duncan is Professor of Statistics in the H. John Heinz III School of Public Policy and Management and the Department of Statistics at Carnegie Mellon University. He was on the faculty of the University of California, Davis (1970-1974), and was a Peace Corps Volunteer in the Philippines (1965-1967), teaching at Mindanao State University. His research centers on information technology and social accountability. He has published more than 50 papers in such journals as *Statistical Science, Management Science, the Journal of the American Statistical Association, Econometrica, and Psychometrika*. He has received National Science Foundation research funding and has lectured in Brazil, Italy, Turkey, Ireland, Mexico, Israel and Japan. He chaired the Panel on Confidentiality and Data Access of the National Academy of Sciences (1989-1993), resulting in the book, *Private Lives and Public Policies: Confidentiality and Accessibility of Government Statistics*. He chaired the American Statistical Association's Committee on Privacy and Confidentiality.

He is a Fellow of the American Statistical Association, an elected member of the International Statistical Institute, and a Fellow of the American Association for the Advancement of Science. In 1996, he was elected *Pittsburgh Statistician of the Year* by the American Statistical Association. He has been editor of the Theory and Methods Section of the Journal of the American Statistical Association. He received a B.S. degree (1963) and M.S. degree (1964) from the University of Chicago and a Ph.D. degree (1970) from the University of Minnesota, all in the field of statistics. He can be e-mailed at George.Duncan@cmu.edu.

Patricia Diamond Fletcher is Assistant Professor at the Department of Information Systems, University of Maryland Baltimore County. She holds a Ph.D. from the School of Information Studies, Syracuse University. She is also a Faculty Associate at the Maryland Institute for Policy Analysis and Research. Her research focuses on information resources management (IRM) and policy in government. She participated in a national study of IRM in state governments, and was a principal investigator for two national studies of IRM, one in county governments, and the other in city governments. She is currently researching the information management policies in U.S. Federal government, especially the impact of the Clinger-Cohen Act. She recently edited a special issue of the *Journal of the American Society for information Science* on the National Information Infrastructure.

G. David Garson is full professor of public administration at North Carolina State University, where he teaches courses on American government, research methodology, computer applications, and geographic information systems. In 1995, he was recipient of the Donald Campbell Award from the Policy Studies Organization, American Political Science Association, for outstanding contributions to policy research methodology and in 1997 of the Aaron Wildavsky Book Award from the same organization. He is author of *Neural Network Analysis for Social Scientists* (forthcoming, 1998), *Computer Technology and Social Issues* (1995), *Geographic Databases and Analytic Mapping* (1992), and is author, coauthor, editor, or coeditor of 17 other books and author or coauthor of over 50 articles. He has also created award-winning American Government computer simulations, CD-ROMs, and four web sites for Prentice-Hall and Simon & Schuster (1995, 1996, 1997, 1998). In 1998 he won the "Web Book Award" from Online Magazine for his web site, "Introduction to American Government." For the last 16 years, he has also served as editor of the *Social Science Computer Review* and is on the editorial board of four additional journals. He also serves as a Visiting Scholar with Academic Systems, Inc., where he heads up a project on interactive economics education. Contact him at David_Garson@ncsu.edu.

Carl Grafton is Professor of Political Science and Public Administration at Auburn University at Montgomery. The author of many articles and book chapters on computer applications in public administration and political science, he is currently Book Review Editor of the *Social Science Computer Review*. Computer applications have been an integral part of his courses on public and nonprofit budgeting and quantitative decision-making for over 15 years.

Richard Heeks (richard.heeks@man.ac.uk) is a lecturer in information systems at the University of Manchester, England in the Institute for Development Policy and Management: a postgraduate center for public sector managers from developing and transitional economies. He has an M.Phil. in information systems and a PhD on IT industry development which led to publication of *India's Software Industry* (Sage Publications, 1996). He is also author of *Personal Bibliographic Indexes and Their Computerization* (Taylor Graham, 1986) and *Computerization in Academic Departments* (Taylor Graham, 1987), and editor of *Technology and Developing Countries* (Frank Cass, 1995). He is managing editor for the working paper series, *Information Systems for Public Sector Management* (located online at http://www.man.ac.uk/idpm/idpm_dp.htm). He has been a consultant to several public sector organizations worldwide. He currently directs the Manchester Masters program in 'Public Sector Management and Information Systems,' and is editing *Reinventing Government in the Information Age* (Routledge, 1999).

Stephen H. Holden is the National Director, Electronic Program Enhancements, for the Internal Revenue Service (IRS). He leads the development of new electronic filing, payment, and communications programs for the IRS. Steve joined the IRS in 1994 and has worked on the IRS's systems modernization efforts during his tenure at the IRS.

Prior to coming to the IRS, Steve worked for ten years at the Office of Management and Budget (OMB), doing a variety of policy, management, and budget analysis work. During that time, he served as the principal author of OMB's government-wide policy for information technology management. Steve's federal civil service career began in 1983 as a Presidential Management Intern.

He holds a bachelor's degree in public management and a Master's of Public Administration from the University of Maine. He earned his Ph.D. in Public Administration and Affairs from Virginia Tech in 1994.

Donald F. Norris is director of the Maryland Institute for Policy Analysis and Research (MIPAR) and professor of Policy Sciences at the University of Maryland Baltimore County (UMBC). He holds a Ph.D. in government from the University of Virginia. Dr. Norris has authored two books (*Microcomputers and Local Government*, 3rd ed., 1989, and *Police Community Relations: A Program that Failed*, 1973), edited one (*United States Energy Reality*, 1978), co-edited another (*Politics of Welfare Reform*, 1994), and has contributed chapters to 15 others. He has published articles in several scholarly journals including: *Public Administration Review, State and Local Government Review, Journal of Urban Affairs, Public Productivity and Management Review, Public Budgeting and Finance, Government Publications Review, Talking Politics, Local Government Studies*, and the *Journal of Rural Studies*. He has also been guest editor for special issues of *State and Local Government Review* and *Journal of Urban Affairs*.

Alana Northrop is Professor of Political Science at California State University, Fullerton and formerly directed its M.P.A. Program. She received her B.A. from Smith College and her Ph.D. from the University of Chicago. Dr. Northrup has worked in the field of information systems for over 20 years, studying local government use of computing in the U.S. Her other research has been on municipal reform, bureaucratic effectiveness, quantitative methods, and the initiative process. Her articles have appeared in the *American Journal of Political Science, Public Administration Review, Public Administration Quarterly, Journal of Criminal Justice*, and the *Social Science Computer Review*. She is currently working on a cross-national study of which countries will benefit from the Information Age.

Anne Permaloff is Professor of Political Science and Public Administration at Auburn University at Montgomery. She is a past president and current member of the board of the Computers and Multimedia Division of the American Political Science Association. Author of several articles and book chapters on computer applications in public administration and political science, she includes computer applications in her courses on research methodology, public policy analysis, and public budgeting.

Charles Prysby is a professor and head of the department of political science at the University of North Carolina at Greensboro. He received his Ph.D. from Michigan State University in 1973. His primary areas of research are in voting behavior, political parties, Southern electoral politics, and contextual effects on political behavior. His articles have appeared in a number of journals and edited books, and he is the coauthor of *Political Behavior and the Local Context* (Praeger, 1991). He also is the coauthor of the computer-based instructional packages on voting behavior in presidential elections published by the American Political Science

Association as part of the SETUPS series. For a number of years, he has taught a graduate course on computer applications in public administration.

Nicole Prysby is an attorney with interests in the area of employment law. She received her J.D. with honors from the University of North Carolina School of Law in 1995. She is a contributing author for several publications in the employment and human resource law area, including the *State by State Guide to Human Resource Law*, and the *Multistate Payroll Guide*, and is a co-author of the *Multistate Guide to Benefits Law* (all Aspen/Panel). She currently is working in the field of environmental consulting, for Perrin Quarles, Associates, in Charlottesville, Virginia. From 1995-1997, she was an attorney in the Public Law Department at the National Legal Research Group, Charlottesville, Virginia.

Bruce Rocheleau (brochele@niu.edu) is Associate Professor of Political Science at Northern Illinois University, DeKalb, Illinois. He teaches and does research concerning information technology and has published numerous articles, chapters, and monographs concerning the use of information technology by governmental organizations. He received his B.A. from the University of Pennsylvania, M.A. from New York University, and Ph.D. from the University of Florida.

Carmine Scavo is Associate Professor of Political Science and Director of the Master in Public Administration Program at East Carolina University in Greenville, NC. He received his Ph.D. in Political Science from the University of Michigan. He routinely teaches courses in Voting Behavior, Urban Management, Intergovernmental Relations, Public Policy, and Policy Analysis. He has published articles in such journals as *Social Science Quarterly*, *Southeastern Political Review*, and the *Journal of Urban Affairs* and chapters in edited volumes. Since 1984, he has been co-author of the American National Election Study (ANES) SETUPS (Supplementary Empirical Teaching Unit in Political Science) series of monographs which are designed to educate undergraduate students in computerized data analysis of survey data. The SETUPS monographs are published quadrennially by the American Political Science Association and are accompanied by a subset of ANES data, archived by the Inter-University Consortium for Political and Social Research (ICPSR).

Sonal J. Seneviratne is Director of Organizational Development & Learning and Assistant Research Professor at the University of Southern California, where he holds the Boaz Research Professorship. He has had ten years' experience in the information systems field both as an systems analyst and information systems manager. His research interests include organizational change and development, the impacts of technology on organizations and public management issues relating to technology and change. His work has appeared in *Public Administration Review* and *Asian Journal of Business and Information Systems.*

Yuhang Shi is Visiting Assistant Professor of Political Science at East Carolina University, Greenville, NC. He received his Ph.D. in Political Science from the State University of New York at Binghamton, New York. He teaches American Government, State and Local Government, Public Policy, and Computer Applications for Political Science and Public Administration.

Ellen Storey Vasu, Ph.D., is the coordinator of the graduate program in Instructional Technology in the College of Education and Psychology at North Carolina State University. From 1974-1983 she was an Associate Director of the Institute for Research in Social Science at UNC Chapel Hill, where she taught in the L.L. Thurstone Psychometric Lab. She currently teaches a doctoral level research methods course in the College of Education and Psychology and has also in the department of Statistics. She has published extensively in the areas of research methods, multivariate statistical analyses, and instructional technology. She can be contacted at Box 7801, NC State University, Raleigh, NC, 27695-7801; e-mail:esvasu@unity.ncsu.edu

Michael L. Vasu, Ph.D., is the Director of the Social Science Research and Computing Laboratory at North Carolina State University. He has twice served as president of the Southern Association for Public Opinion Research (SAPOR). He is the Associate Editor for Public Administration of the *Social Science Computer Review*, and author of numerous books and articles on computing, research methods, and organizational behavior. Professor Vasu, along with Professor Raymond Taylor, shared the second place cash award in the 1998 Franz Edleman Award for Achievements in Operations Research and Management Sciences. He can be reached at Box 8101, NC State University, Raleigh, NC, 27695-8101; e-mail: vasu@social.chass.ncsu.edu

Michael A. Warren is a doctoral candidate in the DPA program at Arizona State University. His dissertation is titled, "Internet Technology Assessment and Deployment: A Comparative Study. He is president of Electronic Archive Services, an information systems firm in Chandler, Arizona. His experience includes almost 20 years in the information technology field. Ten of those years were with the City of Phoenix in various lead technology positions. He recently completed a one year consulting assignment with American Express and is currently leading a year 2000 consulting project at Allied Signal.

Louis F. Weschler is Professor of Public Administration, School of Public Affairs, Arizona State University. He served on the faculties of the University of Southern California, the University of Washington, and the University of California, Davis, before coming to ASU in 1980. Currently, he directs a study of the use of electronic media and computer networks in community-based governance. He also collaborates with City of Phoenix staff in development of a model "electronic village" accessible via the Internet to enhance citizen and community use of city and other public datasets.

Index

A

accepting incoming call-backs 206
access 225
accessing a stored communication 237
administrative records 100
Administrative Review Agency 112
adoption 18, 142, 148
AFIS 140, 141, 142, 144
American Civil Liberties Union 109
American Family Privacy Act of 1997 101
anchor points 202
anonymity 233
ASCII format 211
Association of Public Data Users 108
ATI (automated telephone interviewing) 206
ATM 140
Automated Fingerprint Identification Systems (AFIS) 138, 147
Automated Traffic Control Systems 147
Automated Transaction Machines 147
Automated Vehicle Locator 147

B

bar code technology 141, 147
bar coding 140
BBS 140
Bell Atlantic 126
benefit-cost analysis 179
biased questions 198
Blacksburg Electronic Village (BEV) 126
branching 206
Brooks Act 70
BSP 68
budget 176
budget system 159
budgetary resources 150, 151
bulletin board 147, 251
Bureau of Labor Statistics 104
business administration 63, 76
business process re-engineering 47
business systems planning (BSP) 67
BYTE Research 122

C

call scheduling 206
CAPI 204, 215
CART 209, 210, 211, 212, 215
CART session 210
CART technology 209, 210, 211
case management system (CMS) 204
CASR 203, 204, 215
category development principles 203
CATI 205, 206, 207, 213
CATI systems 206
CD ROM 140, 141, 142, 144, 147
Center for Democracy and Technology 123
Central IT Department 140
centralization 26, 28, 29, 50
centralization-decentralization 26
centralized 25, 26, 28
CIO 26, 27, 29, 30
city governments 137
client/server 120
Clinton administration 72, 74
closer interviewer supervision 206
codebook 201
Comdex 122
Commission to Study the Federal Statistical System 101
common gateway interface (CGI) 208, 249
communication patterns 228
comparison mechanism. 158
complex branching structures 203
complex time series analysis 186
computer assisted drafting 143
computer based training 140, 147
computer hackers 238
Computer Professionals for Social Responsibility 109
computer-aided design (CAD) 220
computer-aided mapping (CAM) 220
computer-assisted interviews 202
computer-assisted personal interviewing (CAPI) 197
computer-assisted survey research (CASR) 197
Computer-assisted telephone interviewing (CATI) 197, 205
computerized attendance system 171
computing education In MPA Programs 8
confidence coefficients 199
confidence interval 199

300 Index

confidentiality 233
Congress 75
constitutional empowerment 105
consumer records 102
content analysis 203
Continuous Audience Response Technology (CART) 197, 214
control mechanism. 159
coordination – 151
corporate information management (CIM) 73
cost accounting MIS 168
Council for Marketing and Opinion Research 109
Council of Professional Associations on Federal St 109
curve smoothing 180
cyberspace 247
cyberspace demographics 128

D

data access 101
data analysis 201
Data and Access Protection Commission 112
data warehousing, 120
data-gathering systems 163
database applications 183
database management 15, 174, 187
database system 172
databases 100
decentralization 25, 50
decentralized 26
decision making 162, 166, 221
democratic accountability 105
Department of Commerce 128
Department of Defense (DOD) 73
desktop publishing 174
dial-up access 140
DIALOG 213
Digital Era Copyright Enhancement Act 102
direct broadcast satellite 142, 144
disasters 23, 33, 34
dissemination 226

E

e-mail 15, 24, 27, 31, 32
e-mail policy 242
ECPA 237, 238
ECPA includes a business exemption 237
education sector MIS 171
electronic commerce 125, 147
electronic data interchange 140, 147
electronic governance 131
electronic mail 140, 141, 144, 147
electronic networks 120

electronic redlining 128
electronic surveys 203
employer-owned system exemption 237
end users 150
ethernet 127
evaluation 229
event-triggered report 164
ex post facto research 209
exception 164
exception report. 163
executive information systems 162
exponential smoothing 181
External Databases 140, 141

F

Family Genetic Privacy and Protection Act 102
fax modems 140, 141, 147
fax-back/reply service 142, 144
Federal Electronic Communications Privacy Act (ECP 237
Federal Electronic Communications Privacy Act of 1 232
federal government 63
Federal Internet Privacy Protection Act of 1997 101
FEDSIM 68
fiber backbone 127
fiber optic cable 129, 140, 141, 144
fixed-choice 200
focus groups 196
FOIA 239, 240, 241
Fourth Amendment 232, 233, 234
Freedom of Information Act 239
FTP (file transfer protocol) 208, 250
functional separation 106

G

Gallup Organization 208
General Accounting Office (GAO) 66, 69, 70, 74, 75, 76
General Services Administration (GSA) 66
Genetic Confidentiality and Nondiscrimination Act 102
geographic information system" (GIS) 16, 140, 147, 174, 220, 252
ghost workers 168
GIS applications 221
global positioning 147
global positioning systems 120
global village 131
Gopher 250
governance 118
government reporting and compliance 169
GPS 140, 142, 144
graphics 15, 174

GSA 66, 68, 69, 70, 75
GSA's Federal Systems Integration and Management C 68

H

handheld computers and PDA's 140, 147
harassment 239
hardware compatibility 18
Health Care Assurance Act of 1997 102
Health Insurance Consumer's Bill of Rights Act of 102
health service 168
healthcare planning 222
Human resources MIS 168
Hypertext Markup Language (HTML) 248

I

IBM 68
ICMA 142, 144
imaging 140, 141
implementation 228
IMTEC 69, 74
income-related MIS 168
independent and dependent variable 209
indexes 198
individual autonomy 105
Industrial Age 118
information 82
Information Age 72, 76, 118
information management 63
Information Management and Technology (IMTEC) 69
information overload 164
Information Quality Analysis (IQA) 68
information resources 82
information resources management 67, 81
information Resources Management Service 66
information revolution 44
information sciences 63, 76
Information Technology and Management Reform Act (75
infrastructure planning 222
inputs 160
Institute for Social Research (ISR) 208
integrated MIS 169
integrated voice, data and video 140
interactive teleconferencing facilities 142, 144
interactive video training 141
interactive voice response 147
Internal Privacy Review Board 111
Internal Revenue Service 103
International Business Machines (IBM) 67
Internet 16, 23, 24, 34, 36, 100
Internet access and use 140
interrupted time series analysis is 186

interviewer bias 198, 203
interviewer training 206
intranet server 142, 144
intranets 120, 147
inventory information systems 169
IRM 67, 68, 69, 70, 71, 72, 73, 74, 75, 76
IRMS 68
ISDN 127
IT management 63, 67, 71, 73, 76

J

Java 250

K

kiosk 142, 140, 144, 147

L

land use planning 222
LANS 140, 144
laptops (Use of) 142, 144
leading edge information technologies 139
legislation 103
level of measurement 201
liability 225
linear programming 183
local area network 141, 142, 144
local government 65
long range IT plan 140, 141, 142, 144, 147

M

Malaysia 166
management information systems (MIS) 64, 157
management information systems and information res 76
management reports 206
management support 19
marketing research 223
Michigan Family Independence Agency 126
Microdata 114
Microsoft Office (1994) 202
Microsoft Word (1994) 213
Minnesota E-Democracy 126
MIS 64, 66, 67, 72
MIS model 166
MN-Democracy 126
MN-Forum 126
mobile data terminals 147
mobile radios and cellular phones 142
monitoring and control systems 158
monitoring mechanism. 158
multimedia 140, 141, 147
multimedia applications 205

municipal functions 146

N

NAPA 70
National Academy of Public Administration (NAPA) 69
National Archive 240
National Association of State Information Resource 88
National Drivers Register 169
national information infrastructure 127
National Opinion Research Center (NORC) 208
needs assessment 224
network computer (NC) 124
non-response problems 198
non-sampling error 198
North Carolina Public Records Act 240

O

object-oriented 120
obscene, hostile, threatening, or harassing commun 243
Office of Management and Budget (OMB) 65
Office of Science and Technology Policy 73
Office of Technology Assessment (OTA) 65
OMB Circular No. A-130 76
ombuds 111
on-line codebook browsing 204
online data 114
open 200
operational definitions 198
operational management. 162
optical character recognition 174
optical disk storage 140, 141, 147
OR/ED LABS 211
organizational change 41
organizational climate 150
organizational impacts 41
organizational issues 227
organizational transformation 41
outcomes: 160
outputs 160
outreach 258

P

Pacific Telesis (PacTel) 130
Panel on Confidentiality and Data Access 106
paper and pencil interviewing (PAPI) 197
paper and pencil surveys 203
Paperwork Reduction Act (PRA) 65, 67, 75
payoffs 147
payroll 163, 168
penetration 147

pensions: 169
periodic report. 164
personal computer (PC) 202
personal digital assistance 142, 144
personnel 18, 150
personnel information system 169
Planned Unit Developments (PUD) 214
point-and-click technology 208
policy guidelines 91
political campaigns 222
political support 228
population parameter 199
portable computers 141, 144
PRA 69, 70
precision 199
precoded question 200
presentation software 174
pretest the questionnaire 201
primacy 200
prior items 206
privacy 101, 226, 233, 238
Privacy Act of 1974 113
Privacy and Information Clearinghouse 111
privacy clauses in their constitutions 234
Privacy or Information Advocate 110
Privacy Protection Study Commission 106
privatization 23, 29, 33, 34
privatize 33
privatized 28
privatizing 27, 34
probability theory 199
project planning 174, 224
promotion 251
public access information technologies 147
public access network to query jurisdiction's data 141
public access technologies 140
public access terminals 147
public administration 197, 63, 64, 74, 76
Public Administration Journals and Textbooks 9, 12
public administrators 76
Public and Private Partnerships 225
public healthcare 171
public management information systems (PMIS) 64
public records 225
public sector 41
public sector strategic planning 84
public service delivery 170
public use terminals 140
purchases 28, 29, 33
purchasing 18, 23, 28, 29, 30, 32, 33, 37

Q

qualitative focus groups 209
question order effects 200

Questionnaire Programming Language (QPL) 206

R

Rand Corporation 129
random digit dialing (RDD) 206
random sampling procedure 207
random selection 199
RDD 206
reapportionment 223
recency effect 200
recruitment and selection 168
regression analysis 181, 184
relational database management 176
reliable responses 200
Remote Sensing Data 147
report writing 201
reports 163
representative democracy 131
representative sample 199
request report 164, 165
Research Triangle Institute 205
respondent-supplied information 206
response set bias 200
restricted access 110
restricted data. 109

S

safeguard of New Employee Information Act of 1998 102
sample statistic 199
sampling 182, 199
sampling error 198, 199, 200
sampling frame 199, 208
satelliteimagery/data 142, 144
scale 198
scanners 140, 141, 189
schools 171
security 19
service delivery 252
Services Worker Support System (SWSS) 126
share 26
shared 30
sharing 23, 25, 28, 30, 31, 37
single moving average 180
smart highway 141
smart public buildings 141
smart states 125
Smart Traffic Monitoring Systems 141
smart-coded toll booths 142, 144
smart-coded Toll Booths and Parking 141
social desirability 200
Social Science Computer Review 197
Social Security Administration 104
split-halves method 202
spreadsheets 15, 174, 181, 184
SPSS (1997) 213
SPSS for Windows (1997) 202
SPSS or SAS file formats 211
state and local government 63
state government 86
state IT plans 94
Statewide Automated Child Welfare System (SACWIS) 126
statewide IT planning 86
statistic 199
statistical inferences 199
statistics packages 174, 184
statutes that protect privacy in personal communic 234
stored communications principle 238
stored communications provision 237
strategic information management 70
strategic IRM planning 82
strategic management 73, 74, 75 162
strategic Ppanning 81, 83, 88
strategic plans 89
strategic triangle 119
strategy 83
subject intimidation 203
survey research 196
surveys 100
system design 227

T

tabular data 114
tctical management 162
Taxation MIS 170
Taxpayer Browsing Protection Act 101
TCP/IP 254
TDE (touchtone dial entry) 206
technology champion 150
teleconferencing 131
teledemocracy 36, 37
Telnet 250
hird party interception of electronic communicati 238
tolerated error 199
top officials 150
total quality management (TQM) 251
total survey error 198, 201
traditional paper and pencil mail surveys 203
training 169, 17
trends 153

U

U.S Census Block 213
U.S. Census Bureau 248, 103
U.S. Sprint 210
unauthorized access to computer systems 234
universal access 128

US Environmental Protection Agency 169

V

valid values 201
value label 201, 202
values 202
variable description 201
variable name 201
variable width 201
video arraignment 142, 144, 147
video-conferencing 130
ViewFacts 211
violation of privacy torts 235
Virginia Freedom of Information Act 241
virtual reality 141, 144
virtual reality training 142, 144

W

WAN 140
Web page 248
Web site design 246
welfare cheats 170
Western Governors' Association 125
Wide Area Network 141, 147
wireless LAN 141
wireless services 142
wireless services (Mobile radios and cellular phon 144
word processing 14, 174
World Wide Web (WWW) 123, 207, 247
World Wide Web applications 147
WWW Site On Internet 142, 144